THE DIVORCE

OF

CATHERINE OF ARAGON.

THE STORY AS TOLD BY THE IMPERIAL AMBASSADORS
RESIDENT AT THE COURT OF HENRY VIII.

IN USUM LAICORUM.

BY

JAMES ANTHONY FROUDE,

LATE REGIUS PROFESSOR OF MODERN HISTORY IN THE UNIVERSITY OF OXFORD.

BEING A SUPPLEMENTARY VOLUME TO THE AUTHOR'S
HISTORY OF ENGLAND.

NEW IMPRESSION.

LONGMANS, GREEN AND CO.
39 PATERNOSTER ROW, LONDON
NEW YORK, BOMBAY, AND CALCUTTA
1909

CONTENTS.

CHAPTER III

CHAPTER IV.

CHAPTER V.

CHAPTER VI.

CHAPTER VII.

CHAPTER VIII.

CHAPTER IX.

CHAPTER X.

THE DIVORCE

OF

CATHERINE OF ARAGON.

INTRODUCTION.

THE mythic element cannot be eliminated out of history. Men who play leading parts on the world's stage gather about them the admiration of friends and the animosity of disappointed rivals or political enemies. The atmosphere becomes charged with legends of what they have said or done—some inventions, some distortions of facts, but rarely or never accurate. Their outward acts, being public, cannot be absolutely misstated; their motives, being known only to themselves, are an open field for imagination; and as the disposition is to believe evil rather than good, the portraits drawn may vary indefinitely, according to the sympathies of the describer, but are seldom too favourable. The more distinguished a man is the more he is talked about. Stories are current about him in

B

his own lifetime, guaranteed apparently by the highest
authorities; related, insisted upon; time, place, and
circumstance accurately given—most of them mere
malicious lies; yet, if written down, to reappear in
memoirs a hundred years hence, they are likely to pass
for authentic, or at least probable. Even where there
is no malice, imagination will still be active. People
believe or disbelieve, repeat or suppress, according to
their own inclinations; and death, which ends the
feuds of unimportant persons, lets loose the tongues
over the characters of the great. Kings are especially
sufferers; when alive they hear only flattery; when
they are gone men revenge themselves by drawing
hideous portraits of them, and the more distinguished
they may have been the more minutely their weaknesses
are dwelt upon. 'C'est un plaisir indicible,' says
Voltaire, 'de donner des décrets contre des souverains
'morts quand on ne peut en lancer contre eulx de leur
'vivant de peur de perdre ses oreilles.' The dead
sovereigns go their way. Their real work for good or
evil lives after them; but they themselves are where
the opinions expressed about their character affect
them no more. To Cæsar or Napoleon it matters
nothing what judgment the world passes upon their
conduct. It is of more importance for the ethical
value of history that acts which as they are related
appear wicked should be duly condemned, that acts
which are represented as having advanced the welfare
of mankind should be duly honoured, than that the
real character of individuals should be correctly ap-

preciated. To appreciate any single man with complete accuracy is impossible. To appreciate him even proximately is extremely difficult. Rulers of kingdoms may have public reasons for what they do, which at the time may be understood or allowed for. Times change, and new interests rise. The circumstances no longer exist which would explain their conduct. The student looks therefore for an explanation in elements which he thinks he understands—in pride, ambition, fear, avarice, jealousy, or sensuality; and, settling the question thus to his own satisfaction, resents or ridicules attempts to look for other motives. So long as his moral judgment is generally correct, he inflicts no injury, and he suffers none. Cruelty and lust are proper objects of abhorrence; he learns to detest them in studying the Tiberius of Tacitus, though the character described by the great Roman historian may have been a mere creation of the hatred of the old Roman aristocracy. The manifesto of the Prince of Orange was a libel against Philip the Second; but the Philip of Protestant tradition is an embodiment of the persecuting spirit of Catholic Europe which it would be now useless to disturb. The tendency of history is to fall into wholesome moral lines whether they be accurate or not, and to interfere with harmless illusions may cause greater errors than it aspires to cure. Crowned offenders are arraigned at the tribunal of history for the crimes which they are alleged to have committed. It may be sometimes shown that the crimes were not crimes at all, that the sufferers had deserved their fate, that the severities

were useful and essential for some great and valuable
purpose. But the reader sees in the apology for acts
which he had regarded as tyrannical a defence of
tyranny itself. Preoccupied with the received interpretation, he finds deeds excused which he had learnt to
execrate; and in learning something which, even if
true, is of no real moment to him, he suffers in the
maiming of his perceptions of the difference between
right and wrong. The whitewashing of the villains
of tradition is, therefore, justly regarded as waste of
labour. If successful, it is of imperfect value; if unsuccessful, it is a misuse of industry which deserves
to be censured. Time is too precious to be squandered
over paradoxes. The dead are gone; the censure
of mankind has written their epitaphs, and so they
may be left. Their true award will be decided elsewhere.

This is the commonsense verdict. When the work
of a man is done and ended; when, except indirectly
and invisibly, he affects the living world no more, the
book is closed, the sentence is passed, and there he may
be allowed to rest. The case is altered, however, when
the dead still live in their actions, when their principles
and the effects of their conduct are still vigorous and
operative, and the movements which they initiated continue to be fought over. It sometimes happens that
mighty revolutions can be traced to the will and resolution of a single man, and that the conflict continues
when he is gone. The personal character of such a man
becomes then of intrinsic importance as an argument

for attack or defence. The changes introduced by
Henry VIII. are still denounced or defended with renewed violence; the ashes of a conflict which seemed
to have been decided are again blown into a flame; and
what manner of man Henry was, and what the statesmen and churchmen were who stood by him and assisted
him in reshaping the English constitution, becomes a
practical question of our own time. By their fruits ye
shall know them. A good tree cannot bear evil fruit,
neither can a corrupt tree bring forth good fruit. Roman
Catholics argue from the act to the man, and from the
man back to the act. The Reformation, they say, was
a rebellion against an authority appointed by God for
the rule of the world; it was a wicked act in itself;
the author or the authors of it were presumably, therefore, themselves wicked; and the worst interpretation of
their conduct is antecedently probable, because a revolt
against the Church of Christ could only have originated
in depraved hearts. Or again, inverting the argument,
they say with sufficient plausibility that the sins and
crimes of the King are acknowledged facts of history;
that from so bad a man no good thing could ever rise;
that Henry was a visible servant of the devil, and therefore the Reformation, of which he was the instrument,
was the devil's work. If the picture drawn of him by
his Catholic contemporaries is correct, the inference is
irresistible. That picture, however, was drawn by those
whose faith he wounded and whose interests he touched,
and therefore might be regarded with suspicion. Religious animosity is fertile in calumny, because it

assumes beforehand that every charge is likely to be
true in proportion to its enormity, and Catholic writers
were credulous of evil when laid to the charge of so
dangerous an adversary. But the Catholics have not
been Henry's only accusers; all sorts and sects have
combined in the general condemnation. The Anglican
High Churchman is as bitter against him as Reginald
Pole himself. He admits and maintains the separation
from Rome which Henry accomplished for him ; but he
abhors as heartily as Pole or Lingard the internal
principles of the Reformation. He resents the control
of the clergy by the civil power. He demands the
restoration of the spiritual privileges which Henry and
his parliaments took away from them. He aspires to
the recovery of ecclesiastical independence. He therefore with equal triumph points to the blots in Henry's
character, and deepens their shade with every accusation,
proved or unproved, which he can find in contemporary
records. With him, too, that a charge was alleged at
the time is evidence sufficient to entitle him to accept
it as a fact.

Again, Protestant writers have been no less unspar-
ing from an imprudent eagerness to detach their cause
from a disreputable ally. In Elizabeth's time it was a
point of honour and loyalty to believe in the innocence
of her mother. If Anne Boleyn was condemned on
forged or false evidence to make way for Jane Seymour,
what appears so clearly to us must have been far
clearer to Henry and his Council; of all abominable
crimes committed by tyrannical princes there was never

one more base or cowardly than Anne's execution; and in insisting on Anne's guiltlessness they have condemned the King, his ministers, and his parliaments. Having discovered him to have murdered his wife, they have found him also to have been a persecutor of the truth. The Reformation in England was at its outset political rather than doctrinal. The avarice and tyranny of the Church officials had galled the limbs of the laity. Their first steps were to break the chains which fretted them, and to put a final end to the temporal power of the clergy. Spiritual liberty came later, and came slowly from the constitution of the English mind. Superstition had been familiarised by custom, protected by natural reverence, and shielded from inquiry by the peculiar horror attaching to unbelief. The nation had been taught from immemorial time that to doubt on the mysteries of faith was the worst crime which man could commit; and while they were willing to discover that on their human side the clergy were but brother mortals of questionable character, they drew a distinction between the Church as a national institution and the doctrines which it taught. An old creed could not yield at once. The King did much; he protected individual Lutherans to the edge of rashness. He gave the nation the English Bible. He made Latimer a bishop. He took away completely and for ever the power of the prelates to punish what they called heresy *ex officio* and on their own authority; but the zeal of the ultra-Protestants broke loose when the restraint was taken off; the sense of the country was offended by the irreverence with which objects and opinions were treated which they regarded as holy, and Parliament, which had put a bit in the mouth of the ecclesiastical courts, was driven to a substitute in the Bill of the Six Articles. The advanced section in popular movements is usually unwise. The characteristic excellence of the English Reformation is, that throughout its course it was restrained by the law, and the Six Articles Bill, tempered as it was in the execution, was a permissible, and perhaps useful, measure in restraint of intemperance. It was the same in Germany. Anabaptists continued to be burnt in Saxony and Hesse long after Luther's revolt; Calvin thought the stake a fitting penalty for doubts upon the Trinity. John Knox, in Scotland, approved of witch-burning and sending mass-priests to the gallows. Henry could not disregard the pronounced feeling of the majority of the English people. He was himself but one of them, and changed slowly as they changed. Yet Protestant tradition has assumed that the bloody whip with six strings was an act of arbitrary ferocity. It considers that the King could, and ought to, have advanced at once into an understanding of the principle of toleration—toleration of the new opinions, and a more severe repression of the old. The Puritans and Evangelicals forgot that he had given them the English Testament. They forgot that by setting his foot upon the bishops he had opened the pulpits to themselves, and they classed him among the persecutors, or else joined in the shallow laughs of the ultramontane Catholics at what they pleased to call his inconsistency.

Thus from all sides a catena of invective has been wrapped about Henry's character. The sensible part of the country held its tongue. The speakers and writers were the passionate and fanatical of both persuasions, and by them the materials were supplied for the Henry VIII. who has been brought down to us by history, while the candid and philosophic thinkers of the last and present centuries have accepted the traditional figure. In their desire to be impartial they have held the balance equal between Catholics and Protestants, inclining slightly to the Catholic side, from a wish to conciliate a respectable body who had been unjustly maligned and oppressed ; while they have lavished invectives upon the early Reformers violent enough to have satisfied even Pole himself, whose rhetoric has formed the base of their declamation.

Liberal philosophy would have had a bad time of it in England, perhaps in all Europe, if there had been no Henry VIII. to take the Pope by the throat. But one service writers like Macaulay have undoubtedly accomplished. They have shown that it is entirely impossible to separate the King from his ministers—to condemn Henry and to spare Cranmer. Protestant writers, from Burnet to Southey, have tried to save the reforming bishops and statesmen at Henry's expense. Cranmer, and Latimer, and Ridley have been described as saints, though their master was a villain. But the cold impartiality of Macaulay has pointed out unanswerably that in all Henry's most questionable acts his own ministers and his prelates were active participants—

that his Privy Council, his parliaments, his judges on
the bench, the juries empanelled to try the victims of
his tyranny, were equally his accomplices; some actively
assisting; the rest, if these acts were really criminal,
permitting themselves to be bribed or terrified into
acquiescence. The leading men of all descriptions, the
nation itself, through the guilt of its representatives,
were all stained in the same detestable colours. It may
be said, indeed, that they were worse than the King
himself. For the King at least may be pleaded the
coarse temptations of a brutal nature; but what pallia-
tion can be urged for the peers and judges who sacrificed Anne Boleyn, or More, or Fisher, according to
the received hypothesis? Not even the excuse of
personal fear of an all-powerful despot. For Henry
had no Janissaries or Prætorians to defend his person
or execute his orders. He had but his hundred yeomen
of the guard, not more numerous than the ordinary
followers of a second-rate noble. The Catholic leaders,
who were infuriated at his attacks upon the Church, and
would if they could have introduced foreign armies to
dethrone him, insisted on his weakness as an encouragement to an easy enterprise. Beyond those few yeomen
they urged that he had no protection save in the
attachment of the subjects whom he was alienating.
What strange influence was such a king able to exercise
that he could overawe the lords and gentry of England,
the learned professions, the municipal authorities?
How was it that he was able to compel them to be the
voluntary instruments of his cruelty? Strangest of

all, he seems to have needed no protection, but rather to have been personally popular, even among those who disapproved his public policy. The air was charged with threats of insurrection, but no conspiracy was ever formed to kill him, like those which so often menaced the life of his daughter. When the North was in arms in the Pilgrimage of Grace, and a question rose among the leaders whether in the event of victory the King was to be deposed, it was found that anyone who proposed to remove him would be torn in pieces by the people.

Granting that Henry VIII. was, as Dickens said of him, 'a spot of blood and grease' on the page of English history, the contemporary generation of Englishmen must have been fit subjects of such a sovereign. Every country, says Carlyle, gets as good a government as it deserves. The England of the Cromwells and the Cranmers, the Howards and the Fitzwilliams, the Wriothesleys and the Pagets, seems to have been made of baser materials than any land of which mankind has preserved a record. Roman Catholics may fairly plead that out of such a race no spiritual reform is likely to have arisen which could benefit any human soul. Of all the arguments which can be alleged for the return of England to the ancient fold, this is surely the most powerful.

Yet England shows no intention of returning. History may say what it pleases, yet England remains tenacious of the liberties which were then won for us, and unconscious of the disgrace attaching to them;

unconscious, also, that the version of the story which
it accepts contains anything which requires explanation.
The legislation of Henry VIII., his Privy Council, and
his parliaments is the Magna Charta of the modern
world. The Act of Appeals and the Act of Supremacy
asserted the national independence, and repudiated the
interference of foreign bishop, prince, or potentate
within the limits of the English empire. The clergy
had held for many centuries an *imperium in imperio.*
Subject themselves to no law but their own, they had
asserted an irresponsible jurisdiction over the souls and
bodies of the people. The Act for the submission of
these persons reduced them to the common condition of
subjects under the control of the law. Popes were no
longer allowed to dispense with ordinary obligations.
Clerical privileges were abolished. The spiritual courts,
with their intolerable varieties of iniquity, were swept
away, or coerced within rational limits. The religious
houses were suppressed, their enormous wealth was
applied for the defence of the realm, and the worse
than Augean dunghill of abuses was cleared out with
resolute hand. These great results were accomplished
in the face of papal curses, in defiance of superstitious
terrors, so despicable when bravely confronted, so terrible while the spectre of supernatural power was still
unexorcised ; in the face, too, of earthly perils which
might make stout hearts shake, of an infuriated priest-
hood stirring the people into rebellion, of an exasperated
Catholic Europe threatening fire and sword in the name
of the Pope. These were distinguished achievements,

not likely to have been done at all by an infamous prince and infamous ministers; yet done so well that their work is incorporated in the constitution almost in the form in which they left it; and this mighty revolution, the greatest and most far-reaching in modern times, was accomplished without a civil war, by firmness of hand, by the action of Parliament, and a resolute enforcement of the law. Nor has the effect of Henry's legislation been confined to England. Every great country, Catholic or Protestant, has practically adopted its chief provisions. Popes no longer pretend a power of deposing princes, absolving subjects from their allegiance, or selling dispensations for offences against the law of the land. Appeals are no longer carried from the national courts to the court of the Rota. The papal treasury is no longer supplied by the plunder of the national clergy, collected by resident papal officials. Bishops and convocations have ceased to legislate above and independent of the secular authority, and clerks who commit crimes bear the same penalties as the profane. The high quality of the Reformation statutes is guaranteed by their endurance; and it is hard to suppose that the politicians who conceived and carried them out were men of base conditions. The question is not of the character of the King. If nothing was at issue but the merits or demerits of a single sovereign, he might be left where he lies. The question is of the characters of the reforming leaders, who, jointly with the King, were the authors of this tremendous and beneficent revolution. Henry in all that he did acted

with these men and through them. Is it possible to
believe that qualities so opposite as the popular theory
requires existed in the same persons ? Is it possible,
for instance, that Cranmer, who composed or translated
the prayers in the English Liturgy, was the miserable
wretch which Macaulay or Lingard describes ? The
era of Elizabeth was the outspring of the movement
which Henry VIII. commenced, and it was the grandest
period in English history. Is it credible that so in-
vigorating a stream flowed from a polluted fountain ?

Before accepting a conclusion so disgraceful—before
consigning the men who achieved so great a victory, and
risked and lost their lives in the battle, to final execration
—it is at least permissible to pause. The difficulty can
only be made light of by impatience, by prejudice, or by
want of thought. To me at any rate, who wished to discover what the real history of the Reformation had been,
it seemed so considerable, that, dismissing the polemical
invectives of later writers, I turned to the accounts of
their conduct which had been left behind by the authors
of it themselves. Among the fortunate anomalies of
the situation, Henry departed from previous custom in
holding annual parliaments. At every step which he
took, either in the rearrangement of the realm or in
his own domestic confusions, he took the Lords and
Commons into his council, and ventured nothing without
their consent. The preambles of the principal statutes
contain a narrative clear and precise of the motives of
everything that he did—a narrative which at least may
have been a true one, which was not put forward as a

defence, but was a mere explanation of acts which on the surface seemed violent and arbitrary. If the explanation is correct, it shows us a time of complications and difficulties, which, on the whole, were successfully encountered. It shows us severe measures severely executed, but directed to public and necessary purpose, involving no sycophancy or baseness, no mean subservience to capricious tyranny, but such as were the natural safeguards during a dangerous convulsion, or remedies of accidents incidental to hereditary monarchy. The story told is clear and distinct; pitiless, but not dishonourable. Between the lines can be read the storm of popular passions, the beating of the national heart when it was stirred to its inmost depths. We see established institutions rooted out, idols overthrown, and injured worshippers exasperated to fury ; the air, as was inevitable at such a crisis, full of flying rumours, some lies, some half lies with fragments of truth attaching to them, bred of malice or dizzy brains, the materials out of which the popular tradition has been built. It was no insular revolution. The stake played for was the liberty of mankind. All Europe was watching England, for England was the hinge on which the fate of the Reformation turned. Could it be crushed in England, the Catholics were assured of universal victory, and therefore tongues and pens were busy everywhere throughout Christendom, Catholic imagination representing Henry as an incarnate Satan, for which, it must be admitted, his domestic misadventures gave them tempting opportunities. So thick

fell the showers of calumny, that, bold as he was, he
at times himself winced under it. He complained to
Charles V. of the libels circulated about him in France
and Flanders. Charles, too, had suffered in the same
way. He answered, humorously, that 'if kings gave
occasion to be spoken about they would be spoken
about; kings were not kings of tongues.' Henry VIII.
was an easy mark for slander; but if all slanders are
to pass as true which are flung at public men whose
policy provides them with an army of calumniators,
the reputation of the best of them is but a spotted rag.
The clergy were the vocal part of Europe. They had
the pulpits; they had the writing of the books and
pamphlets. They had cause to hate Henry, and they
hated him with an intensity of passion which could not
have been more savage had he been the devil himself.
But there are men whose enmity is a compliment.
They libelled Luther almost as freely as they libelled
the English king. I myself, after reading and weighing
all that I could find forty years ago in prints or
manuscripts, concluded that the real facts of Henry's
conduct were to be found in the Statute Book and nowhere else; that the preambles of the Acts of Parliament did actually represent the sincere opinion about
him of the educated laymen of England, who had
better opportunities of knowing the truth than we can
have, and that a modern Englishman may be allowed
to follow their authority without the imputation of
paradox or folly.

With this impression, and with the Statute Book for

a guide, I wrote the opening portion of my ' History of England, from the Fall of Wolsey to the Defeat of the Armada.' The published criticisms upon my work were generally unfavourable. Catholic writers inherited the traditions and the temper of their forefathers, and believed the catena of their own historians. Protestants could not believe in a defence of the author of the Six Articles Bill. Secular reviewers were easily witty at the ' model husband' whom they supposed me to be imposing upon them, and resented the interference with a version of the story authenticated by great names among my predecessors. The public, however, took an interest in what I had to say. The book was read, and continues to be read; at the close of my life, therefore, I have to go once more over the ground; and as I am still substantially alone in maintaining an opinion considered heretical by orthodox historians, I have to decide in what condition I am to leave my work behind me. In the thirty-five years which have elapsed since those early volumes appeared large additions have been made to the materials for the history of the period. The vast collection of manuscripts in the English Record Office, which then were only partially accessible, have been sorted, catalogued, and calendared by the industry of my friends Mr. Brewer and Mr. Gairdner. Private collections in great English houses have been examined and reported on by the Historical Manuscripts Commission. Foreign archives at Paris, Simancas, Rome, Venice, Vienna, and Brussels have been searched to some extent by myself, but in a far larger degree by able scholars specially appointed for the purpose. In the despatches, thus made accessible, of the foreign ambassadors resident at Henry's court we have the invaluable, if not impartial, comments of trained and responsible politicians who related from day to day the events which were passing under their eyes. Being Catholics, and representatives of Catholic powers, they were bitterly hostile to the Reformation—hostile alike on political grounds and religious—and therefore inclined to believe and report the worst that could be said both of it and of its authors. But they wrote before the traditions had become stereotyped; their accounts are fresh and original; and, being men of the world, and writing in confidence to their own masters, they were as veracious as their prejudices would allow them to be. Unconsciously, too, they render another service of infinite importance. Being in close communication with the disaffected English peers and clergy, and engaged with them secretly in promoting rebellion, the ministers of Charles V. reveal with extraordinary clearness the dangers with which the Government had to deal. They make it perfectly plain that the Act of Supremacy, with its stern and peremptory demands, was no more than a legitimate and necessary defence against organised treason.

It was thus inevitable that much would have to be added to what I had already published. When a microscope is applied to the petal of a flower or the wing of an insect, simple outlines and simple surfaces are resolved into complex organisms with curious and

beautiful details. The effect of these despatches is precisely the same—we see with the eyes, we hear with
the ears, of men who were living parts of the scenes
which they describe. Stories afterwards elaborated
into established facts we trace to their origin in rumours
of the hour; we read innumerable anecdotes, some
with the clear stamp of truth on them, many mere
creations of passing wit or malice, no more authentic
than the thousands like them which circulate in modern
society, guaranteed by the positive assertions of personal
witnesses, yet visibly recognisable as lies. Through
all this the reader must pick his way and use his own
judgment. He knows that many things are false which
are reported about his own eminent contemporaries.
He may be equally certain that lies were told as freely
then as now. He will probably allow his sympathies
to guide him. He will accept as fact what fits in with
his creed or his theory. He will share the general
disposition to believe evil, especially about kings and
great men. The exaggerated homage paid to princes,
when they are alive, has to be compensated by suspecting the worst of them as soon as they are gone. But
the perusal of all these documents leaves the broad
aspect of the story, in my opinion, precisely where it
was. It is made more interesting by the greater ful-
ness of particulars; it is made more vivid by the clear
view which they afford of individual persons who before
were no more than names. But I think now, as I
thought forty years ago, that through the confusions
and contradictions of a stormy and angry time, the

statute-book remains the safest guide to follow. If there be any difference, it is that actions which till explained appeared gratuitously cruel, like the execution of Bishop Fisher, are seen beyond dispute to have been reasonable and just. Bishop Fisher is proved by the words of the Spanish Ambassador himself to have invited and pressed the introduction of a foreign Catholic army into England in the Pope's interest.

Thus I find nothing to withdraw in what I then wrote, and little to alter save in correcting some small errors of trivial moment; but, on the other hand, I find much to add; and the question rises in what way I had better do it, with fair consideration for those who have bought the book as it stands. To take the work to pieces and introduce the new material into the text or the notes will impose a necessity of buying a new copy, or of being left with an inferior one, on the many friends who least deserve to be so treated. I have concluded, therefore, on writing an additional volume, where such parts of the story as have had important light thrown upon them can be told over again in ampler form. The body of the history I leave as it stands. It contains what I believe to be a true account of the time, of the immediate causes which brought about the changes of the sixteenth century, and of the characters and principles of the actors in them. I have only to fill up certain deficiencies and throw light into places hitherto left dark. For the rest, I do not pretend to impartiality. I believe the Reformation to have been the greatest incident in English history; the root and

source of the expansive force which has spread the
Anglo-Saxon race over the globe, and imprinted the
English genius and character on the constitution of
mankind. I am unwilling to believe more evil than
I can help of my countrymen who accomplished so
beneficent a work, and in a book written with such
convictions the mythical element cannot be wholly
wanting. Even things which immediately surround
us, things which we see and touch, we do not perceive
as they are; we perceive only our own sensations, and
our sensations are a combined result of certain objects
and of the faculties which apprehend them. Something of ourselves must always be intermixed before
knowledge can reach us; in every conclusion which we
form, in every conviction which is forced upon us, there
is still a subjective element. It is so in physical
science. It is so in art. It is so in our speculations
on our own nature. It is so in religion. It is so even
in pure mathematics. The curved and rectilineal
figures on which we reason are our own creation, and
have no existence exterior to the reasoning mind. Most
of all is it so in history, where we have no direct perceptions to help us, but are dependent on the narratives
of others whose beliefs were necessarily influenced by
their personal dispositions. The first duty of an historian is to be on his guard against his own sympathies;
but he cannot wholly escape their influence. In judging
of the truth of particular statements, the conclusion
which he will form must be based partly upon evidence
and partly upon what he conceives to be likely or

unlikely. In a court of justice, where witnesses can
be cross-examined, uncertain elements can in some
degree be eliminated; yet, after all care is taken,
judges and juries have been often blinded by passion
and prejudice. When we have nothing before us but
rumours set in circulation, we know not by whom or on
what authority, and we are driven to consider proba-
bilities, the Protestant, who believes the Reformation
to have been a victory of truth over falsehood, cannot
come to the same conclusion as the Catholic, who
believes it to have been a curse, or perhaps to the same
conclusion as the indifferent philosopher, who regards
Protestant and Catholic alike with benevolent contempt.
For myself, I can but say that I have discriminated with
such faculty as I possess. I have kept back nothing. I
have consciously distorted nothing which conflicts with
my own views. I have accepted what seems sufficiently
proved. I have rejected what I can find no support for
save in hearsay or prejudice. But whether accepting or
rejecting, I have endeavoured to follow the rule that
incidents must not be lightly accepted as authentic
which are inconsistent with the universal laws of human
nature, and that to disprove a calumny it is sufficient to
show that there is no valid witness for it.

Finally, I do not allow myself to be tempted into
controversy with particular writers whose views disagree
with my own. To contradict in detail every hostile
version of Henry VIII.'s or his ministers' conduct would
be as tedious as it would be irritating and unprofitable.
My censors have been so many that a reply to them all

is impossible, and so distinguished that a selection
would be invidious. Those who wish for invectives
against the King, or Cranmer, or Cromwell can find
them everywhere, from school manuals to the grave
works of elaborate historians. For me, it is enough to
tell the story as it presents itself to my own mind, and
to leave what appears to me to be the truth to speak
for itself.

The English nation throughout their long history
have borne an honourable reputation. Luther quotes
a saying of Maximilian that there were three real
sovereigns in Europe—the Emperor, the King of France,
and the King of England. The Emperor was a king of
kings. If he gave an order to the princes of the Reich,
they obeyed or disobeyed as they pleased. The King
of France was a king of asses. He ordered about his
people at his will, and they obeyed like asses. The
King of England was a king of a loyal nation who
obeyed him with heart and mind as loyal and faithful
subjects. This was the character borne in the world
by the fathers of the generation whom popular historians represent as having dishonoured themselves by
subserviency to a bloodthirsty tyrant. It is at least
possible that popular historians have been mistaken,
and that the subjects of Henry VIII. were neither
much better nor much worse than those who preceded
or came after them.

CHAPTER I.

Prospects of a disputed succession to the crown—Various claimants
—Catherine incapable of having further children—Irregularity
of her marriage with the King—Papal dispensations—First
mention of the divorce—Situation of the Papacy—Charles V.—
Policy of Wolsey—Anglo-French alliance—Imperial troops in
Italy—Appeal of the Pope—Mission of Inigo de Mendoza—
The Bishop of Tarbes—Legitimacy of the Princess Mary called
in question—Secret meeting of the Legate's court—Alarms of
Catherine—Sack of Rome by the Duke of Bourbon—Proposed
reform of the Papacy—The divorce promoted by Wolsey—
Unpopular in England—Attempts of the Emperor to gain
Wolsey.

IN the year 1526 the political prospects of England
became seriously clouded. A disputed succession
had led in the previous century to a desperate civil war.
In that year it became known in private circles that if
Henry VIII. was to die the realm would again be left
without a certain heir, and that the strife of the Roses
might be renewed on an even more distracting scale.
The sons who had been born to Queen Catherine had
died in childbirth or had died immediately after it.
The passionate hope of the country that she might still
produce a male child who would survive had been
constantly disappointed, and now could be entertained
no longer. She was eight years older than her husband.

She had 'certain diseases' which made it impossible
that she should be again pregnant, and Henry had for
two years ceased to cohabit with her. He had two
children still living—the Princess Mary, Catherine's
daughter, then a girl of eleven, and an illegitimate son
born in 1519, the mother being a daughter of Sir John
Blount, and married afterwards to Sir Gilbert Talboys.
By presumptive law the Princess was the next heir; but
no woman had ever sat on the throne of England alone
and in her own right, and it was doubtful whether the
nation would submit to a female sovereign. The boy,
though excluded by his birth from the prospect of the
crown, was yet brought up with exceptional care, called
a prince by his tutors, and probably regarded by his
father as a possible successor should his sister go the
way of her brothers. In 1525, after the King had
deliberately withdrawn from Catherine, he was created
Duke of Richmond—a title of peculiar significance,
since it had been borne by his grandfather, Henry VII.
—and he was granted precedence over the rest of the
peerage. Illegitimacy was a serious, but, it might be
thought, was not an absolute, bar. The Conqueror had
been himself a bastard. The Church, by its habits of
granting dispensations for irregular marriages or of dis-
solving them on pleas of affinity or consanguinity or
other pretext, had confused the distinction between
legitimate and illegitimate. A Church Court had
illegitimatised the children of Edward IV. and Elizabeth
Grey, on the ground of one of Edward's previous connections; yet no one regarded the princes murdered in

the Tower as having been illegitimate in reality; and
to prevent disputes and for an adequate object, the
Duke of Richmond, had he grown to manhood, might,
in the absence of other claims, have been recognised by
Parliament. But the Duke was still a child, and might
die as Henry's other sons had died; and other claims
there were which, in the face of the bar sinister, could
not fail to be asserted. James V. of Scotland was next
in blood, being the son of Henry's eldest sister,
Margaret. There were the Greys, inheriting from the
second sister, Mary. Outside the royal house there
were the still popular representatives of the White Rose,
the Marquis of Exeter, who was Edward IV.'s grandson;
the Countess of Salisbury, daughter of Edward's brother
the Duke of Clarence, and sister of the murdered Earl
of Warwick; and Henry's life was the only obstacle
between the collision of these opposing pretensions.
James, it was quite certain, would not be allowed to
succeed without a struggle. National rivalry forbade it.
Yet it was no less certain that he would try, and would
probably be backed by France. There was but one
escape from convulsions which might easily be the ruin
of the realm. The King was in the flower of his age,
and might naturally look for a Prince of Wales to come
after him if he was married to a woman capable of
bearing one. It is neither unnatural nor, under the
circumstances, a matter to be censured if he and others
began to reflect upon the peculiar character of his
connection with Catherine of Aragon. It is not
sufficiently remembered that the marriage of a widow

with her husband's brother was then, as it is now, forbidden by the laws of all civilised countries. Such a marriage at the present day would be held *ipso facto* invalid and not a marriage at all. An irregular power was then held to rest with the successors of St. Peter to dispense, under certain conditions, with the inhibitory rules. The popes are now understood to have never rightly possessed such an authority, and therefore, according to modern law and sentiment, Henry and Catherine never were husband and wife at all. At the time it was uncertain whether the dispensing power extended so far as to sanction such a union, and when the discussion rose upon it the Roman canonists were themselves divided. Those who maintained the widest view of the papal faculty yet agreed that such a dispensation could only be granted for urgent cause, such as to prevent foreign wars or internal seditions, and no such cause was alleged to have existed when Ferdinand and Henry VII. arranged the marriage between their children. The dispensation had been granted by Pope Julius with reluctance, had been acted upon after considerable hesitation, and was of doubtful validity, since the necessary conditions were absent. The marriages of kings were determined with little reference to the personal affection of the parties. Between Henry and Catherine there was probably as much and as little personal attachment as there usually is in such cases. He respected and perhaps admired her character ; but she was not beautiful, she was not attractive, while she was as proud and intractable as her mother Isabella. Their union had been settled by the two fathers to cement the alliance between England and Spain. Such connections rest on a different foundation from those which are voluntarily entered into between private persons. What is made up for political reasons may pardonably be dissolved when other reasons of a similar kind require it; and when it became clear that Catherine could never bear another child, that the penalty threatened in the Levitical law against marriages of this precise kind had been literally enforced in the death of the male offspring, and that civil war was imminent in consequence upon the King's death, Henry may have doubted in good faith whether she had ever been his wife at all—whether, in fact, the marriage was not of the character which every one would now allow to attach to similar unions. Had there been a Prince of Wales, the question would never have arisen, and Henry, like other kings, would have borne his fate. But there was no prince, and the question had risen, and there was no reason why it should not. There was no trace at the outset of an attachment to another woman. If there had been, there would be little to condemn; but Anne Boleyn, when it was first mooted, was no more to the King than any other lady of the court. He required a wife who could produce a son to secure the succession. The powers which had allowed an irregular marriage could equally dissolve it, and the King felt that he had a right to demand a familiar concession which other sovereigns had often applied for in one form or another, and rarely in vain.

Thus as early as 1526 certainly, and probably as much as a year before, Cardinal Wolsey had been feeling his way at Rome for a separation between Henry and Catherine. On September 7 in that year the Bishop of Bath, who was English Ambassador at Paris, informed the Cardinal of the arrival there of a confidential agent of Pope Clement VII. The agent had spoken to the Bishop on this especial subject, and had informed him that there would be difficulties about it.[1] The 'blessed ' divorce '—*benedictum divorcium* the Bishop calls it— had been already under consideration at Rome. The difficulties were not specified, but the political features of the time obliged Clement to be circumspect, and it was these that were probably referred to. Francis I. had been defeated and taken prisoner by the Imperialists at Pavia. He had been carried to Spain, and had been released at Henry's intercession, under severe conditions, to which he had reluctantly consented, and his sons had been left at Madrid as hostages for the due fulfilment of them. The victorious army, half Spanish, half German, remained under the Duke of Bourbon to complete the conquest of Italy; and Charles V., with his already vast dominions and a treasury which the world believed to be inexhaustibly supplied from the gold mines of the New World, seemed advancing to universal empire.

France in the preceding centuries had been the hereditary enemy of England; Spain and Burgundy

---

[1] *Calendar of State Papers, Hen. VIII., Foreign and Domestic,* vol. iv. Introduction, p. 223.

her hereditary friends. The marriage of Catherine of Aragon had been a special feature of the established alliance. She was given first to Prince Arthur, and then to Henry, as a link in the confederacy which was to hold in check French ambition. Times were changing. Charles V. had been elected Emperor, largely through English influence; but Charles was threatening to be a more serious danger to Europe than France had been. The Italian princes were too weak to resist the conqueror of Pavia. Italy once conquered, the Papacy would become a dependency of the Empire, and, with Charles's German subjects in open revolt against it, the Church would lose its authority, and the organisation of the Catholic world would fall into hopeless decrepitude. So thought Wolsey, the most sharp-sighted of English ministers. He believed that the maintenance of the Papacy was the best defence of order and liberty. The only remedy which he could see was a change of partners. England held the balance between the great rival powers. If the English alliance could be transferred from the Empire to France, the Emperor could be held in check, and his supposed ambition neutralised. Wolsey was utterly mistaken; but the mistake was not an unnatural one. Charles, busy with his Italian wars, had treated the Lutheran schism with suspicious forbearance. Notwithstanding his Indian ingots his finances were disordered. Bourbon's lansquenets had been left to pay themselves by plunder. They had sacked monasteries, pillaged cathedral plate, and ravished nuns with irreverent ferocity. The estates of the Church had been as little spared by them as Lombardy; and to Clement VII. the invasion was another inroad of barbarians, and Bourbon a second Attila. What Bourbon's master meant by it, and what he might intend to do, was as uncertain to Clement as perhaps it was to Charles himself. In the prostrate, degraded, and desperate condition into which the Church was falling, any resolution was possible. To the clearest eyes in Europe the Papacy seemed tottering to its fall, and Charles's hand, if he chose to raise it, might precipitate the catastrophe. To ask a pope at such a time to give mortal offence to the Spanish nation by agreeing to the divorce of Catherine of Aragon was to ask him to sign his death-warrant. No wonder, therefore, that he found difficulties. Yet it was to France and England that Clement had to look for help in his extremities. The divorce perhaps had as yet been no more than a suggestion, a part of a policy which was still in its infancy. It could wait at any rate for a more convenient season. Meantime he sent his secretary, Sanga, to Paris to beg aid; and to Henry personally he made a passionate appeal, imploring him not to desert the Apostolic See in its hour of extreme need. He apologised for his importunacy, but he said he hoped that history would not have to record that Italy had been devastated in the time of Clement VII. to the dishonour of the King and of Wolsey. If France and England failed him, he would himself be ruined. The Emperor would be universal monarch. They would open their eyes at last, but they would open them too late. So

piteous was the entreaty that Henry when he read the
Pope's letter burst into tears.[1]   Clement had not been
idle.   He had brought his own small army into the field
to oppose Bourbon; he joined the Italian League, and
prepared to defend himself.   He was called the father of
Christendom, yet he was at open war with the most
Catholic king.   But Wolsey reasonably considered that
unless the Western powers interfered the end would
come.

If England was to act, she could act only in alliance
with France.   The change of policy was ill understood,
and was not popular among Henry's subjects.   The
divorce as yet had not been spoken of.   No breath of
such a purpose had gone abroad.   But English sentiment was imperial, and could endure with equanimity
even the afflictions of a pope.   The King was more
papal than his people; he allowed Wolsey to guide him,
and negotiations were set on foot at once for a special
treaty with France, one of the conditions of which was
to be the marriage of the Princess Mary—allotted like
a card in a game—either to Francis or to one of his
sons; another condition being that the English crown
should be settled upon her should Henry die without a
legitimate son.   Sir John Russell was simultaneously
despatched to Rome with money to help the Pope in
paying his troops and garrisoning the city.   The ducats
and the 'kind words' which accompanied them 'created

---

[1] *Calendar, Foreign and Domestic, Hen. VII.*, vol. iv. p. 1112.—
Hen. VIII. to Clement VII., Oct.
23, 1526.—*Ib.* p. 1145.   Giberto
to Gambara, Dec. 20, 1526.—*Ib.*
p. 1207.

'incredible joy,' encouraged his Holiness to reject unjust
conditions which had been offered, and restored him,
if for the moment only, 'from death to life.'[1] If
Russell described correctly what he saw in passing
through Italy, Clement had good cause for anxiety.
'The Swabians and Spaniards,' he wrote, 'had com-
'mitted horrible atrocities. They had burnt houses to
'the value of two hundred million ducats, with all the
'churches, images, and priests that fell into their hands.
'They had compelled the priests and monks to violate
'the nuns. Even where they were received without
'opposition they had burned the place; they had not
'spared the boys, and they had carried off the girls; and
'whenever they found the Sacrament of the Church
'they had thrown it into a river or into the vilest place
'they could find. If God did not punish such cruelty
'and wickedness, men would infer that He did not
'trouble Himself about the affairs of this world.'[2]

The news from Italy gave a fresh impulse to
Wolsey's policy and the Anglo-French Alliance, which
was pushed forward in spite of popular disapproval.
The Emperor, unable to pay, and therefore unable to
control his troops, became himself alarmed. He found
himself pressed into a course which was stimulating
the German revolt against the Papacy, and he professed
himself anxious to end the war. Inigo de Mendoza, the
Bishop of Burgos, was despatched to Paris to negotiate

---

[1] Giberto, Bishop of Verona,
to Wolsey, Feb. 10, 1527.—
Calendar, Foreign and Domestic,
vol. iv. pp. 1282-3.
[2] *Ib.,* April 26, 1527, vol. iv.
p. 1376.

for a general pacification. From Paris he was to proceed to London to assure Henry of the Emperor's
inalienable friendship, and above all things to gain over
Wolsey by the means which experience had shown to
be the nearest way to Wolsey's heart. The great
Cardinal was already Charles's pensionary, but the
pension was several years in arrear. Mendoza was to
tell him not only that the arrears should be immediately
paid up, but that a second pension should be secured to
him on the revenues of Milan, and that the Emperor
would make him a further grant of 6,000 ducats
annually out of the income of Spanish bishoprics. No
means was to be spared to divert the hostility of so
dangerous an enemy.[1]

Wolsey was not to be so easily gained. He had
formed large schemes which he did not mean to part
with, and in the matter of pensions Francis I. was as
liberal in promises as Charles. The Pope's prospects
were brightening. Besides the English money, he had
improved his finances by creating six new cardinals,
and making 240,000 crowns out of the disposition of
these sacred offices.[2] A French embassy, with the
Bishop of Tarbes at its head, came to England to
complete the treaty with Henry in the Pope's defence.
Demands were to be made upon the Emperor; if those
demands were refused, war was to follow, and the
cement of the alliance was to be the marriage of Mary

---

[1] Inigo de Mendoza to the
Emperor, Jan. 19, 1527.—*Spanish
Calendar*, vol. iii. pt. 2, p. 24.

[2] Alonzo Sanchez to Charles V.,
May 7, 1527.—*Ib.* p. 176.

with a French prince. It is likely that other secret
projects were in view also of a similar kind. The
marriage of Henry with Catherine had been intended
to secure the continuance of the alliance with Spain.
Royal ladies were the counters with which politicians
played; and probably enough there were thoughts of
placing a French princess in Catherine's place. However this may be, the legality of the King's marriage
with his nominal queen was suddenly and indirectly
raised in the discussion of the terms of the treaty, when
the Bishop of Tarbes inquired whether it was certain
that Catherine's daughter was legitimate.

Mr. Brewer, the careful and admirable editor of the
'Foreign and Domestic Calendar of State Papers,'
doubts whether the Bishop did anything of the kind. I
cannot agree with Mr. Brewer. The Bishop of Tarbes
was among the best-known diplomatists in Europe.
He was actively concerned during subsequent years in
the process of the divorce case in London, in Paris, and
at Rome. The expressions which he used on this
occasion were publicly appealed to by Henry in his
addresses to the peers and to the country, in the public
pleas which he laid before the English prelates, in the
various repeated defences which he made for his conduct.
It is impossible that the Bishop should have been
ignorant of the use which was made of his name, and
impossible equally to suppose that he would have
allowed his name to be used unfairly. The Bishop of
Tarbes was unquestionably the first person to bring the
question publicly forward. It is likely enough, how-

ever, that his introduction of so startling a topic had
been privately arranged between himself and Wolsey
as a prelude to the further steps which were immediately to follow. For the divorce had by this time been
finally resolved on as part of a general scheme for the
alteration of the balance of power. The domestic reasons
for it were as weighty as ever were alleged for similar
separations. The Pope's hesitation, it might be assumed,
would now be overcome, since he had flung himself for
support upon England and France, and his relations with
the Emperor could hardly be worse than they were.

The outer world, and even the persons principally
concerned, were taken entirely by surprise. For the
two years during which it had been under consideration
the secret had been successfully preserved. Not a hint
had reached Catherine herself, and even when the
match had been lighted by the Bishop of Tarbes the
full meaning of it does not seem to have occurred to
her. Mendoza, on his arrival in England, had found
her disturbed; she was irritated at the position which
had been given to the Duke of Richmond; she was
angry, of course, at the French alliance; she complained that she was kept in the dark about public
affairs; she was exerting herself to the utmost among
the friends of the imperial connection to arrest Wolsey's
policy and maintain the ancient traditions; but of the
divorce she had not heard a word. It was to come upon
her like a thunderstroke.[1]

---

[1] Mendoza to Charles V., March 18, 1527.—*Spanish Calendar*, vol.
iii. part 2, p. 110.

Before the drama opens a brief description will not
be out of place of the two persons who were to play the
principal parts on the stage, as they were seen a year
later by Ludovico Falieri, the Venetian ambassador in
England. Of Catherine his account is brief.

'The Queen is of low stature and rather stout; very
'good and very religious; speaks Spanish, French,
'Flemish, and English; more beloved by the Islanders
'than any queen that has ever reigned; about forty-
'five years old, and has been in England thirty years.
'She has had two sons and one daughter. Both the
'sons died in infancy. One daughter survives.'

On the King Falieri is more elaborate.

'In the 8th Henry such beauty of mind and body is
'combined as to surprise and astonish. Grand stature,
'suited to his exalted position, showing the superiority
'of mind and character; a face like an angel's, so fair
'it is; his head bald like Cæsar's, and he wears a beard,
'which is not the English custom. He is accomplished
'in every manly exercise, sits his horse well, tilts with
'his lance, throws the quoit, shoots with his bow
'excellent well; he is a fine tennis player, and he
'practises all these gifts with the greatest industry.
'Such a prince could not fail to have cultivated also his
'character and his intellect. He has been a student
'from his childhood; he knows literature, philosophy,
'and theology; speaks and writes Spanish, French, and
'Italian, besides Latin and English. He is kind,
'gracious, courteous, liberal, especially to men of learn-
'ing, whom he is always ready to help. He appears

'religious also, generally hears two masses a day, and
'on holy days High Mass besides. He is very chari-
'table, giving away ten thousand gold ducats annually
'among orphans, widows, and cripples.' [1]

Such was the King, such the Queen, whom fate and
the preposterous pretensions of the Papacy to dispense
with the established marriage laws had irregularly
mated, and whose separation was to shake the European
world. Pope Clement complained in subsequent years
that the burden of decision should have been thrown in
the first instance upon himself. If the King had proceeded at the outset to try the question in the English
courts ; if a judgment had been given unfavourable to
the marriage, and had he immediately acted upon it,
Queen Catherine might have appealed to the Holy See ;
but accomplished facts were solid things. Her case
might have been indefinitely protracted by legal tech-
nicalities till it died of itself. It would have been a
characteristic method of escape out of the difficulty,
and it was a view which Wolsey himself perhaps at
first entertained. He knew that the Pope was unwilling
to take the first step.

On the 17th of May, 1527, after a discussion of the
Treaty with France, he called a meeting of his Legatine
court at York Place. Archbishop Warham sate with
him as assessor. The King attended, and the Cardinal,
having stated that a question had arisen on the lawful-

---

[1] Report from England, Nov.
10, 1531.—*Venetian Calendar.*
Falieri arrived in England in 1528,
and the general parts of the Report
cover the intervening period.

ness of his marriage, enquired whether the King, for the sake of public morals and the good of his own soul, would allow the objections to be examined into. The King assented, and named a proctor. The Bull of Julius II. was introduced and considered. Wolsey declared that in a case so intricate the canon lawyers must be consulted, and he asked for the opinions of the assembled bishops. The bishops, one only excepted, gave dubious answers. The aged Bishop of Rochester, reputed the holiest and wisest of them, said decidedly that the marriage was good, and the Bull which legalised it sufficient.

These proceedings were not followed up, but the secrecy which had hitherto been observed was no longer possible, and Catherine and her friends learnt now for the first time the measure which was in contemplation. Mendoza, writing on the day following the York Place meeting to the Emperor, informed him, as a fact which he had learnt on reliable authority, that Wolsey, for a final stroke of wickedness, was scheming to divorce the Queen. She was so much alarmed that she did not venture herself to speak of it, but it was certain that the lawyers and bishops had been invited to sign a declaration that, being his brother's widow, she could not be the wife of the King. The Pope, she was afraid, might be tempted to take part against her, or the Cardinal himself might deliver judgment as Papal Legate. Her one hope was in the Emperor. The cause of the action taken against her was her fidelity to the Imperial interests. Nothing as yet had been made formally public, and she begged that the whole matter might be kept as private as possible.[1]

That the Pope would be willing, if he dared, to gratify Henry at Charles's expense was only too likely. The German Lutherans and the German Emperor were at the moment his most dangerous enemies. France and England were the only Powers who seemed willing to assist him, and a week before the meeting of Wolsey's court he had experienced in the most terrible form what the Imperial hostility might bring upon him. On the 7th of that same month of May the army of the Duke of Bourbon had taken Rome by storm. The city was given up to pillage. Reverend cardinals were dragged through the streets on mules' backs, dishonoured and mutilated. Convents of nuns were abandoned to the licentious soldiery. The horrors of the capture may have been exaggerated, but it is quite certain that to holy things or holy persons no respect was paid, and that the atrocities which in those days were usually perpetrated in stormed towns were on this occasion eminently conspicuous. The unfortunate Pope, shut up in the Castle of St. Angelo, looked down from its battlements upon scenes so dreadful that it must have appeared as if the Papacy and the Church itself had been overtaken by the final judgment. We regard the Spaniards as a nation of bigots, we consider it impossible that the countrymen of Charles and Philip could have been animated by any such bitterness against the

---

[1] Inigo de Mendoza to Charles V., May 18, 1527.—*Spanish Calendar,* vol. iii. part 2, p. 193.

centre of Catholic Christendom. Charles himself is not likely to have intended the humiliation of the Holy See. But Clement had reason for his misgivings, and Wolsey's policy was not without excuse. Lope de Soria was Charles's Minister at Genoa, and Lope de Soria's opinions, freely uttered, may have been shared by many a Catholic besides himself. On the 25th of May, a fortnight after the storm, he wrote to his master the following noticeable letter:

'The sack of Rome must be regarded as a visitation 'from God, who permits his servant the Emperor to 'teach his Vicar on earth and other Christian princes 'that their wicked purposes shall be defeated, the unjust 'wars which they have raised shall cease, peace be re-'stored to Christendom, the faith be exalted, and heresy 'extirpated. . . . Should the Emperor think that the 'Church of God is not what it ought to be, and that the 'Pope's temporal power emboldens him to promote war 'among Christian princes, I cannot but remind your 'Majesty that it will not be a sin, but a meritorious 'action, to reform the Church; so that the Pope's 'authority be confined exclusively to his own spiritual 'affairs, and temporal affairs to be left to Cæsar, since 'by right what is God's belongs to God, and what is 'Cæsar's to Cæsar. I have been twenty-eight years 'in Italy, and I have observed that the Popes have 'been the sole cause of all the wars and miseries 'during that time. Your Imperial Majesty, as Supreme 'Lord on earth, is bound to apply a remedy to that evil.' [1]

---

[1] Lope de Soria to Charles V., May 25, 1527.—*Spanish Calendar*, vol. iii. part 2, p. 209.

Heretical English and Germans were not the only persons who could recognize the fitness of the secular supremacy of princes over popes and Churches. Such thoughts must have passed through the mind of Charles himself, and of many more besides him. De Soria's words might have been dictated by Luther or Thomas Cromwell. Had the Emperor at that moment placed himself at the head of the Reformation, all later history would have been different. One statesman at any rate had cause to fear that this might be what was about to happen. Wolsey was the embodiment of everything most objectionable and odious to the laity in the ecclesiastical administration of Europe. To defend the Papacy and to embarrass Charles was the surest method of protecting himself and his order. The divorce was an incident in the situation, but not the least important. Catherine represented the Imperialist interest in England. To put her away was to make the breach with her countrymen and kindred irreparable. He took upon himself to assure the King that after the last outrage the Pope would agree to anything that France and England demanded of him, and would trust to his allies to bear him harmless. That the divorce was a thing reasonable in itself to ask for, and certain to be conceded by any pope who was free to act on his own judgment, was assumed as a matter of course. Sir Gregory Casalis, the English agent at Rome, was instructed to obtain access to Clement in St. Angelo, to convey to him the indignation felt in England at his treatment, and then to insist on the illegality of the King's relations with Catherine. on the King's own scruples of conscience,

and on the anxiety of his subjects that there should be
a male heir to the crown. The 'urgent cause' such
as was necessary to be produced when exceptional
actions were required of the popes was the imminence
or even certainty of civil war if no such heir was
born.

Catherine meanwhile had again communicated with
Mendoza. She had spoken to her husband, and Henry,
since further reticence was impossible, had told her
that they had been living in mortal sin, and that a
separation was necessary. A violent scene had followed,
with natural tears and reproaches.[1] The King endeavoured to console her, but it was not a matter where
consolation could avail. Wolsey advised him to deal
with her gently, till it was seen what the Pope and the
King of France would do in the matter. Wolsey himself was to go immediately to Paris to see Francis, and
consult with him on the measures necessary to be taken
in consequence of the Pope's imprisonment. It was
possible that Clement, finding himself helpless, might
become a puppet in the Emperor's hands. Under such
circumstances he could not be trusted by other countries
with the spiritual authority attaching to his office, and
schemes were being formed for some interim arrangement by which France and England were to constitute
themselves into a separate patriarchate, with Wolsey at
its head as Archbishop of Rouen. Mendoza says that
this proposal had been actually made to Wolsey by the

---

[1] Mendoza to Charles V., July 13, 1527.—*Spanish Calendar*, vol.
ii. part 2, p. 276.

French Ambassador.[1] In Spain it was even believed
to be contemplated as a permanent modification of
the ecclesiastical system. The Imperial Councillors at
Valladolid told the Venetian Minister that the Cardinal
intended to separate the Churches of England and
France from that of Rome, saying that as the Pope was
a prisoner he was not to be obeyed, and that even if
the Emperor released him, he still would not be free
unless his fortresses and territory now in the Emperor's
hands were restored to him.[2] Wolsey had reason for
anxiety, for Catherine and Mendoza were writing to the
Emperor insisting that he should make the Pope revoke
Wolsey's Legatine powers.

In spite of efforts to keep secret the intended divorce,
it soon became known throughout England. The Queen
was personally popular. The nation generally detested
France, and looked on the Emperor as their hereditary
friend. The reasons for the divorce might influence
statesmen, but did not touch the body of the people.
They naturally took the side of an injured wife, and
if Mendoza can be believed (and there is no reason
why he should not be believed), the first impression
was decidedly unfavourable to a project which was regarded as part of the new policy. Mendoza made the
most of the opposition. He told the Emperor that
if six or seven thousand men were landed in Cornwall, forty thousand Englishmen would rise and join

---

[1] Mendoza to Charles V., July 13, 1527.—*Spanish Calendar*, vol. iii. part 2, p. 273.

[2] Andrea Navagero to the Sig-nory, July 17, 1527.—*Venetian Calendar.*

them.[1] He saw Wolsey—he reasoned with him, and wnen he found reason ineffectual, he named the bribe which the Emperor was willing to give. Knowing what Francis was bidding, he baited his hook more liberally. He spoke of the Papacy: 'how the chair was now in the 'Emperor's hands, and the Emperor, if Wolsey deserved 'it, would no doubt promote his elevation.' The glittering temptation was unavailing. The papal chair had been Wolsey's highest ambition, but he remained un-moved. He said that he had served the Emperor in the past out of disinterested regard. He still trusted that the Emperor would replace the Pope and restore the Church. Mendoza's answer was not reassuring to an English statesman. He said that both the spiritual and temporal powers were now centred in his master, and he advised Wolsey, if he desired an arrangement, to extend his journey from France, go on to Spain, and see the Emperor in person. It was precisely this *centering* which those who had charge of English liberties had a right to resent. Divorce or no divorce, they could not allow a power possessed of so much authority in the rest of Christendom to be the servant of a single prince. The divorce was but an illustration of the situation, and such a Papacy as Mendoza contemplated would reduce England and all Catholic Europe into fiefs of the Empire.

---

[1] Mendoza to Charles V., July 17, 1527.—*Spanish Calendar.*

CHAPTER II.

IT was believed at the time—and it was the tradition afterwards—that Wolsey, in his mission to Paris, intended to replace Catherine by a French princess, the more surely to commit Francis to the support of Henry in the divorce, and to strengthen the new alliance. Nothing can be inherently more likely. The ostensible reason, however, was to do away with any difficulties which might have been suggested by the objection of the Bishop of Tarbes to the legitimacy of the Princess Mary. If illegitimate, she would be no fitting bride for the Duke of Orleans. But she had been born *bonâ fide parentum*. There was no intention of infringing her prospective rights or of altering her present position.

Her rank and title were to be secured to her in amplest measure.

The Cardinal went upon his journey with the splendour attaching to his office and befitting a churchman who was aspiring to be the spiritual president of the two kingdoms. On his way to the coast he visited two prelates whose support to his policy was important. Archbishop Warham had been cold about the divorce, if not openly hostile. Wolsey found him 'not much 'changed from his first fashion,' but admitting that, although it might be unpleasant to the Queen, truth and justice must prevail. Bishop Fisher was a more difficult subject. He had spoken in the Legate's court in Catherine's favour. It was from him, as the King supposed, that Catherine herself had learnt what was impending over her. Wolsey called at his palace as he passed through Rochester. He asked the Bishop plainly if he had been in communication with the Queen. The Bishop, after some hesitation, confessed that the Queen had sought his advice, and said that he had declined to give an opinion without the King's command. Before Wolsey left London, at a last interview at York Place, the King had directed him to explain 'the whole matter' to the Bishop. He went through the entire history, mentioned the words of the Bishop of Tarbes, and discussed the question which had risen upon it, on account of which he had been sent into France. Finally, he described the extreme violence with which Catherine had received the intelligence.

The Bishop greatly blamed the conduct of the

Queen, and said he thought that if he might speak to
her he might bring her to submission. He agreed, or
seemed to agree, that the marriage had been irregular,
though he did not himself think that it could now be
broken. Others of the bishops, he thought, agreed
with him; but he was satisfied that the King meant
nothing against the laws of God, and would be fully
justified in submitting his misgivings to the Pope.[1]

Mendoza's and the Queen's letters had meanwhile
been despatched to Spain, to add to the anxieties which
were overwhelming the Emperor. Nothing could have
been less welcome at such a juncture than a family
quarrel with his uncle of England, whose friendship he
was still hoping to retain. The bird that he had caged
at Rome was no convenient prisoner. The capture
of Rome had not been ordered by himself, though
politically he was obliged to maintain it. The time
did not suit for the ambitious Church reforms of Lope
de Soria. Peace would have to be made with the Pope
on some moderate conditions. His own Spain was
hardly quieted after the revolt of the *Comunidades.*
Half Germany was in avowed apostasy from the Church
of Rome. The Turks were overrunning Hungary, and
sweeping the Mediterranean with their pirate fleets,
and the passionate and restless Francis was watching
his opportunity to revenge Pavia and attack his captor
in the Low Countries and in Italy. The great Emperor
was moderate, cautious, prudent to a fault. In a

---

[1] Wolsey to Henry VIII.,
July 5.—*Calendar, Foreign and*
Domestic, vol. iv. part 2. Bishop
Fisher to Paul, *ibid.*, p. 1471.

calmer season he might have been tempted to take the
Church in hand; and none understood better the condition into which it had fallen. But he was wise enough
to know that if a reform of the Papacy was undertaken
at all it must be undertaken with the joint consent of
the other Christian princes, and all his present efforts
were directed to peace. He was Catherine's natural
guardian. Her position in England had been hitherto
a political security for Henry's friendship. It was his
duty and his interest to defend her, and he meant to
do it; not, however, by sending roving expeditions to
land in Cornwall and raise a civil war; all means were
to be tried before that; to attempt such a thing, he
well knew, would throw Europe into a blaze. The
letters found him at Valladolid. He replied, of course,
that he was shocked at a proceeding so unlooked for
and so scandalous, but he charged Mendoza to be
moderate and to confine himself to remonstrance.[1]
He wrote himself to Henry—confidentially, as from
friend to friend, and ciphering his letter with his own
hand. He was unable to believe, he said, that Henry
could contemplate seriously bringing his domestic
discomforts before the world. Even supposing the
marriage illegitimate—even supposing that the Pope
had no power to dispense in such cases—' it would be
' better and more honourable to keep the matter secret,
' and to work out a remedy.' He bade Mendoza remind
the King that to question the dispensing power affected

---

[1] Charles V. to Inigo de Men-
doza, July 29.—*Calendar, Foreign*   *and Domestic,* vol. iv. part 2, p.
1500.

the position of other princes besides his own; that to touch the legitimacy of his daughter would increase the difficulties with the succession, and not remove them. He implored the King 'to keep the matter 'secret, as he would do himself.' Meanwhile, he told Mendoza, for Catherine's comfort, that he had written to demand a mild brief from the Pope to stop the scandal. He had requested him, as Catherine had suggested, to revoke Wolsey's powers, or at least to command that neither he nor any English Court should try the case. If heard at all, it must be heard before his Holiness and the Sacred College.[1] But he could not part with the hope that he might still bring Wolsey to his own and the Queen's side. A council of Cardinals was to meet at Avignon to consider the Pope's captivity. The Cardinal of England was expected to attend. Charles himself might go to Perpignan. Wolsey might meet him there, discuss the state of Europe, and settle the King's secret affair at the same time. Should this be impossible, he charged Mendoza once more to leave no stone unturned to recover Wolsey's friendship. 'In our 'name,' he said, 'you will make him the following offers:—

'1. The payment of all arrears on his several 'pensions, amounting to 9,000 ducats annually.

'2. Six thousand additional ducats annually until 'such a time as a bishoprick or other ecclesiastical 'endowment of the same revenue becomes vacant in 'our kingdom.

---

[1] Charles V. to Inigo de Mendoza, July 29.—*Calendar, Foreign* *and Domestic*, vol. iv. part 2, p. 1500.

' 3. The Duke, who is to have Milan, to give him
' a Marquisate in that Duchy, with an annual rent
' of 12,000 ducats, or 15,000 if the smaller sum be
' not enough ; the said Marquisate to be held by
' the Cardinal during his life, and to pass after him
' to any heir whom he shall appoint.' [1]

As if this was not sufficient, the Emperor paid a yet
further tribute to the supposed all-powerful Cardinal.
He wrote himself to him as to his 'good friend.' He
said that if there was anything in his dominions which
the Cardinal wished to possess he had only to name it,
as he considered Wolsey the best friend that he had in
the world.[2]

For the ministers of great countries deliberately to
sell themselves to foreign princes was the custom of
the age. The measure of public virtue which such a
custom indicates was not exalted ; and among the
changes introduced by the Reformation the abolition or
suspension of it was not the least beneficial. Thomas
Cromwell, when he came to power, set the example of
refusal, and corruption of public men on a scale so
scandalously enormous was no more heard of. Gold,
however, had flowed in upon Wolsey in such enormous
streams and from so many sources that the Emperor's
munificence and attention failed to tempt him. On
reaching Paris he found Francis bent upon war, and

----

[1] Charles V. to Mendoza, Sept.
30, 1527.—*Calendar, Foreign and
Domestic* vol. iv. p. 1569.

[2] The Emperor to the Cardinal
of York, Aug. 31, 1527.—*Spanish
Calendar,* vol. iii. part 2, p. 357.

willing to promise anything for Henry's assistance.
The belief at the French Court was that the Emperor,
hearing that the Churches of England and France
meant to decline from their obedience to the Roman
Communion, would carry the Pope to Spain; that
Clement would probably be poisoned there, and the
Apostolic See would be established permanently in the
Peninsula.[1] Wolsey himself wrote this, and believed
it, or desired Henry to believe it, proving the extreme
uncertainty among the best-informed of contemporary
politicians as to the probable issue of the capture of
Rome. The French Cardinals drew and sent an address
to the Pope, intimating that as long as he was in confinement they could accept no act of his as lawful, and
would not obey it. Wolsey signed at the head of them.
The Cardinals Salviati, Bourbon, Lorraine, and the
Chancellor Cardinal of Sens, signed after him.[2] The
first stroke in the game had been won by Wolsey. Had
the Pope recalled his powers as legate, an immediate
schism might have followed. But a more fatal blow
had been prepared for him by his master in England.
Trusting to the Cardinal's promises that the Pope would
make no difficulty about the divorce, Henry had considered himself at liberty to choose a successor to
Catherine. He had suffered once in having allowed
politics to select a wife for him. This time he intended

---

[1] Wolsey to Henry VIII., Aug.
1527.—*Calendar, Foreign and
Domestic*, vol. iv. part 2.

[2] The Cardinals of France to

Clement VII., Sept. 16, 1527.—
Spanish Calendar, vol. iii. part 2,
p. 383.

to be guided by his own inclination. When Elizabeth afterwards wished to marry Leicester, Lord Sussex said she had better fix after her own liking; there would be the better chance of the heir that her realm was looking for. Her father fixed also after his liking in selecting Elizabeth's mother.

Anne Boleyn was the second daughter of Sir Thomas Boleyn, a Norfolk knight of ancient blood, and himself a person of some distinction in the public service. Lady Boleyn was a Howard, daughter of the Duke of Norfolk. Anne was born in 1507, and by birth and connection was early introduced into the court. When a girl she was taken to Paris to be educated. In 1522 she was brought back to England, became a lady-in-waiting, and, being a witty brilliant young woman, attracted and encouraged the attentions of the fashionable cavaliers of the day. Wyatt, the poet, was among her adorers, and the young Percy, afterwards Earl of Northumberland. It was alleged afterwards that between her and Percy there had been a secret marriage which had been actually consummated. That she had been involved in some dangerous intrigue or other she herself subsequently confessed. But she was attractive, she was witty; she drew Henry's fancy, and the fancy became an ardent passion. Now, for the first time, in Wolsey's absence, the Lady Anne's name appears in connection with the divorce. On the 16th of August Mendoza informed Charles, as a matter of general belief, that if the suit for the divorce was successful the King would marry a daughter of Master Boleyn, whom the Emperor would remember as once ambassador. at the Imperial court.[1] There is no direct evidence that before Wolsey had left England the King had seriously thought of Anne at all. Catherine could have had no suspicion of it, or her jealous indignation would have made itself heard. The Spanish Ambassador spoke of it as a new feature in the case.

The Boleyns were Wolsey's enemies, and belonged to the growing faction most hostile to the Church. The news as it came upon him was utterly distasteful.[2] Anne in turn hated Wolsey, as he probably knew that she would, and she compelled him to stoop to the disgrace of suing for her favour. The inference is reasonable, therefore, that the King took the step which in the event was to produce such momentous consequences when the Cardinal was not at hand to dissuade him. He was not encouraged even by her own family. Her father, as will be seen hereafter, was from the first opposed to his daughter's advancement. He probably knew her character too well. But Henry, when he had taken an idea into his head, was not to be moved from it. The lady was not beautiful : she was rather short than tall, her complexion was dark, her neck long, her

---

[1] Mendoza to Charles V., Aug. 16, 1527.—*Spanish Calendar*, vol. iii. part 2, p. 327.

[2] The date of Henry's resolution to marry Anne is of some consequence, since the general assumption is that it was the origin of the divorce. Rumour of course, said so afterwards, but there is no evidence for it. The early love-letters written by the King to her are assigned by Mr. Brewer to the midsummer of 1527. But they are undated, and therefore the period assigned to them is conjecture merely.

mouth broad, her figure not particularly good. The fascinating features were her long flowing brown hair, a pair of effective dark eyes, and a boldness of character which might have put him on his guard, and did not.

The immediate effect was to cool Wolsey's ardour for the divorce. His mission in France, which opened so splendidly, eventuated in little. The French Cardinals held no meeting at Avignon. They had signed the address to Clement, but they had not made the Cardinal of York into their patriarch. Rouen was not added to his other preferments. Coald he but have proposed a marriage for his sovereign with the Princess of Alençon, all might have been different, but it had fared with him as it fared with the Earl of Warwick, whom Henry's grandfather had sent to France to woo a bride for him, and in his absence married Elizabeth Grey. He perhaps regretted the munificent offers of the Emperor which he had hastily rejected, and he returned to England in the autumn to feel the consequences of the change in his situation. Mr. Brewer labours in vain to prove that Wolsey was unfavourable to the divorce from the beginning. Catherine believed that he was the instigator of it. Mendoza was of the same opinion. Unquestionably he promoted it with all his power, and made it a part of a great policy. To maintain that he was acting thus against his conscience and to please the King is more dishonouring to him than to suppose that he was either the originator or the willing instrument. All, however, was altered when Anne Boleyn came upon the stage, and she made haste to make him feel the change. 'The

'Legate has returned from France,' wrote Mendoza on the 26th of October. He went to visit the King at Richmond, and sent to ask where he could see him. The King was in his chamber. It happened that the lady, who seemed to entertain no great affection for the Cardinal, was in the room with the King, and before the latter could answer the message she said for him, ' Where ' else is the Cardinal to come ? Tell him he may come 'here where the King is.' The Legate felt that such treatment boded no good to him, but concealed his resentment. 'The cause,' said Mendoza, ' is supposed ' to be that the said lady bears the Legate a grudge, for ' other reasons, and because she has discovered that ' during his visit to France the Legate proposed to have ' an alliance for the King found in that country.'[1] Wolsey persuaded Mendoza that the French marriage had been a fiction, but at once he began to endeavour to undo his work, and prevent the dissolution of the marriage with Catherine. He tried to procure an unfavourable opinion from the English Bishops before legal proceedings were commenced. Mendoza, however, doubted his stability if the King persisted in his purpose, and advised that a papal decision on the case should be procured and forwarded as soon as possible.[2]

The Pope's captivity, however, would destroy the value of any judgment which he might give while he continued in durance. The Emperor, encouraged by the intimation that Wolsey was wavering, reverted to

---

[1] Mendoza to Charles V. Oct. 26, 1527.—*Spanish Calendar*, vol. iii. part 2 p. 432.   [2] *Ibid.*

his previous hope. In a special memorandum of measures
to be taken, the most important, notwithstanding the
refusal of the previous offers, was still thought to be to
'bribe the Cardinal.' He must instantly be paid the
arrears of his pensions out of the revenues of the sees of
Palencia and Badajoz. If there was not money enough
in the treasury, a further and larger pension of twelve
or fourteen thousand crowns was to be given to him
out of some rich bishopric in Castile. The Emperor
admitted that he had promised the Cortes to appoint
no more foreigners to Spanish sees, but such a promise
could not be held binding, being in violation of the
liberties of the Church. Every one would see that it
was for the good of the kingdom.

The renewed offer was doubtless conveyed to Wolsey,
but he probably found that he had gone too deep to
retire. If he made such an effort as Mendoza relates,
he must have speedily discovered that it would be
useless. He had encouraged the King in a belief that
the divorce would be granted by the Pope as a matter
of course, and the King, having made up his own mind,
was not to be moved from it. If Wolsey now drew
back, the certain inference would be that he had accepted
an Imperial bribe. There was no resource, therefore,
but to go on.

While Wolsey had been hesitating, the King had,
unknown to him, sent his secretary, Dr. Knight, to
Rome with directions to obtain access if possible to the
Pope, and procure the dispensation which had been
already applied for to enable him to marry a second

time without the formalities of a judgment. Such an expedient would be convenient in many ways. It would leave Catherine's position unaffected and the legitimacy of the Princess Mary unimpugned. Knight went. He found that without a passport he could not even enter the city, still less be allowed an interview. 'With ten thousand crowns he could not bribe his way 'into St. Angelo.' He contrived, however, to have a letter introduced, which the Pope answered by telling Knight to wait in some quiet place. He (the Pope) would 'there send him all the King's requests in as 'ample a form as they were desired.' Knight trusted in a short time 'to have in his custody as much, perfect, 'sped, and under lead, as his Highness had long time 'desired.'[1]

Knight was too sanguine. The Emperor, finding the Pope's detention as a prisoner embarrassing, allowed him, on the 9th of December, to escape to Orvieto, where he was apparently at liberty; but he was only in a larger cage, all his territories being occupied by Imperial troops, and he himself watched by the General of the Observants, and warned at his peril to grant nothing to Catherine's prejudice. Henry's Secretary followed him, saw him, and obtained something which on examination proved to be worthless. The negotiations were left again in Wolsey's hands, and were pressed with all the eagerness of a desperate man.

Pope Clement had ceased to be a free agent. He

---

[1] Knight to Henry VIII., Dec. 4.—*Calendar, Foreign and Domestic,* vol. iv. part 2, pp. 1633-4.

did not look to the rights of the case.   He would gladly
have pleased Henry could he have pleased him without
displeasing Charles.   The case itself was peculiar, and
opinions differed on the rights and wrongs of it.   The
reader must be from time to time reminded that, as
the law of England has stood ever since, a marriage
with a brother's widow was not a marriage.   As the law
of the Church then stood, it was not a marriage unless
permitted by the Pope ; and according to the same law
of England the Pope neither has, nor ever had, any
authority to dispense with the law.   Therefore Henry,
on the abstract contention, was in the right.   He had
married Catherine under an error.   The problem was
to untie the knot with as little suffering to either as the
nature of the case permitted.   That the negotiations
were full of inconsistencies, evasions, and contradictions,
was natural and inevitable.   To cut the knot without
untying it was the only direct course, but that all means
were exhausted before the application of so violent a
remedy was rather a credit than a reproach.

The first inconsistency was in the King.   He did
not regard his marriage as valid ; therefore he thought
himself at liberty to marry again ; but he did not wish
to illegitimatise his daughter or degrade Catherine.   He
disputed the validity of the dispensation of Julius II. ;
yet he required a dispensation from Clement which
was equally questionable to enable him to take a second
wife.   The management of the case having reverted to
Wolsey, fresh instructions were sent to Sir Gregory
Casalis, the regular English agent at the Papal court, to

wait on Clement. Casalis was 'bid consider how much
'the affair concerned the relief of the King's conscience,
'the safety of his soul, the preservation of his life, the
'continuation of his succession, the welfare and repose
'of all his subjects now and hereafter.' The Pope at
Orvieto was personally accessible. Casalis was to represent to him the many difficulties which had arisen in
connection with the marriage, and the certainty of civil
war in England should the King die leaving the succession no better provided for. He was, therefore, to request
the Pope to grant a commission to Wolsey to hear the
case and to decide it, and (perhaps as an alternative) to
sign a dispensation, a draft of which Wolsey enclosed.
The language of the dispensation was peculiar. Wolsey
explained it by saying that 'the King, remembering by
'the example of past times what false claims [to the
'crown] had been put forward, to avoid all colour or
'pretext of the same, desired this of the Pope as abso-
'lutely necessary.' If these two requests were conceded,
Henry undertook on his part to require the Emperor to
set the Pope at liberty, or to declare war against him if
he refused.

A dispensation, which was to evade the real point
at issue, yet to convey to the King a power to take
another wife, was a novelty in itself and likely to be
carefully worded. It has given occasion among modern
historians to important inferences disgraceful to every
one concerned. The sinister meaning supposed to be
obvious to modern critics could not have been concealed
from the Pope himself. Here, therefore, follow the

words which have been fastened on as for ever fatal to the intelligence and character of Henry and his Ministers.

The Pope, after reviewing the later history of England, the distractions caused by rival claimants of the crown, after admitting the necessity of guarding against the designs of the ambitious, and empowering Henry to marry again, was made to address the King in these words [1] :—

' In order to take away all occasion from evil doers, we ' do in the plenitude of our power hereby suspend *hâc vice* ' all canons forbidding marriage in the fourth degree, also ' all canons *de impedimento publicæ honestatis* preventing ' marriage in consequence of clandestine espousals, further ' all canons relating to precontracts clandestinely made ' but not consummated, also all canons affecting impedi-' ments created by affinity rising *ex illicito coitu,* in any ' degree even in the first, so far as the marriage to be ' contracted by you, the petitioner, can be objected to or ' in any wise be impugned by the same. Further, to ' avoid canonical objections on the side of the woman by ' reason of former contract clandestinely made, or impedi-' ment of public honesty or justice arising from such ' clandestine contract, or of any affinity contracted in any ' degree even the first, *ex illicito coitu :* and in the event ' that it has proceeded beyond the second or third degrees ' of consanguinity, whereby otherwise you, the petitioner, ' would not be allowed by the canons to contract mar-

---

[1] I follow Mr. Brewer's translation.

'riage, we hereby license you to take such woman for
'wife, and suffer you and the woman to marry free from
'all ecclesiastical objections and censures.'

The explanation given by Wolsey of the wording
of this document is that it was intended to preclude
any objections which might be raised to the prejudice
of the offspring of a marriage in itself irregular. It was
therefore made as comprehensive as possible.   Dr.
Lingard, followed by Mr. Brewer, and other writers see
in it a transparent personal application to the situation
in which Henry intended to place himself in making a
wife of Anne Boleyn. Two years subsequent to the
period when this dispensation was asked for, when the
question of the divorce had developed into a battle
between England and the Papacy, and the passions of
Catholics and Reformers were boiling over in recrimi-
nation and invective, the King's plea that he was parting
from Catherine out of conscience was met by stories set
floating in society that the King himself had previously
intrigued with the mother and sister of the lady whom
he intended to marry. Precisely the same obstacle
existed, therefore, to his marriage with Anne, being
further aggravated by incest. No attempt was ever
made to prove these charges; no particulars were given
of time or place. No witnesses were produced, nor
other evidence, though to prove them would have been
of infinite importance. Queen Catherine, who if any
one must have known it if the accusation was true,
never alludes to Mary Boleyn in the fiercest of her
denunciations. It was heard of only in the conversation

of disaffected priests or secret visitors to the Spanish Ambassador, and was made public only in the manifesto of Reginald Pole, which accompanied Paul III.'s Bull for Henry's deposition. Even this authority, which was not much in itself, is made less by the fact that in the first draft of 'Pole's Book,' sent to England to be examined in 1535, the story is not mentioned. Evidently, therefore, Pole had not then heard of it or did not believe it. The guilt with the mother is now abandoned as too monstrous. The guilt with the sister is peremptorily insisted on, and the words of the dispensation are appealed to as no longer leaving room for doubt. To what else, it is asked, can such extraordinary expressions refer unless to some disgraceful personal *liaison?*

The uninstructed who draw inferences of fact from the verbiage of legal documents will discover often what are called 'mare's nests.' I will request the reader to consider what this supposition involves. The dispensation would have to be copied into the Roman registers, subject to the inspection of the acutest canon lawyers in the world. If the meaning is so clear to us, it must have been clear to them. We are, therefore, to believe that Henry, when demanding to be separated from Catherine, as an escape from mortal sin, for the relief of his conscience and the surety of his succession, was gratuitously putting the Pope in possession of a secret which had only to be published to extinguish him and his plea in an outburst of scorn and laughter.

There was no need for such an acknowledgment, for

the intrigue could not be proved. It could not be required for the legitimation of the children that were to be born; for a man of Wolsey's ability must have known that no dispensation would be held valid that was granted after so preposterous a confidence. It was as if a man putting in a claim for some great property, before the case came on for trial privately informed both judge and jury that it was based on forgery.

We are called on to explain further, why, when all Europe was shaken by the controversy, no hint is to be found in any public document of a fact which, if true, would be decisive; and yet more extraordinary, why the Pope and the Curia, when driven to bay in all the exasperation of a furious controversy, left a weapon unused which would have assured them an easy victory. Wolsey was not a fool. Is it conceivable that he would have composed a document so fatal and have drawn the Pope's pointed attention to it? My credulity does not extend so far. We cannot prove a negative; we cannot prove that Henry had not intrigued with Mary Boleyn, or with all the ladies of his court. But the language of the dispensation cannot be adduced as an evidence of it, unless King, Pope, and all the interested world had parted with their senses.

As to the story itself, there is no ground for distinguishing between the mother and the daughter. When it was first set circulating both were named together. The mother only has been dropped, lest the improbability should seem too violent for belief. That Mary Boleyn had been the King's mistress before or after her own marriage is now asserted as an ascertained fact by respectable historians—a fact sufficient, can it be proved, to cover with infamy for ever the English separation from Rome, King, Ministers, Parliaments, Bishops, and every one concerned with it. The effectiveness of the weapon commends it to Catholic controversialists. I have only to repeat that the evidence for the charge is nothing but the floating gossip of Catholic society, never heard of, never whispered, till the second stage of the quarrel, when it had developed into a passionate contest; never even then alleged in a form in which it could be met and answered. It could not have been hid from Queen Catherine if it was known to Reginald Pole. We have many letters of Catherine, eloquent on the story of her wrongs; letters to the Emperor, letters to the Pope; yet no word of Mary Boleyn. What reason can be given save that it was a legend which grew out of the temper of the time? Nothing could be more plausible than to meet the King's plea of conscience with an allegation which made it ridiculous. But in the public pleadings of a cause which was discussed in every capital in Europe by the keenest lawyers and diplomatists of the age, an accusation which, if maintained, would have been absolutely decisive, is never alluded to in any public document till the question had passed beyond the stage of discussion. The silence of all responsible persons is sufficient proof of its nature. It was a mere floating calumny, born of wind and malice.

Mr. Brewer does indeed imagine that he has

D

discovered what he describes as a tacit confession on Henry's part. When the Act of Appeals was before the House of Commons which ended the papal jurisdiction in England, a small knot of Opposition members used to meet privately to deliberate how to oppose it. Among these one of the most active was Sir George Throgmorton, a man who afterwards, with his brother Michael, made himself useful to Cromwell and played with both parties, but was then against the divorce and against all the measures which grew out of it. Throgmorton, according to his own account, had been admitted to an interview with the King and Cromwell. In 1537, after the Pilgrimage of Grace, while the ashes of the rebellion were still smouldering, after Michael Throgmorton had betrayed Cromwell's confidence and gone over to Reginald Pole, Sir George was reported to have used certain expressions to Sir Thomas Dyngley and to two other gentlemen, which he was called on by the Council to explain. The letter to the King in which he replied is still extant. He said that he had been sent for by the King after a speech on the Act of Appeals, 'and that he saw his Grace's conscience was ' troubled about having married his brother's wife.' He professed to have said to Dyngley that he had told the King that if he did marry Queen Anne his conscience would be more troubled at length, for it was thought he had meddled both with the mother and the sister; that his Grace said: ' Never with the mother,' and my Lord Privy Seal (Cromwell), standing by, said, ' nor with the ' sister neither, so put that out of your mind.' Mr.

Brewer construes this into an admission of the King
that Mary Boleyn had been his mistress, and omits, of
course, by inadvertence, that Throgmorton, being asked
why he had told this story to Dyngley, answered that
'he spake it only out of vainglory, to show he was one
'that durst speak for the Commonwealth.' Nothing
is more common than for 'vainglorious' men, when
admitted to conversation with kings, to make the most
of what they said themselves, and to report not very
accurately what was said to them. Had the conversation been authentic, Throgmorton would naturally have
appealed to Cromwell's recollection. But Mr. Brewer
accepts the version of a confessed boaster as if it was a
complete and trustworthy account of what had actually
passed. He does not ask himself whether if the King
or Cromwell had given their version it might not have
borne another complexion. Henry was not a safe
person to take liberties with. Is it likely that if one of
his subjects, who was actively opposing him in Parliament, had taxed him with an enormous crime, he
would have made a confession which Throgmorton
had only to repeat in the House of Commons to ruin
him and his cause? Mr. Brewer should have added
also that the authority which he gave for the story
was no better than Father Peto, afterwards Cardinal
Peto, as bitter an enemy of the Reformation as Pole
himself. Most serious of all, Mr. Brewer omits to
mention that Throgmorton was submitted afterwards
to a severe cross-examination before a Committee of
Council, the effect of which, if he had spoken truly,

could only be to establish the authenticity of a disgraceful charge.[1]

The last evidence alleged is the confession made by Anne Boleyn, after her condemnation, of some mystery which had invalidated her marriage with the King and had been made the ground of an Act of Parliament. The confession was not published, and Catholic opinion concluded, and concludes still, that it must have been the Mary Boleyn intrigue. Catholic opinion does not pause to inquire whether Anne could have been said to confess an offence of the King and her sister. The cross-examination of Throgmorton turns the conjecture into an absurdity. When asked, in 1537, whom he ever heard say such a thing, he would have had but to appeal to the proceedings in Parliament in the year immediately preceding.

Is it likely finally that if Throgmorton's examination proves what Mr. Brewer thinks it proves, a record of it would have been preserved among the official State Papers ?

If all the stories current about Henry VIII. were to be discussed with as much detail as I have allowed

---

[1] 1. When he says, ' It is ' thought,' let him be examined whom he ever heard say any such thing of the King. 2. Where, when, and why he spoke those words to Sir Wm. Essex and Sir Wm. Barentyne. 3. Whether he communicated the matter to any other. 5, 6. Whether he thought the words true and why. 7, 8. Whether he did not think the words very slanderous to any man's good name. 10, 15. Whether he thinks such reports conducive to the peace of the Commonweal, or fitting for a true subject to spread. — *Calendar, Foreign and Domestic,* 1537, p. 333.

to this, the world would not contain the books which should be written. An Irish lawyer told me in my youth to believe nothing which I heard in that country which had not been sifted in a court of justice, and only half of that. Legend is as the air invulnerable, and blows aimed at it, if not 'malicious mockery' are waste of effort. Charges of scandalous immorality are precious to controversialists, for if they are disproved ever so completely the stain adheres.

CHAPTER III.

Anxiety of the Pope to satisfy the King—Fears of the Emperor—
Proposed alternatives—France and England declare war in the
Pope's defence—Campeggio to be sent to England—The King's
account of the Pope's conduct—The Pope's distress and alarm
—The secret decretal—Instructions to Campeggio.

THE story returns to Orvieto. The dispensation was
promised on condition that it should not be immediately acted on.[1] Catherine having refused to acquiesce in a private arrangement, Wolsey again pressed
the Pope for a commission to decide the cause in
England, and to bind himself at the same time not to
revoke it, but to confirm any judgment which he might
himself give. 'There were secret causes,' he said,
'which could not be committed to writing which made
'such a concession imperative: certain diseases in the
'Queen defying all remedy, for which, as for other causes,
'the King would never again live with her as his wife.'

The Pope, smarting from ill-treatment and grateful
for the help of France and England, professed himself
earnestly anxious to do what Henry desired. But he

---

[1] *Calendar, Foreign and Domestic*, vol. iv. part 2, p. 1672.

was still virtually a prisoner.   He had been obliged by
the General of the Observants, when in St. Angelo, to
promise to do nothing, 'whereby the King's divorce
'might be judged in his own dominions.'   He pleaded
for time.   He promised a commission of some kind, but
he said he was undone if action was taken upon it while
the Germans and Spaniards remained in Italy.   He
saw evident ruin before him, he said, but he professed
to be willing to run the hazard rather than that Wolsey
should suspect him of ingratitude.   He implored the
Cardinal, *cum suspiriis et lacrymis,* not to precipitate
him for ever, and precipitated he would be if, on
receiving the commission, the Cardinal at once began
the process.[1]   A fortnight later Casalis described a long
conversation with the Pope and Cardinals on the course
to be pursued.   Henry had desired that a second Legate
should be sent from Rome to act with Wolsey.   To consent to this would directly compromise the Papal Court.
Clement had no objection to the going forward with
the cause, but he did not wish to be himself responsible.
He signed an imperfect commission not inconsistent
with his promise to the General of the Observants.   On
this Wolsey might act or, if he preferred it, might
proceed on his own Legatine authority.   For himself,
instead of engaging to confirm Wolsey's sentence, he
said that no doctor could better resolve the point at
issue than the King himself.   If he was resolved, said
the Pope, let him commit his cause to the Legate, marry

---

[1] *Calendar, Foreign and Domestic,* vol. iv. part 2, p. 1672.

again, follow up the trial, and then let a public application be made for a Legate to be sent from the Consistory. If the Queen was cited first, she would put in
no answer, save to protest against the place and judges.
The Imperialists would demand a prohibition, and then
the King could not marry, or, if he did, the offspring
would be illegitimate. They would also demand a
commission for the cause to be heard at Rome, which
the Pope would be unable to refuse. But the King
being actually married again, they could not ask for a
prohibition. They could only ask that the cause should
be re-examined at Rome, when the Pope would give
sentence and a judgment could be passed which would
satisfy the whole world.[1] This was the Pope's own
advice, but he did not wish it to be known that it had
come from himself. Casalis might select the Legate to
England after the first steps had been taken. Campeggio he thought the fittest, being already an English
bishop.[2] At any rate, the Pope bade Casalis say he
would do his best to satisfy the King, though he knew
that the Emperor would never forgive him.

It is not certain what would have followed had
Henry acted on the Pope's suggestion. The judgment
which Clement promised might have been in his favour.
Clement evidently wished him to think that it would.

---

[1] Casalis to Wolsey, January
13, 1528.—*Calendar, Foreign and
Domestic*, vol. iv. part 2, p. 1694.

[2] Three foreigners held English
sees, not one of which either of
them had probably ever visited.

Campeggio was Bishop of Salisbury; Ghinucci, the auditor of
the Rota, was Bishop of Worcester; and Catherine's Spanish
confessor, who had come with her
to England, was Bishop of Llandaff.

But he might, after all, have found himself required to take Catherine back. Either alternative was possible. At any rate he did not mean, if he could help it, to have recourse to violent methods. Charles himself, though he intended to prevent, if he could, a legal decision against his aunt, had hinted at the possibility and even desirableness of a private arrangement, if Catherine would agree. Catherine, unfortunately, would agree to nothing, but stood resolutely upon her rights, and Charles was forced to stand by her. Henry was equally obstinate, and the Pope was between the rock and the whirlpool.

The Pope had promised, however, and had promised with apparent sincerity. The Papal states remaining occupied by the Imperial troops, Henry carried out his own part of the engagement by joining France in a declaration of war against the Emperor. Toison d'or and Clarencieulx appeared before Charles at Burgos on the 22nd of January, Charles sitting on his throne to receive their defiance. Toison d'or said that the Emperor had opened Christendom to the Turks, had imprisoned the Pope, had allowed his armies to sack Rome and plunder churches and monasteries, had insulted the holy relics, slain or robbed princes of the Church, cardinals, patriarchs, archbishops, outraged nunneries and convents, had encouraged Lutheran heretics in committing these atrocities, &c. For these reasons France declared open war with the Emperor. The English herald—he was accused afterwards of having exceeded his instructions — was almost as

peremptory. Henry, in earlier times, had lent Charles
large sums of money, which had not been repaid.
Clarencieulx said that, unless the Pope was released
and the debt settled, the King of England must make
common cause with his brother of France. Six weeks'
interval was allowed for the Emperor to consider his
answer before hostilities on the side of England should
commence.

The Emperor replied with calmness and dignity.
War with France was inevitable. As to England, he
felt like Cicero, when doubting whether he should
quarrel with Cæsar, that it was inconvenient to be in
debt to an enemy. If England attacked him he said
he would defend himself, but he declined to accept
the defiance. Mendoza was not recalled from London.
At the end of the six weeks the situation was prolonged
by successive truces till the peace of Cambray. But
Henry had kept his word to the Pope. England
appeared by the side of France in the lists as the
armed champion of the Papacy, and the Pope was
expected to fulfil his promises without disguise or
subterfuge.

Clement's method of proceeding with the divorce
was rejected. The dispensation and commission which
had been amended with a view to it were rejected also
as worthless. Dr. Fox and Stephen Gardiner were
despatched to Orvieto with fuller powers and witn a
message peremptory and even menacing. They were
again to impress on the Pope the danger of a disputed
succession. They were to hint that, if relief was

refused in deference to the Emperor, England might decline from obedience to the Holy See. The Pope must, therefore, pass the commission and the dispensa-tion in the form in which it had been sent from England. If he objected that it was unusual, they were to announce that the cause was of great moment. The King would not be defrauded of his expectation through fear of the Emperor. If he could not obtain justice from the Pope, he would be compelled to seek it elsewhere.[1]

The language of these instructions shows that the King and Wolsey understood the Proteus that they were dealing with, and the necessity of binding his hands if he was not to slip from them. It was not now the fountain of justice, the august head of Christendom, that they were addressing, but a shifty old man, clad by circumstances with the robe of authority, but whose will was the will of the power which happened to be strongest in Italy. It was not tolerable that the Emperor should dictate on a question which touched the vital interests of an independent kingdom.

Spanish diplomatists had afterwards to excuse and explain away Clement's concessions on the ground that they were signed when he was angry at his imprisonment, had been extorted by threats, and were therefore of no validity. He struggled hard to avoid committing himself. The unwelcome documents

---

[1] Wolsey to Gardiner and Fox, February —, 1528. — *Calendar*, | *Foreign and Domestic*, vol. iv. part 2, p. 1740.

were recast into various forms. The dispensation was not signed after all, but in the place of it other briefs were signed of even graver importance. The Pope yielded to the demand to send a second Legate to try the cause with Wolsey in England, where it was assumed as a matter of course that judgment would be given for the King. The Legate chosen was Campeggio, who was himself, as was said, an English bishop. The Pope also did express in writing his own opinion on the cause as favourable to the King's plea. What passed at Orvieto was thus afterwards compendiously related by Henry in a published statement of his case.

'On his first scruple the King sent to the Bishop of Rome, as Christ's Vicar, who had the keys of knowledge, to dissolve his doubts. The said Bishop refused to take any knowledge of it, and desired the King to apply for a commission to be sent into the realm, authorised to determine the cause, thus pretending that it might no wise be entreated at Rome, but only within the King's own realm. He delegated his whole powers to Campeggio and Wolsey, giving them also a special commission in form of a decretal, wherein he declared the King's marriage null and empowered him to marry again. In the open commission also he gave them full authority to give sentence for the King. Secretly he gave them instructions to burn the commission decretal and not proceed upon it; (but) at the time of sending the commission he also sent the King a brief, written in his own hand, admitting the justice of his cause, and promising *sanctissime sub verbo Pontificis* that he would never advocate it to Rome.'[1]

Engagements which he intended to keep or break according to the turns of the war between Francis and Charles did not press very heavily perhaps on Clement's conscience, but they were not extorted from him without many agonies. 'He has granted the commission,' Casalis wrote. 'He is not unwilling to please the King and Wolsey, but fears the Spaniards more than ever he did. The Friar-General has forbidden him in the Emperor's name to grant the King's request. He fears for his life from the Imperialists if the Emperor knows of it. Before he would grant the brief he said, weeping, that it would be his utter ruin. The Venetians and Florentines desired his destruction. His sole hope of life was from the Emperor. He asked me to swear whether the King would desert him or not. Satisfied on this point, he granted the brief, saying that he placed himself in the King's arms, as he would be drawn into perpetual war with the Emperor. Wolsey might dispose of him and the Papacy as if he were Pope himself.'[2]

The Emperor had insisted, at Catherine's desire, that the cause should not be heard in England. The Pope had agreed that it should be heard in England. Consent had been wrung from him, but his consent had

---

[1] Embassy to the German Princes, January 5, 1534.—*Calendar, Foreign and Domestic,* vol. vii. p. 10.

[2] Casalis to Peter Vannes, April, 1538.—*Calendar, Foreign and Domestic,* vol. iv. part 2, p. 1842.

been given, and Campeggio was to go and make the best of it. His open commission was as ample as words could make it. He and Wolsey were to hear the cause and decide it. The secret 'decretal' which he had wept over while he signed it declared, before the cause was heard, the sentence which was to be given, and he had pledged his solemn word not to revoke the hearing to Rome. All that Clement could do was to instruct the Legate before he started to waste time on his way, and, on his arrival in England, to use his skill to 'accommodate matters,' and to persuade the Queen— if he found her persuadable—to save him from his embarrassments by taking the veil. This was a course which Charles himself in his private mind would have recommended, but was too honourable to advise it. The fatal decretal was to be seen only by a very few persons, and then, as Henry said, Campeggio was to burn it. He was instructed also to pass no sentence without first referring back to Rome, and, if driven to extremity, was to find an excuse for postponing a decision; very natural conduct on the part of a weak, frightened mortal—conduct not unlike that of his predecessor, Alexander III., in the quarrel between Becket and Henry II.—but in both cases purely human, not such as might have been looked for in a divinely guided Vicar of Christ.

CHAPTER IV.

Anne Boleyn—Letters to her from the King—The Convent at
Wilton—The Divorce—The Pope's promises—Arrival of
Campeggio in England—Reception at the Bridewell Palace—
Proposal to Catherine to take the veil—Her refusal—Uncer-
tainty of the succession—A singular expedient—Alarms of
Wolsey—The true issue—Speech of the King in the City—
Threats of the Emperor—Defects in the Bull of Pope Julius—
Alleged discovery of a brief supplying them—Distress of
Clement.

THE marriage with Anne Boleyn was now a fixed
idea in Henry's mind. He had become passionately attached to her, though not perhaps she to him.
The evidence of his feeling remains in a series of letters
to her—how preserved for public inspection no one
knows. Some of them were said to have been stolen by
Campeggio. Perhaps they were sold to him; at any
rate, they survive. A critic in the *Edinburgh Review*
described them as such as 'might have been written by
'a pot-boy to his girl.' The pot-boy must have been
a singular specimen of his kind. One, at any rate,
remains to show that, though Henry was in love, he
did not allow his love to blind him to his duty as a
prince. The lady, though obliged to wait for the full

gratification of her ambition, had been using her influence to advance her friends, while Wolsey brought
upon himself the rebuke of his master by insufficient
care in the distribution of Church patronage. The
correspondence throws an unexpected light upon the
King's character.

The Abbess of Wilton had died. The situation was
a pleasant one. Among the sisters who aspired to the
vacant office was a certain Eleanor Carey, a near connection of Anne, and a favourite with her. The appointment rested virtually with the Crown. The Lady Anne
spoke to the King. The King deputed Wolsey to inquire
into the fitness of the various candidates, with a favourable recommendation of Eleanor Carey's claims. The
inquiry was made, and the result gives us a glimpse
into the habits of the devout recluses in these sacred
institutions.[1]

'As for the matter of Wilton,' wrote Henry to Anne,
'my Lord Cardinal here had the nuns before him, and
'examined them in the presence of Master Bell, who
'assures me that she whom we would have had Abbess
'has confessed herself to have had two children by two
'different priests, and has since been kept not long ago
'by a servant of Lord Broke that was. Wherefore I
'would not for all the gold in the world clog your con-
'science nor mine, to make her ruler of a house which is
'of so ungodly demeanour, nor I trust you would not that,

---

[1] Henry VIII. to Anne Boleyn, June or July, 1528.—*Calendar,* | *Foreign and Domestic,* vol. iv part 2, p. 1960.

'neither for brother nor sister,[1] I should so distain mine
'honour or conscience. And as touching the Prioress
'[Isabella Jordan] or Dame Eleanor's elder sister, though
'there is not any evident cause proved against them, and
'the Prioress is so old that of many years she could not
'be as she was named, yet notwithstanding, to do you
'pleasure I have done that neither of them shall have
'it, but that some other good and well-disposed woman
'shall have it, whereby the house shall be better reformed,
'whereof I assure you it hath much need, and God much
'the better served.'

This letter is followed by another to the Cardinal.
Wolsey, in whose hands the King had left the matter,
in a second letter which is lost, instead of looking out
for the 'good and well-disposed woman,' though Isabella
Jordan's reputation was doubtful, yet chose to appoint
her, and the King's observations upon this action of his
are worth attending to, as addressed by such a person as
Henry is supposed to have been to a Cardinal Archbishop
and Legate of the Holy See. Many of the letters signed
by the King were the composition of his ministers and
secretaries. This to Wolsey was his own.

'The great affection and love I bear you, causeth
'me, using the doctrine of my Master, *quem diligo castigo*,
'thus plainly as now ensueth to break to you my mind,
'ensuring you that neither sinister report, affection to
'my own pleasure, interest, nor mediation of any other
'body beareth part in this case, wherefore whatsoever I

---

[1] Eleanor Carey was the sister of Mary Boleyn's husband.

' do say, I pray you think it spoken of no displeasure,
' but of him that would you as much good both of body
' and soul as you would yourself.

' Methinks it is not the right train of a trusty loving
' friend and servant when the matter is put by the master's
' consent into his arbitre and judgement—especially in a
' matter wherein his master hath both royalty and interest,
' to elect and choose a person who was by him defended.
' And yet another thing which displeaseth me more.
' That is to cloke your offence made by ignorance of my
' pleasure, saying that you expressly knew not my de-
' terminate mind in that behalf.   Alas, my lord, what
' can be more evident or plainer than these words, speci-
' ally to a wise man—" His Grace careth not who, but
' " referreth it all to you, so that none of those who either
' " be or have been spotted with incontinence, like as by
' " report the Prioress hath been in her youth, have it ; "
' and also in another place in the letter, " And therefore
' " his Highness thinketh her not meet for that purpose ; "
' thirdly, in another place in the same letter by these
' words, " And though his Grace speaketh not of it so
' " openly, yet meseemeth his pleasure is that in no wise
' " the Prioress have it, nor yet Dame Eleanor's eldest
' " sister, for many considerations the which your Grace
' " can and will best consider."

' Ah, my Lord, it is a double offence both to do ill
' and to colour it too; but with men that have wit it
' cannot be accepted so.   Wherefore, good my Lord, use
' no more that way with me, for there is no man living
' that more hateth it.   These things having been thus

'committed, either I must have reserved them *in pectore*,
'whereby more displeasure might happen to breed, or
'else thus roundly and plainly to declare them to you,
'because I do think that *cum amico et familiari sincere*
'*semper est agendum*, and especially the master to his
'best beloved servant and friend, for in so doing the one
'shall be more circumspect in his doing, the other shall
'declare and show the lothness that is in him to have
'any occasion to be displeased with him.

   'And as touching the redress of Religion [convent
'discipline], if it be observed and continued, undoubtedly
'it is a gracious act.   Notwithstanding, if all reports be
'true, *ab imbecillis imbecilla expectantur.* How be it, Mr.
'Bell hath informed me that the Prioress's age, personage
'and manner, *præ se fert gravitatem.* I pray God it be
'so indeed, seeing she is preferred to that room. I under-
'stand furthermore, which is greatly to my comfort, that
'you have ordered yourself to Godward as religiously and
'virtuously as any Prelate or father of Christ's Church
'can do, where in so doing and persevering there can be
'nothing more acceptable to God, more honour to your-
'self, nor more desired of your friends, among the which
'I reckon myself not the least. . . .

   'I pray you, my Lord, think it not that it is upon
'any displeasure that I write this unto you. For surely
'it is for my discharge before God, being in the room
'that I am in, and secondly for the great zeal I bear
'unto you, not undeserved in your behalf. Wherefore
'I pray you take it so; and I assure you, your fault
'acknowledged, there shall remain in me no spark of

' displeasure, trusting hereafter you shall recompense that
' with a thing much more acceptable to me. And thus
' fare you well; advertising you that, thanked be God,
' I and all my folk be, and have been since we came
' to Ampthill, which was on Saturday last, July 11, in
' marvellous good health and clearness of air.

'Written with the hand of him that is, and shall be
' your loving Sovereign Lord and friend,—HENRY R.'[1]

Campeggio meanwhile was loitering on his way as
he had been directed, pretending illness, pretending
difficulties of the road. In sending him at all the Pope
had broken his promise to Charles. He engaged, however, that no sentence should be given which had not
been submitted first to Charles's approval. The Emperor,
anxious to avoid a complete rupture with England, let
the Legate go forward, but he directed Mendoza to
inform Wolsey that he must defend his aunt's honour ;
her cause was his and he would hold it as such.[2] Wolsey,
though afraid of the consequence of opposing the divorce
to himself and the Church, yet at heart had ceased to
desire it. Mendoza reported that English opinion was
still unfavourable, and that he did not believe that the
commission would have any result. The Pope would
interpose delays. Wolsey would allow and recognise
them. Both Legates would agree privately to keep the
matter in suspense. The English Cardinal appeared
to be against the Queen, but every one knew that

---

[1] *Calendar, Foreign and Do-mestic,* vol. iv., Introduction, pp. 388-9.

[2] The Emperor to Mendoza, July 5, 1528.—*Spanish Calendar,* vol. iii. part 2, p. 728.

secretly he was now on her side.[1] Catherine only was
seriously frightened. She had doubtless been informed
of the secret decretal by which the Pope appeared to
have prejudged her cause. She supposed that the Pope
meant it, and did not understand how lightly such
engagements sate upon him. The same Clement, when
Benvenuto Cellini reproached him for breaking his word,
replied, smiling, that the Pope had power to bind and
to loose. Catherine came before long to know him
better and to understand the bearings of this singular
privilege; but as yet she thought that words meant
what they seemed to say. When she heard that
Campeggio was actually coming, she wrote passionately
to the Emperor, flinging herself upon him for protection.
Charles calmed her alarm. She was not, he said, to be
condemned without a hearing. The Pope had assured
him that the Legates should determine nothing to her
detriment. The case should be decided at Rome, as
she had desired. Campeggio's orders were to advise
that it should be dropped. Apart from his present
infatuation, the King was a good Christian and would
act as one. If he persisted, she might rely on the Pope's
protection. She must consent to nothing which would
imply the dissolution of her marriage. If the worst
came, the King would be made conscious of his duties.[2]

In the middle of October the Legate arrived. He
had been ill in earnest from gout and was still suffering.

---

[1] Mendoza to the Emperor,
September 18, 1528.—*Ibid.* vol.
iii. part 2, p. 788.

[2] Charles V. to Queen Catherine, September 1, 1528.—*Spanish
Calendar*, vol. iii. part 2, p. 779.

He had to rest two days in Calais before he could face
the Channel. The passage was wild. A deputation of
Peers and Bishops waited to receive him at Dover.
Respectful demonstrations had been prepared at the
towns through which he was to pass, and a state ceremonial was to accompany his entrance into London.
But he was, or pretended to be, too sick to allow himself
to be seen. He was eight days on the road from the
coast, and on reaching his destination he was carried
privately in a state barge to the house provided for his
residence. Wolsey called the next morning. The King
was absent, but returned two days later to the Bridewell
palace. There Campeggio waited on him, accompanied
by Wolsey. The weather continued to frown. 'I wish,'
wrote Gerardo Molza to the Marchioness of Mantua,
'that you could have seen the two Cardinals abreast,
'one on his mule, the other carried in his chair, the rain
'falling fast so that we were all drenched.' The King,
simple man, believed that the documents which he held
secured him. The Pope in sending the Legate had
acted in the teeth of the Emperor's prohibition, and no
one guessed how the affair had been soothed down.
The farce was well played, and the language used was
what Henry expected. Messer Floriano, one of Campeggio's suit, made a grand oration, setting out the
storming of Rome, the perils of the Church, and the
misery of Italy, with moving eloquence. The crowd
was so dense in the hall of audience that some of the
Italians lost their shoes, and had to step back barefoot
to their lodgings through the wet streets.

The Legate was exhausted by the exertion, but he was not allowed to rest, and the serious part of the business began at once behind the scenes. He had hoped, as the Emperor said, that the case might be dropped. He found Henry immoveable. 'An angel 'from heaven,' he wrote on the 17th of October,[1] 'would 'not be able to persuade the King that his marriage 'was not invalid. The matter had come to such a pass 'that it could no longer be borne with. The Cardinal 'of York and the whole kingdom insisted that the 'question must be settled in some way.' One road out of the difficulty alone presented itself. The Emperor had insisted that the marriage should not be dissolved by Catherine's consent, objecting reasonably that a judgment invalidating it would shake other royal marriages besides hers. But no such judgment would be necessary if Catherine could be induced to enter 'lax religion,' to take vows of chastity which, at her age and under her conditions of health, would be a mere form. The Pope could then allow Henry to take another wife without offence to any one. The legitimacy of the Princess would not be touched, and the King undertook that the succession should be settled upon her if he had no male heir. The Queen in consenting would lose nothing, for the King had for two years lived apart from her, and would never return to cohabitation. The Emperor would be delivered from an obligation infinitely inconvenient to him, and his

[1] Campeggio to Salviati and to Sanga, October 17, 1528.—*Cal-* *endar, Foreign and Domestic,* vol. iv. part 2, pp. 2099—2102.

own honour and the honour of Spain would be equally untouched.

These arguments were laid before the Queen by both the Legates, and urged with all their eloquence. In the interests of the realm, in the interests of Europe, in the interests of the Church, in her own and her daughter's interest as well, it would have been wiser if she had complied. Perhaps she would have complied had the King's plea been confined, as at first, to the political exigencies of the succession. But the open and premature choice of the lady who was to take her place was an indignity not to be borne. She had the pride of her race. Her obstinacy was a match for her husband's. She was shaken for a moment by the impassioned entreaties of Campeggio, and she did not at once absolutely refuse. The Legate postponed the opening of his court. He referred to Rome for further instructions, complaining of the responsibility which was thrown upon him. Being on the spot he was able to measure the danger of disappointing the King after the secret commission, the secret decretal, and the Pope's private letter telling Henry that he was right. Campeggio wrote to Salviati, after his first interview with Catherine, that he did not yet despair. Something might be done if the Emperor would advise her to comply. He asked Fisher to help him, and Fisher seemed not wholly unwilling; but, after a few days' reflection, Catherine told him that before she would consent she would be torn limb from limb; she would have an authoritative sentence from the Pope, and would accept nothing else; nothing should make her alter her opinion, and if after death she could return to life, she would die over again rather than change it.[1]

Wolsey was in equal anxiety. He had set the stone rolling, but he could not stop it. If Clement failed the King now, after all that he had promised, he might not only bring ruin on Wolsey himself, but might bring on the overthrow of the temporal power of the Church of England. Catherine was personally popular; but in the middle classes of the laity, among the peers and gentlemen of England, the exactions of the Church courts, the Pope's agents and collectors, the despotic tyranny of the Bishops, had created a resentment the extent of which none knew better than he. The entire gigantic system of clerical dominion, of which Wolsey was himself the pillar and representative, was tottering to its fall. If the King was driven to bay, the favour of a good-natured people for a suffering woman would be a poor shelter either for the Church or for him. Campeggio turned to Wolsey for advice on Catherine's final refusal. The Pope, he said, had hoped that Wolsey would advise the King to yield. Wolsey had advised. He told Cavendish that he had gone on his knees to the King, but he could only say to Campeggio that 'the King—fortified and justified by reasons, 'writings, and counsels of many learned men who 'feared God—would never yield.' If he was to find

---

[1] Campeggio to Salviati, October 26, 1528.—*Calendar, Foreign and Domestic*, vol. iv. part 2, p. 2108.

that the Pope had been playing with him, and the
succession was to be left undetermined, 'the Church
'would be ruined and the realm would be in infinite
'peril.'

How great, how real, was the dread of a disputed
succession, appears from an extraordinary expedient
which had suggested itself to Campeggio himself, and
which he declares that some perplexed politicians had
seriously contemplated. 'They have thought,' he wrote
on the 28th of October, 'of marrying the Princess Mary
'to the King's natural son [the Duke of Richmond] if
'it could be done by dispensation from His Holiness.'
The Legate said that at first he had himself thought of
this as a means of establishing the succession; but he
did not believe it would satisfy the King's desire.[1] If
anything could be more astonishing than a proposal for
the marriage of a brother and sister, it was the reception
which the suggestion met with at Rome. The Pope's
secretary replied that 'with regard to the dispensation
'for marrying the son to the daughter of the King, if on
'the succession being so established the King would
'abandon the divorce, the Pope would be much more
'inclined to grant it.'[2]

Clement's estimate of the extent of the dispensing
power was large. But the situation was desperate. He
had entangled himself in the meshes. He had promised
what he had no intention of performing. He was find-

---

[1] Campeggio to Sanga, Oct. 28.
—*Calendar, Foreign and Domestic*,
vol. iv. part 2, p. 2113.

[2] Sanga to Campeggio, Dec. —,
1528.—*Ibid.* vol. iv. part 2 p.
2210.

ing that he had been trifling with a lion, and that the
lion was beginning to rouse himself. Again and again
Wolsey urged the dangers upon him. He wrote on the
1st of November to Casalis that 'the King's honour was
'touched, having been so great a benefactor to the Holy
'See. The Pope would alienate all faith and devotion
'to the Apostolic See. The sparks of opposition which
'had been extinguished with such care and vigilance
'would blaze out to the utmost anger of all, both in
'England and elsewhere.'[1] Clement and his Cardinals
heard, but imperfectly believed. 'He tells us,' wrote
Sanga, 'that if the divorce is not granted the authority
'of the Apostolic See in England will be annihilated; he
'is eager to save it because his own greatness is bound
'up with ours.' The Curia was incredulous, and thought
that Wolsey was only alarmed for himself. Wolsey,
however, was right. Although opinions might have
varied on the merits of the King's request, people were
beginning to ask what value as a supreme judge a
pope could have, who could not decide on a point of
canon law.

The excitement was growing. Certain knowledge of
what was going on was confined to the few who had
access to the secret correspondence, and they knew only
what was meant for their own eyes. All parties, English and Imperial alike, distrusted the Pope. He had
impartially lied to both, and could be depended on by
neither, except so far as they could influence his fears.

---

[1] Wolsey to Casalis, Nov. 1, 1528.—*Calendar, Foreign and Domestic*,
vol. iv. part 2, p. 2120.

Catherine was still the favourite with the London citizens. She had been seen accidentally in a gallery of the Palace, and had been enthusiastically cheered. The King found it necessary to explain himself. On the 8th of November he summoned the Lord Mayor and Aldermen, the Privy Council, and a body of Peers, and laid the situation before them from his own point of view. He spoke of his long friendship with the Emperor, and of his hope that it would not be broken, and again of his alliance with France, and of his desire to be at peace with all the world. ' He had wished,' he said, ' to ' attach France more closely to him by marrying his ' daughter to a French prince, and the French Ambas- ' sador, in considering the proposal, had raised the ' question of her legitimacy. His own mind had long ' misgiven him on the lawfulness of his marriage. M. ' de Tarbes' words had added to his uneasiness. The ' succession to the crown was uncertain; he had con- ' sulted his bishops and lawyers, and they had assured ' him that he had been living in mortal sin. . . . He ' meant only to do what was right, and he warned his ' subjects to be careful of forming hasty judgments on ' their Prince's actions.'

Apart from the present question the King was extremely popular, and reports arriving from Spain touched the national pride. There was a talk of calling Parliament. Mendoza and Catherine again urged Charles to speak plainly. The Pope must inhibit Parliament from interfering. The Nuncio in London would present the order, and Parliament, they thought, would submit.[1] They were mistaking the national temper. Mendoza's letters had persuaded the Spanish Council that the whole of England was in opposition to the King. The Spanish Chancellor had said publicly that if the cause was proceeded with there would be war, and 'the King would be dethroned by his own 'subjects.' The words were reported to Wolsey, and were confirmed by an English agent, Sylvester Darius, who had been sent to Valladolid on business connected with the truce.[2] Darius had spoken to the Chancellor on the probability of England taking active part with France. 'Why do you talk of the King of England?' the Chancellor had answered; 'if we wished, we could 'expel him from his kingdom in three months. What 'force had the King? his own subjects would expel him. 'He knew how matters were.'[3] It was one thing for a free people to hold independent opinions on the arrangements of their own royal family. It was another to be threatened with civil war at the instigation of a foreign sovereign. Wolsey quoted the dangerous language at a public meeting in London; and a voice answered, 'The 'Emperor has lost the hearts of a hundred thousand 'Englishmen.'[4] A fresh firebrand was thrown into the flames immediately after. The national pride was

---

[1] Catherine to Charles V., Nov. 24, 1528.—*Spanish Calendar*, vol. iii. part 2, p. 855.

[2] Mendoza to Charles V., Dec. 2, 1528.—*Ib.* p. 862; Jan. 16, 1529, *ib.* p. 878.

[3] Sylvester Darius to Wolsey, Nov. 25, 1528.—*Calendar, Foreign and Domestic*, vol. iv. pt. 2, p. 2126.

[4] Du Bellay to Montmorency, Dec. 9, 1528.—*Ibid.* p. 2177.

touched on a side where it was already sensitive from interest. There were 15,000 Flemish artisans in London. English workmen had been jealous of their skill, and had long looked askance at them. The cry rose that they had an army of traitors in their midst who must be instantly expelled. The Flemings' houses were searched for arms, and watched by a guard, and the working city population, traders, shopkeepers, mechanics, apprentices, came over to the King's side and remained there.

Meantime the cause itself hung fire. A new feature had been introduced to enable Campeggio to decline to proceed and the Pope to withdraw decently from his promises. The original Bull of Pope Julius permitting the marriage had been found to contain irregularities of form which were supposed fatal to it. The validity of the objection was not denied, but was met by the production of a brief alleged to have been found in Spain, and bearing the same date with the Bull, which exactly met that objection. No trace of such a brief could be found in the Vatican Register. It had informalities of its own, and its genuineness was justly suspected, but it answered the purpose of a new circumstance. A copy only was sent to England, which was shown by Catherine in triumph to Henry, but the original was detained. It would be sent to Rome, but not to London; without it Campeggio could pretend inability to move, and meanwhile he could refuse to proceed on his commission. Subterfuges which answer for the moment revenge themselves in the end. Having been once raised, it was absolutely necessary that a question immediately affecting the succession should be settled in some way, and many of the peers who had been hitherto cool began to back the King's demands. An address was drawn up, having among others the Duke of Norfolk's signature, telling the Pope that the divorce must be conceded, and complaints were sent through Casalis against Campeggio's dilatoriness. The King, he was to say, would not submit to be deluded.

Casalis delivered his message, and describes the effect which it produced. 'The Pope,' he wrote, 'very 'angry, laid his hand on my arm and forbade me to 'proceed, saying there was but too good ground for 'complaint, and he was deluded by his own councillors. 'He had granted the decretal only to be shown to the 'King, and then burnt. Wolsey now wished to divulge 'it. He saw what would follow, and would gladly recall 'what had been done, even with the loss of one of his 'fingers.'

Casalis replied that Wolsey wished only to show it to a few persons whose secrecy might be depended on. Was it not demanded for that purpose ? Why had the Pope changed his mind ? The Pope, only the more excited, said he saw the Bull would be the ruin of him, and he would make no more concessions. Casalis prayed him to consider. Waving his arms violently, Clement said, 'I do consider. I consider the ruin which 'is hanging over me. I repent what I have done. If 'heresies arise, is it my fault ? I will not violate my 'conscience. Let them, if they like, send the Legate

'back, because he will not proceed. They can do as
'they please, provided they do not make me responsible.'

Did the Pope mean, then, Casalis asked, that the
commission should not proceed? The Pope could not
say as much as that; he had told Campeggio, he said,
to dissuade the King and persuade the Queen. 'What
harm could there be,' Casalis inquired, 'in showing the
decretal, under oath, to a few of the Privy Council?'

The Pope said the decretal ought to have been
burnt, and refused to discuss the matter further.[1]

---

[1] John Casalis to Wolsey, Dec. 17, 1528.—*Calendar, Foreign and
Domestic,* vol. iv. part 2, p. 2186.

CHAPTER V.

Demands of the Imperial Agent at Rome—The alleged Brief—
Illness of the Pope—Aspirations of Wolsey—The Pope
recovers—Imperial menaces—Clement between the anvil and
the hammer—Appeal of Henry to Francis—The trial of the
cause to proceed—Instructions to Campeggio—Opinion at
Rome—Recall of Mendoza—Final interview between Mendoza
and the King.

HUMAN pity is due to the unfortunate Pope—Vicar
of Christ, supreme judge in Europe, whose
decrees were the inspirations of the Holy Ghost—
spinning like a whipped top under the alternate lashes
of the King of England and the Emperor. He had
hoped that his decretal would not be known. It could
not be concealed from Mendoza, who discovered, putting
the worst interpretation upon it, ' that the Pope and
' King had been endeavouring to intimidate the Queen
' into retiring into a convent.' Finding that he, too,
could put no faith in Clement, the Emperor's representative at Rome now forced a new promise from him.
The proceedings in England were not to be opened
without a fresh direct order from the Pope, and this
the Pope was to be forbidden to give. If the King was

E

obstinate and the Queen demanded it, Campeggio was
to leave England, and, notwithstanding his engagements
to the contrary, Clement was to advocate the cause to
Rome. The new brief was sufficient plea. Without it
the Legates could come to no conclusion, 'the whole
'right of the Queen being based upon its contents.'
The Emperor had it in his hands, and by refusing to
allow it to be examined, except at Rome, might prevent
them from moving.

There was little doubt that the brief had been forged
for the occasion. The Pope having sent a commission
to England, the King considered that he had a right to
the production of documents essential to the case. He
required Catherine to write to Charles to ask for it.
Catherine did as he desired, and the messenger who
carried her letter to the Spanish Court was sworn to
carry no private or separate missive from her. Mendoza
dared not write by the same hand himself, lest his
despatches should be examined. He made the messenger, therefore, learn a few words by heart, telling the
Emperor that the Queen's letter was not to be attended
to. 'We thought,' he said, 'that the man's oath was
'thus saved.'[1] Thus time drifted on. The new year
came, and no progress had been made, though Campeggio had been three months in England. The Pope,
more helpless than dishonest, continued to assure the
King that he would do all that by law could be required of him, and as much as he could do *ex plenitu-*

---

[1] Mendoza to Charles V., Feb. 4, 1529.—*Spanish Calendar*, vol. iii.
part 2.

dine potestatis. No peril should prevent him. 'If
'the King thought his resigning the Papacy would
'conduce to his purpose, he could be content, for the
'love he bore his Highness, rather than fail to do the
'same.'

If the Pope was so well disposed, the King could
not see where the difficulty lay. The Queen had refused his entreaty that she should enter religion. Why
should not the Pope, then, allow the decretal to be put
in execution? But Cardinal Salviati informed Casalis
that a sentence given in virtue of the decretal would
have no effect, but would only cause the Pope's deposition.[1] Visibly and unpleasantly it became now
apparent to Henry to what issues the struggle was
tending. He had not expected it. Wolsey had told
him that the Pope would yield; and the Pope had
promised what was asked; but his promises were
turning to vapour. Wolsey had said that the Emperor
could not afford to quarrel with him. The King found
that war with the Emperor in earnest was likely
enough unless he himself drew back, and draw back he
would not. The poor Pope was as anxious as Henry.
He had spoken of resigning. He was near being
spared the trouble. Harassed beyond his strength, he
fell ill, and was expected to die; and before Wolsey
there was now apparently the strange alternative
either of utter disgrace or of himself ascending the

---

[1] Knight and Benet to Wolsey, Jan. 8, 1529.—*Calendar, Foreign and Domestic,* vol. iv. part 3, p. 2262.

chair of St. Peter as Clement's successor. His election, perhaps, was really among the chances of the situation. The Cardinals had not forgiven the sack of Rome. A French or English candidate had a fair prospect of success, and Wolsey could command the French interest. He had boundless money, and money in the Sacred College was only not omnipotent. He undertook, if he was chosen, to resign his enormous English preferments and reside at Rome, and the vacancy of his three bishoprics and his abbey would pour a cataract of gold into the Cardinals' purses. The Bulls for English bishoprics had to be paid for on a scale which startled Wolsey himself. Already archbishop of York, bishop of Winchester, and abbot of St. Albans, he had just been presented to Durham. He had paid 8,000 ducats to 'expedite' his Bulls for Winchester. The Cardinals demanded 13,000 ducats for Durham. The ducat was worth five shillings, and five shillings in 1528 were worth fifty shillings of modern money. At such a rate were English preferments bled to support the College of Cardinals; and if all these great benefices were again vacated there would be a fine harvest to be gathered. For a week or two the splendid vision suspended even the agitation over the divorce; but the Pope revived, and the Legates and he had to resume their ungrateful burden.

It was still really uncertain what Clement would do. Weak, impulsive men often leave their course to fate or chance to decide for them. Casalis, when he was able to attend to business again, told him in Wolsey's name

that he must take warning from his late danger. 'By
'the wilfully suffering a thing of such high importance
'to be unreformed to the doing whereof Almighty God
'worked so openly he would incur God's displeasure
'and peril his soul.' The Imperialists were as anxious
as Wolsey, and equally distrustful. In the Sacred
College English gold was an influence not to be despised, and Henry had more to give than Charles.
Micer Mai, the Imperial agent at Rome, found, as the
spring came on, that the Italian Cardinals were growing
cold. Salviati insisted to him that Catherine must go
into a convent. Casalis denounced the new brief as a
forgery, and the Sacred College seemed to be of the
same opinion. The fiery Mai complained in the Pope's
presence of the scant courtesy which the Ministers of
the Emperor were meeting with, while the insolent
and overbearing were regaled like the Prodigal Son.[1]
The Pope assured him that, come what might, he
would never authorise the divorce; but Mai only
partially believed him. At trying moments Mai was
even inclining to take the same view of the Papacy
as Lope de Soria. 'At other times,' he said, 'many
'things could be got out of the Pope by sheer intimi-
'dation; but now that could not be tried, for he would
'fall into despair, and the Imperialists would lose him
'altogether. They owed him something for what he
'had done for them before, otherwise he would be of

---

[1] Mai to Charles V., April 3, 1529.—*Spanish Calendar*, vol. iii.
part 2, p. 973.

'opinion that it would be for God's service to reduce
'them to their spiritual powers.'[1]

Occasionally Mai's temper broke through, and he
used language worth observing. One of the Cardinals
had spoken slightingly of the Emperor.

'I did not call on his Holiness,' he wrote to Charles,
'but sent him a message, adding that, if ever it came to
'my notice that the same Cardinal, or any member of
'the College, had dared to speak in such an indecent
'manner of the Emperor, I took my most solemn oath
'that I would have him beheaded or burnt alive within
'his own apartment. I had this time refrained out of
'respect for his Holiness; but should the insult be
'repeated I would not hesitate. They might do as they
'would with their Bulls and other rogueries—grant or
'refuse them as they liked; but they were not to speak
'evil of princes, or make themselves judges in the
'affairs of kingdoms.'[2]

This remarkable message was conveyed to the Pope,
who seemed rather pleased than otherwise. Mai, however, observed that the revolt of the Lutherans was not
to be wondered at, and in what they said of Rome he
considered that they were entirely right, except on
points of faith.[3]

---

[1] Micer Mai to the Emperor, May 11, 1529.—*Spanish Calendar*, vol. iv. part 1, p. 20.

[2] In Spanish the words are even more emphatically contemptuous: 'Y que ennoramala que se curasen 'de sus bulas y de sus bellaquerias, 'si las querian dar ó no dar, y que 'no pongan lengua en los reyes y 'querir ser jueces de la subjeccion 'de los reynos.'

[3] Micer Mai to the Emperor, June 5, 1529.—*Spanish Calendar*, vol. iv. part 1, p. 60.

Cardinals had been roughly handled in the sack of the Holy City at but a year's distance. The possibility was extremely real. The Imperial Minister, it appeared, could still command the services of the Spanish garrisons in the Papal territories if severity was needed, and the members of the Sacred College had good reason to be uneasy; but King Henry might reasonably object to the trial of his cause in a country where the assessors of the supreme judge were liable to summary execution if they were insubordinate. That Charles could allow his representative to write in such terms to him proves that he and Mai, and Henry himself, were in tolerable agreement on Church questions. The Pope knew it; one of his chief fears was that the Emperor, France, England, and the German Princes, might come to an understanding to his own disadvantage. Perhaps it might have been so had not the divorce kept Henry and Charles apart. Campeggio wrote to Sanga on the 3rd of April that certain advances had been made by the Lutherans to Henry, in which they promised to relinquish all heresies on articles of faith, and to believe according to Divine law if he and the King of France would reduce the ecclesiastical state to the condition of the Primitive Church, taking from it all its temporalities. He had told the King that this was the Devil dressed in angel's clothing, a mere design against the property of the Church; and that it had been ruled by councils and theologians that it was right for the Church to hold temporal property. The King said those rules had been made by Churchmen themselves, and now the

laity must interfere. He said also that Churchmen
were said to be leading wicked lives, especially about
the Court of Rome.[1]

Growled at on both sides, in terror for himself, in
terror for the Church, the Pope drifted on, hoping for
some accident to save him which never came, and
wishing perhaps that his illness had made an end of
him.

The Emperor complained of Campeggio as partial
to the King because he held an English bishopric. ' If
' the Pope leaves the succession undetermined,' insisted
Wolsey, on the other side, ' no Prince would tolerate
' such an injury.' ' Nothing was done,' wrote the Pope's
secretary to Campeggio, ' and nothing would be done.
' The Pope was in great trouble between the English
' and Imperial Ambassadors. He wished to please the
' King, but the King and Cardinal must not expect him
' to move till they had forced the Venetians to restore
' the Papal territories.' Stephen Gardiner, who knew
Clement well and watched him from day to day, said :
' He was a man who never resolved anything unless
' compelled by some violent affection. He was in great
' perplexity, and seemed willing to gratify the King
' if he could, but when it came to the point did nothing.
' He would be glad if the King's cause could be
' determined in England by the Legates; and if the
' Emperor made any suit against what should be done

---

[1] Campeggio to Sanga, April 3, 1529.—*Calendar, Foreign and
Domestic* vol. iv. p. 2379.

'there, they would serve him as they now served the
'King, and put off the time. So matters would go on,
'unless Campeggio would frankly promise to give sen-
'tence in the King's favour; otherwise such delays
'would be found as the counterfeit Brief had caused.' [1]
Sir Francis Bryan, who was also at the Papal court,
wrote to the King that the Pope would do nothing for
him, and whoever had told the King that he would,
had not done him the best service. 'He was very
'sorry to write thus, but the King must not be fed
'with their flattering words.' [2]

To wait longer on the Pope's action was now seen
in England to be useless. The Pope dared not offend
the Emperor further, and the Emperor had interposed
to prohibit future action. Clement had himself several
times suggested that the best way was to decide the
case first in England in the Legate's court, and leave
Catherine to appeal; he had promised Charles that no
judgment should be given in England by the Legates;
but he had worn so double a face that no one could say
which truly belonged to him. Gardiner and Bryan
were recalled. The King, finding the Pope's ingratitude, 'resolved to dissemble with him, and proceed on
'the commission granted to Wolsey and Campeggio.' [3]
The Cardinal of York encouraged his brother Legate by
assuring him that if the marriage was now dissolved

[1] Gardiner to Henry VIII.,
April 21.—*Calendar, Foreign and
Domestic,* vol. iv. p. 2415.
    [2] Bryan to Henry VIII.—*Ibid.*

p. 2418.
    [3] Wolsey to Gardiner, May 5,
1529.—*Ibid.* p. 2442.

means would be found to satisfy the Emperor. Catherine would be left with her state undiminished, would have anything that she desired 'except the person of the 'King.' The Emperor's natural daughter might be married to the Duke of Richmond, and all would be well.[1]

So Wolsey wrote, but his mind was less easy than he pretended. Unless Henry was supported actively by the French, he knew that the Pope would fail him in the end; and Francis had been disappointed in the hope that Henry would stand actively by him in the war. Without effectual help from that quarter, Wolsey saw that he was himself undone. The French Ambassador represented to his Court that Wolsey was sincerely attached to the French alliance, that the King had only been induced to enterprise the affair by the assurance which the Cardinal had always given that he had nothing to fear from the Emperor; Wolsey had advanced the divorce as a '*means to break off for ever* '*the alliance with the Emperor*'; and Francis, by now declaring himself, would confer a very great favour on the King, and would oblige Wolsey as much as if he had made him pope.[2] His master was not only now concerned for the discharge of his conscience and his desire to have issue, but the very safety and independence of England was at stake. He could not have

---

[1] Campeggio to Salviati, May 12, 1529.—*Calendar, Foreign and Domestic*, p. 2451.

[2] Du Bellay to Montmorency, May 22, 1529.—*Ibid.* vol. iv. p. 2469.

it said that he left the succession to the throne un-
cleared for the threats of his enemy.[1]

The Duke of Suffolk was despatched to Paris to
bring Francis to the point.   Francis professed the
warmest goodwill to his brother of England.   He
undertook to advise the Pope.   He assured Suffolk that
if the Emperor attempted force Henry would find him
at his side; but further he would not pledge himself.
The time was past for a Wolsey patriarchate, and
Francis, curiously enough, expressed doubts whether
Wolsey was not after all betraying Henry.   'There are
'some,' he said, ' which the King my brother doth trust
'in that matter that would it should never take effect.
'Campeggio told me he did not think the divorce would
'be brought about, but should be dissembled well enough.
'When the Cardinal of England was with me, as far as I
'could perceive, he desired the divorce might take place,
'for he loved not the Queen; but I advise my brother
'not to trust any man too much, and to look to his own
'matters.   The Cardinal has great intelligence with the
'Pope, and Campeggio and they are not inclined to it.' [2]

Things could not go on thus for ever.   There would
have been an excuse for Clement, if with a conscience
of his high office he had refused to anticipate a judgment till the case had been heard and considered.   But
from the first the right or wrong of the cause itself had
been disregarded as of no moment.   Nothing had been

---

[1] Du Bellay to Montmorency, May 28, 1529.—*Calendar, Foreign and Domestic,* vol. iv. pp. 2476-7.

[2] The Duke of Suffolk to Henry VIII., June 4, 1529.—*Ibid.* p. 2491.

thought of but the alternate dangers to be anticipated from the King or the Emperor. Had the French driven the Imperialists out of Italy, the divorce would have been granted without further question. The supreme tribunal in Christendom was transparently influenced by no motive save interest or fear. Clement, in fact, had anticipated judgment, though he dared not avow it. He had appointed a commission, and by the secret decretal had ruled what the decision was to be. The decretal could not be produced, but, with or without it, the King insisted that the court should sit. Campeggio had been sent to try the cause, and try it he should. Notice was given that the suit was to be heard at the end of June. Wolsey perhaps had chosen a date not far from the close of term, that the vacation might suspend the process, and give time for further delay.

Since a trial of some kind could not be avoided, final instructions were sent from Rome to Campeggio. 'If,' wrote Sanga to him, 'the Pope was not certain 'that he remembered the injunctions which he gave him 'by word of mouth, and which had been written to him 'many times, he would be very anxious. His Holiness 'had always desired that the cause should be protracted 'in order to find some means by which he could satisfy 'the King without proceeding to sentence. The citation 'of the cause to Rome, which he had so often insisted 'on, had been deferred, not because it was doubted 'whether the matter could be treated with less scandal 'at Rome than there, but because His Holiness had

'ever shrunk from a step which would offend the King.
'But, since Campeggio had not been able to prevent the
'commencement of the proceedings, His Holiness warned
'him that the process must be slow, and that no sen-
'tence must in any manner be pronounced.   He would
'not lack a thousand means and pretexts, if on no
'other point, at least upon the brief which had been
'produced.' [1]

According to Casalis the view taken of the general
situation at Rome was this.

'The Pope would not declare openly for the Emperor
'till he saw how matters went.   He thought the
'Emperor would come to Italy, and if there was a war
'would be victorious, so that it would be for His
'Holiness's advantage to obtain his friendship before-
'hand.   If peace was made the Emperor would dictate
'terms, and more was to be hoped from his help than
'from the French King.   The Emperor was the enemy
'of the Allies, and sought to recover the honour which
'he lost by the sack of Rome by making himself pro-
'tector of the Pope.' [2]

Wolsey's dream was over, and with it the dreams of
Lope de Soria and Micer Mai. The fine project to unite
France and England in defence of the Papacy was
proving baseless as the sand on which it was built.
Henry VIII. was to lead the reform of the Church in
England.   Charles, instead of beheading cardinals, was

---

[1] Sanga to Campeggio, May 29, 1529.—*Calendar, Foreign and Domestic*, vol. iv. p. 2479.

[2] Casalis to Wolsey, June 13, 1529.—*Ibid.* pp. 2507-8.

to become the champion of the Roman hierarchy. The
air was clearing. The parties in the great game were
drifting into their natural situations. The fate which
lay before Wolsey himself, the fate which lay before the
Church of England, of the worst corruptions of which
he was himself the chief protector and example, his own
conscience enabled him too surely to foresee.

Mendoza was recalled, and before leaving had an
interview with the King. 'The Emperor,' he said,
'was obliged to defend his aunt. It was a private affair,
'which touched the honour of his family.' The King
answered that the Emperor had no right to interfere. He
did not meddle himself with the private affairs of other
princes. Mendoza was unable to guess what was likely
to happen. The suit was to go on. If a prohibitory
mandate arrived from the Pope, it was uncertain whether
Wolsey would obey it, and it was doubtful also whether
any such mandate would be sent. He suspected
Clement of possible deliberate treachery. He believed
that orders had been sent to the Legate to proceed, and
give sentence in virtue of the first commission. In that
case the sentence would certainly be against the Queen,
and not a moment must be lost in pressing an appeal
to Rome.[1]

---

[1] Mendoza to Charles V., June 17, 1529.—*Spanish Calendar*, vol. iv.
part 1, p. 96.

CHAPTER VI.

The Court at Blackfriars—The point at issue—The Pope's competency as judge — Catherine appeals to Rome — Imperial pressure upon Clement—The Emperor insists on the Pope's admission of the appeal—Henry demands sentence—Interference of Bishop Fisher—The Legates refuse to give judgment—The Court broken up—Peace of Cambray.

THE great scene in the hall at the Blackfriars when the cause of Henry VIII. and Catherine of Aragon was pleaded before Wolsey and Campeggio is too well known to require further description. To the Legates it was a splendid farce. They knew that it was to end in nothing. The world outside, even the parties chiefly concerned, were uncertain what the Pope intended, and waited for the event to determine their subsequent conduct. There was more at issue than the immediate question before the Court. The point really at stake was, whether the interests of the English nation could be trusted any longer to a judge who was degrading his office by allowing himself to be influenced by personal fears and interests; who, when called on to permit sentence to be delivered, by delegates whom he had himself appointed, yet confessed himself unable, or

unwilling, to decide whether it should be delivered or
not.   Abstractedly Henry's demand was right.   A
marriage with a brother's wife was not lawful, and no
Papal dispensation could make it so; but long custom
had sanctioned what in itself was forbidden.   The Pope
could plead the undisputed usage of centuries, and if
when the case was first submitted to him he had un-
equivocally answered that a marriage contracted *bonâ
fide* under his predecessor's sanction could not be broken,
English opinion, it is likely, would have sustained him,
even at the risk of a disputed succession, and the King
himself would have dropped his suit.   But the Pope, as
a weak mortal, had wished to please a powerful sovereign.
He had entertained the King's petition; he had hesitated,
had professed inability to come to a conclusion, finally
had declared that justice was on the King's side, and had
promised that it should be so declared.   If he now drew
back, broke his engagements, and raised new difficulties
in the settlement of a doubt which the long discussion of
it had made serious; if he allowed it to be seen that his
change of purpose was due to the menaces of another
secular Prince, was such a judge to be any longer tolerated ?   Was not the Papacy itself degenerate, and unfit
to exercise any longer the authority which it had been
allowed to assume?   This aspect of the matter was
not a farce at all.   The Papal supremacy itself was on
its trial.

On the 16th of June the King and Queen were cited
to appear in court.   Catherine was unprepared.   She
had been assured by the Emperor that her cause should

not be tried in England. She called on Campeggio to explain. Campeggio answered that the Pope having deputed two Legates for the process, could not revoke their commission without grave consideration. He exhorted her to pray God to enlighten her to take some good advice, considering the times. He was not without hope that, at the last extremity, she would yield and take the vows. But she did not in the least accede to his hints, and no one could tell what she meant to do.[1] She soon showed what she meant to do. On the 18th the court sate. Henry appeared by a proctor, who said for him that he had scruples about the validity of his marriage, which he required to be resolved. Catherine attended in person, rose, and delivered a brief protest against the place of trial and the competency of the judges. Wolsey was an English subject, Campeggio held an English bishopric. They were not impartial. She demanded to be heard at Rome, delivered her protest in writing, and withdrew.

It was at once answered for the King that he could not plead in a city where the Emperor was master. The court adjourned for three days that the Cardinals might consider. On the 21st they sate again. The scene became more august. Henry came now himself, and took his place under a canopy at the Legates' right hand. Catherine attended again, and sate in equal state at their left. Henry spoke. He said he believed that he had been in mortal sin. He could bear it no longer,

---

[1] Campeggio to Salviati, June 16, 1529.—*Calendar, Foreign and Domestic,* vol. iv. p. 2509.

and required judgment. Wolsey replied that they
would do what was just; and then Catherine left her
seat, crossed in front of them, and knelt at her husband's
feet. She had been his lawful wife, she said, for twenty
years, and had not deserved to be repudiated and put to
shame. She begged him to remember their daughter,
to remember her own relations, Charles and Ferdinand,
who would be gravely offended. Crowds of women,
gathered about the palace gates, had cheered her as
she came in, and bade her care for nothing. If
women had to decide the case, said the French Ambassador, the Queen would win. Their voices availed
nothing. She was told that her protest could not be
admitted. She then left the court, was thrice summoned to come back, and, as she refused, was pronounced contumacious.

For the King to appear as a suitor at Rome was
justly regarded as impossible. Casalis was directed to
tell Clement that, being in the Emperor's hands, he
could not be accepted as a judge in the case, and that
sovereign princes were exempted by prerogative from
pleading in courts outside their own dominions. If he
admitted the Queen's appeal, he would lose the devotion
of the King and of England to the See Apostolic, and
would destroy Wolsey for ever.[1] Had the Legates been
in earnest there would have been no time to learn
whether the appeal was allowed at Rome or not; they
would have gone on and given sentence under their

---

[1] Wolsey to Casalis, June 22, 1529. — *Calendar, Foreign and Domestic*, vol. iv. p. 2526.

commission. It appeared as if this was what they intended to do. The court continued sitting. Catherine
being contumacious, there was nothing left to delay the
conclusion. She was in despair; she believed herself
betrayed. Mendoza, who might have comforted her,
was gone. She wrote to him that she was lost unless
the Emperor or the Pope interposed. Even Campeggio
seemed to be ignorant how he was to avoid a decision.
Campeggio, the French Ambassador wrote, was already
half conquered. If Francis would send a word to him,
he might gather courage to pass sentence, and Henry
would be brought to his knees in gratitude. The very
Pope, perhaps, in his heart would not have been displeased if the Legates had disobeyed the orders which he
had given, and had proceeded to judgment, as he had
often desired that they might. Micer Mai's accounts to
Charles of the shifts of the poor old man, as the accounts
from England reached him, are almost pathetic. Pope,
Cardinals, canon lawyers, Mai regarded as equally feeble,
if not as equally treacherous. One reads with wonder
the Spaniard's real estimate of the persons for whose
sake and in whose name Charles and Philip were to
paint Europe red with blood.

'Salviati,' said Mai, 'who, though a great rogue,
'has not wit enough to hide his tricks, showed me the
'minute of a letter they had written to Campeggio: a
'more stupid or rascally composition could not have been
'concocted in hell.'[1] Campeggio was directed in this

---

[1] 'La mas necia y bellaca carta que se pudiera hacer en el Infierno.'

letter to reveal to no one that he had received orders not to give sentence. He was to go on making delays, which was what 'those people desired,' because, if he was to say that he would make no declaration in the affair, the Archbishop of York would act by himself, the Pope's mandate having been originally addressed to the two Legates conjointly or to one individually. The letter had gone on to direct Campeggio, if he could not manage this, to carry on the proceedings until the final sentence, but not deliver sentence without first consulting Rome. If possible, he was to keep this part of his instructions secret, for fear of displeasing the King.

'I lost all patience,' Mai continued. 'Andrea de 'Burgo and I went to the Pope, and told him we had 'seen the instructions sent to Campeggio, which were of 'such a nature that if we were to inform your Majesty 'of their contents you would undoubtedly resent the 'manner in which you were being treated. We would 'not do that, but we would speak our minds plainly. 'The letter to Campeggio was a breach of faith so 'often pledged by his Holiness to your Majesty that 'the divorce suit should be advocated to Rome. The 'violation of such a promise and the writing to Cam- 'peggio to go on with the proceeding was a greater 'insult and offence to your Majesty than the com- 'mission given to him in the first instance. It was a 'wonder to see how lightly his Holiness held promises 'made in accordance with justice and reason. An offence 'of such a kind bore so much on the honour of your

'Majesty and the princes of the Imperial family, that
'your Majesty would not put up with it. The King
'would have but to ask Campeggio whether he would
'or would not give sentence, and, if he refused, the duty
'would then devolve on the other Legate. His Holi-
'ness should be careful how he added fuel to the fire
'now raging in Christendom.'[1]

It was not enough for Mai that the cause should be
revoked to Rome. The English agents said that if an
independent sovereign was to be forced to plead at
Rome, the Pope must at least hear the suit in person.
He must not refer it to the Rota. Mai would not
hear of this. To the Rota it must go and nowhere
else. The Pope might mean well, but he might die
and be succeeded by a pope of another sort, or the
English might regain the influence they once had, and
indeed had still, in the Papal court. They were great
favourites, bribing right and left and spending money
freely.[2] What was a miserable pope to do? Casalis,
and Dr. Benet who had joined him from England,
pointed out the inevitable consequences if he allowed
himself to be governed by the Emperor. The Pope
replied with lamentations that none saw that better
than he, but he was so placed between the hammer and
the anvil, that, though he wished to please the King,
the whole storm would fall on him. The Emperor
would not endure an insult to his family, and had said

---

[1] Mai to Charles V., August 4,
1529.—*Spanish Calendar*, vol. iv.
part I, page 155 (abridged).

[2] Same to the same, August 28.
—*Ibid.* p. 182.

that he regarded the cause more than all his kingdoms. Those were only ornaments of fortune, while this touched his honour. He would postpone the advocation for a few days, but it could not be refused. He was in the Emperor's power, and the Emperor could do as he pleased with him.

The few days' respite meant a hope that news of some decisive act might arrive meanwhile from England. The King must determine, Casalis and Benet thought, whether it would be better to suspend the process at his own request, or to proceed to sentence before the advocation.[1] The Pope, the Commissioners added, was well disposed to the King, and would not refuse to shed his blood for him ; but in this cause and at this time he said it was impossible.

While matters were going thus at Rome, the suit in England went forward. The Cardinals availed themselves of every excuse for delay ; but in the presence of Catherine's determined refusal to recognize the court, delay became daily more difficult. The King pressed for judgment ; formal obstacles were exhausted, and the Roman Legate must either produce his last instructions, which he had been ordered not to reveal, or there was nothing left for him to urge as a reason for further hesitation. It was not supposed that in the face of a distinct promise the Pope would revoke the commission. Campeggio and Wolsey were sitting with full powers to hear and determine. Determine, it seemed, they must ;

---

[1] Benet, Casalis, and Vannes to Henry VIII.—*Calendar, Foreign and Domestic*, vol. iv. pp. 2567-8.

when, at the fifth session, uncalled on and unlooked for,
the Bishop of Rochester rose and addressed the court.
The King, he said, had declared that his only intention was to have justice done, and to relieve himself of
a scruple of conscience, and had invited the judges and
everyone else to throw light upon a cause which distressed and perplexed him. He [the Bishop], having
given two years' diligent study to the question, felt
himself bound in consequence to declare his opinion,
and not risk the damnation of his soul by withholding
it. He undertook, therefore, to declare and demonstrate
that the marriage of the King and Queen could be
dissolved by no power, human or divine, and for that
conclusion he was ready to lay down his life. The Baptist
had held it glorious to die in a cause of marriage, when
marriage was not so holy as it had been made by the
shedding of Christ's blood. He was prepared to encounter any peril for the truth, and he ended by presenting
his arguments in a written form.[1]

The Bishop's allusion to the Baptist was neither respectful nor felicitous. It implied that Henry, who as
yet at least had punished no one for speaking freely,
was no better than a Herod. Henry's case was that to
marry a brother's wife was not lawful, and the Baptist
was of the same opinion. The Legates answered quietly
that the cause had not been committed to Fisher, and
that it was not for him to pronounce judicially upon it.
Wolsey complained that the Bishop had given him no

---

[1] Campeggio to Salviati, June 29, 1529.—*Calendar, Foreign and
Domestic*, vol. iv. p. 2538.

notice of his intended interference. They continued to examine witnesses as if nothing had happened. But Fisher's action was not without effect. He was much respected. The public was divided on the merits of the general question. Many still thought the meaning of it to be merely that the King was tired of an old wife and wanted a young one. Courage is infectious, and comment grew loud and unfavourable. The popular voice might have been disregarded. But Campeggio, who had perhaps really wavered, not knowing what Clement wished him to do, gathered heart from Fisher's demonstration. 'We are hurried on,' he wrote to Salviati on the 13th of July, 'always faster than a trot, 'so that some expect a sentence in ten days. . . . I 'will not fail in my duty or office, nor rashly or willingly 'give offence to any one. When giving sentence I will 'have only God before my eyes, and the honour of the 'Holy See.' [1] A week later Du Bellay said that things were almost as the King wished, and the end was expected immediately, when Campeggio acted on the Pope's last verbal instructions at their parting at Rome. He was told to go on to the last, but must pause at the final extremity. He obeyed. When nothing was left but to pronounce judgment, he refused to speak it, and said that he must refer back to the Holy See. Wolsey declined to act without him, and Campeggio, when pressed, if we can believe his own account of what he said, answered : 'Very well, I vote in favour of the

---

[1] *Calendar, Foreign and Domestic,* vol. iv. p. 2581.

'marriage and the Queen. If my colleague agrees, well
'and good. If not, there can be no sentence, for we
'must both agree.'[1]

Wolsey's feelings must be conjectured, for he never
revealed them. To the Commissioners at Rome he
wrote: 'Such discrepancies and contrariety of opinion
'has ensued here that the cause will be long delayed.
'In a week the process will have to cease, and two
'months of vacation ensue. Other counsels, therefore,
'are necessary, and it is important to act as if the
'advocation was granted. Campeggio unites with me to
'urge the Pope, if it must be granted, to qualify the
'language; for if the King be cited to appear in person
'or by proxy, and his prerogative be interfered with,
'none of his subjects will tolerate it; or if he appears
'in Italy it will be at the head of a formidable army.[2]
'A citation of the King to Rome on threat of excommu-
'nication is no more tolerable than the whole loss of the
'King's dignity. If, therefore, the Pope has granted any
'such advocation, it must be revoked. If it arrives
'here before such a revocation, no mention of it shall
'be made, not even to the King.'[3]

This was Wolsey's last effort. Before his despatch
could reach Rome the resolution was taken. Had it

---

[1] Mai to Charles V., Sept. 3,
1529.—*Spanish Calendar*, vol. iv.
part I, p. 195.

[2] This was not an idle boast. A
united army of French and English
might easily have marched across
the Alps; and nothing would have

pleased Francis better than to have
led such an army, with his brother
of England at his side, to drive
out the Emperor.

[3] Wolsey to Benet, &c., July
27.—*Calendar, Foreign and Domestic*, vol. iv. p. 2591.

arrived in time, it would have made no difference while
Micer Mai was able to threaten to behead Cardinals
in their own apartments. The cause was advoked, as
it was called—reserved to be heard in the Rota. The
Legates' commission was cancelled. The court at
Blackfriars was dissolved, as Campeggio said, in anger,
shame, and disappointment. He had fulfilled his orders
not without some alarm for himself as he thought of his
bishopric of Salisbury.

Catherine, springing from despondency into triumph,
imagined that all was over. The suit, she thought,
would be instantly recommenced at Rome, and the Pope
would give judgment in her favour without further
form. She was to learn a harsher lesson, and would have
consulted better for her happiness if she had yielded to
the Pope's advice and retired into seclusion. While the
Legates were sitting in London, another conference was
being held at Cambray, to arrange conditions of European peace. France and the Empire adjusted their
quarrels for another interval. The Pope and the
Italian Princes were included—England was included
also—and the divorce, the point of central discord
between Henry and the Emperor, was passed over in
silence as too dangerous to be touched.

CHAPTER VII.

Call of Parliament—Wolsey to be called to account—Anxiety of
the Emperor to prevent a quarrel—Mission of Eustace Chapuys
—Long interview with the King—Alarm of Catherine—
Growth of Lutheranism—The English Clergy—Lord Darcy's
Articles against Wolsey—Wolsey's fall—Departure of Cam-
peggio—Letter of Henry to the Pope—Action of Parliament
—Intended reform of the Church—Alienation of English
feeling from the Papacy.

ON the collapse of the commission it was at once
announced that the King would summon a Parliament. For many years Wolsey had governed England
as he pleased. The King was now to take the reins in
his own hands. The long-suffering laity were to make
their voices heard, and the great Cardinal understood
too well that he was to be called to account for his
stewardship. The Queen, who could think of nothing
but her own wrongs, conceived that the object must be
some fresh violence to herself. She had requested the
Pope to issue a minatory brief forbidding Parliament
to meddle with her. She had mistaken the purpose of
its meeting, and she had mistaken the King's character.
Important as the divorce question might be, a great
nation had other things to think of which had

waited too long. It had originated in an ambitious scheme of Wolsey to alter the balance of power in Europe, and to form a new combination which the English generally disliked. Had his policy been successful he would have been continued in office, with various consequences which might or might not have been of advantage to the country. But he had failed miserably. He had drawn the King into a quarrel with his hereditary ally. He had entangled him, by ungrounded assurances, in a network of embarrassments, which had been made worse by the premature and indecent advancement of the Queen's intended successor. For this the Cardinal was not responsible. It was the King's own doing, and he had bitterly to pay for it. But Wolsey had misled his master into believing that there would be no difficulty. In the last critical moment he had not stood by him as the King had a right to expect; and, in the result, Henry found himself summoned to appear as a party before the Pope, the Pope himself being openly and confessedly a creature in the hands of the Emperor. No English sovereign had ever before been placed in a situation so degrading.

Parliament was to meet for other objects—objects which could not be attained while Wolsey was in power, and were themselves of incalculable consequence. But Anne Boleyn was an embarrassment, and Henry did for the moment hesitate whether it might not be better to abandon her. He had no desire to break the unity of Christendom or to disturb the peace of his own kingdom for the sake of a pretty woman. The Duke of Norfolk, though he was Anne's uncle, if he did not oppose her intended elevation, did nothing to encourage it. Her father, Lord Wiltshire, had been against it from the first. The Peers and the people would be the sufferers from a disputed succession, but they seemed willing to encounter the risk, or at least they showed no eagerness for the King's marriage with this particular person. If Reginald Pole is to be believed, the King did once inform the Council that he would go no further with it. The Emperor, to make retreat easy to him, had allowed nothing to be said on the subject at Cambray, and had instructed the Pope to hold his hand and make no further movement. He sent a new Ambassador to England, on a mission of *doulceur et amytié.* Eustace Chapuys, the Minister whom he selected, was not perhaps the best selection which he could have made, and Lord Paget, who knew him well, has left an account of him not very favourable. ' For Chapuys,' he said, ' I never took him for a wise ' man, but for one that used to speak *cum summâ* ' *licentiâ* whatsoever came *in buccam*, without respect of ' honesty or truth, so it might serve his turn, and of ' that fashion it is small mastery to be a wise man. ' He is a great practicer, with which honest term we ' cover tale-telling, lying, dissimuling, and flattering.' [1] Chapuys being the authority for many of the scandals about Henry, this description of him by a competent

---

[1] Paget to Petre.—*State Papers, Henry VIII.*, vol. x. p. 466.

observer may be borne in remembrance; but there can
be no question that Charles sent him to England on an
embassy of peace, and one diplomatist is not always
perhaps the fairest judge of another of the same trade.
The King's hesitation, if he ever did hesitate, was not
of long duration. He had been treated like a child,
tricked, played with, trifled with, and he was a dangerous
person to deal with in so light a fashion. Chapuys
reached London in the beginning of September. On
landing he found the citation to Rome had not been
officially notified to the King, as a morsel too big for
him to swallow.[1] The King received him politely,
invited him to dine in the palace, and allowed him
afterwards to be introduced to Catherine, who was still
residing at the court. Three days after he had a long
interview with Henry. His commission, he said, was
to smooth all differences between the King and his
master. The King responded with equal graciousness,
but turned the conversation upon those differences
themselves. The Emperor, he said, had not used him
well. The advocation to Rome was absurd. He had
written himself to the Pope with his own hand, telling
him it was not only expedient but absolutely necessary
that the cause should be tried in England. The Roman
territories were still in the occupation of the Imperial
troops. The Pope had committed it to two of his
Cardinals, had solemnly promised that it should not be

<hr/>

[1] Chapuys to the Regent Margaret, September 18, 1529.—*Spanish
Calendar*, vol. iv. part 1, p. 214.

revoked, and that he would confirm any sentence which the Legates should pronounce. These engagements the Emperor had obliged the Pope to break. He himself had not proceeded upon light grounds. He was a conscientious Prince, he said, who preferred his own salvation to all worldly advantages, as appeared sufficiently from his conduct in the affair. Had he been differently situated and not attentive to his conscience, he might have adopted other measures, which he had not taken and never would take.[1] Chapuys attempted to defend Clement. 'Enough of that Pope,' Henry sharply interrupted. 'This is not the first time that 'he has changed his mind. I have long known his 'versatile and fickle nature.'[2] The Pope, he went on, 'would never dare pronounce sentence, unless it favoured 'the Emperor.'

Catherine was eagerly communicative. Chapuys learned from her that the King had offered that the case should be heard at Cambray—which she had, of course, refused. She was much alarmed about the Parliament, 'the King having played his cards so well 'that he would have a majority of votes in his favour.' It was quite certain that he meant to persevere. She professed outwardly that she was personally attached to the King; yet she desired Chapuys expressly to caution the Emperor against believing that his conduct had anything to do with conscience. The idea of separation,

---

[1] Chapuys to Charles V., Sept. 2.—*Spanish Calendar*, vol. v. part 2, p. 225.   [2] *Ib.* p. 229.

she said, had originated entirely in his own iniquity and malice, and when the treaty of Cambray was completed, he had announced it to her with the words : ' My peace ' with the Emperor is made : it will last as long as you ' choose.' [1]

Chapuys had been charged to ascertain the feeling of the English people. He found them generally well affected to the Queen. But the Lutheran heresy was creeping in. The Duke of Suffolk had spoken bitterly of Papal legates, and Chapuys believed if they had nothing to fear but the Pope's malediction, there were great numbers who would follow the Duke's advice and make Popes of the King and Bishops, all to have the divorce case tried in England.[2] The Queen was afraid of pressing her appeal, fearing that if the Commons in Parliament heard that the King had been summoned to Rome, measures injurious to her might easily be proposed and carried.[3] Even the Duke of Norfolk was not satisfactory. He professed to be devoted to the Emperor; he said he would willingly have lost a hand so that the divorce question should never have been raised ; but it was an affair of theology and canon law and he had not meddled with it. If the Emperor had remained neutral, instead of interfering, it would have been sooner settled.[4]

But, for the instant, the interests of the people of England were fixed on a subject more immediately close

---

[1] Chapuys to Charles V., Sept. 2, 1529.—*Spanish Calendar*, vol. vi. part i, pp. 236-7.

[2] *Ibid.* p. 236.
[3] *Ibid.* p. 274.
[4] *Ibid.* p. 294.

to them. The sins of the clergy had at last found them
out. They pretended to be a supernatural order, to
hold the keys of heaven and hell, to be persons too
sacred for ordinary authority to touch. Their vices
and their tyranny had made them and their fantastic
assumptions no longer bearable, and all Europe was
in revolt against the scandals of the Church and
Churchmen. The ecclesiastical courts, as the pretended
guardians of morality, had the laity at their mercy;
and every offence, real or imaginary, was converted into
an occasion of extortion. The courts were themselves
nests of corruption; while the lives and habits of the
order which they represented made ridiculous their
affectations of superiority to common men. Clement's
conduct of the divorce case was only a supreme instance
of the methods in which the clerical tribunals administered what they called justice. An authority
equally oblivious of the common principles of right and
wrong was extended over the private lives and language
of every family in Catholic Christendom. In England
the cup was full and the day of reckoning had arrived.
I have related in the first volume of my history of the
period the meeting of the Parliament of 1529, and I
have printed there the Petition of the Commons to the
Crown, with the Bishops' reply to it.[1] I need not
repeat what has been written already. A few more
words are needed, however, to explain the animosity

---

[1] The transcripts of these documents were furnished to me by the late Sir Francis Palgrave, who was then Keeper of the Records.

which broke out against Wolsey. The great Cardinal
was the living embodiment of the detested ecclesiastical
domination, and a representation in his own person of
the worst abuses complained of. He had been a
vigorous Minister, full of large schemes and high
ambitions. He had been conscious of much that was
wrong. He had checked the eagerness of the bench of
Bishops to interfere with opinion, had suppressed many
of the most disorderly smaller monasteries, and had
founded colleges out of their revenues. But he had left
his own life unreformed, as an example of avarice and
pride. As Legate he had absorbed the control of the
entire ecclesiastical organisation. He had trampled on
the Peers. On himself he had piled benefice upon
benefice. He held three great bishoprics, and, in
addition to them, the wealthiest of the abbeys. York
or Durham he had never entered; Winchester he may
have visited in intervals of business; and he resided
occasionally at the Manor of the More, which belonged
to St. Albans : but this was all his personal connection
with offices to which duties were attached which he
would have admitted to be sacred, if, perhaps, with
a smile. As Legate and Lord Chancellor he disposed
of the whole patronage of the realm. Every priest
or abbot who needed a license had to pay Wolsey for
it. His officials were busy in every diocese. Every
will that was to be proved, every marriage within the
forbidden degrees, had to pass under their eyes, and
from their courts streams richer than Pactolus flowed
into Wolsey's coffers. Foreign princes, as we have seen.

were eager to pile pensions upon him. His wealth
was known to be enormous. How enormous was now
to be revealed. Even his own son—for a son he had
—was charged upon the commonwealth. The worst
iniquity of the times was the appointing children to
the cure of souls. Wolsey's boy was educated at Paris,
and held benefices worth 1,500 crowns a year, or 3,000
pounds of modern English money. A political mistake had now destroyed his credit. His enemies
were encouraged to speak, and the storm burst upon
him.

A list of detailed complaints against him survives
which is curious alike from its contents, the time at
which it was drawn up, and the person by whom it was
composed—the old Lord Darcy of Templehurst, the
leader afterwards in the Pilgrimage of Grace. Darcy
was an earnest Catholic. He had fought in his youth
under Ferdinand at the conquest of Granada. He was
a dear friend of Ferdinand's daughter, and an earnest
supporter, against Wolsey, of the Imperial alliance.
His paper is long and the charges are thrown together
without order. The date is the 1st of July, when the
Legates' court had begun its sittings and was to end, as
he might well suppose, in Catherine's ruin. They express the bitterness of Darcy's feelings. The briefest
epitome is all that can be attempted of an indictment
which extended over the whole of Wolsey's public career.
It commences thus :—

'Hereafter followeth, by protestation, articles against
'the Cardinal of York, shewed by me, Thomas Darcy,

'only to discharge my oath and bounden duty to God
'and the King, and of no malice.

' 1. All articles that touches God and his Church and
'his acts against the same.

' 2. All that touches the King's estate, honour and
'prerogative, and against his laws.

' 3. Lack of justice, and using himself by his
'authority as Chancellor faculties legatine and cardinal;
'what wrongs, exactions he hath used.

' 4. All his authorities, legatine and other, purchased
'of the Pope, and offices and grants that he hath of the
'King's grace, special commissions and instructions sent
'into every shire; he, and the Cardinal's servants, to
'be straitly examined of his unlawful acts.'

Following vaguely this distribution, Darcy proceeds
with his catalogue of wrongs.   Half the list is of
reforms commenced and unfinished, everything disturbed and nothing set right, to 'the ruffling of the
'good order of the realm.'   Of direct offences we find
Wolsey unexpectedly accused of having broken the
Præmunire statute by introducing faculties from Rome
and allowing the Pope to levy money in the realm
contrary to the King's prerogative royal, while for
himself, by 'colour of his powers as Cardinal legate *a*
'*latere* and faculties spiritual and temporal, he had as-
'sembled marvellous and mighty sums of money.'   Of
bishops, abbots, priors, deans, &c., he had received
(other sums) for promotion spiritual since his entry.
He had appropriated the plate and jewels of the suppressed abbeys.   He had raised the 'probate duty' all

over the realm, the duty going into his own coffers. He had laid importable charges on the nobles of the realm. He had Towered, Fleeted, and put to the walls of Calais a number of the noblemen of England, and many of them for light causes. He had promoted none but such as served about the King to bring to pass his purposes, or were of his council in such things as an honest man would not vouchsafe to be acquainted with. He had hanged, pressed, and banished more men since he was in authority than had suffered death by way of justice in all Christendom besides. He had wasted the King's treasure, &c. He had levied mighty sums of other houses of religion, some for dread to be pulled down, and others by his feigned visitations under colour of virtuous reformation. As Chancellor 'he had taken 'up all the great matters depending in suit to determine 'after his discretion, and would suffer no way to take 'effect that had been devised by other men.' In other times ' the best prelate in the realm was contented with ' one bishoprick.' Darcy demanded that the duties of bishops should be looked into. They should hold no temporal offices, nor meddle with temporal affairs. They should seek no dispensation from the Pope. The tenure of land in England should be looked into, to find what temporal lands were in spiritual men's hands, by what titles, for what purposes, and whether it was followed or no. The King's Grace should proceed to determine all reformations, of spiritual and temporal, within his realm. Never more Legate nor Cardinal should be in England: these legacies and

faculties should be clearly annulled and made frus-
trate, and search and enquiry be made what had been
levied thereby. He recommended that at once and
without notice Wolsey's papers and accounts should be
seized. 'Then matters much unknown would come
'forth surely concerning his affairs with Pope, Emperor,
'the French King, other Princes, and within the realm.'[1]

Many of Darcy's charges are really creditable to
Wolsey, many more are exaggerated; but of the oppres-
sive character of his courts, and of the immense revenue
which he drew from them, no denial was possible. The
special interest of the composition, however, is that it
expresses precisely the temper of the Parliament of 1529.
It enables us to understand how the Chancellorship
came to be accepted by Sir Thomas More. It contains
the views of conservative Catholic English statesmen
who, while they had no sympathy with changes of doctrine, were weary of ecclesiastical domination, who desired
to restrict the rights of the Pope in England within the
limits fixed by the laws of the Plantagenets, to relieve
the clergy of their temporal powers and employments,
and reduce them to their spiritual functions. Micer
Mai and De Soria had said the same thing; Charles V.,
likely enough, shared their opinion, though he could not
see his way towards acting upon it. In England it
could be acted upon, and it was.

There is no occasion to repeat the well-known tale

_____

[1] Cardinal Wolsey and Lord Darcy, July 1, 1529.—*Calendar, Foreign
and Domestic,* vol. iv. pp. 2548-62.

of the fall of Wolsey. He resigned the seals on the
18th of October; his property was seized and examined
into. The Venetian Ambassador reported that his ordinary income was found to have been 150,000 crowns,
besides pensions, gifts from foreign princes, and irregular
contributions from home. His personal effects were
worth half a million more. He said that it had been all
gathered for the King; if the King was pleased to take
it before his end, the King was welcome to it.

The King was thenceforward his own first minister;
the Duke of Norfolk became President of the Council;
Suffolk was Vice-President, and Sir Thomas More Lord
Chancellor. But the King intended to rule with
Parliament to advise and to help him. Catherine told
Chapuys, in fear for herself, that the elections to the
Lower House had been influenced to her own injury.
She was mistaken, for the elections had not turned on the
divorce. The object of the meeting of the Legislature
was to reform the clergy, and upon this all parties
among the laity were agreed. It may be (though the
Queen could not know it) that exertions were made to
counteract or control the local influences of individual
nobles or prelates. If the object was to secure a real
representation of popular feeling, it was right and
necessary to protect the electors against the power of
particular persons. But it is at least clear that this
Parliament came up charged with the grievances of
which Darcy's indictment was the epitome.

The Houses met on the 3rd of November, and went
at once to business. I can add nothing to what I have

written elsewhere on the acts of the first session. Wolsey was impeached; the Peers would have attainted him or sent him to trial for high treason; the Commons were more moderate, listening to Cromwell, who faced unpopularity by defending gallantly his old patron. But the King himself did not wish the fallen Cardinal to be pressed too hard; and it was said that, determined to protect him, he forbade the attainder. He had determined to pardon him, and an attainder would have made pardon more difficult. Very interesting accounts of Wolsey's own behaviour in his calamity are found in the letters of the foreign Ambassadors. Du Bellay saw him on the 17th of October, the day before he surrendered the Great Seal, and found him entirely broken. He wept; he 'hoped ' the French King and Madam would have pity on him.' His face had lost its fire; ' he did not desire legate- ' ship, seal of office, or power; he was ready to give ' up everything, to his shirt, and live in a hermitage, if ' the King would not keep him in his displeasure.' He wished Francis to write to Henry in his favour. He had been the chief instrument of the present amity with France; and such a service ought not to have given a bad impression of him. Suspicions were abroad that he had received large presents from the French Court; they were probably true, for he said ' he hoped Madam would not do him an injury if it ' were spoken of.' [1]

---

[1] Du Bellay to Montmorency, Oct. 17, 1529.—*Calendar, Foreign* | *and Domestic,* vol. iv. part 3, p 2675.

Nothing could be more piteous. The poor old man was like a hunted animal; lately lord of the world, and now 'none so poor to do him reverence.' Darcy had raised the question of the Præmunire. The ancient Statute of Provisors had forbidden the introduction of Bulls from Rome, and the statute was awake again. He was made to confess that the penalties of Præmunire— confiscation of goods and imprisonment — had been incurred by him when he published the Bull which made him Legate, and by the use of which he had unlawfully vexed the greater number of the prelates of the realm, and the King's other subjects.

His brother Legate, Campeggio, had remained for some weeks in London after the dissolution of the court. But England was no place for him in the hurly-burly which had broken loose. He went, and had to submit to the indignity of having his luggage searched at Dover. The cause alleged was a fear that he might be taking with him some of Wolsey's jewels. Tradition said that he had obtained possession of the letters of the King to Anne Boleyn, and that it was through him that they reached the Vatican. At any rate, the locks were forced, the trunks inspected, and nothing of importance was found in them.[1] Campeggio complained to the King of the violation of his privilege as ambassador. Henry told him ironically that he had suffered no wrong: his legateship was gone when the cause was revoked ; he

---

[1] Chapuys to the Emperor, Oct. 25, 1529.—*Spanish Calendar*, vol. iv. pt. I, p. 304.

had no other commission : he was an English bishop,
and so far, therefore, an English subject. But a courteous apology was made for the unnecessary violence
which had been used ;[1] Campeggio's ruffled plumes were
smoothed, and he wrote to Salviati from Paris with the
latest news of Wolsey, telling him ' that the King would
' not go to extremes, but would act considerately in the
' matter, as he was accustomed to do in all his actions.'[2]

Although no mention was made in Parliament of
the divorce, the subject, of course, could not sleep. The
question of the succession to the crown having been
made so prominent, it would, and must, sooner or later,
come before the Legislature to be settled, and had
already become a topic of general consideration and
anxiety. Mary's legitimacy had been impugned. Falieri,
writing from London and reporting what he heard in
society, said that ' by English law females were excluded
' from the throne.' Custom might say so, for no female
had, in fact, ever sat on the throne ; but enacted law or
rule there was none : it was only one uncertainty the
more. At any rate, Falieri said that the King had determined to go on with the divorce, that he might have
a legitimate male heir.

Henry's experience of Clement had taught him that
he need not fear any further immediate steps. The
advocation of the cause implied of itself a desire for
longer delay, and, with more patience than might have

---

[1] Hen. VIII. to Campeggio,
Oct. 22, 1529.—*Calendar, Foreign
and Domestic*, vol. iv. p. 2677.

[2] To Salviati, Nov. 5.—*Ibid.*
p. 2702.

been looked for in such a disappointment, he had resolved to wait for what the Pope would do. That an
English sovereign should plead before the Rota at Rome
was, of course, preposterous. The suggestion of it was
an insult. But other means might be found. He had
himself proposed Cambray as a neutral spot for a first
commission; he really believed that the Pope was at
heart on his side, and therefore did not wish to quarrel
with him. When Campeggio was leaving England the
King wrote to Clement more politely than might have
been expected. He did not insist that the English
commission should be renewed.

   ' We could have wished,' he said, 'not less for your
' sake than our own, that all things had been so expe-
' dited as corresponded to our expectation, not rashly
' conceived, but according to your promises. As it is,
' we have to regard with grief and wonder the incredible
' confusion which has arisen. If a Pope can relax Divine
' laws at his pleasure, surely he has as much power over
' human laws. We have been so often deceived by your
' Holiness's promises that no dependence can be placed
' on them. Our dignity has not been consulted in the
' treatment which we have met with. If your Holiness
' will keep the cause now advoked to Rome in your own
' hands, until it can be decided by impartial judges, and
' in an indifferent place, in a manner satisfactory to our
' scruples, we will forget what is past, and repay kindness
' by kindness.' [1]

---

[1] Hen. VIII. to Clement VII.—*Calendar, Foreign and Domestic*,
vol. iv. p. 2660.

As the Pope had professed to be ignorant of the
extent of his dispensing power, the King proposed to
submit this part of the question to the canon lawyers
of Europe. The Nuncios, meanwhile, in Paris and
London advised that the Pope and the Emperor should
write in a friendly way to the King. Charles was believed in England to have said 'that the King should
'stick to his wife in spite of his beard.' He had not
used such words, and ought to disclaim them, but he
might endeavour to persuade the King to let the divorce
drop.

The Parliament meanwhile had been fiercely busy
in cutting down the Church courts—abolishing or limit-
ing the various forms of extortion by which the laity
had been plundered. The clergy were required to reside
upon their benefices. 'Pluralities' were restricted.
The business of the session had been a series of Clergy
Discipline Acts. The Bishop of Rochester especially
clamoured over the 'want of faith' which such Acts
exhibited, but nothing had been done of which the Pope
could complain, nothing of which, perhaps, he did not
secretly approve. Catherine, through her agents at
Rome, demanded instant sentence in her cause. The
Pope's inclination seemed again on Henry's side. He
described an interview with the Emperor, who had
urged Catherine's case. He professed to have replied
that he must be cautious when the case was not clear.
Many things, he said, made for the King. All the
divines were against the power of the Pope to dispense.
Of the canon lawyers, some were against it ; and those

who were not against it considered that the dispensing powers could only be used for a very urgent cause, as, to prevent the ruin of a kingdom. The Pope's function was to judge whether such a cause had arisen; but no such inquiry was made when the dispensation of Julius was granted. The Emperor must not be surprised if he could do no more for the Queen.[1]

The Emperor himself thought of nothing less than taking his uncle 'by the beard.' He wished to be reconciled to him if he could find a way to it. For one thing, he was in sore need of help against the Turks, and Chapuys was directed to ascertain if Henry would give him money. Henry's reply was not encouraging, and sounded ominously, as if his mind was making perilous progress on the great questions of the day. He said it would be a foolish thing for him to remit money to the Emperor and help him to maintain three armies in Italy, which ought to be elsewhere. He had consulted his Parliament, and had found he could not grant it. The said money might be turned to other use, and be employed to promote dissension among Christian Princes.[2] At a subsequent interview the conversation was renewed and took a more general turn. The King spoke of the Court of Rome—the ambitious magnificence of which, he said, 'had been the ' cause of so many wars, discords, and heresies.' Had the Pope and Cardinals, he said, observed the precepts of

---

[1] Casalis to Henry VIII., Dec. 26, 1529.—*Calendar, Foreign and Domestic*, vol. iv. p. 2722.

[2] Chapuys to Charles V., Dec. 6, 1529.—*Spanish Calendar*, vol. iv. part i, p. 344.

the Gospel and attended to the example of the Fathers of the Church [several of whom the King mentioned, to Chapuys' surprise], they would have led a different life, and not have scandalised Christendom by their acts and manners. So far, Luther had told nothing but the truth; and had Luther limited himself to inveighing against the vices, abuses, and errors of the clergy, instead of attacking the Sacraments of the Church, everyone would have gone with him; he would himself have written in his favour, and taken pen in hand in his defence. Into the Church in his own dominions he hoped, little by little, to introduce reforms and end the scandal.[1]

These expressions were dangerous enough, but there was worse to follow. 'Henry maintained that the only 'power which Churchmen had over laymen was abso- 'lution from sin'; Chapuys found that he had told the Queen that he was now waiting for the opinions of the foreign doctors; when he had obtained these he would forward them to Rome; and should not the Pope, in conformity with the opinions so expressed, declare the marriage null and void, he would denounce the Pope as a heretic and marry whom he pleased.[2]

'The Lady Anne,' Chapuys said, 'was growing im- 'patient, complaining that she was wasting her time and 'youth to no purpose.' The House of Commons had already 'clipped the claws' of the clergy, and it was not impossible that, on the plea of the various and con-

---

[1] Chapuys to Charles V., Dec. 6, 1529.—*Spanish Calendar*, vol. iv. part I, p. 344.   [2] *Ibid.* p. 351.

tradictory judgments on the matter, they and the people might consent to the divorce.

The hope that the King might be held back by national disapproval was thus seen to be waning. The national pride had been touched by the citation of an English sovereign to plead before a foreign court. Charles V. feared that the Pope, alarmed at the prospect of losing England, would 'commit some new 'folly' which might lead to war.[1] The English Nuncio in fact informed Chapuys, much to the latter's astonishment, that the Pope had ordered him to find means to reconcile the King and the Emperor. Chapuys thought the story most unlikely. The Emperor would never have trusted the Pope with such a commission, nor was the Pope a promising mediator, seeing that he was more hated in England than might have been supposed.

There were evident signs now that the country meant to support the King. The Duke of Norfolk told the Ambassador that unless the Emperor would permit his master to divorce the Queen and take another wife, there was no remedy left. The King's scruples of conscience, instead of abating, were on the increase, owing to the opinions of others who thought as he did, and no one in the world could turn him.[2] Chapuys thought it more likely than not that the question would be introduced at once into Parliament, where he had heard

[1] Charles V. to Ferdinand, Jan. 11, 1530.—*Calendar, Foreign and Domestic,* vol. iv. p. 2742.

[2] Chapuys to Charles V., Dec. 9, 1529.—*Spanish Calendar,* vol. iv. part 1, p. 359.

that a majority had been bribed or gained over to the King's side. With the consent of the Commons he would consider himself secure all round. Should the Pope pronounce in favour of the Queen, the English would say that the sentence was unjust, for, besides the suspicion and ill-will they had towards the Pope and other ecclesiastical judges, they would allege that in confirming the Bull of Pope Julius, the Pope and Cardinals would be only influenced by their own interest ' to increase the authority of the Pope, and ' procure him money by such dispensations.'[1]

At this moment Chapuys feared some precipitate step on Henry's part. Norfolk, whom he saw frequently, told him that ' there was nothing which the King ' would not grant the Emperor to obtain his consent, ' even to becoming his slave for ever.'[2] ' The reform of ' the clergy was partly owing to the anger of the people ' at the advocation of the cause to Rome.' ' Nearly all ' the people hated the priests,' Chapuys said—an important testimony from an unwilling witness. Peers and Commons might be brought to agree that Popes could grant no dispensations in marriages or anything else, and so save their money. If there was nothing to restrain them but respect for the Pope, they would not care much for him, and the Holy See would have no more obedience in England than in Germany. The Duke of Norfolk talked as menacingly as the rest. He said publicly to the Ambassador ' that the Pope himself

---

[1] Chapuys to Charles V., Dec. 9, 1529.—*Spanish Calendar*, vol. iv. part 1, p. 361. [2] *Ibid.* p. 366.

'had been the first to perceive the invalidity of the
'marriage, had written to say that it could not stand,
'and would so declare himself, or have it legally de-
'clared . . . . and now, being in the Emperor's power,
'the same Pope would have the case tried and determined
'only as the Emperor wished.'[1]

Under these circumstances Chapuys could only
advise that means should be taken to weaken or defer
the action of Parliament. The Cambray proposal might
be revived, or a suggestion made that the cause should
be argued before the Sorbonne at Paris. The Duke of
Norfolk could perhaps be gained over; but, unfortunately,
he and Queen Catherine were not on good terms. The
Duke was afraid also—the words show how complicated
were the threads which ruled the situation—that, should
the King dismiss the Lady Anne, the Cardinal would
in all probability regain his influence, owing to his
uncommon ability and the King's readiness to restore
him to favour. Everyone perceived the King bore the
Cardinal no real ill-will, and should the King's affection
for the lady abate in the least, the Cardinal would
soon find means of settling the divorce in a manner
which would cost the opposite party their lives.[2] In
this letter of Chapuys is the first allusion which I have
found to the Mary Boleyn scandal, then beginning to
be heard of in circles opposed to the divorce : 'People
'say,' he wrote, 'that it is the King's evil destiny that

---

[1] Chapuys to Charles V., Dec. 9, 1529.—*Spanish Calendar*, vol. iv.
part I, p. 367.   [2] *Ibid.* p. 368.

'impels him; for had he, as he asserts, only attended to
'the voice of conscience, there would have been still
'greater affinity to contend with in this intended mar-
'riage than in that of the Queen his wife.'[1]   The story
is referred to as a fresh feature of the case, which had
not before been heard of.

---

[1] Chapuys to Charles V., Dec. 9, 1529.—*Spanish Calendar*, vol. iv.
part I, p. 369.

CHAPTER VIII.

Hope of Wolsey to return to power—Anger of Anne Boleyn and the Duke of Norfolk—Charles V. at Bologna—Issue of a prohibitory brief—The Pope secretly on Henry's side—Collection of opinions—Norfolk warns Chapuys—State of feeling in England—Intrigues of Wolsey—His illness and death.

THE momentous year of 1529 wore out. Parliament rose before Christmas; Peers and Commons dispersed to their homes; and the chief parties in the drama were still undetermined what next to do. The Duke of Norfolk was afraid of Wolsey's return to power. It was less impossible than it seemed. A parliamentary impeachment, though let fall, ought to have been fatal; but none knew better than Wolsey by how transitory a link the parties who had combined for his ruin were really held together. More and Darcy had little sympathy with the advanced Reformers whose eyes were fixed on Germany. They agreed in cutting down the temporal encroachments of the clergy; they agreed in nothing besides. The King had treated Wolsey with exceptional forbearance. He had left him the Archbishopric of York, with an income equal in modern money to eight or ten thousand pounds a year, and had made him large presents besides of money, furniture, and jewels. Finding himself so leniently dealt with, the Cardinal recovered heart, and believed evidently that his day was not over. In a letter to Gardiner, written in January, 1530, he complained as a hardship of having been made to surrender Winchester and St. Albans. He had not 'deserved to lose them,' he said, 'and had not expected to lose them on his submission. 'His long services deserved at least a pension.'[1] The King agreed, or seemed to agree; for a further grant of 3,000 crowns was allowed him, charged on the See of Winchester. Anne Boleyn was furious. The Duke of Norfolk swore that ' sooner than suffer Wolsey's return ' to office he would eat him up alive.'[2] Though he had never seen his diocese, the Cardinal was making no haste to go thither. He lingered on at Esher, expecting to be sent for, and it is evident from the alarm of his rivals that there was real likelihood of it. The Lady Anne so hated him that she quarrelled with her uncle Norfolk for not having pressed his attainder. Catherine liked him equally ill, for she regarded him as the cause of her sufferings. He had been ' disevangelised,' as Norfolk called it; but Henry missed at every turn his dexterity and readiness of hand. He had monopolised the whole business of the realm; the subordinate officials everywhere were his creatures, and the threads of every branch of administration had centred in his

---

[1] Wolsey to Gardiner, Jan. 1530. — *Calendar, Foreign and Domestic,* vol. iv. p. 2763.

[2] Chapuys to Charles V., Feb 6, 1530. —*Spanish Calendar,* vol. iv. pp. 449-50.

cabinet; without him there was universal confusion. The French Court was strongly in his favour. He had himself made the Anglo-French alliance; and the Anglo-French alliance was still a necessity to Henry, if he meant to defy the Emperor and retain an influence at Rome. The King wished, if he could, to keep on terms with the Pope, and Wolsey if any one, could keep the Papal Court within limits of moderation.

The situation was thus more critical than ever. Catherine knew not what to look for. Those among the peers who, like Norfolk, would naturally have been her friends, and would have preferred that the divorce should never have been spoken of, yet saw no reason why on a private ground the Emperor should light up a European war again. They conceived that by protesting he had done enough for his honour, and that he ought to advise his aunt to give away. According to Chapuys, attempts were privately made to obtain a declaration of opinion from the House of Commons before Parliament rose.[1] He says that the attempts were unsuccessful. It may have been so.

But Chapuys could not hope that the unwillingness would last. Charles was determined to stand by Catherine to all extremities. Henry was threatening to marry his mistress whether the Pope consented or not, professing to care not a straw, and almost calling the Pope a heretic. The Pope did not wish to be a party to a scandal, but also would be sorry to see the

---

[1] Chapuys to Charles V., Jan. 31, 1529.—*Spanish Calendar*, vol. iv. p 387.

King lose all submission and reverence to the See of
Rome. For himself, the Emperor said he could not
see how the affair would end, 'but he was certain that
Henry would persist, and war would probably come
of it.' He directed his brother Ferdinand to avoid
irritating the German Lutherans, as France might
probably take part with England.[1] Fresh efforts were
made to persuade Catherine to take the veil. They
were as unsuccessful as before.[2]

The Emperor was now in Italy. He had gone to
Bologna for his coronation on the conclusion of the
Peace of Cambray, and the Pope was to be made to feel
the weight of his Imperial presence. Henry used the
occasion to send a deputation to Bologna, composed of
the Earl of Wiltshire, Anne's father, who was personally
known to Charles, Dr. Cranmer, then coming into
prominence, and Stokesly, the Bishop of London, who,
having been first on Catherine's side, had been converted. They were directed to lay before the Emperor
the motives for the King's action, to protest against his
interference, and to explain the certain consequences if
he persisted in supporting the Queen.

The Emperor gave a cold answer, and declined to
hear the Earl's instructions, while the Pope, the Earl
said, was led by the Emperor, and dared not displease
him. The second act of the drama was now to open,
and Clement was made to strike the first blow. In con-

---

[1] Charles V. to Ferdinand,
Jan. 11, 1530.—*Ibid.* vol. iv. part
1, pp 405-6.

[2] Chapuys to Charles V., Feb.
6, 1530.—*Calendar, Foreign and
Domestic,* vol. iv. p. 2780.

sequence of the reports from Catherine and Chapuys
that Henry was collecting the opinions of the canonists
of Europe, and intended to act on them if favourable, a
brief was issued on the 7th of March ordering the King
to restore Catherine to her rights, and prohibiting him
from making a second marriage while the suit was
undetermined. The divines and lawyers of Catholic
Europe were at the same time threatened with excommunication if they presumed to declare themselves
favourable to the divorce. But though the voice was
Clement's, the hand was the Emperor's. Clement was
being dragged along against his will, and was still
'facing both ways' in honest or dishonest irresolution.
While issuing the brief under compulsion, he said
precisely the opposite in his communication with the
French Ambassador, the Bishop of Tarbes. The Ambassador was able to assure his own master that the Pope
would never give sentence in Catherine's favour. In
direct contradiction of the brief, the Bishop wrote ' that
' the Pope had told him more than three times in secret
' he would be glad if the marriage between Henry and
' Anne was already made, either by dispensation of the
' English Legate or otherwise, provided it was not by
' his authority or in diminution of his powers of dis-
' pensation and limitation of divine law.' [1] In England
the Pope had still his own Nuncio—a Nuncio who, as
Chapuys declared, was 'heart and soul' with the King.
He was the brother of Sir Gregory Casalis, Henry's

---

[1] Bishop of Tarbes to Francis
I., from Bologna, March 27, 1530. | —*Calendar, Foreign and Domestic,*
vol. iv. p. 2826.

agent at Rome, and Henry was said to have promised
him a bishopric as soon as his cause should be won.
The Pope could not have been ignorant of the disposition of his own Minister.

Chapuys reported a mysterious State secret which
had reached him through Catherine's physician. The
Smalcaldic League was about to be formed among the
Protestant Princes of Germany. Francis was inviting
the King to support them and to join with himself in
encouraging them to dethrone the Emperor ; the King
was said to have agreed on the ground that the Pope
and the Emperor had behaved ill to him, and the
probability was that both France and England in the
end would become Lutheran.

Had there been nothing else, the Queen's sterility
was held a sufficient ground for the divorce. If she had
been barren from the first, the marriage would have
been held invalid at once. Now that the hope of
succession was gone, the Pope, it was said, ought to
have ended it.[1]

The King had been busy all the winter carrying out
his project of collecting the opinions of the learned.
The Pope's prohibition not having been issued in
England, his own Bishops, the Universities, and the
canonists had declared themselves in favour of the
divorce. The assent had not in all instances been given
very willingly. Oxford and Cambridge had attempted
a feeble resistance, and at Oxford the Commissioners

---

[1] Chapuys to Charles V., Dec. 31, 1529.—*Spanish Calendar*, vol. iv.
part I, p. 394.

had been pelted with stones. Still, given it had been, and the conservative Peers and gentry were coming to the same conclusion. The King was known to be wishing to recall Wolsey. The return of Wolsey to power might imply the acceptance of the French policy; perhaps the alliance with the Lutherans— at any rate, war with the Emperor. The Duke of Norfolk and his friends were English aristocrats, adherents of the old traditions, dreading and despising German revolutionists; but they believed that the King and the Emperor could only be drawn together by Charles's consent to the divorce. The King, Norfolk said to Chapuys, was so much bent on it that no one but God could turn him. He believed it imperative for the welfare of the realm that his master should marry again and have male succession; he would give all that he possessed for an hour's interview with the Emperor; if his Majesty would but consent to the marriage, the friendship between him and the King would then be indissoluble;[1] the divorce was nothing by the side of the larger interests at issue; 'the King,' it was rumoured, 'had written, or was about to write, 'to the Archbishop of Canterbury, that if the Pope 'persisted in refusing justice, his own and all Church 'authority would be at an end in England;' the nobles and people, provoked and hurt at the advocation of the suit to Rome, were daily more and more incensed against Churchmen, and would become Lutherans in

---

[1] Chapuys to Charles V., Jan. 12, 1530.—*Spanish Calendar*, vol. iv. part 1, p. 417.

the end.[1] The Pope had confessed that the presence
of the Imperial army in Italy left him no liberty. If
revolution came, the Emperor would be the cause of it.
The Duke spoke with the indignation of an Englishman
at a rumour that the Emperor had 'threatened to use
all his power in the Queen's support.' Such menaces,
he said, were useless, and the nation would not endure
them. Foreign princes had no authority over English
kings.

Chapuys did not mend matters by saying that the
Emperor was not thinking of employing force, for he did
not believe that the King would give occasion for it.
The Emperor's interference, indeed, would be unnecessary, for the Duke must be aware that if the divorce
was proceeded with there would be a civil war in
England.[2] Chapuys was vain of his insight into things
and characters. Like so many of his successors, he
mistook the opinion of a passionate clique of priests
and priest-ridden malcontents for the general sentiment
of the nation. They told him, as they told other
Spanish ambassadors after him, that all the world
thought as they did. Fanatics always think so; and
the belief that they were right proved in the end the
ruin of the Spanish empire. In the present instance,
however, Chapuys may be pardoned for his error.
Norfolk imagined that Wolsey was scheming for a
return to power on the old anti-Imperial lines. Wolsey
was following a more dangerous line of his own. Im-

---

[1] Chapuys to Charles V., Jan. 20, 1530.—*Spanish Calendar*, vol. iv.
part 1, p. 436.   [2] *Ibid.* April 23, 1530, p. 511.

patient with the delay in his restoration, he imagined that by embroiling matters more fatally he could make his own help indispensable; and he was drifting into what can only be called treachery—treachery specially dishonourable to him. Wolsey, the originator of the divorce and the French alliance, had now become the friend of Catherine and the secret adviser of Chapuys. He had welcomed, had perhaps advised, the issue of the prohibitory Papal brief. Copies of it were sent for from Flanders to be shown in England. 'The 'Queen,' wrote Chapuys on the 10th of May,[1] 'is now 'firmer than ever, and believes the King will not dare 'make the other marriage; if he does, which may God 'prevent, I suspect he will repent and be thankful to 'return to his first marriage, if by so doing he could be 'freed from his second. *This is the opinion of Cardinal 'Wolsey and of many others.* The Cardinal would have 'given his archbishopric that this had been done two 'years ago. He would have been better revenged on 'the intrigue which has ruined him.'

These words, taken by themselves, prove that Wolsey was now in the confidence of Catherine's friends, but would not justify further inference. Another letter which follows leaves no room for doubt.

On the 15th of June Chapuys writes again.[2] 'I 'have a letter from the Cardinal's physician, in which 'he tells me that his master, not knowing exactly the 'state of the Queen's affairs, cannot give any special

---

[1] Chapuys to Charles V., April 23, 1530.—*Spanish Calendar*, vol. iv. part I, p. 533.   [2] *Ibid.* p. 600.

'advice upon them; but with fuller information would
'counsel and direct as if he was to gain Paradise by it,
'as on her depended his happiness, honour, and peace
'of mind. As things stood he thought that the Pope
'should proceed to the weightier censures, and should
'call in the secular arm; there was want of nerve in
'the way in which things were handled.'[1]   The calling
in the secular arm meant invasion and open war. To
advise it was treasonable in any English subject. There
may be circumstances under which treason of such a
kind might be morally defended. No defence, moral or
political, can be made for Wolsey; and it was the more
discreditable because at this time he was professing
the utmost devotion to his King, and endeavouring to
secure his confidence. Three different petitions Norfolk
discovered him to have sent in, 'desiring as much
'authority as ever he had.' Norfolk no doubt watched
him, and may have learnt enough to suspect what he
was doing. The whispers and the messages through the
intriguing physician had not gone unobserved. The King
persisted in his generous confidence, and could not be
persuaded that his old friend could be really treacherous,[2]

---

[1] ' J'ay reçeu lettres du medicin
'du Cardinal, par lesquelles il
'm'advertit que son maystre pour
'non sçavoir en quelles termes
'sont les affaires de la Reyne, il
' ne scauroit particulierement quel
'conseil donner et que estant in-
' forme, il y vouldroit donner con-
' seil et addresse comme ce estoit
'pour gagner paradis. Car de la

'depend son bien, honneur et
' repoz, et qu'il lui semble pour
'maintenant que l'on debvroyt
'proceder a plus grandes censures
'et a la *invocation du bras secu-*
'*lier.* Car maintenant il n'y a
'nul nerf.'
[2] T. Arundel to Wolsey, Oct.
16, 1530.—*Calendar, Foreign and
Domestic,* vol. iv. p. 3013.

but he consented to send him down to his diocese. Wolsey went, still affecting his old magnificence, with a train of six hundred knights and gentlemen; but he never reached his cathedral city. Chapuys heard, to his alarm, that the physician was arrested and was in the Tower. He congratulated himself that, were all revealed which had passed between him and Wolsey, nothing could be discovered which would compromise his own safety. But it was true that Wolsey's physician had betrayed his master, revealing secrets which he had bound himself never to tell. He had confessed, so Chapuys learnt, that the Cardinal had advised the Pope to excommunicate the King, if he did not send away the 'Lady' from the court, hoping thus 'to raise the country and obtain the management.'[1] Too evidently the Cardinal had been intriguing, and not honourably, merely for his own purposes. He might have persuaded himself that the divorce would be injurious to the country; but after the part which he had played it was not for him to advise the Pope to strike at his master, whom he had himself tempted to go so deep with it. The King was convinced at last. Orders were sent down to arrest him and bring him back to London. He knew that all was now over with him, and that he would not be again forgiven. He refused to take food, and died on his way at Leicester Abbey on St. Andrew's Day. He was buried, it was observed, in the same church where the body lay of

[1] Chapuys to Charles V., Nov. 27, 1530.—*Spanish Calendar*, vol. iv. part 1, p. 3035.

Richard III. One report said that he had starved himself; another that he had taken poison. Chapuys says ' that he died like a good Christian, protesting that ' he had done nothing against the King.' His designs had failed, whatever they might have been, and he ended his great career struggling ineffectually to conjure back into the vase the spirit which he had himself let loose.

CHAPTER IX.

Danger of challenging the Papal dispensing power—The Royal family of Spain—Address of the English Peers to the Pope—Compromise proposed by the Duke of Norfolk—The English Agents at Rome—Arrival of a new Nuncio in England—His interview with the King—Chapuys advises the King's excommunication—Position of the English clergy—Statute of Provisors—The clergy in a Præmunire—Remonstrances of the Nuncio—Despair of Catherine—Her letter to the Pope—Henry prepares for war—The introduction of briefs from Rome forbidden—Warnings given to the Spanish Ambassador and the Nuncio.

THE question whether the Pope had power to license marriages within the forbidden degrees affected interests immeasurably wider than the domestic difficulties of Henry VIII. Innumerable connections had been contracted, in reliance upon Papal dispensations, the issue of which would be illegitimate if the authority was declared to be insufficient. The Emperor himself was immediately and personally concerned. Emmanuel of Portugal had been three times married. His first wife was Isabel, daughter of Ferdinand and Isabella, Catherine's sister and Charles's aunt. His second wife was her sister Maria; his third, Charles's sister Eleanor. Charles's own Empress was the child of the

second of these marriages, and they had all been contracted under dispensations from Rome. A sudden
change of the law or the recognition in a single instance
that the Pope's authority in such matters might be
challenged would create universal disturbance; and it
was not for Catherine's sake alone that the Emperor
had so peremptorily resisted Henry's demand. The
difficulty would have been evaded had Catherine agreed
to take the vows; and Henry himself, when Catherine
refused, had been so far conscious of the objection that
he had hitherto based his demand on the irregularity
of the original Bull of Pope Julius. Clement had said
often that a way could be found if Charles would consent; but Charles had not consented. In England, the
marriage having been once challenged, a decision of
some kind was necessary to avoid a disputed succession,
and larger issues had now to be raised. The Emperor
having dismissed the English Embassy at Bologna with
scant courtesy, the Pope, as we have seen, had fallen
back secretly on his old wish that Henry would take
the matter into his own hands, disregard the inhibition,
and marry as he pleased, without throwing the responsibility on himself. Henry, however, after the assurances
which the Pope had given him, was determined that
he should not escape in this way. He had gained or
extorted a favourable opinion from his own learned
corporations. Francis had assisted him to a similar
opinion from the University of Paris. Confident in
these authorities, a great body of English peers, spiritual
and temporal, now presented a formal demand to Clement

that the King's petition should be conceded, and intimated that if it was again refused they must seek a remedy for themselves. Wolsey himself signed, for the petition was drawn in the summer before his death. Archbishop Warham signed, followed by bishops, abbots, dukes, earls, and barons. Some, doubtless, had to strain their consciences, but the act as a whole must be taken as their own. The King, unless he was supported by the people, had no means of forcing them, or of punishing them if they refused. Norfolk still laboured desperately to work upon Chapuys. He told him, before the address was despatched, that, as there seemed no other way of bringing the business to an end, he would sacrifice the greater part of what he owned in the world if God would be pleased to take to himself the Queen and his niece also,[1] for the King would never enjoy peace of mind till he had made another marriage, for the relief of his conscience and the tranquillity of his realm, which could only be secured by male posterity to succeed to the crown.

The King, Norfolk said, could not plead at Rome, which was garrisoned by a Spanish army, and the Pope would do the Emperor's bidding if it was to dance in the streets in a clown's coat; the Queen objected to a trial in England; but could not a neutral place be found with impartial judges? Might not the Cardinal of Liège be trusted, and the Bishop of Tarbes?

The blunt and honest Norfolk was an indifferent

---

[1] Anne Boleyn.

successor to the dexterous Cardinal. To wish that Catherine and Anne Boleyn were both dead was a natural, but not a valuable, aspiration. A neutral place of trial was, no doubt, desirable, and the Cardinal of Liège might be admissible, but de Tarbes would not do at all. 'He had been one of the first,' Chapuys remarked, 'to put the fancy in the King's head.' [1]

At Rome the diplomatic fencing continued, the Pope secretly longing to 'commit some folly' and to come to terms with Henry, while the Imperial agents kept their claws fixed upon him. In October Mai reported that Henry's representatives were insisting that Clement should dissolve the marriage without legal process, on the ground that the kingdom must have an heir, and because the King protested that he was living in mortal sin. If this could not be done, the Pope should at least promise that if the King married he should not be proceeded against. The Pope seemed too much inclined to listen ; [2] but with Mai at his shoulder, he could not afford to be valiant. He was made to answer that he had done his best; he could not reject the Queen's appeal ; the King had not named a proctor to appear for him, and therefore delay had been unavoidable ; the threat of the Peers in their address that unless the divorce was granted they would seek a remedy else-where, was unworthy of them, and could not have been

---

[1] Chapuys to Charles V., July 11, 1530. — *Spanish Calendar*, vol. iv. part 1, p. 630.

[2] Mai to Charles V., Oct. 2

and Oct. 10, 1530.—*Calendar, Foreign and Domestic*, vol. iv. pp. 3002, 3009.

sanctioned by the King; he had always wished to comply with the King's requests when it could be done with justice.[1]

True to his policy of doing nothing and trusting to time, Clement hoped to tire Henry out by smooth words and hopes indirectly conveyed; but he was slowly swept on by the tide, and, when forced to act at all, had to act at Mai's dictation. The Nuncio in England had been too openly on Henry's side. A change was necessary. John Casalis was recalled. The Baron de Burgo was sent to succeed him, who was expected to be of sterner material. Chapuys had ascertained from two legal friends in the House of Commons that, when the next session opened, the divorce would be brought before Parliament, and that Parliament would stand by the King; also that M. du Bellay had come from Paris with promises from Francis to settle matters with the Pope afterwards, if the King cut the knot and married.[2] Unless the Emperor gave way, of which there was no hope, or unless the Pope dared the Emperor's displeasure, to which Clement was as disinclined as ever, a breach with the Papacy seemed now unavoidable. His Holiness still hoped, however, that there might be a third alternative.

The new Nuncio reached England in the middle of September. He reported briefly that at his first interview the King told him that, unless the cause was

---

[1] Answer of the Pope, Sept. 27, 1530.—*Calendar, Foreign and Domestic*, vol. iv. p. 2291.

[2] Chapuys to Charles V., Sept. 4, 1530.—*Spanish Calendar*, vol. iv. part I, p. 707.

committed to the Archbishop of Canterbury and the English Bishops, he would act for himself, since he knew that the Pope had promised the Emperor to declare for the Queen. Chapuys supplied the Emperor with fuller particulars of the interview. The Nuncio had declared to the King that, in view of the injury likely to ensue to the authority of the Church, 'his Holiness would rather die or resign the Papacy 'than that the cause should not be settled to the mutual 'satisfaction of those concerned in it.' The King, instead of replying graciously, as the Nuncio expected, had broken into violent abuse of the Pope himself and the whole Roman Court. The Church, Henry had said, required a thorough reformation, and the Church should have it. The Pope alone was to blame for the difficulty in which he found himself. He had sent him a brief from Orvieto, admitting the divorce to be a necessity, and now he had promised the Emperor, as he knew from good authority, that judgment should be given for the Queen. He would not endure such treatment. He would never consent that the cause should be decided at Rome, or in any place where either Pope or Emperor had jurisdiction. It was an ancient privilege of England 'that no cause having its origin in that 'kingdom should be advoked to another.' If the Pope would not do him justice, he would appeal to his Parliament, which was about to assemble, and if the Emperor threatened him with war, he hoped to be able to defend himself. The Nuncio had deprecated precipitate action. If the King would only do nothing, the Pope, he said, would pause also, till an amicable settlement could be arrived at; but the King would promise nothing; 'he would act as seemed best to 'himself.'

Henry being thus peremptory, Chapuys and the Nuncio had to consider what was to be done. The Pope, before the Nuncio's despatch, had received private advices from Wolsey, of which the Baron de Burgo had been informed. The evil, Wolsey had admitted, was too far gone for gentle treatment: it needed cautery and incision; but they must proceed cautiously. If the Pope used threats, the King would go at once to Parliament; there would then be war, in which France would take a part. Might not a personal interview be brought about between the King and the Emperor? The Nuncio could not see his way, but was willing to be guided by Chapuys. Chapuys was for instant action on the Pope's part. Moderation, he said, was useless. He believed (of course Wolsey had told him so) that, if the Pope would deliver sentence at Rome immediately, the King would find no one in the realm, or out of it, to help him in the quarrel against the Church. The responsibility ought not to be thrown upon the Emperor. The Pope must speak, and all good Catholics would be at his side.[1] The Nuncio agreed. The clergy in England were irritated and alarmed, and the opportunity was favourable. The Nuncio and the Ambassadors decided between them that the Pope was to be

---

[1] Chapuys to Charles, Sept. 20, 1530.—*Spanish Calendar*, vol. iv. part 1, p. 726.

advised to end the cause at once, threaten the King
with excommunication, and let a copy of the brief be
in England before Parliament opened.

Chapuys, well as he thought that he understood
England, had something to learn about it which was
to be a disagreeable surprise. He had imagined that
the Pope's authority, when boldly asserted there, had
never been successfully resisted. Tradition remembered Anselm and Becket. It had forgotten the legislation of the Edwards and of Richard II. According to
Chapuys, the Pope was to issue a brief forbidding Parliament to meddle in the divorce case. There were
laws on the statute book which forbade the interference
of the Pope under any circumstances in the internal
affairs of the English realm. Should the Pope, by bull
or brief, by presentation to offices of the Church or by
delegation of his authority, attempt to exercise direct
jurisdiction in England to the prejudice of the rights of
the Crown, all persons who introduced such bulls or
briefs, who recognised the Pope's pretensions or acted
on his orders, fell under Præmunire—a vague but
terrible consequence, almost as fatal as a proved charge
of treason. The statutes had been long obsolete. The
sword was in its scabbard. Wolsey had forgotten their
existence when he sought and accepted the position of
Legate of the Holy See. Henry had forgotten them
when he applied for a Legatine commission to try his
cause in London. The clergy who had claimed to be
independent of the State, to be an *imperium in imperio*
with the Pope at their head, the officials who had made

the name of a Church court execrated in every county
in England—all had forgotten them. But the Acts
themselves were unrepealed, and survived as a monu-
ment of the spirit of a past generation. Doubtless
it was known that the Pope was being urged to
violence. Doubtless it was known that large numbers
of the clergy were prepared to stand by him, in terror
at the threatened Reformation. The blow was to be
parried by an appeal to the historical precedents of
the realm. These impatient persons were to learn
that, instead of joining in attack upon the King, they
would have enough to do to purchase their pardons
for their own offences. The well-tempered steel sprang
to light again bright as ever, and while the Nuncio was
dreaming of excommunication and interdict, he learnt
to his astonishment that the subject coming before
Parliament was not the divorce of the Queen, but the
position of the whole spiritualty of the realm.

By recognising Wolsey as Legate from the Holy
See the entire clergy were found to be under Præmunire.
On the divorce, perhaps, or on excommunication arising
out of it, there might still have been a difference of
opinion in Parliament; but the Papal authority was
now to be argued there on the lines of the past de-
velopment of English liberty. Notice of what was
coming was given at the beginning of October by a
proclamation warning all persons of the illegality of
introducing briefs from Rome. The Nuncio rushed to
the council chamber; he saw the Dukes of Norfolk and
Suffolk; he asked passionately what was meant? what

was the Pope accused of? what English privileges had he violated? why had he not been warned beforehand? The two Dukes answered 'that they cared nothing for 'Pope or Popes in England—not even if St. Peter 'himself came to life again. The King was Emperor 'and Pope in his own dominions. The Pope was 'alienating the English people, and, if he wished to 'recover their affection, he must deserve it by attending 'to their petitions.' [1]

The Nuncio assumed a bold face and told them they would find themselves mistaken if they thought they could intimidate the Holy See. He applied to the King. Henry told him that nothing had been published to the Pope's injury. He was merely using his prerogative to guard against opposition to the ordinances which he had made, or was about to make, for the reformation of the clergy. He had gone promptly to work, lest the Pope should issue an inhibition. The Nuncio knew not what to make of it. Queen Catherine was greatly disturbed; she feared the edict was a proof that the King was not afraid of the Pope after all. On the whole, the Nuncio considered that an attempt was being made to frighten him, and he sent off fresh letters advising the Pope to proceed at once to pass sentence.[2]

Henry was, in fact, checkmating them all. With the help of the revived Statute of Provisors he was able to raise the whole question of the Pope's authority in

---

[1] Chapuys to Charles V., Oct. 1, 1530.—*Spanish Calendar*, vol. iv. part 1, p. 734.   [2] *Ibid.*

England without fresh legislation on present points of difference. Parliament, which was to have met in October, was prorogued till January, to mature the intended measures. The King went to Hampton Court. He sent for the Nuncio to come to him. He told him that by the citation to Rome the Pope had violated the privileges of sovereign princes, and had broken the promise which he had given him in writing at Orvieto. If the Pope showed no more consideration for him, he would have to show that the Pope's pretension to authority was a usurpation, and very serious consequences would then follow.

The King, the Nuncio said, spoke with much show of regret and with tears in his eyes. He added that the present Parliament had been called at the request of the nation for the restraint of the clergy. They were so hated throughout the realm, both by nobles and people, that, but for his protection, they would be utterly destroyed. He should wait to take action till February, to see whether the Pope would meanwhile change his conduct towards him.[1]

Norfolk, to whom the Nuncio went next, gave him no comfort; he said that, 'though Queen Catherine 'was a good woman, her coming to England had been 'the curse of the country;' God had shown his displeasure at the marriage by denying the King a male heir; if the King should die without a son, old feuds

---

[1] Chapuys to Charles V., Oct. 15, 1530.—*Spanish Calendar*, vol. iv. part 1, p. 759.

would be reopened and the realm would be plunged
into misery. It was not tolerable that the vital
interests of England should be sacrificed to the Emperor.
He advised the Nuncio to use his influence with the
Pope. 'The King's severity might then perhaps be
'modified.'

One more direct appeal was made by Henry himself
to Clement. 'Finding his just demands neglected, the
'requests of the King of France unattended to, and the
'address of his nobles depised and derided,' he perceived,
he said, that the Pope was wholly devoted to the
Emperor's will, and ordained, prorogued and altered to
serve the times. He required the Pope, therefore, to
set down in writing his grounds for rejecting his suit.
He demanded once more that the cause should be heard
in England before indifferent judges. 'The laws of the
'realm would not suffer the contrary;' he abhorred
'contention, but would not brook denial.'[1]

Queen Catherine was in despair. The hearing of
the cause had again been postponed at Rome. A party
in her favour had been formed in the House of Commons, but were at a loss what course to follow. If the
Pope would give a decision they would know what to
do, but the delay of sentence seemed to imply that he
was himself uncertain where the right really lay. They
questioned Chapuys whether any directions had arrived
from Rome on which to rest their opposition, hoping

---

[1] Henry VIII. to Clement
VII., Dec. 6, 1530.—*Calendar,*   *Foreign and Domestic,* vol. iv. p.
3055.

perhaps that an inhibitory brief had been issued. Opposition, they feared, would be useless without further action at the Papal Court.

'The Pope,' Chapuys said, 'had been so dilatory 'and so dissembling that he was not in favour with 'either side.'[1] A change was passing over public feeling. Every day gave strength to the King's cause. Archbishop Warham, who had been hitherto for the Queen, was beginning to waver, and even to think that he might try the suit in his own court.[2] The Queen, the Nuncio, the Bishop of Rochester, and the friends who remained staunch to her agreed unanimously that the boldest course would be the wisest. Immediate sentence at Rome in the Queen's favour was the only remedy. Gentleness was thrown away. Let the King see that the Pope was really in earnest, and he would not venture to go further. Catherine herself wrote to Clement with the passion of a suffering woman. 'Delay,' she said, 'would be the cause of a new hell upon earth, 'the remedy for which would be worse than the worst 'that had ever yet been tried.'[3] She did not blame the King. The fault was with the wicked counsellors who misled him. Once delivered out of their hands, he would be as dutiful a son of the Church as he had ever been.[4]

It is noticeable throughout that each of the two

---

[1] Chapuys to Charles V., Dec. 21, 1530.—*Spanish Calendar*, vol. iv. part 1, p. 853.
[2] *Ibid.*

[3] Catherine to the Pope, Dec. 17, 1530.—*Ibid.* p. 855.
[4] *Ibid.*

parties assumed that the Pope's judgment when he gave it must be on its own side. The King demanded a sentence in favour of the divorce ; the Queen and the Emperor a sentence that the marriage was good. The Pope was to try the cause ; but neither admitted that the right or the wrong was doubtful, or that the Pope must hear the arguments before he could decide. Doubtless they were justified in so regarding the Pope's tribunal. The trial would be undertaken, if a trial there was to be, with a foregone conclusion ; but what kind of a court of justice could the Rota be if it could be so spoken of, and its master so be addressed ?

Most idolatries pass through the same stage. The idol is whipped before he is finally discarded. Until lately the Holy Ghost was invited to assist the Cathedral Chapters in the choice of a Bishop, but must choose the person already named by the Prime Minister under pain of Præmunire. Men should choose their idols better. Reasonable beings are not fit objects of such treatment. Much is to be said in favour of stuffed straw or the graven image, which the scourge itself cannot force to speak. Anne Boleyn was jubilant. ' She ' is braver than a lion,' wrote Chapuys. She said to one of the Queen's ladies that she wished all the Spaniards in the world were in the sea. The lady told her such language was disrespectful to her mistress. She said she cared nothing for the Queen, and would rather see her hanged than acknowledge her as her mistress.[1]

---

[1] Chapuys to Charles V., Jan. 1, 1531.—*Calendar, Foreign and Domestic*, vol. v. p. 10.

Clement, goaded by Micer Mai, issued at last a second brief, repeating the terms of the first, again forbidding the second marriage, and threatening Parliaments, Bishops, and Divines in England if they dared to interfere. But between a brief and the execution of it was a long interval. Sentence on the original cause he would not pass; and in leaving his final decision doubtful he left opinion free to the rest of the world. The brief was to be presented by the Nuncio. The Pope accompanied it with a deprecatory, and not undignified, letter to Henry from himself.[1] Chapuys feared that 'by his loose talk' Clement was secretly encouraging the King. The brief might bring on a crisis. He did not relish the prospect of remaining in England 'in the boiling vortex likely to be opened.' But as the Queen insisted that he should stay, he pressed unceasingly for 'excommunication and interdict.' 'The 'Emperor might then make effectual war with the 'English. They would lose their trade with Spain and 'Flanders, and the disaffection to the King and Council 'would be greatly increased.'[2]

On the spot and surrounded by an atmosphere of passion, Chapuys was in favour of war. The Emperor, still unwilling to part with the hereditary friendship of England, was almost as reluctant as Clement. He had supposed that Henry was influenced by a passing infatuation, that by supporting Catherine he would

[1] *Calendar, Foreign and Domestic,* vol. v. p. 12.
[2] Chapuys to Charles, Dec. 21,

1530.—*Spanish Calendar,* vol. iv part 1, p. 854.

please the greater part of the nation, and ultimately, perhaps, secure the gratitude of Henry himself. He had not allowed for the changes which were passing over the mind of the English people. He had not foreseen the gathering indignation of a proud race jealous of their liberties when they saw him dictating to the Spiritual Judge of Europe on a question which touched their own security. But he had gone too far to draw back. He found himself sustained, not only by Spanish opinion, but by the part of his subjects about whom he had felt most uneasy. The Italian universities had for the most part gone with Paris and declared against the dispensing power. In Germany Henry had been disappointed. The King of England had been an old antagonist of Luther. Sir Thomas More, as Chancellor, had been enforcing the heresy laws against Luther's English proselytes with increased severity. The Lutherans in turn declared decidedly against Henry's divorce. The Emperor was their feudal sovereign. They saw no reason for entering into a new quarrel with him on a cause which, so far as they understood, was none of their own. Henry was evidently alarmed. Chapuys reported that he was busy building ships, casting cannon, repairing fortresses, and replenishing the Tower arsenal, as if conscious that he might have serious work before him. The Emperor still clung to the belief that he would be afraid to persevere, and Chapuys himself began to think that the Emperor might be more right than himself, and that the storm might pass off. No sign, however, appeared of yielding. The new brief was known to have been issued, and to have been forwarded to the Nuncio. Not contented with the warning already given by proclamation, Norfolk on the 13th of January sent for Chapuys to draw his attention once more to the law. The introduction of briefs from Rome touching the honour and authority of the Crown was forbidden by Act of Parliament. It was understood that 'certain 'decretals' had been procured by the Queen's friends, and were about to be published. The Duke desired the Ambassador to know that if the Pope came in person to present such briefs he would be torn in pieces by the people. It was not a new question. Popes had tried in past times to usurp authority in England. The King's predecessors had always resisted, and the present King would resist also. Kings were before Popes. The King was master in his own dominions. If any such decretal came into the Ambassador's hands, the Duke warned him not to issue it.[1]

Imperialist officials were more accustomed to dictate to others than to submit to commands. Chapuys was brave, and, when occasion required, could be haughty to insolence. He thanked the Duke for giving him the notice. 'He would not argue,' he said, 'on the 'authority possessed by Popes over disobedient kings 'and kingdoms. It was a notorious fact in full practice 'at that very time. His curiosity had not extended so

[1] Chapuys to Charles V., January 13, 1531.—*Spanish Calendar*, vol. iv. part 2, p. 22.

'far as the study of the English statute book, and on
'such points he must refer the Council to the Nuncio.
'For himself he could only say he thought they would
'have done better if they had not given occasion for
'such "briefs" from the Pope. The Emperor would
'not consent to an unreasonable sentence against the
'King, for he regarded him as his ally and friend, but he
'could assure the Duke that if his master was to direct
'him to assist the publication of any Papal brief in
'England he would unquestionably execute his Majesty's
'commands. As to the nation at large, he did not think
'they would resist the Pope's decretals. He thought, on
'the contrary, they would help their execution with all
'their power. Truth and justice must reign everywhere,
'even among thieves and in hell. The Church of Christ
'was never so unprovided with defenders as to be unable
'to carry the world with her, and the English would
'have no right to complain if the Emperor, having ex-
'hausted all means of conciliation, caused justice to take
'her course.'[1]

Such language could bear but one meaning.
Chapuys perhaps intended to frighten Norfolk. The
Duke was suspected to be less staunch in support of the
King than he professed to be in Council. The Duchess
was a fiery partisan of Catherine, and a close intimate of
the Ambassador himself. He thought that he had produced an impression; but Norfolk answered at last that,

---

[1] Chapuys to Charles V., January 13, 1531.—*Spanish Calendar*, vol.
iv. part 2, p. 23.

'if the King could take another wife he certainly
' would ; ' the Pope had no business to interfere, except
in cases of heresy.[1] To the Nuncio the Duke gave the
same warning which he had given to the Ambassador,
drawing special attention to the pains and penalties to
which disobedience would make him liable. The Nuncio
answered, like Chapuys, that at whatever cost he would
obey the Pope's orders, and ' would die if necessary for
' his lord and master.'

---

[1] Chapuys to Charles V., January 13, 1531.—*Spanish Calendar,*
vol. iv. part 2, p. 26.

CHAPTER X.

A STRUGGLE was now inevitable between the King and the Pope, and the result of it would depend on the sentiments of the English nation. Chapuys and the Nuncio believed the majority of the people to be loyally attached to the see of Rome. To the Pope as pope the King and Council were willing to submit; but a pope who was the vassal and mouthpiece of another secular sovereign, they believed the country would support them in refusing to acknowledge. Was Chapuys right or was the King? The Parliament about to open would decide. In the clergy of England the Pope had a ready-made army completely at his devotion. In asserting their independence of civil control the clerical order had been conscious that they could not stand alone, and had attached

themselves with special devotion to their Spiritual
Sovereign at Rome. They might complain of annates
and first-fruits and other tributes which they were
made to pay; but the Pope's support they knew to be
essential to the maintenance of their professional
privileges; and in any contest which might arise they
were certain to be found on the side of the Holy See.
The hero of the imagination of every English priest
was Becket of Canterbury. In theory he regarded the
secular prince as ruling only by delegation from the
Supreme Pontiff, and as liable in case of contumacy to
be deposed. In case of quarrel between the clergy and
the State the enormous influence of the Church was
pledged to the order and to its chief at Rome.

The spiritualty were already exasperated by the
clipping of their claws in the last session. From the
Bishop of Rochester, who represented clerical opinion in
its most accentuated form, from great ladies, and from a
party of the nobles with whom, as Catherine's friends, he
mainly associated, Chapuys had heard unanimous censures of the King's conduct. These persons told him
that the whole nation agreed with them, and certainly
the opposition of a body so powerful as the clergy was
by itself formidable. Before it came to war, therefore,
with the Pontiff, the King had prepared his measures
to disarm the Pontiff's legionaries. To clip their
claws was not enough. Their mouths had to be held
with bit and bridle. Parliament, after repeated proro-
gations, was opened at last in January. Convocation,
which was called simultaneously, was put formally in

possession of a fact which had appeared on the first rumour of it incredible—that the whole body of the clergy lay under Præmunire for having recognised Cardinal Wolsey's legation and the Papal Bull by which it was instituted. It was an intimation that the old English laws were awake again. The clergy were subjects of the Crown, not of the Pope, and to impress the fact upon their minds they learnt that legally their property was forfeited, that they would obtain their pardon only on paying a fine of a hundred thousand pounds, and on distinctly acknowledging the King as the Supreme Head of the Church of England. Chapuys's correspondence explained the motives of the Government in extorting the confession; and justified the arbitrary use which was made of the Præmunire. The Pope was being urged to excommunicate the King and declare him deposed. The clergy, through whom the Pope would act, were to be forced to admit that they were subjects of the Crown and were bound to obey the laws of their country. It was in no idle vanity, no ambitious caprice that Henry VIII. demanded the title which has been so much debated. It was as a practical assertion of the unity and independence of the realm. England was to have but one sovereign supreme within her own limits, with whom no foreign prince, secular or spiritual, had a right to interfere; and an acknowledgment of their obligation was demanded in ample form from the order which looked elsewhere for its superior. The black regiments were to be compelled to swear allegiance to the proper sovereign.

Clement's mind had always misgiven him that, if he pushed Henry too far, mischief would befall him. He had refused the last brief till it was extorted from him.[1] As if Mai had not been pressing and vehement enough, Catherine had now at Rome a special representative of her own, Dr. Ortiz, a bitter Catholic theologian with the qualities which belong to that profession. Mai and Ortiz together, listening to no excuse, drove the Pope on from day to day, demanding sentence with its inevitable consequence. The Cardinals were alarmed. One of them told Mai that, in his opinion, the original dispensation really was void, that Julius had no faculty to dispense in such a case. The Pope suggested that the affair might be suspended for two years. It might then, perhaps, drop and be forgotten. He enquired whether, if the King consented to plead by proxy before him, the Emperor would agree to *any accommodation*. Should the case go on, it might last fifteen or twenty years. All the Cardinals, said Mai, nay, the Pope himself, would like to put off the affair entirely, to avoid trouble.[2] The Court of Rome had, in fact, discovered at last that matters were really serious, that Henry would not be played with, and that the quarrel must be peaceably settled. Mai and Ortiz were furious. They insisted on immediate action. Delay, they said, would be injurious to the Queen. Their orders were to urge the Pope to proceed and pass sentence, whether the parties

---

[1] Muxetula to Charles V., Jan. 12, 1531.—*Calendar, Foreign and Domestic*, vol. v. p. 18.

[2] Mai to Covos, Feb. 13, 1531. —*Spanish Calendar*, vol. iv. part 2, p. 59.

appeared or not. They hinted that very soon there would be no more trouble from England; they had been told, and they believed, that, with the clergy on Catherine's side, a Papal decree would end the whole business.

Their confidence was shaken and their activity rudely arrested by the news of the Præmunire and the demand for the submission of the English clergy. Too well the meaning of it was understood. On Chapuys and the Nuncio it fell like a thunderbolt. They held an anxious consultation, and they agreed on the least wise measure which they could possibly have adopted. The Nuncio, as representing the majesty of the Holy See, determined to go himself to Convocation, and exhort the Bishops to uphold the Church and resist the King and the House of Commons. He actually went, and was much astonished at the reception which he met with. The right reverend body was so ' scandalised' at his intrusion that they entreated him to withdraw, without giving him time to declare his errand. They told him that, if he had anything to say, ' he must address himself to the Archbishop of Canter- ' bury, who was not then present.' The Nuncio had to withdraw precipitately. In his vexation he had not even the prudence to depart quietly, but insisted on thrusting on the Bishop of London the words which he had meant to speak.[1]

The Bishops and clergy themselves were compelled

---

[1] Chapuys to the Emperor, Jan. 23, 1531.—*Spanish Calendar,* vol. iv. part 2, p. 39.

to submit to the inevitable.   The law under which they
suffered had marked an epoch of successful resistance
to Papal usurpation.   The revival of it was to mark
another and a greater.   They struggled long enough and
violently enough to deprive their resistance of dignity,
and then, 'swearing they would never consent,' consented.   They agreed to pay the hundred thousand
pounds as the price of their pardon.   They agreed, in
accepting it, to acknowledge the King as Supreme Head
of the English Church, and, to ease their conscience,
they were allowed to introduce as a qualifying phrase,
quantum per legem Christi licet.   But the law of Christ
would avail them little for their special privileges.
It would have to be interpreted by the rejection of
another form which they had desired to substitute and
were not allowed.   For '*legem Christi*' they had desired
to read '*legem Ecclesiæ*.'·   The supposed claims of the
Church were precisely what they were to be compelled
to disavow.

It was done.   The enchantment was gone from
them.   They had become as other men, shorn Samsons
and no longer dangerous.   The Pope might say what
he pleased.   The clergy were now the King's servants,
and not the Pope's, and must either support the Crown
or become confessed traitors.   Thus when the brief
arrived, the Nuncio was allowed to present it.   The
King took it with a smile and passed it on to the Privy
Council, talked to him good-humouredly of indifferent
matters, and had never been more polite.   In a light
way he told the Nuncio that he knew of his attempt to

persuade the Bishops to agree to nothing to the Pope's
prejudice; but his anxiety was unnecessary; no injury
would be done to the Pope, unless the Pope brought it
upon himself. The King's graciousness was but too
intelligible. To Catherine and Chapuys and all their
friends the meaning of it was that Henry had made
himself 'Pope' in England. The Queen foresaw her
own fate as too sure to follow. She feared 'that, since
'the King was not ashamed of doing such monstrous
'things, and there being no one who could or dared
'contradict him, he might, one of these days, undertake
'some further outrage against her own person.' [1]

The blame of the defeat was thrown on the unfortunate Clement. The Pope's timidity and dissimulation,
wrote Chapuys, had produced the effect which he had
all along foretold. It had prejudiced the Queen's
interests and his own authority. Her cause was
making no progress. The Pope had promised Mai that
if the King disobeyed his first brief and allowed Anne
Boleyn to remain at court he would excommunicate
him, and now all that he had done had been to issue
another conditional brief less strong than the first, and
the Lady was left defiant and with as much authority
as ever. The Queen had begun to think that the Pope
had no desire to settle the matter, and, as Norfolk
observed to Chapuys, was glad that the Princes should
be at discord, for fear they might combine to reform
the clergy. If the Pope had directly ordered the

---

[1] Chapuys to Charles V., Feb. 14, 1531.—*Spanish Calendar*, vol. iv.
part 2, p. 63.

King to separate from the Lady Anne, the King would never have claimed the supremacy [1] which had caused such universal consternation. The Chancellor [Sir Thomas More] was so horrified at it, Chapuys said, that he would quit office as soon as possible. The Bishop of Rochester was sick with grief. He opposed as much as he could; but they threatened to fling him and his friends into the river, so he had to yield at last, and had taken to his bed in despair. The Bishops, it was thought, would now do anything against the Queen which they were ordered, especially seeing how cold and indifferent the Pope seemed about her fate. The Nuncio had questioned the King about the nature of his new Papacy. The King told him that if the Pope showed him proper respect he might retain his lawful authority, ' otherwise he knew what he would ' himself do.' [2]

The last words were explained in another letter in which Chapuys said that the Lady Anne was supporting the Lutherans. They had been treated to prison and stake while More had held the seals. On More's retirement they were now to have an easier time of it. Between them and the King there was the link of a common enemy in the Pope, and the King was showing a disposition to protect them. The revival of the Præmunire created embarrassments of many kinds.

---

[1] Chapuys to Charles V., Feb. 21, 1530.—*Spanish Calendar*, vol. iv. part 2, p. 69 ; and *Calendar, Foreign and Domestic*, vol. v. p. 49. There are a few verbal differences between the two versions.

[2] Chapuys to Charles V., Feb. 21, 1530.—*Ibid.*

The Pope had officials of his own in England and
Ireland, whom he appointed himself, and could not realise
the extent of the change which he had brought on.   It
is amusing to find him in the midst of the storm peacefully soliciting Henry for help against the Turks, and
the Nuncio paying friendly visits to the palace.   Henry
told him that he had made a final appeal to Rome and
was waiting to see the result.   The Pope might excommunicate him if he pleased ; he cared nothing for his
excommunication ; the Emperor might, no doubt, hurt
him ; but he was not sure that the Emperor desired to
hurt him, or, if it came to that, he could defend himself
and the realm.   Norfolk was equally decided.   They knew,
he said, that the Queen and the Emperor were pressing
the Pope for sentence, but it was time lost.   If the Pope
issued ten thousand excommunications, no notice would
be taken of them.   The Archbishop and not the Pope
was the lawful judge in English causes.   Chapuys
expressed a hope that a day would come when the King
would listen to his true friends again, &c.   'You will
' see before long,' replied the Duke, 'that the Emperor
' will repent of not having consented to the divorce.'[1]

In fact, the Emperor had begun to repent already, or,
if not to repent, yet to be perplexed with the addition
which his action had brought upon him to his many
burdens.   The Præmunire and the successful establishment of the authority of the Crown over the clergy had
startled all Europe.   The King and Parliament, it had

---

[1] Chapuys to Charles V., March
22, 1531.—*Spanish Calendar*, vol.   iv. part i, p. 94. *Ibid.—Calendar,
Foreign and Domestic*, vol. v. p. 68.

been universally supposed, would yield before a threat of excommunication. When it appeared that they were as careless of the Pope's curses as Luther and the Elector of Saxony, the affair wore another aspect. Even the Imperialist Cardinals in the Consistory came round to the Pope's own view and wished to let the cause rest for two or three years. Mai feared that such a course might lead to *Novedades* or revolution, but admitted that much might be said for it, especially considering the difficulties in Germany. He ceased to press the Pope for immediate sentence, and Dr. Ortiz, Catherine's passionate agent, complained that he found the Emperor's Ambassador growing cold and less eager to support his own arguments.[1] Catherine, seeing her clerical friends prostrated, could but renew her entreaties to her own relations. Her position was growing daily weaker. The nation, seeing the Pope confining himself to weak threats and unable or unwilling to declare her marriage valid, was rapidly concluding that on the main question the King was right, and that to throw the realm into a convulsion for an uncertainty was not tolerable. No appeal had as yet been made to Parliament, but 'the King of France,' Catherine wrote to Charles, 'has asked the Pope to 'delay sentence. If this be allowed, the means now 'employed by these people to gain the consent of the 'nation to his second marriage are such that they will

---

[1] Micer Mai to Covos, March 28, 1531.—*Spanish Calendar*, vol. iv. part I, p. 105. Ortiz to the Archbishop of Santiago, April 11, 1531.—*Ibid.* p. 116.

'obtain what they desire and accomplish my ruin at the
'next session. If the delay be not already granted, I
'entreat your Highness not to consent to it. Insist that
'the Pope shall give judgment before next October,
'when Parliament will meet again. Forgive my impor-
'tunity. I cannot rest till justice is done to me. For the
'love of Heaven let it be done before the time I name.
'I myself, if it must be so, shall go to Parliament and
'declare before its members the justice of my case.' [1]

The harassed Pope was obstinately cautious, and
occasionally even turned upon his persecutors. Mai
now urged him to call a General Council and settle all
questions. The word 'council' rang painfully in Papal
ears. Why did not the Emperor make war upon the
Lutherans? he pettishly asked. Mai told him the
Lutherans were rich and stubborn and strong, and it
would be an endless work. Why not then, said Clement, begin with the Swiss, who were not so strong?
Mai answered that it could not be. The heretics everywhere made common cause, and the Emperor could not
fight them all single-handed. The Pope sighed, and
said he feared there would be little help from France
and England.[2]

In England events moved steadily on, without hesitation, yet without precipitation. The Bishops were
not yet agreed on the divorce. At the close of the
session (March, 1531) Sir Thomas More read in the

---

[1] Queen Catherine to the Emperor, April 5, 1531.—*Spanish
Calendar*, vol. iv. part 1, p. 112.

[2] Micer Mai to Charles V.,
April 21, 1531.—*Ibid.* p. 130.

Upper House the opinions which had been collected
from the Universities at home and abroad, and a debate
ensued upon them. . . . London and Lincoln were on
the King's side. St. Asaph and Bath were of opinion
that Parliament had no right to interfere. Norfolk cut
the argument short by saying that the documents had
been introduced merely to be read. There was no proposal before the House. More said briefly that the King
knew what his opinion was, and that he need not repeat
it. The judgments were sent down to the House of
Commons, where Chapuys persuaded himself that they
were heard with more displeasure than approval. The
session ended, and Parliament was prorogued till the
following autumn. The Emperor himself wrote to More.
The letter was forwarded through Chapuys, who wished
to deliver it in person. More declined his visit and
declined the letter. If it was placed in his hand, he
said, he must communicate it to the King. Parliament
having risen, there was again a breathing time.[1]

So far as the persons of the two ladies were concerned
who were the central figures in the quarrel, there was
little difference of opinion in England. The Duke of
Norfolk, who represented the feelings of the great body
of the nation, thought that the interests of the succession made the divorce a necessity. The realm could
not be left exposed to the risk of another civil war.
He was jealous of the honour and liberties of the
country, and ill liked to see a question which touched

---

[1] Chapuys to Charles V., April 2, 1531.—*Calendar, Foreign and
Domestic*, vol. v. p. 83.

them so nearly left to the pleasure of the Emperor. But Norfolk as much admired Catherine as he disliked his niece, and there were probably few English statesmen who did not regret that a public cause should have been tainted by a love-affair. All the leading men regretted that the King had fastened his choice upon a person neither liked nor respected. Anne's antecedents were unfavourable. Her elevation had turned her brain; she had made herself detested for her insolence and dreaded for her intrigues. Catherine, on the other hand, was a princess of royal birth and stainless honour. The Duke observed to the Marquis of Exeter that it was a wonder to see her courage—nothing seemed to frighten her: 'the Devil and no other,' he said, 'must have 'originated so wretched a business.' The same view of the matter was growing at Rome in the Pope and among the Cardinals. The Bishop of Tarbes, who represented Francis at the Papal Court, warned Clement that the loss of England might be the loss of France also. If the King of England, he said, was driven to desperation, the miserable divorce suit would be the ruin of the world; Francis would and must stand by him if the Pope proceeded to excommunication. His impatience with his marriage might be unreasonable, but was no adequate ground for the convulsion of Catholic Christendom. Clement was at heart of the same opinion. The course which he wished to follow was to delay indefinitely. A formal suspension would not be needed. They had only to go on slowly. The King would then most likely marry, and the cause would drop. Andrea

de Burgo, Ferdinand's Ambassador, said that the
Emperor was strong enough to settle the matter by
himself. 'Not so strong as you think,' Clement
observed. 'Between the Turks and the Lutherans the
'Emperor may have trouble enoᵗ gh of his own.' [1]

The Pope's unwillingness was well understood in
England. He made another faint effort to save Catherine; he ordered the Nuncio to announce to Henry
that the brief must be obeyed, or 'justice would have
'its course.' Believing that the message would be
resented, the Nuncio hesitated to deliver it, but, encouraged by Chapuys, at last demanded audience and
informed Henry in the Pope's name what he was to
expect if he persisted. Henry shortly answered that the
Pope was losing his time. He already knew what the
Nuncio had come to tell him, but, once for all, he would
never accept the Pope as his judge in an affair concerning himself and the English nation. The Pope
may excommunicate me, he said. 'I care not a fig for
'his excommunication. Let him do as he wills at Rome.
'I will do here as I will. . . . I take the Pope to be a
'worthy man on the whole, but ever since the last war
'he has been so afraid of the Emperor that he dares not
'act against his wishes.' [2]

The most obvious resource was to adopt the suggestion already made that the case should be transferred to
Cambray, or to some other spot not open to objection,

---

[1] Micer Mai to Charles V.,
May 25, 1531.—*Spanish Calendar*,
vol. iv. part 2, p. 165.

[2] Chapuys to Charles V., June
6, 1531.—*Spanish Calendar*, vol.
iv. part 2, p. 170.

where it could be heard with impartiality. Clement himself was weary of the struggle, and eager to escape from it by any reasonable means. If Catherine would agree, Charles was unlikely to hesitate ; but, though weary and worn out with disappointments, she was a resolute woman, and as long as she persisted the Emperor was determined not to desert her. With small hope of success, but as an experiment which it was thought desirable to try, a deputation of Peers and Bishops were commissioned to see Catherine, to ask her to withdraw her demand for an immediate sentence, and consent that the cause should be tried in a neutral place; while the Pope, through his Legate in Spain, made a similar proposition to Charles. The Queen heard that they were coming, and prepared for them by causing several ' masses of the Holy Ghost' to be said, that she might be enlightened how to answer. The delegates arrived shortly after the masses were completed, the two Dukes, Lord Exeter, Earls, Barons, Bishops, and canon lawyers, thirty of them in all. Norfolk spoke for the rest. He said that the King had been treated with contempt and vituperation by the Pope on her account; he had been cited to appear personally at Rome—a measure never before enforced by any pope against an English king. He could not go; he could not leave his kingdom—nor could the dispute be settled by the Pope's insistence on it. A fitter place and fitter judges must be chosen by the mutual consent of the parties, or she would be the cause of trouble and scandal to them and their posterity.

The Duke entreated her to consider the consequences of refusal—to remember the many good services which the King had rendered to her father and to the Emperor, and to allow the constitution of some other court before which the King could plead.

In itself the demand was reasonable. It was impossible for a king of England to plead before the Pope in the power, as he was, of the Emperor, who was himself a party interested in the dispute. A neutral place might have been easily found. Neutral judges might be less easily procurable; but none could be less fit than his Holiness. The Queen, however, replied stoutly as ever that her cause should be judged by the Pope and by no one else; not that she expected any favour at his hands; so far the Pope had shown himself so partial to the King that more could not be asked of him; she, and not the King, had cause to complain of his Holiness; but the Pope held the place and had the power of God upon earth, and was the image of eternal truth. To him, and only to him, she remitted her case. If trouble came, it would be the work of others, not of her. She allowed that in past times the King had assisted her relations. The Emperor had not denied it, and was the King's true friend. With a scornful allusion to the Supremum Caput, she said, the King might be Lord and Master in temporal matters, but the Pope was the true Sovereign and Vicar of God in matters spiritual, of which matrimony was one.[1]

---

[1] Chapuys to Charles V., June 6, 1531.—*Spanish Calendar*, vol. iv. part 2, p. 172.

H

The Spanish Legate had succeeded no better with Charles, who returned a peremptory refusal; but so little confidence had the Emperor in the true Sovereign and Vicar of God that he insisted not merely that the Pope *should try the case, but should try it in his own presence, lest the Queen's interests should suffer injury.* The request itself indicated a disposition on the Pope's part to evade his duty. Charles gave him to understand, in language sufficiently peremptory, that he intended that duty to be done.[1]

In this direction there was no hope. Catherine had been even more emphatic with the deputation. After her reply to Norfolk, the bishops and lawyers took up the word. She always denied that she had been Prince Arthur's actual wife. She herself on all occasions courted the subject, and was not afraid of indelicacy. The Church doctors responded. They said she had slept with Prince Arthur, and the presumptions were against her. She bade them go plead their presumptions at Rome, where they would have others than a woman to answer them. She was astonished, she said, to see so many great people gathered against a lone lady without friends or counsel.

Among the great persons before her she had still some staunch friends. Anne Boleyn was detested by them all; and those who, like Norfolk, wished her, for her own sake, to be less uncompromising could not refuse to admire the gallant spirit of Isabella's daughter.

[1] Answer to the Papal Legate respecting the Cause of England, July, 1531.—*Spanish Calendar,* vol. iv. part 2, p. 203.

But, alas! the refusal to allow the cause to be heard in
a free city, before an impartial tribunal, was equivalent
to a consciousness that, unless by a court under the
Emperor's control, an unfavourable judgment was to be
looked for.   They could not any one of them allow
their Sovereign to plead where an Imperial Minister
could threaten the lives of uncompliant Cardinals. But,
unless every knightly feeling had been dead in them,
they could not have refused their sympathy. Had the
Pope spoken plainly from the first, most of the Peers
would perhaps have stood by the lady before them
with voice and sword. But the Pope had allowed
that the King was in the right. He had drawn back
only under compulsion, and even at that moment was
only prevented by fear from deciding on the King's
side. Glad as they might have been had the question never been raised, they could not submit their
Prince to the indignity of a condemnation by a coerced tribunal—a tribunal which was to be trusted
to proceed only, as it now appeared, in the Emperor's
own presence.

They carried the answer back to their master. ' I
' feared it would be so,' he said, ' knowing as I do the
' heart and temper of the Queen. We must now provide
' in some other way.'

Norfolk, who wished well to the Queen, regretted
that she had taken a course so little likely to profit
her. ' The Emperor's action,' he said, ' in causing the
' King to be cited to Rome was outrageous and unpre-
' cedented. The cause ought to be tried in England,

' and the Queen had been unwise in rejecting the advice
' of the Peers.' [1]

The Emperor on reflection reconsidered his own first
refusal to allow the cause to be transferred ; to insist
on the trial being conducted before himself was really
intolerable, and he drew a more moderate reply ; but
he still persisted that the Pope alone should hear the
case, and decide it in the Queen's favour. ' The affair,'
he said, ' was of such a nature as to admit of no solution
' save the declaring that a marriage contracted with the
' authority and license of the Holy See was valid and in-
' dissoluble. As the patron and defender of the Apostolic
' See he was more in duty bound than any other Prince
' to remove and defend all small offences and disputes.'
In fact he still advanced a claim of sovereign jurisdiction
which it was impossible for England to allow.[2]

Catherine was well aware that the Pope had been
a party to the request for the removal of her cause,
and bitterly she railed at him. Charles sent her a
copy of his own answer. It reassured her, if she had
doubted ; she saw that, let Clement struggle how he
would, she could be confident that her nephew would
compel him to decide for her. The Pope, she announced,
was responsible for all that had happened by refusing
to do her justice. This last move showed that he was
as little disposed to apply the remedy [3] as he had been.

---

[1] Chapuys to Charles V., June
24, 1531.—*Calendar, Foreign and
Domestic,* vol. v. pp. 144-5.

[2] The Emperor's Answer to the
Legate, July 26, 1531.—*Spanish
Calendar,* vol. iv. part 2, p. 218.

[3] Catherine's phrase for the excommunication of her husband.

If the cause was removed from Rome, the judges, whoever they might be, would declare that black was white.[1]

Up to this time Catherine had continued at the Court with her own apartments, and with the Princess Mary as her companion. She had refused the only available means of a peaceful arrangement, and was standing out, avowedly resting on the Emperor's protection. She was not reticent. She spoke out freely of her wrongs and her expectations. To separate mother and daughter would have been a needless aggravation had the suit been between private individuals. But Mary was a public person with her own rights on the succession. It was found necessary to remove Catherine from London and to place the Princess out of reach of her influence. Moor Park, which had been a country-house of Wolsey's, was assigned for the Queen's residence, while Mary was sent to the palace at Richmond. Catherine was too proud to resist when resistance would be useless, but she said she would prefer the Tower.[2] The Nuncio remonstrated. He advised the King 'to recall her to 'the Court and shut a hundred thousand tongues.' The King replied, 'nearly in tears,' that he had sent her away because she used such high words and was always threatening him with the Emperor.[3] Of Mary, Henry

---

[1] Queen Catherine to Charles V., July 28.—*Spanish Calendar*, vol. iv. part 2, p. 220.

[2] *Spanish Calendar*, vol. iv.

part 2, p. 239.

[3] Chapuys to Charles V., January 4, 1532.—*Calendar, Foreign and Domestic*, vol. v. p. 335.

was personally fond. He met her one day in Richmond
Park, spoke affectionately to her, and regretted that he
saw her so seldom. She cannot be where the Lady is,
said Chapuys, 'because the Lady has declared that she
'will not have it, nor hear of her.' She would not even
allow the King to speak to Mary without being watched
on the occasion just mentioned. She sent two of her
people to report what passed between them.[1]

---

[1] Chapuys to Charles V., October 1, 1531.—*Spanish Calendar*, vol.
v. part 2, p. 256.

CHAPTER XI.

Proposals for the reunion of Christendom—Warning addressed
to the Pope—Address of the English nobles to Queen
Catherine—Advances of Clement to Henry—Embarrassments
of the Pope and the Emperor—Unwillingness of the Pope to
decide against the King—Business in Parliament—Reform of
the English Church—Death of Archbishop Warham—Bishop
Fisher and Chapuys—Question of annates—Papal Briefs—
The Pope urged to excommunicate Henry—The Pope refuses
—Anger of Queen Catherine's Agent.

THE unity of Christendom was not to be broken in
pieces without an effort to preserve it. Charles V.
was attempting impossibilities in his own dominions,
labouring for terms on which the Lutheran States might
return to the Church. He had brought the Pope to
consent to the 'communion in both kinds,' and to the
'marriage of priests'—a vast concession, which had
been extorted by Micer Mai in the intervals of the discussions on the divorce. Efforts which fail are forgotten,
but they represent endeavours at least honourable.
Catherine was absorbed in her own grievances. Charles
gave them as much attention as he could spare, but had
other things to think of. As long as he could prevent
Clement from taking any fatal step, he supposed that

he had done enough. He had at least done all that he
could, and he had evidently allowed Chapuys to persuade
him that Henry's course would be arrested at the last
extremity by his own subjects. He left Mai to watch
the Pope, and Ortiz to urge for sentence; but when the
pressure of his own hand relaxed his agents could effect
but little. The English Parliament was to open again
in January. The King's Commissioners at Rome
informed the Consistory that if it was decided finally to
try the cause at Rome they were to take their leave,
and the King would thenceforward regard the Pope
as his public enemy.[1] The threat ' produced a great
' impression.' The Pope had no wish to be Henry's
enemy in order to please the Emperor. Mai and Ortiz
told him that the English menaces were but words; he
had but to speak and England would submit. The
Pope did not believe it, and became again ' lax and
' procrastinating.'[2]

The English nobles made a last effort to move
Catherine. Lord Sussex, Sir William Fitzwilliam,
and Lee, Archbishop of York, who had been her warm
supporter, waited on her at Moor Park to urge her, if
she would not allow the case to be tried at Cambray, to
permit it to be settled by a commission of bishops and
lawyers. The Pope confessedly was not free to give
his own opinion, and English causes could not be ruled
by the Emperor. If Catherine had consented, it is by
no means certain that Anne Boleyn would have been

---

[1] Mai to Covos, Oct. 24, 1531.—*Spanish Calendar*, vol. iv. part 2,
p. 276.   [2] *Ibid.*

any more heard of. A love which had waited for five years could not have been unconquerable ; and it was possible and even probable in the existing state of opinion that some other arrangement might have been made for the succession. The difficulty rose from Catherine's determination to force the King before a tribunal where the national pride would not permit him to plead. The independence of England was threatened, and those who might have been her friends were disarmed of their power to help her. Unfortunately for herself, perhaps fortunately for the English race which was yet to be born, she remained still inflexible. 'The 'King's plea of conscience,' she said, 'was not honest. 'He was acting on passion, pure and simple ; and 'English judges would say black was white.' Sussex and Fitzwilliam knelt to entreat her to reconsider her answer. She too knelt and prayed them for God's honour and glory to persuade the King to return to her, as she was his lawful wife. All present were in tears, but there was no remedy. Chapuys said that the coldness and indifference with which the affair was treated at Rome was paralysing her defenders. The question could not stand in debate for ever, and, unless the Pope acted promptly and resolutely, he feared that some strong act was not far distant.[1]

She was destroying her own chance. She persisted in relying on a defence which was itself fatal to her.

'God knows what I suffer from these people,' she

---

[1] Chapuys to Charles V., Oct. 16, 1531.—*Spanish Calendar*, vol. iv. part 2, p. 263.

wrote to the Emperor, ' enough to kill ten men, much
' more a shattered woman who has done no harm. I can
' do nothing but appeal to God and your Majesty, on
' whom alone my remedy depends. For the love of God
' procure a final sentence from his Holiness as soon as
' possible. The utmost diligence is required. May God
' forgive him for the many delays which he has granted
' and which alone are the cause of my extremity ! I am
' the King's lawful wife, and while I live I will say no
' other. The Pope's tardiness makes many on my side
' waver, and those who would say the truth dare not.
' Speak out yourself, that my friends may not think I
' am abandoned by all the world.' [1]

Well might Catherine despair of Clement. While
she was expecting him to excommunicate her husband,
he was instructing his Nuncio to treat that husband as
his most trusted friend. He invited Henry to assist in
the Turkish war ; he consulted him about the protection of Savoy from the Swiss Protestants ; he
apologised to him for the language which he was
obliged to use on the great matter. Henry, contemptuous and cool, ' not showing the passion which he
' had shown at other times,' replied that the Pope must
be jesting in inviting him, far off as he was, to go to
war with the Turk. If Christendom was in danger he
would bear his part with the other Princes. As to
Savoy, the Duke had disregarded the wishes of France

---

[1] Catherine to Charles V., Nov.
6, 1531.—*Spanish Calendar*, vol.
iv. part 2, p. 279. I must remind
the reader that I have to compress
the substance both of this and
many other letters.

and must take the consequences. For the rest, the
message which he had sent through his Ambassador at
Rome was no more than the truth. 'If,' said he to the
Nuncio, 'I ask a thing which I think right, the answer
'is "The law forbids." If the Emperor ask a thing,
'law and rules are changed to please him. The Pope
'has greatly wronged me. I have no particular ani-
'mosity against him. After all, he does not bear me
'much ill will. The fear of the Emperor makes him
'do things which he would not otherwise do. Proceed-
'ings may be taken against me at Rome. I care not.
'If sentence is given against me, I know what to do.' [1]

The Pope never meant to give sentence if he could
help it. Every day brought Parliament nearer, and he
drove Mai distracted with his evasions. 'I have said
'all that I could to his Holiness and the Cardinals
'without offending them,' he reported to Charles. 'Your
'Majesty may believe me when I say that these devils
'are to a man against us. Some take side openly, being
'of the French or English faction; others will be easily
'corrupted, for every day I hear the English Ambassador
'receives bills for thousands of ducats, which are said
'to go in bribery.' [2]

Promises were given in plenty, but no action followed, and Ortiz had the same story to tell Catherine.
'Your Ambassador at Rome,' she wrote to her nephew,
'thinks the Pope as cold and indifferent as when the

[1] Chapuys to Charles V., Dec. 4, 1531.—*Spanish Calendar*, vol. iv part 2, p. 320.

[2] Mai to Charles V., Dec. 12. —*Ibid.* part 1, p. 328.

' suit began. I am amazed at his Holiness. How can
' he allow a suit so scandalous to remain so long un-
' decided ? His conduct cuts me to the soul. You know
' who has caused all this mischief. Were the King once
' free from the snare in which he has been caught, he
' would confess that God had restored his reason. His
' misleaders goad him on like a bull in the arena. Pity
' that a man so good and virtuous should be thus
' deceived ! God enlighten his mind !'[1]

To the Emperor himself, perhaps, the problem was
growing more difficult than he expected. He himself
at last pressed for sentence, but sentence was nothing
unless followed by excommunication if it was disobeyed,
and the Pope did not choose to use his thunder if
there was to be no thunderbolt to accompany it. The
Cardinal Legate in Spain assured him that the Emperor
would employ all his force in the execution of the
censures. The Pope said that he prized that promise
as ' a word from heaven.' But though Charles might
think the English King was doing what was wrong
and unjust, was it so wrong and so unjust that fire and
sword were to be let loose through Christendom ?
Chapuys and Catherine were convinced that there
would be no need of such fierce remedies. They might
be right, but how if they were not right ? How if
England supported the King ? The Emperor could not
be certain that even his own subjects would approve of
a war for such an object. Three years later, when the

---

[1] Catherine to Charles V., Dec. 15, 1531. —*Spanish Calendar*, vol.
iv. part 1, p. 331.

moment for action had arrived, if action was to be taken at all, it will be seen that the Spanish Council of State took precisely this view of the matter, and saw no reason for breaking the peace of Europe for what, after all, was but 'a family quarrel.' The Pope was cautious. He knew better than his passionate advisers how matters really stood. The Pope may promise, Mai said, 'but as long as the world remains in its troubled 'state, these people will be glad of any excuse to prolong 'the settlement.' January came, when the English Parliament was to meet, and the note was still the same. The Pope says, wrote Mai, that we must not press the English too hard. I have exhausted all that I could say without a rupture. I told him he was discrediting the Queen's case and your Majesty's authority. I made him understand that I should be obliged to apply elsewhere for the justice that was denied me at Rome. He owns that I am right, but Consistory follows Consistory and more delays are allowed. We can but press on as we have always done and urge your Majesty's displeasure.[1]

If a sentence could not be had, Ortiz insisted on the issue of another minatory brief. Anne Boleyn must be sent from the Court. The King must be made to confess his errors. The Pope assented; said loudly that he would do justice; though England and France should revolt from the Holy See in consequence, a brief should go, and, if it was disobeyed, he would proceed

---

[1] Mai to the Emperor, Jan. 15, 1532.—*Spanish Calendar*, vol. iv. part 1, p. 360.

to excommunicate : 'the Kings of England and France
'were so bound together that if he lost one he lost both,
'but he would venture notwithstanding.' But like the
Cardinals who condemned Giordano Bruno, Clement
was more afraid of passing judgment than Henry of
hearing it passed. The brief was written and was
sent, but it contained nothing but mild expostulation.[1]
All the distractions of the world were laid at the door
of the well-meaning, uncertain, wavering Clement. La
Pommeraye, the French Ambassador in London, said
(Chapuys vouches for the words) that 'nothing could
'have been so easy as to bring all Christian Princes to
'agree had not that devil of a Pope embroiled and sown
'dissension through Christendom.'[2]

In England alone were to be found clear purpose and
steadiness of action. The divorce in England was an
important feature in the quarrel with the Papacy, but
it was but a single element in the great stream of Reformation, and the main anxiety of King and people
was not fixed on Catherine, but on the mighty changes
which were rushing forward. When a Parliament was
first summoned, on the fall of Wolsey, the Queen had
assumed that it was called for nothing else but to em-
power the King to separate from her. So she thought
at the beginning, so she continued to think. Yet
session had followed session, and the Legislature had
found other work to deal with. They had manacled

---

[1] Clement VII. to Henry VIII., Jan. 25, 1532.—*Calendar, Foreign and Domestic*, vol. v. p. 358.

[2] *Spanish Calendar*, vol. iv. part 1, p. 368.

the wrists of her friends, the clergy; but that was all, and she was to have yet another year of respite. The 'blind passion' which is supposed to have governed Henry's conduct was singularly deliberate. Seven years had passed since he had ceased cohabitation with Catherine, and five since he had fallen under the fascination of the impatient Anne; yet he went on as composedly with public business as if Anne had never smiled on him, and he was still content to wait for this particular satisfaction. As long as hope remained of saving the unity of Christendom without degrading England into a vassal State of the Empire, Henry did not mean to break it. He had occupied himself, in concert with the Parliament, with reforming the internal disorders and checking the audacious usurpations of the National Church. He had, so far, been enthusiastically supported by the immense majority of the laity, and was about to make a further advance in the same direction.

The third Session opened on the 13th of January, Peers, Prelates, and Commons being present in full number. By this time a small but active opposition had been formed in the Lower House to resist measures too violently anti-clerical. They met occasionally to concert operations at the Queen's Head by Temple Bar. The Bishops, who had been stunned by the Præmunire, were recovering heart and intending to show fight. Tunstal of Durham, who had been reflecting on the Royal Supremacy during the recess, repented of his consent, and had written his misgivings to the King.

The King used the opportunity to make a remarkable reply.

' People conceive,' he said, ' that we are minded to
' separate our Church of England from the Church of
' Rome, and you think the consequences ought to be
' considered.   My Lord, as touching schism, we are
' informed by virtuous and learned men that, considering
' what the Church of Rome is, it is no schism to separate
' from her, and adhere to the Word of God.   The lives
' of Christ and the Pope are very opposite, and therefore
' to follow the Pope is to forsake Christ.   It is to be
' trusted the Papacy will shortly vanish away, if it be not
' reformed ; but, God willing, we shall never separate
' from the Universal body of Christian men.' [1]

Archbishop Warham also had failed to realise the
meaning of his consent to the Royal Supremacy.   He
had consecrated the Bishop of St. Asaph on the receipt
of a nomination from Rome before the bulls had been
presented to the King.   He learnt that he was again
under a Præmunire.   The aged Primate, fallen on evil
times, drew the heads of a defence which he intended
to make, but never did make, in the House of Lords.
Archbishops, he said, were not bound to enquire whether
Bishops had exhibited their bulls or not.   It had not
been the custom.   If the Archbishop could not give the
spiritualities to one who was pronounced a bishop at
Rome till the King had granted him his temporalities,
the spiritual powers of the Archbishops would depend

---

[1] Henry VIII. to the Bishop of   pressed.—*Calendar, Foreign and*
Durham, Feb. 24, 1532.   Com-   *Domestic,* vol. v. p. 387.

on the temporal power of the Prince, and would be of little or no effect, which was against God's law. In consecrating the Bishop of St. Asaph he had acted as the Pope's Commissary. The act itself was the Pope's act. The point for which the King contended was one of the Articles which Henry II. sought to extort at Clarendon, and which he was afterwards compelled to abandon. The liberties of the Church were guaranteed by Magna Charta, and the Sovereigns who had violated them, Henry II., Edward III., Richard II., had come to an ill end. The lay Peers had threatened that they would defend the matter with their swords. The lay Peers should remember what befell the knights who slew St. Thomas. The Archbishop said he would rather be hewn in pieces than confess this Article, for which St. Thomas died, to be a Præmunire.[1]

Warham was to learn that the spirit of Henry II. was alive again in the present Henry, and that the Constitutions of Clarendon, then premature, were to become the law of the land.

Fisher of Rochester had received no summons to attend the present Parliament; but he sent word to the Imperial Ambassador that he would be in his place, whether called up or not, that he might defend Catherine should any measure be introduced which affected her. He begged Chapuys not to mention his name in his despatches, except in cipher. If they met in public, Chapuys must not speak to him or appear to know him.

---

[1] Archbishop Warham, 1532.—*Calendar, Foreign and Domestic*, vol. v. p. 541.

He on his part would pass Chapuys without notice till
the present tyranny was overpast. Bishop Fisher was
entering upon dangerous courses which were to lead
him into traitorous efforts to introduce an invading army
into England and to bring his own head to the block.
History has only pity for these unfortunate old men,
and does not care to remember that, if they could
have had their way, a bloodier persecution than the
Marian would have made a swift end of the Reformation.

I need not repeat what I have written elsewhere on
the acts of this Session.[1] A few details only deserve
further notice. The privilege of the clergy to commit
felony without punishment was at last abolished.
Felonious clerks were thenceforward to suffer like
secular criminals. An accident provided an illus-
trative example. A priest was executed in London for
chipping the coin, having been first drawn through the
streets in the usual way. Thirty women sued in vain
for his pardon. He was hanged in his habit, without
being degraded, against the protest of the Bishop—' a
' thing never done before since the island was Christian.' [2]
The Constitutions of Clarendon were to be enforced at
last. The Arches court and the Bishops' courts were
reformed on similar lines, their methods and their
charges being brought within reasonable limits. Priests
were no longer allowed to evade the Mortmain Acts by

---

[1] *History of England*, vol. i.
p. 342, &c.

[2] Carlo Capello to the Signory,

July 10, 1532.—*Venetian Calendar*,
vol. iv. p. 342.

working on death-bed terrors. The exactions for mor-
tuaries, legacy duties, and probate duties, long a pleasant
source of revenue, were abolished or cut down. The
clergy in their synods had passed what laws they
pleased and enforced them with spiritual terrors. The
clergy were informed that they would no longer be
allowed to meet in synod without Royal license, and
that their laws would be revised by laymen. Chapuys
wittily observed that the clergy were thus being made
of less account than cordwainers, who could at least
enact their own statutes.

A purpose of larger moment was announced by
Henry for future execution. More's chancellorship
had been distinguished by heresy-prosecutions. The
stake in those three years had been more often lighted
than under all the administration of Wolsey. It was
as if the Bishops had vented on those poor victims
their irritation at the rude treatment of their privileges. The King said that the clergy's province was
with souls, not with bodies. They were not in future
to arrest men on suspicion, imprison, examine, and
punish at their mere pleasure. There was an outcry, in
which the Chancellor joined. The King suspended his
resolution for the moment, but did not abandon it. He
was specially displeased with More, from whom he had expected better things. He intended to persist. 'May God,'
exclaimed the orthodox and shocked Chapuys, ' send
'such a remedy as the intensity of the evil requires!' [1]

---

[1] Chapuys to Charles V., May 13, 1532.—*Spanish Calendar*, vol. iv.
part 1, p. 446.

None of Henry's misdeeds shocked Chapuys so deeply as the tolerating heresy.

The Royal Supremacy had been accepted by Convocation. It was not yet confirmed by Parliament. Norfolk felt the pulses of the Peers. He called a meeting at Norfolk House. He described the Pope's conduct. He insisted on the usual topics—that matrimonial causes were of temporal jurisdiction, not spiritual; that the King was sovereign in his own dominions, &c., &c., and he invited the Peers' opinions. The Peers were cold. Lord Darcy had spoken freely against the Pope in his indictment of Wolsey. It seemed his ardour was abating. He said the King and Council must manage matters without letting loose a cat among the legs of the rest of them.[1] The meeting generally agreed with Darcy, and was not pressed further. Papal privilege came before Parliament in a more welcome form when a bill was introduced to withdraw annates or first fruits of benefices which had been claimed and paid as a tribute to the Holy See. The imposition was a grievance. There were no annates in Spain. The Papal collectors were detested. The House of Commons made no difficulty. The Nuncio complained to the King. The King told him that it was not he who brought forward these measures. They were moved by

---

[1] 'Le Roy et son Conseil sça-voient bien qu'il y en avoient a faire sans vouloir mestre le chat entre les jambes dautres.' Chapuys to the Emperor, February 14, 1532.—*Spanish Calendar*, vol. iv. part 1, p. 384 ; *Calendar, Foreign and Domestic*, vol. v. p. 381.

the people, who hated the Pope marvellously.[1] In the
Upper House the Bishops stood by their spiritual chief
this time unanimously. Among the mitred Abbots there
was division of opinion. The abbeys had been the chief
sufferers from annates and had complained of the
exaction for centuries. All the lay Peers, except Lord
Arundel, supported the Government. The bill was
passed, but passed conditionally, leaving power to the
Crown to arrange a compromise if the Pope would
agree to treat. For the next year the annates were
paid in full, as usual, to give time for his Holiness to
consider himself.[2]

Thus steadily the Parliament moved on. Archbishop Warham, who was dying broken-hearted, dictated
a feeble protest from his bed against all which had been
done by it in derogation of the Pope or in limitation of
the privileges of the Church. More had fought through
the session, but, finding resistance useless, resigned the
chancellorship. He saw what was coming. He could
not prevent it. If he retained his office he found that
he must either go against his conscience or increase the
displeasure of the King.[3] He preferred to retire.

---

[1] Chapuys to Charles V., Feb.
28, 1532.—*Calendar, Foreign and
Domestic*, vol. v. p. 392.

[2] An address purporting to have
been presented by Convocation on
this occasion, not only complaining
of the annates, but inviting a complete separation from the See of
Rome, was perhaps no more than
a draft submitted to the already

sorely humiliated body, and not
accepted by it.—*History of England*, vol. i. pp. 354-5. The French
Ambassador says distinctly that the
clergy agreed to nothing, but their
refusal was treated as of no consequence.

[3] Chapuys to Charles V., May
22, 1532.—*Calendar, Foreign and
Domestic*, vol. v. p. 476.

In this way, at least in England, the situation was clearing, and parties and individuals were drifting into definite positions. Montfalconet,[1] writing to Charles in May, said that he had been in England and had seen Queen Catherine, who was still clamouring for the Pope's sentence. Every one, he continued, speaking for the Catholic party, whom alone he had seen, was angry with the Pope, and angry with the Emperor for not pressing him further. Peers, clergy, laity, all loved the Queen. She was patient. She thought that if she could but see the King all might yet be well. Were the sentence once delivered, she was satisfied that he would submit.[2] The French Ambassador in London, on the other hand, recommended Francis to force the Pope to hold his hand. He told Chapuys that France must and would take Henry's part if a rupture came. The Emperor had no right to throw Europe into confusion for the sake of a woman. If the King of England wished to marry again, he should do as Louis XII. had done under the same circumstances—take the woman that he liked and waste no more time and money.[3]

At Rome the Pope had been fingering his briefs with hesitating heart. The first, which he had issued under Charles's eye at Bologna, had been comparatively

---

[1] Maître d'hôtel to the Emperor and Governor of Brescia.

[2] Montfalconet to Charles V., May, 1532.—*Calendar, Foreign and Domestic*, vol. v. p. 479.

[3] Chapuys to the Emperor, April 16, 1532.—*Spanish Calendar*, vol. iv. part 1, p. 425. In 1499 Louis XII. repudiated his first wife, Jeanne de France, and married Anne of Brittany, widow of Charles VIII.

firm. He had there ordered Henry to take Catherine
back under penalty of excommunication. The last,
though so hardly extracted from him, was meagre and
insignificant. The King, when it was presented, merely
laughed at it. 'The Pope,' he said, 'complains that I have
'sent the Queen away. If his Holiness considers her as
'my wife, the right of punishing her for the rudeness of
'her behaviour belongs to me and not to him.'[1]

Ortiz, finding it hopeless to expect a decision on the
marriage itself from the Pope, demanded excommunication on the plea of disobedience to the Bologna brief.
He had succeeded, or thought he had succeeded, in
bringing the Pope to the point. The excommunication
was drawn up, 'but when it was to be engrossed and
'sealed the enemy of mankind prevented its completion
'in a manner only known to God.' Ortiz continued to
urge. The document could be sent secretly to the
Emperor, to be used at his discretion. 'If the Emperor
'thought fit to issue it, bearing, as it did, God's authority,
'God in such cases would infallibly send his terrors upon
'earth and provide that no ill should come of it.'[2] The
Pope was less certain that God would act as Ortiz
undertook for him, and continued to offend the Lord by
delay. In vain Catherine's representative railed at
him, in vain told him that he would commit a great sin
and offence against God if he did not excommunicate a
King who was in mortal sin, keeping a mistress at his
Court. The Pope rationally answered that there was

---

[1] *Spanish Calendar*, vol. iv
part I. p. 447

[2] Ortiz to Charles V., May,
1532.—*Ibid.* p. 438.

no evidence of mortal sin. 'It was the custom in 'England for Princes to converse intimately with ladies. 'He could not prove that, in the present case, there was 'anything worse, and the King might allege his con- 'science as a reason for not treating the Queen as a 'husband.'[1] Ortiz insisted that the devil had got hold of the King in the shape of that woman, and unless the Pope obliged him to put her away, the Pope would be damned. But it was an absurdity to excommunicate the King and declare him to have forfeited his crown when the original cause of the quarrel was still un-decided. The King might prove after all to be right, as modern law and custom has in fact declared him to have been.

Charles himself felt that such a position could not be maintained. Henry was evidently not frightened. There was no sign that the English people were turning against him. If a bull of excommunication was issued, Charles himself would be called on to execute it, and it was necessary to be sure of his ground.

Ortiz raged on. 'I told his Holiness,' he wrote, 'that if he did not excommunicate the King I would 'stand up at the day of judgment and accuse him 'before God.'[2] Charles was obliged to tell Ortiz that he must be more moderate. A further difficulty had risen in Rome itself. If the cause was tried at Rome, was it to be tried before the Cardinals in consistory or before

---

[1] *Calendar, Foreign and Do-mestic,* vol. v. p. 539.

[2] Ortiz to Charles V., July 28,

1532.—*Spanish Calendar*, vol. iv. part I, p. 486.

the court of the Rota ? The Cardinals were men of the world. Micer Mai's opinion was that from the Rota only a judgment could be with certainty expected in the Queen's favour.[1] The winds are against us, he wrote to Secretary Covos; what is done one day is undone the next. The Cardinals will not stir, but quietly pocket the ducats which come from the Emperor, and the larger sums which come from the English, who are lavish in spending. The Pope will not break with France. He says he has so many ties with the Kings of France and England that he must pretend goodwill to the latter for fear they both break off from the Church, as they have threatened to do.[2]

---

[1] Ortiz to Charles V., July 28, 1532.—*Spanish Calendar*, vol. iv. part I, p. 414.　　　　　　　　[2] *Ibid.* p. 469.

CHAPTER XII.

Henry advised to marry without waiting for sentence—Meeting
of Henry and Francis—Anne Boleyn present at the interview
—Value of Anne to the French Court—Pressure on the Pope
by the Agents of the Emperor—Complaints of Catherine—
Engagements of Francis—Action of Clement—The King
conditionally excommunicated—Demand for final sentence—
Cranmer appointed Archbishop of Canterbury—Marriage of
Henry and Anne Boleyn—Supposed connivance of the Pope—
The Nuncio attends Parliament—The Act of Appeals—The
Emperor entreated to intervene—Chapuys and the King.

THE Pope had promised Ortiz that nothing should
be said of the intended excommunication till the
brief was complete. He betrayed the secret to the
English Agents, by whom it was conveyed to Henry
The French Ambassador had advised the King to
hesitate no longer, but to marry and end the controversy
The Pope himself had several times in private expresse
the same wish. But Henry, in love though he i
supposed to have been, determined to see Francis i
person before he took a step which could not be re
called. He desired to know distinctly how far Franc
was prepared to go along with him in defying th
Papal censures. An interview between the two King

at such a crisis would also show the world that their alliance was a practical fact, and that if the Emperor declared war in execution of the censures he would have France for an enemy as well as England.

The intended meeting was announced at the end of August, and, strange to say, there was still a belief prevailing that a marriage would come of it between the King and a French princess, and that Anne would be disappointed after all. 'If it be so,' wrote Chapuys, 'the Lady Anne is under a singular delusion, for she 'writes to her friends that at this interview all that she 'has been so long wishing for will be accomplished.' One thing was clear, both to the Imperial Ambassador and the Nuncio, that the Pope by his long trifling had brought himself into a situation where he must either have to consent to a judgment against Catherine or encounter as best he could the combination of two of the most powerful Princes in Christendom. The least that he could do was to issue an inhibition against the King's marriage either with Anne or with the French-woman.

The Pope's danger was real enough, but Anne Boleyn had nothing to fear for herself. She was to form part of the cortège. She was to go, and to be received at the French court as Henry's bride-elect, and she was created Marchioness of Pembroke for the occasion. Queen Catherine believed that the marriage would be completed at the interview with a publicity which would make Francis an accomplice. The Emperor was incredulous. Reluctantly he had been driven to the conclusion that Henry was really in earnest, and he still thought it impossible that such an outrage as a marriage could be seriously contemplated while the divorce was still undecided.[1] Yet contemplated it evidently was. Politically the effect would have been important, and it is not certain that Francis would not have encouraged a step which would be taken as an open insult by Charles. The objection, so Chapuys heard, came from the lady herself, who desired to be married in state with the usual formalities in London.[2] Invited to the interview, however, she certainly was by Francis. The French Queen sent her a present of jewels. The Sieur de Langey came with special compliments from the King to request her attendance. She had been a useful instrument in dividing Henry from the Emperor, and his master, De Langey said, desired to thank her for the inestimable services which she had rendered and was daily rendering him. He wished to keep her devoted to his interests. Wolsey himself had not been more valuable to him. He had not to pay her a pension of 25,000 crowns, as he had done to the Cardinal. Therefore he meant to pay her in flattery and in forwarding the divorce at Rome.[3]

In vain Catherine poured out to Clement her wailing

---

[1] Charles V. to Mary of Hungary, Nov. 7, 1532.—*Calendar, Foreign and Domestic*, vol. v. p. 642.

[2] Chapuys to Charles V., Oct. 1, 1532.—*Calendar, Foreign and Domestic*, vol. v. p. 592.

[3] *Spanish Calendar*, vol. iv. part 1, p. 512.

cries for sentence—sentence without a moment's delay.
Less than ever could the Pope be brought to move.
He must wait and see what came of the meeting of the
Kings, and whether the Emperor got the better of the
Turks. It was the harder to bear because she had
persuaded herself, and had persuaded Ortiz, that, if
the King was once excommunicated, the whole of
England would rise against him for his contumacious
disobedience.[1]

The interview which took place in October between
the Kings of France and England was a momentous
incident in the struggle, for it did, in fact, decide Henry
to take the final step. The scene itself, the festivities,
the regal reception of Anne, the Nun of Kent and the
discovery of the singular influence which an hysterical
impostor had been able to exercise in the higher circles
of English life, have already been described by me, and
I can add nothing to what I have already written. A
more particular account, however, must be given of
a French Commission which was immediately after
despatched to Rome. Francis had not completely
satisfied Henry. He had repeated the advice of his
Ambassadors. He had encouraged the King to marry
at once. He had reiterated his promises of support
if the Emperor declared war. Even an engagement
which Henry had desired to obtain from him, to unite
France with England in a separate communion, should
the Pope proceed to violence, Francis had seemed to

---

[1] Ortiz to the Emperor, Sept 30, 1532.—*Spanish Calendar*, vol. iv.
part 1, p. 523.

give, and had wished his good brother to believe it. But his language had been less explicit on this point than on the other.

The Bishop of Tarbes, now Cardinal Grammont, was sent to Rome, with Cardinal Tournon, direct from the interview, with open instructions to demand a General Council, to inform the Pope that if he refused the two Kings would call a Council themselves and invite the Lutheran Princes to join them, and that, if the Pope excommunicated Henry, he would go to Rome for absolution so well accompanied that the Pope would be glad to grant it.[1] If Catherine's friends in Rome were rightly informed, the Cardinals had brought also a secret commission, which went the full extent of Henry's expectation. The Pope was to be required to fulfil at once the promise which he had given at Orvieto, and to give judgment for the divorce ; ' otherwise the Kings of France and England would ' abrogate the Papal authority in their several realms.' The Pope, confident that the alternative before him was the loss of the two kingdoms, was preparing to yield.[2] Henry certainly returned to England with an understanding that Francis and himself were perfectly united, and would adopt the same course, whatever that might be. A report went abroad that, relying on these assurances, he had brought his hesitation to an end, and immediately after landing made Anne secretly his

---

[1] Instructions to Cardinals Grammont and Tournon, Nov. 13, 1532.—*Calendar, Foreign and Domestic*, vol. v. p. 648.

[2] Chapuys to Charles V., Nov. 10.—*Ibid.* p. 644.

wife. The rumour was premature, but the resolution
was taken. The Pope, the King said, was making
himself the tool of the Emperor. The Emperor was
judge, and not the Pope; and neither he nor his people
would endure it. He would maintain the liberties of
his country, and the Pope, if he tried violence, would
find his mistake.[1]

It is not easy to believe that on a point of such vast
consequence Henry could have misunderstood what
Francis said, and he considered afterwards that he had
been deliberately deceived; but under any aspect the
meeting was a demonstration against the Papacy.
Micer Mai, who watched the Pope from day to day,
declared that his behaviour was enough to drive him
out of his senses. Mai and Ortiz had at last forced
another brief out of him—not a direct excommunication,
but an excommunication which was to follow on further
disobedience. They had compelled him to put it in
writing that he might have committed himself before
the French Cardinals' arrival. But when it was written
he would not let it out of his hands. He was to meet
the Emperor again at Bologna, and till he had learnt
from Charles's own lips what he was prepared to do,
it was unfair and unreasonable, he said, to require an
act which might fatally commit him. He was not,
however, to be allowed to escape. Catherine, when
she heard of the despatch of the Cardinals, again flung
herself on her nephew's protection. She insisted that

---

[1] Chapuys to Charles V., Nov. 10.—*Calendar, Foreign and Domestic,*
vol. v. p. 667.

the Pope should speak out. The French must not be
listened to. There was nothing to be afraid of. 'The
'English themselves carried no lightning except to
'strike her.' [1] Letters from Ortiz brought her news of
the Pope's continued indecision—an indecision fatal, as
she considered it, to the Church and to herself.
Rumours reached her that the King had actually
married, and she poured out her miseries to Chapuys.
'The letters from Rome,' she said, 'reopen all my
'wounds. They show there is no justice foɪ me or my
'daughter. It is withheld from us for political con-
'siderations. I do not ask his Holiness to declare
'war—a war I would rather die than provoke; but I
'have been appealing to the Vicar of God for justice for
'six years, and I cannot have it. I refused the pro-
'posals made to me two years ago by the King and
'Council. Must I accept them now? Since then I
'have received fresh injuries. I am separated from my
'lord, and he has married another woman without
'obtaining a divorce; and this last act has been done
'while the suit is still pending, and in defiance of him
'who has the power of God upon earth. I cover these
'lines with my tears as I write. I confide in you as
'my friend. Help me to bear the cross of my tribula-
'tion. Write to the Emperor. Bid him insist that
'judgment be pronounced. The next Parliament, I
'am told, will decide if I and my daughter are to suffer
'martyrdom. I hope God will accept it as an act of

---

[1] To the Emperor, Nov. 11.—*Spanish Calendar*, vol. iv. part 1,
p. 554.

'merit by us, as we shall suffer for the sake of the 'truth.' [1]

Catherine might say, and might mean, that she did not wish to be the cause of a war. But unless war was to be the alternative of her husband's submission, the Papal thunders would be as ineffectual as she supposed the English to be. The Emperor had not decided what he would do. He may still have clung to the hope that a decision would not be necessary, but he forced or persuaded the Pope to disregard the danger. The brief was issued, bearing the date at which it was drawn, and was transmitted to Flanders as the nearest point to England for publication.

In removing the Queen from his company without waiting for the decision of his cause, and cohabiting with a certain Anne, Clement told the King that he was insulting Divine justice and the Papal authority. He had already warned him, but his monition had not been respected. Again, therefore, he exhorted him on pain of excommunication to take Catherine back as his Queen, and put Anne away within a month of the presentation of the present letter. If the King still disobeyed, the Pope declared both him and Anne to be, *ipso facto,* excommunicated at the expiration of the term fixed, and forbade him to divorce himself by his own authority.[2]

---

[1] Queen Catherine to Chapuys, Nov. 22, 1532. Compressed.— *Spanish Calendar,* vol iv. part 1, p. 291. The editor dates this letter Nov. 1531. He has mis-

taken the year. No report had gone abroad that the King was married to Anne before his return from France.

[2] Clement VII. to Henry

I

It might seem that the end had now come, and that
in a month the King, and the subjects who continued
loyal to him, would incur all the consequences of the
Papal censures. But the proceedings of the Court of
Rome were enveloped in formalities. Conditional
excommunications affected the spiritual status of the
persons denounced, but went no further. A second
Bull of Excommunication was still requisite, declaring
the King deposed and his subjects absolved from their
allegiance, before the secular arm could be called in;
and this last desperate remedy could not decently be
resorted to, with the approval even of the Catholic
opinion of Europe, until it had been decided whether
Catherine was really legal queen. The enthusiastic
Ortiz, however, believed that judgment on ' the principal
' cause ' would now be immediately given, and that the
victory was won. He enclosed to the Empress a letter
from Catherine to him, ' to be preserved as a relic,
' since she would one day be canonised.' ' May God
' inspire the King of England,' he said, ' to acknowledge
' the error into which the Enemy of Mankind has led
' him, and amend his past conduct; otherwise it must
' follow that his disobedience to the Pope's injunction
' and his infidelity to God once proved, he will be de-
' prived of his kingdom and the execution of the
' sentence committed to his Imperial Majesty. This
' done, all those in England who fear God will rise in
' arms, and the King will be punished as he deserves,

VIII., Nov. 15, 1532 ; second date, Dec. 23.—*Calendar, Foreign and
Domestic,* vol. v. p. 650.

'the present brief operating as a formal sentence against
'him. On the main cause, there being no one in Rome
'to answer for the opposite party, sentence cannot long
'be delayed.' [1]

Ortiz was too sanguine and the vision soon faded.
The brief sounded formidable, but it said no more than
had been contained or implied in another which
Clement had issued three years before. He had allowed
the first to be disregarded. He might equally allow
the last. Each step which he had taken had been
forced upon him, and his reluctance was not diminished.
Chapuys thought that he had given a brief instead of
passing sentence because he could recall one and could
not recall the other; that 'he was playing both with
'the King and the Emperor;' and in England, as well
as elsewhere, it was thought 'that there was some
'secret intelligence between him and the King.' The
Pope and the Emperor had met at Bologna and
Charles's language had been as emphatic as Catherine
desired; yet even at Bologna itself and during the
conference Clement had assured the English Agents
that there was still a prospect of compromise. It was
even rumoured that the Emperor would allow the
cause to be referred back to England, if securities could
be found to protect the rights of the Princess Mary;
nay, that he had gone so far as to say, 'that, if the
'King made a suitable marriage, and not a love-

---

[1] Ortiz to the Empress, Jan. 19, 1533.—*Spanish Calendar*, vol.
iv. part 1, pp. 579-80.

'marriage, he would bring the Pope and Catherine to 'allow the first marriage to be annulled.' [1]

In London the talk continued of the removal of the suit from Rome to Cambray. The Nuncio and the King were observed to be much together and on improved terms, the Nuncio openly saying that his Holiness wished to be relieved of the business. It was even considered still possible that the Pope might concede the dispensation to the King which had been originally asked for, to marry again without legal process. If, wrote Chapuys, who thoroughly distrusted Clement, the King once gains the point of not being obliged to appear at Rome, the Pope will have the less shame in granting the dispensation by absolute power, as it is made out that the King's right is so evident; and if his Holiness refuses it, the King will be more his enemy than ever. A sentence is the only sovereign remedy, and the Queen says the King would not resist, if only from fear of his subjects, who are not only well disposed to her and to your Majesty, but for the most part are good Catholics and would not endure excommunication and interdict. If a tumult arose, I know not if the Lady, who is hated by all the world, would escape with life and jewels. But, unless the Pope takes care, he will lose his authority here, and his censures will not be regarded.[2]

---

[1] Carlo Capello to the Signory, March 15, 1533.—*Venetian Calendar*, vol. iv. p. 389.

[2] Chapuys to Charles V., Feb. 9, 1533, vol. vi. p. 62. The same letter will be found in the *Spanish*

It was true that Anne was ill-liked in England, and the King, in choosing her, was testing the question of his marriage in the least popular form which it could have assumed. The Venetian Ambassador mentions that one evening 'seven or eight thousand women 'went out of London to seize Boleyn's daughter,' who was supping at a villa on the river, the King not being with her. Many men were among them in women's clothes. Henry, however, showed no sign of change of purpose. He had presented her to the French Court as his intended Queen. And on such a matter he was not to be moved by the personal objections of his subjects. The month allowed in the brief went by. She was still at the court, and the continued negotiations with the Nuncio convinced Catherine's friends that there was mischief at work behind the scenes. Their uneasiness was increased by the selection which was now made of a successor to Archbishop Warham.

Thomas Cranmer had been Lord Wiltshire's private chaplain, and had at one time been his daughter's tutor. He had attended her father on his Embassy to the Emperor, had been active in collecting opinions on the Continent favourable to the divorce, and had been resident ambassador at the Imperial court. He had been much in Germany. He was personally acquainted with Luther. He had even married, and, though he could not produce his wife openly, the con-

---

Calendar with some differences in the translation. The original French is in parts obscure.

nection was well known. Protestant priests in taking
wives were asserting only their natural liberty. Luther
had married, and had married a nun. An example
laudable at Wittenberg could not be censurable in
London by those who held Luther excused. The
German clergy had released themselves from their vows,
as an improvement on the concubinage which had long
and generally prevailed. Wolsey had a son and was
not ashamed of him, even charging his education on
English benefices. Clerical marriages were forbidden
only by the Church law, which Parliament had never
been invited to sanction, and though Cranmer could not
introduce a wife into society he was at least as fit for
archiepiscopal rank as the great Cardinal. He was a
man of high natural gifts, and ardent to replace superstition and corruption by purer teaching. The English
Liturgy survives to tell us what Cranmer was. His
nomination to the Primacy took the world by surprise,
for as yet he had held no higher preferment than an
archdeaconry ; but the reorganisation of the Church was
to begin ; Parliament was to meet again in February,
and the King needed all the help that he could find in
the House of Lords. The Bishops were still but half
conquered. A man of intellect and learning was required at the head of them. ‘ King Henry loved a
‘man,’ it was said. He knew Cranmer and valued him.
The appointment was made known in the first month
of the new year. Before the new Primate could be in-
stalled a Bull of Confirmation was still legally necessary
from Rome. The King was in haste. The annates

due on the vacancy of the see of Canterbury were despatched at once, the King himself advancing the money and taking no advantage of the late Act. Such unusual precipitancy raised suspicions that something more was contemplated in which Cranmer's help would be needed.

The knot had, in fact, been cut which Henry had been so long struggling to untie. The Lady Anne had aspired to being the central figure of a grand ceremony. Her nuptials were to be attended with the pomp and splendour of a royal marriage. Public feeling was in too critical a condition to permit what might have been resented; and, lest the prize should escape her after all, she had brought down her pride to agree to a private service. When it was performed, and by whom, was never known. The date usually received was 'on or 'before the 25th of January.' Chapuys says that Cranmer himself officiated in the presence of the lady's father, mother and brother, two other friends of the lady, and a Canterbury priest.[1] But Chapuys was relating only the story current at the time in society. Nothing authentic has been ascertained. The fact that the marriage had taken place was concealed till the divorce could be pronounced by a Court protected by Act of Parliament, and perhaps with the hope that the announcement could be softened by the news that the nation might hope for an heir.

Despatch was thus necessary with Cranmer's Bulls.

[1] Chapuys to the Emperor, Feb. 23, 1533.—*Spanish Calendar*, vol. iv. part 1, p. 609.

He himself spoke without reserve on the right of the King to remarry, ' being ready to maintain it with his ' life.' Chapuys and the Nuncio both wrote to request the Pope not to be in a hurry with the confirmation of so dangerous a person.[1] The Pope seemed determined to justify the suspicions entertained of him by his eagerness to meet Henry's wishes. It is certain that the warning had reached him.[2] He sent the Bulls with all the speed he could. He knew, perhaps, what they were needed for.

Henry meanwhile was preparing to meet the Parliament, when the secret would have to be communicated to the world. The modern reader will conceive that no other subject could have occupied his mind. The relative importance of things varies with the distance from which we view them. He was King of England first. His domestic anxieties held still the second place. Before the opening, as the matter of greatest consequence, a draft Act was prepared to carry out the object which in the last year he had failed in securing— ' an Act to restrain bishops from citing or arresting ' any of the King's subjects to appear before them, ' unless the bishop or his commissary was free from ' private grudge against the accused, unless there were ' three, or at least two, credible witnesses, and a copy ' of the libel had in all cases been delivered to the ' accused, with the names of the accusers.' Such an

---

[1] *Calendar, Foreign and Domestic*, vol. vi. p. 65.

[2] Ghinucci and Lee to Henry

VIII., March 11, 1533.—*Ibid.* p. 100.

Act was needed. It was not to shield what was still regarded as impiety, for Frith was burned a few months later for a denial of the Real Presence, which Luther himself called heresy. It was to check the arbitrary and indiscriminate tyranny of a sour, exasperated party, who were pursuing everyone with fire and sword who presumed to oppose them. More, writing to Erasmus, said he had purposely stated in his epitaph that he had been hard upon the heretics. He so hated that folk that, unless they repented, he preferred their enmity, so mischievous were they to the world.[1]

The spirit of More was alive and dangerous. To Catholic minds there could be no surer evidence that the King was given over to the Evil One than leniency to heretics. They were the more disturbed to see how close the intimacy had grown between him and the Pope's representative. The Nuncio was constantly closeted with Henry or the Council. When Chapuys remonstrated, he said ' he was a poor gentleman, living ' on his salary, and could not do otherwise.' ' The Pope ' had advised him to neglect no opportunity of promot- ' ing the welfare of religion.' ' Practices,' Chapuys ascertained, were still going forward, and the Nuncio was at the bottom of them. The Nuncio assured him that he had exhorted the King to take Catherine back. The King had replied that he would not, and that reconciliation was impossible. Yet the secret communi- cations did not cease, and the astonishment and alarm

---

[1] More to Erasmus.—*Calendar, Foreign and Domestic,* vol. vi. p. 144.

increased when the Nuncio consented to accompany
the King to the opening of Parliament. He was conducted in state in the Royal barge from Greenwich
Henry sat on the throne, the Nuncio had a chair on
his right, and the French Ambassador on his left. The
object was to show the nation how little was really
meant by the threat of excommunication, to intimidate
the Bishops, and to make the clergy understand the
extent of favours which they could expect from the
Nuncio's master. The Nuncio's appearance was not
limited to a single occasion. During the progress of
the Session he attended the debates in the House of
Commons. Norfolk gave him notice of the days on
which the Pope would not be directly mentioned, that
he might be present without scandal. The Duke admitted a wish for the world to see that the King and
the Court of Rome understood each other. ' By this
' presumption,' said Chapuys, ' they expect to make
' their profit as regards the people and the prelates who
' have hitherto supported the Holy See, who now, for
' the above reason, dare not speak, fearing to go against
' the Pope.' [1]

The world wondered and was satisfied. The Opposition was paralysed. The Bishop of Rochester complained to the Nuncio, and received nothing but
regrets and promises which were not observed. Again,
a council was held of Peers, Bishops, and lawyers to
consider the divorce, when it was agreed at last that

---

[1] Chapuys to Charles V., Feb.
15.—*Calendar, Foreign and Do-*
mestic, vol. vi. p. 73. *Spanish*
Calendar, vol. iv. part 2, p. 600.

the cause might be tried in the Archbishop of Canterbury's court, and that the arrival of the Bulls would
be accepted as a sign of the Pope's tacit connivance.
Chapuys had failed to stop them. 'The Queen,' he
said, 'was thunderstruck, and complained bitterly of
'his Holiness. He had left her to languish for three
'and a half years since her appeal, and, instead of
'giving sentence, had now devised a scheme to prolong
'her misery and bastardise her daughter. She knew
'the King's character. If sentence was once given
'there would be no scandal. The King would obey, or,
'if he did not, which she thought impossible, she
'would die happy, knowing that the Pope had declared
'for her. Her own mind would be at rest, and the
'Princess would not lose her right. The Pope was
'entirely mistaken if he thought that he would induce
'the King to modify his action against the Church.
'The Lady and her father, who were staunch Lutherans,
'were urging him on. The sentence alone would make
'him pause. He dared not disobey, and if the people
'rose the Lady would find a rough handling.' This,
Chapuys said, was the Queen's opinion, which she had
commanded him to communicate to the Emperor. For
himself, he could only repeat his request that the Bulls
for Canterbury should be delayed till the sentence was
ready for delivery. If the Pope knew Cranmer's reputation as a heretic, he would be in no haste to confirm
him.[1]

---

[1] Chapuys to Charles V., Feb. 9, 1533. Compressed.—*Spanish
Calendar*, vol. iv. part 2, pp. 592—600.

Clement knew well enough what Cranmer was, and the Bulls had been despatched promptly before the Emperor could interfere. The King meanwhile had committed himself, and now went straight forward. He allowed his marriage to be known. Lord Wiltshire had withdrawn his opposition to it.[1] Lord Rochford, Anne's brother, was sent at the beginning of March to Paris, to say that the King had acted on the advice given him by his good brother at their last interview. He had taken a wife for the establishment of his realm in the hope of having male issue. He trusted, therefore, that Francis would remember his promise. In citing him to Rome the Pope had violated the rights of Sovereign Princes. It touched them all, and, if allowed, would give the Pope universal authority. The time was past when such pretensions could be tolerated.[2]

At home he prepared for the worst. The fleet was further increased, new ships were put on the stocks ; the yeomanry were armed, drilled, and equipped, and England rang with sounds of preparation for war ; while in Parliament the famous Act was introduced which was to form the constitutional basis of national inde-

---

[1] Chapuys here mentions this very curious fact: 'The Earl of ' Wiltshire,' he wrote on Feb. 15, ' has never declared himself up to ' this moment. On the contrary, he has hitherto, as the Duke of ' Norfolk has frequently told me, ' tried to dissuade the King rather ' than otherwise from the mar-' riage.'—*Spanish Calendar*, vol. iv. part 2, p. 602.

[2] Henry VIII. to Francis I., March 11, 1533. — *Calendar, Foreign and Domestic*, vol. vi. p. 103.

pendence, and to end for ever the Papal jurisdiction
in England. From the time that Convocation had
acknowledged the King to be the Head of the Church
the question of appeals to Rome had been virtually
before the country. It was now to be settled, and
English law-suits were henceforth to be heard and
decided within the limits of the empire. The Sibyl's
pages were being rent out one by one. The Præmunire
had been revived, and the Pope's claim of independent
right to interfere by bull or brief in English affairs had
been struck rudely down. Tribute in the shape of
annates went next; the appellate jurisdiction was now
to follow. Little would then be left save spiritual
precedence, and this might not be of long continuance.
There had been words enough. The time had come to
act. On the introduction of the Act of Appeals the
King spoke out to Chapuys as if the spirit of the
Plantagenets was awake in him. 'He said a thousand
'things in disparagement of the Pope, complaining of
'the authority and power he unduly assumed over the
'kingdoms of Christendom. He professed to have seen
'a book from the Papal library, in which it was main-
'tained that all Christian princes were only feudatories
'of the Pope. He himself, he said, intended to put a
'remedy to such inordinate ambition, and repair the
'errors of Henry II. and John, who had been tricked
'into making England tributary to the Holy See.'
'The Emperor,' he said, 'not only demanded justice,
'but would have justice done in his own way, and
'according to his own caprice. For himself, he thought

'of resuming to the Crown the lands of the clergy,
'which his predecessors had alienated without right.'
Chapuys advised him to wait for a General Council
before he tried such high measures. 'But the King
'could not be persuaded' that a council was needed for
such a purpose.[1]

The Act of Appeals touched too many interests to
be passed without opposition. Private persons as well
as princes had appealed to the Roman law-courts, and
suits pending or determined there might be reopened at
home and produce confusion unless provided for. However complacent the Pope might appear, it could not be
supposed that he would bear patiently the open renun-
ciation of his authority. Excommunication was half
perceived to be a spectre; but spectres had not wholly
lost their terrors. With an excommunication pronounced
in earnest might come interdict and stoppage of trade,
perhaps war and rebellion at home; and one of the
members for London said that if the King would refer
the question between himself and the Queen to a
General Council, the City of London would give him
two hundred thousand pounds. The arrival of Cranmer's
Bulls, while the Act was still under discussion, moderated the alarm. The Pope evidently was in no warlike
humour. At the bottom of his heart he had throughout
been in Henry's favour; he hoped probably that a time
might come when he could say so, and that all this
hostile legislation would then be repealed. When the

---

[1] Chapuys to Charles V., March 15, 1533.—*Spanish Calendar*, vol.
iv. part 2 p. 619.

excitement was at its hottest, and it was known at
Rome, not only that the last brief had been defied, but
that the King was about to marry the Lady, the Pope
had borne the news with singular calmness.   After all,
he said to the Count de Cifuentes, if the marriage is
completed, we have only to think of a remedy.   The
remedy, Cifuentes said, was for the Pope to do justice ;
the King had been encouraged in his rash course
by the toleration with which he had been treated
and the constant delays.   Clement answered that he
would certainly do justice; but if the marriage was
' a fact accomplished,' he wished to know what the
Emperor meant to do.   Cifuentes told him that
his Holiness must do his part first, and then the
Emperor would ' act as became a powerful and wise
' Prince.' [1]

The Pope had heard this language before.   The
Emperor was afraid of going to war with England, and
the Pope knew it.   The alternative, therefore, was
either to make some concession to Henry or to let him
go on as he pleased, bringing the Holy See into contempt by exposing its weakness : and either course would
be equally dispiriting to the Queen and his own friends
in England.   ' Everybody,' wrote Chapuys, ' cries murder
' on the Pope for his delays, and for not detaining the
' Archbishop's Bulls till the definitive sentence had been
' given.   He was warned of the danger of granting them.
' There is not a lord in the Court of either side who does

---

[1] *Calendar, Foreign and Domestic*, April 21, 1533, vol. iv. p. 171.

'not say publicly his Holiness will betray the Emperor.
'The Dukes of Norfolk and Suffolk speak of it with more
'assurance, saying they know it well and could give good
'evidence of it.'[1]

The Act of Appeals, though strongly resisted in the
House of Commons for fear of the consequences, was
evidently to pass; and it was now understood that, as
soon as it became law, Cranmer was to try the divorce
suit and to give final judgment. The Pope's extraordinary conduct had paralysed opposition. The clergy,
like some wild animal hardly broken in, were made to
parade their docility and to approve beforehand the
Archbishop's intended action. It was to be done in
haste, for Anne was *enceinte*. The members of the
Synod were allowed scant time even to eat their
dinners; they were so harassed that no one opened his
mouth to contradict, except the Bishop of Rochester,
and Rochester had no weight, being alone against all
the rest. So docile was the assembly and so imperious
the King that the Queen and all her supporters now
regarded her cause as lost.[2] Ortiz wrote from Rome
to Charles that, 'though he was bound to believe the
'contrary, he feared the Pope had sent, or might send,
'absolution to the King.' Something might be done
underhand to revoke the last brief, although the Pope
knew what an evil thing it would be, and how ignomi-
nious to the Holy See.[3]

---

[1] Chapuys to Charles V., March
31.—*Calendar, Foreign and Domestic*, vol. vi. p. 128.

[2] *Ibid.*

[3] Dr. Ortiz to Charles V., April
14, 1533.—*Ibid.* pp. 159-60.

The reforming party in England laughed at the expected interdict. The Pope, they said, would not dare to
try it, or, if he did, Christian princes would not trouble
themselves about him. The King said, significantly,
to the Nuncio that he was only defending himself:
'if the Pope gave him occasion to reconsider the
'matter, he might undo what was being aimed at his
'authority.'[1]

The Bill passed more rapidly through its later
stages. The Papal jurisdiction was ended. Anyone
who introduced Briefs of Excommunication or Interdict
into the realm was declared guilty of high treason. The
Bishop of Rochester, becoming violent, was committed
to friendly custody under charge of Gardiner, now
Bishop of Winchester. Appeals to the Pope on any
matter, secular or spiritual, were forbidden thenceforward, and the Act was made retrospective, applying to
suits already in progress. All was thus over. The
Archbishop's sentence was known beforehand, and Anne
Boleyn was to be crowned at Whitsuntide. Force was
now the only remedy, and the constitutional opposition
converted itself into conspiracy, to continue in that form
till the end of the century. The King was convinced
that the strength and energy of the country was with
him. When told that there would be an invasion, he
said that the English could never be conquered as long
as they held together. Chapuys was convinced equally
that they would not hold together. The clergy, and a

---

[1] Chapuys to Charles V., March 31, 1533.—*Spanish Calendar*, vol.
iv. part 2, p. 626.

section of the peers with whom he chiefly associated, spoke all in one tone, and he supposed that the language which they used to him represented a universal opinion. Thenceforward he and his English friends began to urge on the Emperor the necessity of armed intervention, and assured him that he had only to declare himself to find the whole nation at his back.

'Englishmen, high and low,' Chapuys wrote, ' desire 'your Majesty to send an army to destroy the venomous 'influence of the Lady and her adherents, and reform 'the realm. Forgive my boldness, but your Majesty 'ought not to hesitate. When this accursed Anne has 'her foot in the stirrup, she will do the Queen and the 'Princess all the hurt she can. She boasts that she will have the Princess in her own train; one day, perhaps, she will poison her, or will marry her to some varlet, 'while the realm itself will be made over to heresy. A conquest would be perfectly easy. The King has no trained army. All of the higher ranks and all the 'nobles are for your Majesty, except the Duke of Norfolk 'and two or three besides. Let the Pope call in the secular arm, stop the trade, encourage the Scots, send 'to sea a few ships, and the thing will be over. No 'injustice will be done, and, without this, England will 'be estranged from the Holy Faith and will become 'Lutheran. The King points the way and lends them wings, and the Archbishop of Canterbury does worse. 'There is no danger of French interference. France will wait to see the issue, and will give you no more trouble 'if this King receives his due. Again forgive me, but

'pity for the Queen and Princess obliges me to speak
'plainly.' [1]

The King could hardly be ignorant of the communications between the disaffected nobles and the Imperial
Ambassador, but no outward sign appeared that he was
aware of them. Lord Mountjoy, however, was sent
with a guard to watch Catherine's residence, and, the
decisive Act being passed through Parliament, the
Dukes of Norfolk and Suffolk, with Lord Exeter and
the Earl of Oxford, repaired to her once more to invite
her, since she must see that further resistance was
useless, to withdraw her appeal, and to tell her that, on
her compliance, every arrangement should be made for
her state and comfort, with an establishment suited to
her rank. Chapuys demanded an audience of the King
to remonstrate, and a remarkable conversation ensued.
The Ambassador said he had heard of the proceedings
in Convocation and in Parliament. It was his duty to
speak. If the King had no regard for men whom he
despised, he hoped that he would have respect to God.
'God and his conscience,' Henry answered calmly, 'were
'on perfectly good terms.' Chapuys expressed a doubt,
and the King assured him that he was entirely sincere.
Chapuys said he could not believe that at a time when
Europe was distracted with heresies the King of England
would set so evil an example. The King rejoined that,
if the world found his new marriage strange, he himself

---

[1] Chapuys to Charles V., April
10, 1533. Compressed.—*Calendar,
Foreign and Domestic,* vol. vi. pp.
149-51. *Spanish Calendar,* vol. iv.
part 2, p. 630.

found it more strange that Pope Julius should have granted a dispensation for his marriage with his brother's wife. He must have an heir to succeed him in his realm. The Emperor had no right to prevent him. The Ambassador spoke of the Princess. To provide a husband for the Princess would be the fittest means to secure the succession. Henry said he would have children of his own, and Chapuys ventured on more dangerous ground than he was aware of by hinting that he could not be sure of that. 'Am I not a man,' the King said sharply, ' am I not a man like others ? Am ' I not a man ? ' Thrice repeating the words. ' But,' he added, ' I will not let you into my secrets.' The Ambassador inquired whether he intended to remain on friendly terms with the Emperor. The King asked him with a frown what he meant by that. On his replying that the Emperor's friendship depended on the treatment of the Queen, the King said coldly that the Emperor had no right to interfere with the laws and constitution of England.

Chapuys persisted. The Emperor, he said, did not wish to meddle with his laws, unless they personally affected the Queen. The King wanted to force her to abandon her appeal, and it was not to be expected that she would submit to statutes which had been carried by compulsion.

The King grew impatient. The statutes, he said, had been passed in Parliament, and the Queen as a subject must obey them.

The Ambassador retorted that new laws could not

be retrospective; and, as to the Queen being a subject,
if she was his wife she was his subject; if she was not
his wife, she was not his subject.

This was true, and Henry was to be made to feel
the dilemma. He contented himself, however, with
saying that she must have patience, and obey the laws
of the realm. The Emperor had injured him by hinder-
ing his marriage and preventing him from having male
succession. The Queen was no more his wife than she
was Chapuys's. He would do as he pleased, and if the
Emperor made war on him he would fight.

Chapuys inquired whether, if an interdict was issued,
and the Spaniards and Flemings resident in England
obeyed it, his statutes would apply to them.

The King did not answer; but, turning to some one
present, he said : ' You have heard the Ambassador
' hint at excommunication. It is not I that am excom-
' municated, but the Emperor, who has kept me so long
' in mortal sin. That is an excommunication which the
' Pope cannot take off.' [1]

To the lords who carried the message to Catherine
she replied as she had always done—that queen she
was, and she would never call herself by any other
name. As to her establishment, she wanted nothing
but a confessor, a doctor, and a couple of maids. If
that was too much, she would go about the world and
beg alms for the love of God.

---

[1] Chapuys to Charles V., April 16, 1533.—*Calendar, Foreign and Domestic*, vol. vi. p. 163, &c., abridged. Also *Spanish Calendar*, vol. iv. part 2, p. 635.

'The King,' Chapuys said, ' was naturally kind and
' generous,' but the ' Lady Anne had so perverted him
' that he did not seem the same man.' Unless the
Emperor acted in earnest, she would make an end of
Catherine, as she had done of Wolsey, whom she did
not hate with half as much intensity. ' All seems like
' a dream,' he said. ' Her own party do not know whether
' to laugh or cry at it. Every day people ask me when
' I am going away. As long as I remain here it will
' be always thought your Majesty has consented to the
' marriage.'

CHAPTER XIII.

The King's claim—The obstinacy of Catherine—The Court at Dunstable—Judgment given by Cranmer—Debate in the Spanish Council of State—Objections to armed interference—The English opposition—Warning given to Chapuys—Chapuys and the Privy Council—Conversation with Cromwell—Coronation of Anne Boleyn—Discussions at Rome—Bull *supra Attentatis*—Confusion of the Catholic Powers—Libels against Henry—Personal history of Cromwell—Birth of Elizabeth—The King's disappointment—Bishop Fisher desires the introduction of a Spanish army into England—Growth of Lutheranism.

IF circumstances can be imagined to justify the use of the dispensing power claimed and exercised by the Papacy, Henry VIII. had been entitled to demand assistance from Clement VII. in the situation in which he had found himself with Catherine of Aragon. He had been committed when little more than a boy, for political reasons, to a marriage of dubious legality. In the prime of his life he found himself fastened to a woman eight years older than himself; the children whom she had borne to him all dead, except one daughter; his wife past the age when she could hope to be again a mother; the kingdom with the certainty of civil war

before it should the King die without a male heir. In
hereditary monarchies, where the sovereign is the centre
of the State, the interests of the nation have to be considered in the arrangements of his family. Henry had
been married irregularly to Catherine to strengthen the
alliance between England and Spain. When, as a result,
a disputed succession and a renewal of the civil wars
were seen to be inevitable, the King had a distinct right
to ask to be relieved of the connection by the same
irregular methods. The *causa urgentissima*, for which
the dispensing power was allowed, was present in the
highest degree, and that power ought to have been
made use of. That it was not made use of was due to a
control exerted upon the Pope by the Emperor, whose
pride had been offended ; and that such an influence
could be employed for such a purpose vitiated the
tribunal which had been trusted with a peculiar and
exceptional authority. The Pope had not concealed his
conviction that the demand was legitimate in itself,
or that, in refusing, he was yielding to intimidation,
and the inevitable consequences had followed. Royal
persons who receive from birth and station remarkable
favours of fortune, occasionally have to submit to inconveniences attaching to their rank ; and, when the
occasion rises, they generally meet with little ceremony.
At the outset the utmost efforts had been made to spare
Catherine's feelings. Both the King and the Pope
desired to avoid a judgment on the validity of her
marriage. An heir to the crown was needed, and from
her there was no hope of further issue. If at the begin-

ning she had been found incapable of bearing a child, the marriage would have been dissolved of itself. Essentially the condition was the same. Technical difficulties could be disposed of by a Papal dispensation. She would have remained queen, her honour unaffected, the legitimacy of Mary unimpugned, the relations between the Holy See and the Crown and Church of England undisturbed. The obstinacy of Catherine herself, the Emperor's determination to support her, and the Pope's cowardice, prevented a reasonable arrangement; and thus the right of the Pope himself to the spiritual sovereignty of Europe came necessarily under question, when it implied the subjugation of independent princes to another power by which the Court of Rome was dominated.

Such a question once raised could have but one answer from the English nation. Every resource had been tried to the extreme limit of forbearance, and all had failed before the indomitable will of a single woman. A request admitted to be just had been met by excommunication and threats of force. With entire fitness, the King and Parliament had replied by withdrawing their recognition of a corrupt tribunal, and determining thenceforward to try and to judge their own suits in their own courts.

Thus, on the 10th of May, Cranmer, with three Bishops as assessors, sate at Dunstable under the Royal licence to hear the cause which had so long been the talk of Europe, and Catherine, who was at Ampthill, was cited to appear. She consulted Chapuys on the answer which she was to make. Chapuys advised her

not to notice the summons. 'Nothing done by such a
'Court could prejudice her,' he said, 'unless she renounced
'her appeal to Rome.' As she made no plea, judgment
was promptly given.[1] The divorce was complete so far
as English law could decide it, and it was doubtful to
the last whether the Pope was not at heart a consenting
party. The sentence had been, of course, anticipated.
On the 27th of April Chapuys informed the Emperor how
matters then stood.

'Had his Holiness done as he was advised, and
'inserted a clause in the Archbishop's Bulls forbidding
'the Archbishop to meddle in the case, he would have
'prevented much mischief. He chose to take his own
'way, and thus the English repeat what they have said
'all along : that in the end the Pope would deceive
'your Majesty. . . . The thing now to be done is to
'force from the Pope a quick and sudden decision of
'the case, so as to silence those who affirm that he is
'only procrastinating till he can decide in favour of
'the King, or who think that your Majesty will then
'acquiesce, and that there will be no danger of war.
'. . . I have often tried to ascertain from the Queen
'what alternative she is looking to, seeing that gentle-
'ness produces no effect. I have found her hitherto so
'scrupulous in her profession of respect and affection for
'the King that she thinks she will be damned eternally
'if she takes a step which may lead to war. Latterly,
'however, she has let me know that she would like to

---

[1] I have related elsewhere the story of the Dunstable trial, and do not repeat it.—*History of England*, vol. i. pp. 441 - 447.

' see some other remedy tried, though she refers every-
' thing to me.' [1]

The proceedings at Dunstable may have added to
Catherine's growing willingness for the ' other remedy.'
She was no longer an English subject in the eye of
the law, and might hold herself free to act as she
pleased. Simultaneously, however, a consultation was
going forward about her and her affairs in the Spanish
Cabinet which was not promising for Chapuys's views.
The Spanish Ambassador in London, it was said, was
urging for war with England. The history of the
divorce case was briefly stated. The delay of judgment
had been caused by the King's protest that he could not
appear at Rome. That point had been decided against
the King. The Pope had promised the Emperor that
he would proceed at once to sentence, but had not done it.
Brief on brief had been presented to the King, ordering
him to separate from Anne Boleyn *pendente lite*, but
the King had paid no attention to them—had married
the Lady and divorced the Queen. The Emperor was
the Queen's nearest relation. What was he to do?
There were three expedients before him : legal process,
force, and law and force combined. The first was the
best; but the King and the realm would refuse the
tribunal, and *the Pope always had been, and still was,
very cold and indifferent in the matter, and most tolerant
to the English King.* Open force, in the existing state
of Christendom, was dangerous. To begin an aggres-

---

[1] Chapuys to Charles V., April 27, 1533. Abridged.—*Spanish Calendar*, vol. iv. part 2, p. 648.

sion was always a questionable step. Although the
King had married ' Anne de Bulans,' he had used no
violence against the Queen, nor done anything to
justify an armed attack upon him. The question was ' a
' private one,' and the Emperor must consider what he
owed to the public welfare. Should the third course
be adopted, the Pope would have to pronounce judgment and call in the secular arm. All Christian
princes would then be bound to help him, and the
Emperor, as the first among them, would have to place
himself at the head of the enterprise. ' But would it
' not be better and more convenient to avoid, for the
' present, harsh measures, which might bring on war
' and injure trade, and insist only on further censures
' and a sentence of deposition against the King ? Should
' the Pope require to know beforehand what the Em-
' peror would do to enforce the execution, it would be
' enough to tell the Pope that he must do his part first;
' any further engagement would imply that the sentence
' on the principal cause had been decided beforehand.
' Finally, it would have to be determined whether the
' Queen was to remain in England or to leave it.'

These were the questions before the Cabinet. A
Privy Councillor, perhaps Granvelle (the name is not
mentioned), gave his own opinion, which was seemingly
adopted.

All these ways were to be tried. The Pope must
proceed with the suit. Force must be suspended for
the present, *the cause being a personal one, and having
already begun when peace was made at Cambray.* The

Pope must conclude the principal matter, or at least insist on the revocation of what had been done since the suit commenced, and then, perhaps, force would not be required at all. The advice of the Consulta on the answer to be given to the Pope, should he require to know the Emperor's intentions, was exactly right. Nothing more need be said than that the Emperor would not forget the obligations which devolved on him as an obedient son of the Church. The Queen, meanwhile, must remain in England. If she came away, a rupture would be inevitable.

The speaker advised further that a special embassy should be sent to England to remonstrate with the King.

This, however, if unsuccessful, it was felt would lead to war; and opposite to the words the Emperor himself wrote on the margin an emphatic *No.*[1]

The mention of the peace of Cambray is important. The divorce had reached an acute stage before the peace was concluded. It had not been spoken of there, and the Emperor was diplomatically precluded from producing it as a fresh injury. Both he and the Council were evidently unwilling to act. The Pope knew their reluctance, and did not mean, if he could help it, to flourish his spiritual weapons without a sword to support them.

The King wrote to inform Charles of his marriage. 'In the face of the Scotch pretensions to the succes-

---

[1] *Spanish Calendar*, vol. iv. part 2, pp. 650—658.

' sion,' he said, ' other heirs of his body were required
' for the security of the Crown. The thing was
' done, and the Pope must make the best of it.' This
was precisely what the Pope was inclined to do.
Cifuentes thought that, though he seemed troubled,
' he was really pleased.' [1]   ' He said positively that,
' if he was to declare the King of England deprived
' of his crown, the Emperor must bind himself to see
' the sentence executed.' [2] Charles had no intention
of binding himself, nor would his Cabinet advise him
to bind himself. The time was past when Most
Catholic Princes could put armies in motion to execute
the decrees of the Bishop of Rome. The theory
might linger, but the facts were changed. Philip II.
tried the experiment half a century later, but it
did not answer to him. A fresh order of things had
risen in Europe, and passionate Catholics could not
understand it. Dr. Ortiz shrieked that ' the King,
' by his marriage, was guilty of heresy and schism ; '
the Emperor ought to use the opportunity, without
waiting for further declarations from the Pope, and
unsheath the sword which God had placed in his
hands.[3] English Peers and Prelates, impatient of the
rising strength of the Commons and of the growth of
Lutheranism, besieged Chapuys with entreaties for
an Imperial force to be landed. They told him that

---

[1] The Count de Cifuentes to
Charles V., May 7, 1533.—*Calendar, Foreign and Domestic*, vol.
vi. pp. 203-4.

[2] *Ibid.* May 10.
[3] Ortiz to Charles V., May 3,
1533.—*Spanish Calendar*, vol. iv.
part 2, p. 659.

Richard III. was not so hated by the people as Henry, but that, without help from abroad, they dared not declare themselves.[1] Why could they not dare ? The King had no janissaries about his throne. Why could they not stand up in the House of Lords and refuse to sanction the measures which they disapproved ? Why, except that they were *not* the people. Numbers might still be on their side, but the daring, the intellect, the fighting-strength of England was against them, and the fresh air of dawning freedom chilled their blood. The modern creed is that majorities have a right to rule. If, out of every hundred men, four-fifths will vote on one side, but will not fight without help from the sword of the stranger, and the remaining fifth will both vote and fight—fight domestic cowards and foreign foes combined—which has the right to rule ? The theory may be imperfect ; but it is easy to foresee which will rule in fact. The marriage with Anne was formally communicated in the House of Lords. There were some murmurs. The King rose from the throne and said it had been necessary for the welfare of the realm. Peers and Commons acquiesced, and no more was said. The coronation of the new Queen was fixed for the 19th of May.

If the great men who had been so eager with Chapuys were poltroons, Chapuys himself was none. Rumours were flying that the Emperor was coming to waste England, destroy the Royal family, and place a foreign Prince on the throne. The Ambassador

---

[1] Chapuys to Charles V., May 18, 1533.—*Calendar, Foreign and Domestic,* vol. vi. pp. 225-6.

addressed a letter to Henry, saying that he held powers to take action for the preservation of the Queen's rights; and he gave him notice that he intended to enter immediately on the duties of his office.[1] Henry showed no displeasure at so bold a communication, but sent Thomas Cromwell to him, who was now fast rising into consequence, to remind him that, large as was the latitude allowed to Ambassadors, he must not violate the rights of the Crown, and to warn him to be careful. He was then summoned before the Privy Council. Norfolk had previously cautioned him against introducing briefs or letters from the Pope, telling him that if he did he would be torn in pieces by the people. The Council demanded to see the powers which he said that he possessed. He produced directions which he had received to watch over the Queen's rights, and he then remarked on the several briefs by which the King was virtually excommunicated. Lord Wiltshire told him that if any subject had so acted he would have found himself in the Tower. The King wished him well; but if he wore two faces, and meddled with what did not concern him, he might fall into trouble.

Chapuys replied that the Council were like the eels of Melun, which cried out before they were skinned. He had done nothing, so far. He had not presented any 'Apostolic letters.' As to two faces, the Earl meant, he supposed, that he was about to act as the Queen's Proctor as well as Ambassador; he was not a lawyer;

---

[1] Chapuys to Henry VIII., May 5, 1533.—*Spanish Calendar*, vol. iv. part 2, p. 668.

'inconvenience' which the Emperor pointed out.[1] His impatient English friends whom he called 'the people' were still obliged to submit in patience, while the King went on upon his way in the great business of the realm, amidst the 'impress of shipwrights,' the 'daily 'cast of cannon,' and foreign mart of implements for war. An embassy was sent to Germany to treat for an alliance with the Smalcaldic League. A book was issued, with the authority of the Privy Council, on the authority of kings and priests, showing that bishops and priests were equal, and that princes must rule them both. The Scotch Ambassador told Chapuys that if such a book had been published in his country the author of it would have been burnt.[2] Parliament met to pass the Bill, of which Henry had introduced a draft in the previous session, to restrict the Bishops' powers of punishing heretics. Dr. Nixe, the old Bishop of Norwich, had lately burnt Thomas Bilney on his own authority, without waiting for the King's writ. Henry had the Bishop arrested, tried him before a lay judge, confiscated his property, and imprisoned him in the Tower. Parliament made such exploits as that of Dr. Nixe impossible for the future.

Act followed Act on the same lines. The Pope's Bulls were dispensed with on appointments to vacant sees. The King's nomination was to suffice. The tributes to Rome, which had been levied hitherto in infinite variety

---

[1] *Spanish Calendar*, vol. v. p. 32.

[2] Chapuys to Charles V., Jan.

3, 1534.—*Spanish Calendar*, vol. v. p. 1.

of form, were to be swept finally away, and with them an
Act was introduced of final separation from the Papacy.
Were it only in defiance of the Pope, Chapuys said,
such measures impending would matter little, for the
motive was understood; but the preachers were teaching Lutheranism in the pulpits, drawing crowds to hear
them, and, unless the root could be torn out, the realm
would be lost.

Before the closing stroke was dealt in England the
last scene of the tragi-comedy had to be played out in
Rome itself. On the Pope's return from Marseilles the
thunderbolt was expected to fall. The faithful Du
Bellay rushed off to arrest the uplifted arm. He found
Clement wrangling as before with Cifuentes, and Cifuentes, in despair, considering that, if justice would not
move the Pope, other means would have to be found.
The English Acts of Parliament were not frightening
Clement. To them he had become used. But he knew
by this time for certain that, if he deprived Henry,
the Emperor would do nothing. Why, said he, in
quiet irony, to the Emperor's Minister, does not your
master proceed on the Brief *de Attentatis?* It would
be as useful to him as the sentence which he asks for.
By that the King has forfeited his throne. Cifuentes
had to tell him, what he himself was equally aware
of, that it was not so held in England. Until the main
cause had been decided it was uncertain whether the
marriage with Anne Boleyn might not be lawful after all.[1]

---

[1] Cifuentes to Charles V., Jan. 23, 1534.—*Spanish Calendar*, vol.
v. p. 17.

In one of his varying moods the Pope had said at
Marseilles that, if Henry had sent a proctor to plead
for him at Rome, sentence would have been given in
his favour.[1] It was doubtful whether even the Emperor
was really determined, so ambiguous had been his
answers when he was asked if he would execute the
Bull. Du Bellay arrived in the midst of the suspense.
He had brought an earnest message from Francis, praying that judgment might be stayed. As this was the
last effort to prevent the separation of England the
particulars have a certain interest.

In an interview with the Pope Du Bellay said that
when he left London he believed that the rupture was
inevitable. His own sovereign, however, had sent him
to represent to the Holy See that the King of England
was on the eve of forming a treaty with the Lutheran
Princes. The King of France did not pretend to an
opinion on the right or wrong of his brother of
England's case; but he wished to warn his Holiness
that means ought to be found to prevent such an injury
to the Church.

The Pope answered that he had thought long and
painfully on what he ought to do, and had delayed
sentence as long as he was able. The Queen was angry
and accused him of having been the cause of all that
had happened. If the King of France had any further
proposal to offer, he was ready to hear it. If not, the
sentence must be pronounced.

---

[1] Chapuys to Charles V., Jan. 28, 1534.—*Spanish Calendar*, vol. v.
p. 24.

Cifuentes, finding Clement again hesitating, pointed out to him the violent acts which were being done in England, the encouragement of heresy, the cruel treatment of the Queen and Princess, and the risk to the Queen's life if nothing was done to help her. Clement sent for Du Bellay again and inquired more particularly if he had brought no practical suggestion with him. Du Bellay could only say that he had himself brought none; but he trusted that the Pope might devise something, as, without it, not England only but other countries would be irretrievably lost to the Holy See. The Pope said he could think of nothing; and in his account of what had passed to Cifuentes he declared that he had told Du Bellay that he meant to proceed.

Cifuentes was not satisfied. He saw that the Pope was still reluctant. He knew that there were intrigues among the Cardinals. He said that Henry was only making use of France to intimidate him. He asserted, with the deluding confidence which blinded the whole Catholic party, that the revolt of England was the act of the King and not of the people. He was certain, he said, that, although the Bishop pretended that he had no expedient to propose, he had one which he dared not disclose. He could not bring the Pope to a resolution. A further delay of six weeks was granted. Messengers were despatched to England, and English Commissioners were sent in answer. They had no concessions to offer, nor were any concessions expected of them. They lingered on the way. The six weeks expired and they had not arrived. The Spanish party in the Consistory were peremptory. They satisfied the Pope's last scruples by assuring him, vaguely, that he might rely upon the Emperor, and on March 23, with an outburst of general enthusiasm, the Bull was issued which declared valid the marriage of Henry and Catherine, the King to be excommunicated if he disobeyed, and to have forfeited the allegiance of his subjects.

The secular arm was not yet called in, and, before Charles could be required to move, one more step would still be needed. But essentially, and on the main cause of the trouble, the Pope had at last spoken, and spoken finally.[1] The passionate and devout Ortiz poured out on the occasion the emotions of grateful Catholicity. 'The Emperor,' he wrote, 'had won the ' greatest of his victories—a victory over Hell. There ' had been difficulties even to the last. Campeggio had ' opposed, but at last had yielded to the truth. The ' Pope repented of his delay, but now feared he had ' committed a great sin in hesitating so long. The ' holy martyr, the Queen of England, had been saved. ' The Cardinals in past years had been bribed by the 'French King; by the influence of the Holy Spirit ' they had all decided in the Queen's favour. Their ' conscience told them they could not vote against ' her.'[2]

---

[1] Cifuentes to Charles V., March 24.—*Spanish Calendar,* vol. v. p. 84.

[2] Ortiz to Charles V., March 24, 1534.—*Ibid.* vol. v. p. 89.

In England the news of the decision had not been waited for. Two days after the issue of the Bull, the Act abolishing the Pope's authority was read the last time in the House of Lords, to the regret, said Chapuys, of a minority of good men, who could not carry the House along with them.

CHAPTER XV.

The Papal curse—Determined attitude of the Princess Mary—
Chapuys desires to be heard in Parliament—Interview with
the King—Permission refused—The Act of Succession—
Catherine loses the title of Queen—More and Fisher refuse to
swear to the statute—Prospects of rebellion in Ireland—The
Emperor unwilling to interfere—Perplexity of the Catholic
party—Chapuys before the Privy Council—Insists on Catherine's rights—Singular defence of the Pope's action—Chapuys's
intrigues—Defiant attitude of Catherine—Fears for her life—
Condition of Europe—Prospect of war between France and
the Empire—Unwillingness of the Emperor to interfere in
England—Disappointment of Catherine—Visit of Chapuys to
Kimbolton.

PRETENDERS to supernatural powers usually confine the display of their skill to the presence of
friends and believers. The exercise of such powers to
silence opponents or to convince incredulity may be
alleged to have existed in the past, or may be foretold as
to happen in the future ; in the actual present prudent
men are cautious of experiments which, if they fail,
bring them only into ridicule. Excommunication had
real terrors when a frightened world was willing to execute its penalties—when the object of the censure was
cut off from the services of religion and was regarded

as a pariah and an outlaw. The Princes of Europe had real cause to fear the curse of the Pope when their own subjects might withdraw their obedience and the Christian Powers were ready to take arms to coerce them. But Clement knew that his own thunders would find no such support, and he lacked the confidence of Dr. Ortiz that Heaven, if men failed, would avenge its own wrongs. He had not been permitted even to invite the Emperor formally to enforce the sentence which he had been compelled to pronounce. Protestant Germany had been left unpunished in its heresy. The curse had passed harmless over Luther and Luther's supporters. In England he was assured that his authority was still believed in, and that the King would be brought to judgment by his subjects. But there were no outward signs of it. His Bulls could no longer be introduced there. His clergy might at heart be loyal to him; but they had submitted to the Crown and the Parliament. His name was struck out of the service-books, and the business of life went on as if he had never spoken; the business of life, and also the business of the Government: for, the Pope being disposed of, the vital question of the succession to the crown had still to be formally arranged.

Since the Emperor would not act, Chapuys had been feeling his way with the Scotch. If James chose to assert himself, the Ambassador had promised him the Emperor's support. ' He might marry the Princess ' Mary, and the Emperor would welcome the union of

' the crowns of Scotland and England.' [1] Had Mary submitted to her father, her claim to a place in the line of inheritance would not have been taken from her, for she had been born *bonâ fide parentum* and in no reasonable sense could be held illegitimate. But she had remained immoveable. In small things as well as great she had been unnecessarily irritating. Her wardrobe had required replenishing, and she had refused to receive anything which was not given to her as Princess. Anne Boleyn accused her aunt of being too lenient, Mrs. Shelton having refused to make herself the instrument of Anne's violence. Chapuys feared the ' accursed ' Lady ' might be tempted into a more detestable course. But, any way, the nation had broken with the Pope, and Mary could not be left with the prospect of succeeding to the crown while she denied the competency of the English Parliament and the English courts of justice. A bill, therefore, was introduced to make the necessary provisions, establishing the succession in the child, and future children, of Anne.

Catherine could not yet believe that Parliament would assent. Parliament, she thought, had never yet heard the truth. She directed Chapuys to apply for permission to appear at the bar of the House of Lords and speak for her and the Princess.

After the failure of the Nuncio with Convocation Chapuys had little hope that he would be listened to ; but Catherine insisted on his making the attempt, since

---

[1] Chapuys to Charles V. Feb. 21, 1534.—*Spanish Calendar*, vol. v. pp. 53-54.

a refusal, she thought, would be construed into an admission of her right.

The Ambassador wrote to the Council. They desired to know what he proposed to say, and he was allowed a private interview with the Duke of Norfolk. He told the Duke that he wished merely to give a history of the divorce case and would say nothing to irritate. The Duke said he would speak to the King; but the Emperor, considering all that the King had done for him, had not treated him well; they would sooner he had gone to war at once than crossed and thwarted them at so many turns. Chapuys protested that war had never been thought of, and it was arranged that he should see the King and himself present his request. Before he entered the presence Norfolk warned him to be careful of his words, as he was to speak on matters so odious and unpleasing that all the sugars and sauces in the world could not make them palatable. The King, however, was gracious. Chapuys boldly entered on the treatment of the Queen and Princess. He had heard, he said, that the subject was to be laid before Parliament, and he desired to present his remonstrances to the Lords and Commons themselves.

The King replied civilly that, as Chapuys must be aware, his first marriage had been judicially declared null; the Lady Catherine, therefore, could not any longer be called queen, nor the Lady Mary his legitimate daughter. As to Chapuys's request, it was not the custom in England for strangers to speak in Parliament.

Chapuys urged that the Archbishop's sentence was

worth no more than the Bishop of Bath's sentence ille-
gitimatising the children of Edward IV. Parliament
would, no doubt, vote as the King pleased; but, as to
custom, no such occasion had ever arisen before, and
Parliament was not competent to decide questions which
belonged only to spiritual judges. The Princess was
indisputably legitimate, as at the time of her birth no
doubt existed on the lawfulness of her mother's marriage.

This was a sound argument, and Henry seemed to
admit the force of it. But he said that neither Pope
nor princes had a right to interfere with the laws and
institutions of England. Secular judges were perfectly
well able to deal with matrimonial causes. The Princess
Elizabeth was next in succession till a son was born to
him. That son he soon hoped to have. In short, he
declined to allow Chapuys to make a speech in the
House of Lords ; so Chapuys dropped the subject,
and interceded for permission to the Princess Mary
to reside with her mother. He said frankly that, if
harm came to her while in the charge of her present
governess, the world would not be satisfied. Of course
he knew that for all the gold in the world the King
would not injure his daughter; but, even if she died of
an ordinary illness, suspicions would be entertained of
foul play. With real courage Chapuys reminded Henry
that the knights who killed Becket had been encouraged
by the knowledge that the King was displeased with
him. The enemies of the Princess, perceiving that she
was out of favour, and aware of the hatred [1] felt for her

---

[1] *Haine novercule.*

by the Lady Anne, might be similarly tempted to make away with her while she was in Mrs. Shelton's charge.

If Chapuys really used this language (and the account of it is his own), Henry VIII. was more forbearing than history has represented him. He turned the subject, and complained, as Norfolk had done, of the Emperor's ingratitude. Chapuys said he had nothing to fear from the Emperor, unless he gave occasion for it. He smiled sardonically, and replied that, if he had been vindictive, there had been occasions when he could have revenged himself. It was enough, however, if the world knew how injured he had been. He then closed the conversation, dismissed his visitor, and told him he must be satisfied with the patience with which he had been heard.[1]

The Bill for the settlement of the crown was thus discussed without Chapuys's assistance. The terms of it and the reasons for it are familiar to all readers of English history. The King's efforts to obtain an heir male had, so far, only complicated an already dangerous problem. Though the marriage with Catherine had been set aside in an English court, the right of such a court to pronounce upon it was not yet familiar to the nation generally. The Pope had given an opposite sentence ; many of the peers and commons, the Duke of Norfolk among them, though reconciled to the divorce, had not yet made up their minds to schism [2] ;

---

[1] Chapuys to Charles V., Feb. 26, 1534. Abridged. — *Spanish Calendar*, vol. v. p. 59, &c.

[2] Chapuys to Charles V., March 7, 1534.—*Ibid.* p. 73.

and Mary had still many friends who were otherwise
loyal to her father.   But, after the experience of the last
century, Englishmen of all persuasions were frightened
at the prospect of a disputed succession, which only a
peremptory Act of Parliament could effectively dispose
of.   The Bill, therefore, passed at last with little opposition.   Cranmer's judgment was confirmed as against
the Pope's.   The marriage with Catherine was declared
null, the marriage with Anne valid, and Anne's children
the lawful heirs of the crown.   The Act alone was not
enough.   The disclosures brought to light in the affair
of the Nun of Kent, the disaffection then revealed, and
the rank of the persons implicated in it, necessitated
further precautions.   Any doubt which might have
existed on the extent and character of the conspiracy
is removed for ever by the Spanish Ambassador's letters.
The Pope was threatening to absolve English subjects
from their allegiance : how far he might be able to
influence their minds had as yet to be seen ; a Commission, therefore, was appointed to require and receive
the oaths of all persons whom there was reason to
suspect, that they would maintain the succession as
determined in the Act.

The sentence from Rome had not arrived when the
Bill became law, and no action was taken upon it till
the terms in which Clement had spoken were specifically
known.   Catherine, however, seemed to think that the
further she could provoke Henry to harsh measures,
the nearer would be her own deliverance.   She had
always persuaded herself that judgment once given at

Rome for her, the King would yield. The Act of Succession was thus specially galling, and with the same violent unwisdom which she had shown from the first, and against the direct advice of Chapuys, she had decided that the time was come for Mary ' to show ' her teeth to the King.' [1]

It was not for her to expose her daughter to perils which she professed to believe were threatening the lives of both of them. But Mary obeyed her but too well. While the Succession Bill was before the two Houses, Anne, probably at Henry's instance, went to Hatfield to invite her to receive her as Queen, promising, if she complied, that she should be treated better than she had ever been. Mary's answer was that she knew no Queen but her mother; if the King's mistress, so she designated Anne, would intercede with her father for her, she would be grateful. The Lady, Chapuys heard, had said in a rage that she would put down that proud Spanish blood and do her worst with her. Nor was this all. The determined girl refused to be included in Elizabeth's household, or pay her the respect attaching to her birth. Elizabeth soon after being removed from Hatfield to the More, Mary declined to go with her, and obliged the gentlemen in attendance to place her by force in Mrs. Shelton's litter. The Ambassador felt the folly of such ineffectual resistance. Never, he said, would he have advised her to run such a risk of exasperating the King, while the Lady Anne was never ceasing day or night to injure her. His own advice

---

[1] Chapuys to Charles V., March 30.—*Spanish Calendar*, vol. v. p. 96.

had been that when violence was threatened she should yield; but he had been overruled by Catherine.[1]

Chapuys's intercourse with the Court was now restricted. He was received when he applied for a formal interview; but for his information on what was passing there, he was left to secret friends or to his diplomatic colleagues. He asked the French Ambassador how the King took the Pope's sentence. The Ambassador said the King did not care in the least, which Chapuys was unable to believe. The action of the Parliament alarmed and shocked him. Among the hardest blows was the taking from the Bishops the powers of punishing heretics—a violation, as it appeared to him, of common right and the constitution of the realm. The sharp treatment of Bishop Nixe he regarded as an outrage and a crime. The Easter preachers were ordered to denounce the Pope in their sermons. Chapuys shuddered at their language. 'They surpassed them-'selves in the abominations which they uttered.' Worse than sermons followed. On the arrival of the 'sentence,' the Commission began its work in requiring the oath to the Succession Act. Those whose names had been compromised in the revelation of the Nun were naturally the first to be put to the test. Fisher, who had been found guilty of misprision of treason, had so far been left unpunished. It is uncertain whether the Government was aware of his communications with Chapuys, but enough was known to justify suspicion. The oath was offered him. He refused to take it, and he was

---

[1] Chapuys to Charles V., 1534.—*Spanish Calendar*, vol. v. p. 96.

committed to the Tower in earnest. He had been
sentenced to imprisonment before, but had been so far
left at liberty. Sir Thomas More might have been let
alone, for there was no fear that he would lend himself
to active treason. He too, however, was required to
swear, and declined, and followed Fisher to the same
place. The Pope had declared war against the King,
and his adherents had become the King's enemies.
Chapuys himself was suspected. His encouragement
of disaffection could not have been wholly concealed.
He believed that his despatches had been opened in
Calais, and that Cromwell had read them. There
had been a Scotch war. As the Emperor was disinclined
to stir, Chapuys had looked on James as a possibly
useful instrument in disturbing Henry's peace. A
Scottish Commission was in London to arrange a
treaty, 'as they had found England too strong for
'them alone.' The Ambassador, more eager than ever,
tried his best to dissuade the Chief Commissioner
from agreeing to terms, pointing out the condition of
the kingdom and the advantage to Scotland in joining
in an attack on the King. The Scotchman listened, and
promised to be secret. Chapuys assured him of the
Emperor's gratitude,[1] and, though the treaty was concluded, he consoled the Ambassador by saying 'that
'the peace would not prevent his master from waging
'war on the English. Pleas in plenty could easily be
'found.'[2]

---

[1] Chapuys to Charles V., April 22.—*Spanish Calendar*, vol. v.
pp. 126, 127.　　　　[2] *Ibid.* May 14, p. 151.

Ireland was a yet more promising field of operations. On the first rumour of the divorce the Earl of Desmond had offered his services to the Emperor. Chapuys discovered a more promising champion of the Church in Lord Thomas Fitzgerald, whom he described as 'a 'youth of high promise.' If the Pope would send the censures to Dublin, he undertook that Lord Thomas would publish them, and would be found a useful friend.

Again, in spite of refusal, he urged the Emperor to take action himself. Harm, he said, would befall the Queen and Princess, if there was longer delay; Mrs. Shelton had told Mary that she would lose her head if she persisted in disobedience; the people loved them well, but were afraid to move without support. The Lutherans were increasing, and would soon be dangerously strong. The present was the time to act. The King thought he could hold the recusants down by obliging them to swear to his statute ; but if the chance was allowed, they would show their real minds.[1]

One difficulty remained in the way of action. The Pope, though he had given judgment, had not yet called in the secular arm which was supposed to be necessary as a preliminary, and all parties, save Catherine and her passionate advisers, were unwilling that a step should be taken from which there would be no returning. The Emperor did not wish it. Francis, irritated at the refusal to listen to Du Bellay, told the Pope that he was

---

[1] Chapuys to Charles V., April 22.—*Spanish Calendar*, vol. v. pp. 125-31.

throwing England away. The Pope, wrote the Cardinal of Jaen to Secretary Covos, is restive. If we push him too hard, he may go over to the enemy.[1] Charles ordered Cifuentes to keep strictly to his instructions. The evident hesitation amused and encouraged the English Cabinet. 'Which Pope do you mean?' said the Duke of Norfolk to the Scotch Ambassador, who had spoken of Clement as an arbiter on some point in dispute, 'the Pope of Rome or the Pope of Lambeth?' Henry, finding Francis had not wholly deserted him, 'praised God' at a public dinner for having given him so good a brother in the King of France.

Under these circumstances, the Catholic party in England were alarmed and perplexed. Catherine had been undeceived at last in her expectation that the King would submit when the Pope had spoken. She informed Chapuys that she now *saw it was necessary to use stronger remedies*. What these remedies should be Chapuys said she dared not write, lest her letters should be intercepted. She was aware, too, that the Emperor knew best what should be done. Something must be tried, however, and speedily; for the King was acting vigorously, and to wait would be to be lost. A startling difference of opinion also was beginning to show itself even among the Queen's friends. Some might turn round, Chapuys said, as they feared the Emperor, in *helping her, would set up again the Pope's authority, which they called tyrannical.* It was the alarm at

---

[2] Chapuys to Charles V., May 21, 1534.—*Spanish Calendar*, vol. v p. 167.

this which enabled the King to hold his subjects together.[1]

Though Mary had 'shown her teeth' at her mother's bidding, she had not provoked her father to further severities. He asked Mrs. Shelton if her pride was subdued. Mrs. Shelton saying there were no signs of it, he ordered that she should be more kindly treated; and he sent her a message that, if she was obedient, he would find some royal marriage for her. She answered that God had not so blinded her that she should confess that her father and mother had lived in adultery. The words, perhaps, lost nothing in the repeating; but the King said, and said rightly, that it was her mother's influence. Catherine had persuaded her that his kindness was treachery, and that there was a purpose to poison her.[2]

A serious question, however, had risen about the Statute of Succession. The oath had been universally taken by every one to whom it had been offered save More and Fisher. The reason for demanding it was the notorious intention of the Catholic party to take arms in Catherine's and Mary's interests. Were others to be sworn, and were the two ladies chiefly concerned to be exempted? Catherine, in ceasing to be queen, might be held to have recovered her rights as a foreigner. But she had remained in England by her own wish, and at the desire of the Emperor, to assist in fighting out the battle. Mary was undoubtedly a subject,

---

[1] Chapuys to Charles V., May 14, 1534.—*Spanish Calendar*, vol. v. pp. 153, 154.   [2] *Ibid.*

and Catherine and she had both intimated that if the
oath was demanded of them they would not take it.
The Peers and Bishops were called together to consider
the matter, and, as Catherine was a Spanish Princess,
Chapuys was invited to attend.

The council-room was thronged. The Ambassador
was introduced, and a copy of the statute was placed
before him. He was informed that English subjects
generally had voluntarily sworn to obey it. Two
ladies only, Madam Catherine and Madam Mary, had
declined, and the pains and penalties were pointed out
to him which they might incur if they persisted.

Chapuys had been refused an opportunity of speaking his opinion in Parliament. It was now sponta-
neously offered him. He might, if he had pleased,
have denounced the hardship of compelling the Queen
and her daughter to assent personally to a statute
which took their rights from them. The preamble
declared the King's marriage with Catherine to have
been invalid, and in swearing to the Act of Succession
she would be abandoning her entire plea. There was
no intention, however, of forcing the oath upon the
mother. Mary was the person aimed at; and Mary
might have been spared also, if she had not ' shown her
' teeth ' so plainly. Chapuys, however, spoke out boldly
on the whole question. The King, he said, could not
deprive the Princess of her place as heir to the crown,
nor was the English Parliament competent to decide as
to the validity of a marriage. The preamble of the
statute was a lie. He would have proved it had he been

permitted to speak there. People had sworn because
they were afraid, and did not wish to be martyrs; and
the oath being imposed by force, they knew that it could
be no more binding than the oaths which he had lately
taken to the Pope had bound the Archbishop of Canterbury. For a general answer, he produced the Pope's
sentence. The obstinacy which they complained of, he
said, was in them, and not in the ladies. He could not
persuade the ladies to swear; if he could, he would not,
unless under orders from the Emperor; and he warned
the Council that if they tried further violence they must
be prepared to find the Emperor and Ferdinand their
open enemies; the Emperor regarded the Queen as his
mother, and the Princess as his sister; and, though he
allowed that he was speaking without instructions, he
intimated distinctly that the Emperor would not fail to
protect them, and protect the cause of the Church, which
had been intertwined with theirs.

Chapuys was bold, bolder perhaps than the Council
had expected. The Bishop of Durham rose after a
short pause. He had been Catherine's advocate, and, as
Chapuys said, was one of the most learned and honest
prelates in the realm. But he, too, had come to see that
the cause now at issue was the independence of England.
He said that the statute had been well considered. It
had been passed for the quiet of the realm, and must
be obeyed. On Chapuys rejoining that the quiet of the
realm required the King's return to his wife, Tunstall
mentioned the promises which had been made at the
beginning of the suit, and produced the decretal which

the Pope had given at Orvieto, declaring the marriage
with Catherine invalid.   Chapuys, in his answer,
admitted, unconsciously, the justice of the English plea.
He said the decretal had been issued when the Pope
had just escaped from St. Angelo, and was angry and
exasperated against the Emperor.   As to other promises,
he might or might not have made them.   If he said he
would give judgment in the King's favour, he might
have meant merely such a judgment as would be good
for the King; or perhaps he was doing as criminal judges
often did—holding out hopes to prisoners to tempt
confessions from them.   Such practices were legitimate
and laudable.

The English argument was that a judge such as
Chapuys described was not to be trusted with English
suits.   Henry himself could not have put the case more
effectively.   The Bishop of London spoke, and the
Archbishop of York, and then Sampson (the Dean of
the Chapel Royal), who affirmed bluntly that the Pope
had no inherent rights over England.   Man had given
him his authority, and man might take it from him.
Chapuys replied that the King had found it established
when he came to the throne, and had himself recognised
it in referring his cause to the Pope.   Cranmer was
present, but took no direct part.   He brought out,
however, the true issue, by suggesting, through Tunstall, that the Pope had incapacitated himself by submitting to be controlled by the Emperor.   This was
the point of the matter.   To allow an English suit to
be decided by Charles V. was to make England a vassal

state of the Empire. To this Chapuys had no valid
answer, for none could be given; and he discreetly
turned the argument by reflecting on the unfitness of
Cranmer also.

So far the laymen on the Council had left the
discussion to the Bishops, and the Ambassador thought
that he had the best of it. The Duke of Norfolk, he
imagined, thought so too; for the Duke rose after the
taunts at the Archbishop. The King's second marriage,
he said, was a *fait accompli*, and to argue further over
it was loss of time. They had passed their statute, and
he, for one, would maintain it to the last drop of his
blood. To refuse obedience was high treason; and, the
fact being so, the ladies must submit to the law. The
King himself could not disobey an Act which concerned
the tranquillity of the realm.

Chapuys would not yield. He said their laws were
like the laws of Mahomet—laws of the sword—being so
far worse, that Mahomet did not make his subjects swear
to them. Not with entire honesty—for he knew now
that Catherine had consented to the use of force—he
added, that they could have small confidence in their
own strength if they were afraid of two poor weak
women, who had neither means nor will to trouble
them.

The Council said that they would report to the
King, and so the conversation ended. Chapuys spoke
afterwards privately to Cromwell. He renewed his
warning that, if violence was used, there would be real
danger. Cromwell said he would do his best. But

there was a general fear that something harsh would
be tried at the instigation of the 'accursed concubine.'
Probably the question would be submitted to Parliament, or as some thought the Queen and Princess would
be sent to the Tower.[1] Conceiving extremities to be
close, Chapuys asked the Scotch Ambassador whether,
if a mandate came from the Pope against England, the
Scots would obey it. Certainly they would obey it,
was the answer, though they might pretend to regret
the necessity.

Violence such as Chapuys anticipated was not in
contemplation. The opinion of Europe would have
been outraged, if there had been no more genuine
reason for moderation. An appeal was tried on Catherine
herself. The Archbishop of York and the Bishop of
Durham, both of whom had been her friends, went down
to her to explain the nature of the statute and persuade
her to obedience. Two accounts remain of the interview
—that of the Bishops, and another supplied to Chapuys
by the Queen's friends. The Bishops said that she was
in great choler and agony, interrupted them with violent
speeches, declared that she was the King's lawful wife,
that between her and Prince Arthur there had been
never more than a formal connection. The Pope had
declared for her. The Archbishop of Canterbury was a
shadow. The Acts of Parliament did not concern her.[2]

---

[1] Chapuys to Charles V., May
19, 1534.—*Spanish Calendar*, vol.
v. pp. 155-66.

[2] Lee and Tunstall to Henry

VIII., May 21, 1534.—*Calendar
Foreign and Domestic*, vol. vii. p.
270.

Chapuys's story is not very different, though two elderly prelates, once her staunch supporters, could hardly have been as brutal as he describes. After various rough speeches, he said that the Bishops not only referred to the penalties of the statute (they themselves admitted this), but told her that if she persisted she might be put to death. She had answered that if any of them had a warrant to execute her they might do it at once. She begged only that the ceremony should be public, in the face of the people, and that she might not be murdered in her room.[1]

The mission had been rather to advise than to exact, and special demands were rather made on Catherine's side than the King's. Not only she would not swear herself to the statute, but she insisted that her household should be exempted also. She required a confessor, chaplains, physician, men-servants, as many women as the King would allow, and they were to take no oath save to the King and to her. Henry made less difficulty than might have been looked for—less than he would have been entitled to make had he known to what purpose these attendants would be used. The oath was for his native subjects; it was not exacted from herself, or by implication from her confessor, who was a Spaniard, or from her foreign servants.[2] If she would be reason-

---

[1] Chapuys to Charles V., May 29, 1534.—*Spanish Calendar*, vol. v. p. 169.

[2] Thus much was certainly meant by the King's words: 'He 'could not allow any of his native 'subjects to refuse to take the 'oath.'—*Calendar, Foreign and Domestic*, vol. vii. p. 272.

able he said that some of her requests might be granted. She might order her household as she pleased, if they would swear fidelity to him, and to herself as Princess Dowager. But he could not allow them to be sworn to her as Queen.

Chapuys's business was to make the worst of the story to the Emperor. The Court was at Richmond. Chapuys went thither, presented a complaint to the Council, and demanded an interview with the King. Henry would not see him, but sent him a message that he would inquire into what had passed, and would send him an answer. Chapuys, who had been for two years urging war in vain, exaggerated the new injuries. Others, and perhaps he himself, really believed the Queen's life to be in danger. 'Every one,' he wrote, after describing what had taken place, 'fears that mischief will now befall her; the concubine has said she will never rest till she is put out of the way. It is 'monstrous and almost incredible, yet such is the King's 'obstinacy, and the wickedness of this accursed woman, 'that everything may be apprehended.' [1] Anne, it is likely, was really dangerous. The King, so far as can be outwardly traced, was making the best of an unpleasant situation. The Council promised Chapuys that his remonstrances should be attended to. The Queen was left to herself, with no more petty persecutions, to manage her household in her own way. They might swear or not swear as pleased themselves and

---

[1] *Spanish Calendar*, vol. v. p. 172.

her; and with passionate loyalty they remained devoted to her service, assisting her in the conduct of a correspondence which every day became more dangerous.

The European sky meanwhile was blackening with coming storms. Francis had not forgotten Pavia, and as little could allow England to be conquered by Charles as Charles could allow France to be bribed by the promise of Calais. His agents continued busy at Rome keeping a hand on the Pope; a fresh interview was proposed between the French King and Henry, who was to meet him at Calais again in the summer; and an aggressive Anglo-French alliance was a possibility which the Emperor had still to fear. He had small confidence in the representations of Chapuys, and had brought himself to hope that by smooth measures Henry might still be recovered. A joint embassy might be sent to England from himself and the Pope to remonstrate on the schism. If nothing else came of it, their own position would be set right before the world and in the eyes of English opinion. Clement, however, now made difficulties, and had no desire to help Charles out of his embarrassments. Charles had forced a judgment out of him without promising to execute it. Charles might now realise the inconvenience of having driven him on against his own inclination. Cifuentes had again received instructions to delay the issue of the Brief of Execution, or the calling in the secular arm. The Pope felt that he had been made use of and had been cheated, and was naturally resentful. Cifuentes made his proposal. Clement, 'with the placid manner

'which he generally showed when a subject was dis-
'agreeable to him,' 'said that the embassy might go if
'the Emperor wished. . . It would not be of the slightest
'use . . . but it might do no harm. He must, of course,
'however, first consult the King of France.' Cifuentes
not liking the mention of France, the Pope went on
maliciously to say that, if he had not gone to Marseilles,
France would certainly have broken with the Church,
as England had done, and would have set up a patriarchate of its own. Indeed he was afraid it might yet
come to that. The King of France had told him how
he had been pressed to consent, and had made a merit
of refusing. Cifuentes could but remark on the singular
character of the King of France's religious convictions.[1]

The embassy was not sent to England, and the Pope
kept back his invocation of the secular arm till a prince
could be found who would act. No one would be the
first to move, and the meeting of the two kings at Calais
was indefinitely postponed. Francis complained of
Henry's arbitrary manner, 'speaking to me at times as
'if I were his subject.' The explanation given to the
world of the abandonment of the interview was that
Henry found it inconvenient to leave the realm. A
letter of Chapuys explains where the special inconvenience lay. The Lady Anne would be Regent in his
absence, and could not be trusted in her present humour.
'I have received word from a trustworthy source,' he
wrote on the 23rd of June to the Emperor, 'that the

---

[1] Cifuentes to Charles V. June 6, 1534.—*Spanish Calendar*, vol.
v. pp. 174 et seq.

'concubine has said more than once, and with great
'assurance, that the moment the King crosses the
'Channel to the interview, and she is left Regent, she
'will put the Princess to death by sword or otherwise.
'Her brother, Lord Rochford, telling her she would
'offend the King, she answered she cared not if she did.
'She would do it if she was burnt or flayed alive after-
'wards. The Princess knows her danger, but it gives
'her no concern. She puts her trust in God.'

Imperfect credit must be given to stories set current
by malicious credulity. But the existence of such stories
shows the reputation which Anne had earned for herself,
and which in part she deserves. Chapuys reiterated his
warnings.

'Pardon my importunity,' he continued, 'but, unless
'your Majesty looks promptly to it, things will be past
'remedy. Lutheranism spreads fast, and the King
'calculates that it will make the people stand by him
'and will gain the Germans. So long as danger is not
'feared from without, Parliament will agree to all that
'he wishes. Were your Majesty even to overlook all
'that he has done, he would persist in the same way.
'Good Catholics are of opinion that the readiest way to
'bridle France and Germany is to begin in England.
'It can be done with ease. The people only wait for
'your Majesty to give the signal.' [1]

The inaction of the Emperor was incomprehensible
to Catherine's friends. To herself it was distracting.

---

[1] Chapuys to Charles V., June 23, 1534. Abridged.—*Spanish Calendar*, vol. v. pp. 198-9.

She had fed upon the hope that when the Pope had given judgment her trial would be at an end; that the voice of Catholic Europe would compel the King to submit. The Roman lightning had flashed, but the thunderbolt had not fallen. The English laity, long waiting in suspense, had begun to think, as Chapuys feared they would, that the Pope was the shadow, and Cranmer the substance. Cut off from the world, she thought she was forsaken, or that the Emperor's care for her would not carry him to the point of interference. If no voice was raised in her favour in her own Spain, the Spanish Ambassador might at least show that her countrymen had not forgotten her. She sent pressing messages to Chapuys, begging him to visit her; and Chapuys, impatient himself of his master's hesitating policy, resolved to go. He applied for permission to the Council. It was refused. But the Council could not forbid his making a summer pilgrimage to our Lady of Walsingham, and the road lay near Kimbolton. He wrote to Cromwell that, leave or no leave, he was going into Norfolk, and meant to call there. The porters might refuse him entrance if they pleased. He gave him fair notice. It should not be said that he had acted underhand.

It was the middle of July. Making as much display as possible, with a retinue of sixty horses and accompanied by a party of Spaniards resident in London, the Ambassador rode ostentatiously through the City, and started on the great North Road. Spending a night on the way, he arrived on the second evening within

a few miles of Catherine's residence. At this point he
was overtaken by two gentlemen of the household, with
an intimation that he would not be admitted. He
demanded to see their orders, and, the orders not being
produced, he said that, being so near the end of his
journey, he did not mean to turn back. He would have
persisted, but a message came to him from the Queen
herself, or from one of her people, to say that she could
not receive him; he could proceed to Walsingham if
he pleased, but he must not approach within bowshot
of the Castle. Some peremptory command must have
reached her. A second secret message followed, that,
although she had not dared to say so, she was grateful
for his visit; and, though he must not come on himself,
a party of his suite might show themselves before the
gates.

Thus the next morning, under the bright July sky,
a picturesque Spanish cavalcade was seen parading
under the windows of Kimbolton, 'to the great con-
'solation of the ladies of the household, who spoke to
'them from the battlements; and with astonishment
'and joy among the peasantry, as if the Messiah had
'actually come.' The Walsingham pilgrimage was
abandoned, lest it should be thought to have been the
real object of the journey; and Chapuys, with polite
irony, sent the King word that he had relinquished it
in deference to his Majesty's wishes. He returned to
London by another road, to make a wider impression
upon the people.

'The Emperor,' he said in relating his expedition,

'would now see how matters stood. The Queen might
'be almost called the King's prisoner. The house,' he
said, 'was well kept and well found, though there were
'complaints of shortness of provisions. She had five
'or six servants, and as many ladies-in-waiting, besides
'the men whom she looked on as her guards.' [1]

---

[1] Chapuys to Charles V., July 27, 1534.—*Spanish Calendar* vol.
v. pp. 219-20.

he had no such ambition. Then, speaking in Latin, because part of the Council did not understand French, he dwelt on the old friendship between the Emperor and the King. He said that the part which the Emperor had taken about the divorce was as much for the sake of the King and the realm as for the sake of the Queen, although the Queen and Princess were as a mother and a sister to him. He went through the case; he said their statutes were void in themselves, and, even if valid, could not be retrospective. The Archbishop had been just sworn to the Pope. He had broken his oath, and was under excommunication,[1] and was, therefore, disqualified to act. He reminded the Council of the Wars of the Roses, and told them they were sharpening the thorns for fresh struggles.

Doctor Foxe (the King's Almoner, afterwards bishop) replied that the King could not live with his brother's wife without sin, and had therefore left her. It was a fact accomplished, and no longer to be argued. To challenge the action of the Archbishop was to challenge the law of the land, and was not to be allowed. The Pope had no authority in England, spiritual or temporal. The introduction of bulls or briefs from Rome was unlawful, and could not be sheltered behind immunities of ambassadors. Chapuys was the representative of the Emperor, not of the Pope, and Foxe cautioned him against creating disturbances in the realm.

To this Chapuys quietly answered that he would

---

[1] Cranmer had sworn the usual oath, but with a reservation that his first duty was to his Sovereign and the laws of his country.

K

do his duty, let the consequences be what they might.
Being again warned, he said he would wait for two or
three days, within which he looked for a satisfactory
reply from the King.

In leaving the council-room, he said, in imperious
fashion, as if he were addressing a set of criminals, that
reports were current about the Emperor which he desired
to notice. Some declared that he had consented to the
marriage with the Lady Anne, others that he meant
to make war. Both allegations alike were false and
malicious. So far from wishing to injure England, the
Emperor wished to help and support it, and could not
believe that he would ever be obliged to act otherwise;
and as to consenting to the divorce, if the Pope declared
for it he would submit to the Pope's judgment; otherwise the world would not turn him from the path which
he meant to follow. He was acting as the King's best
friend, as the King would acknowledge if he could forget
his passion for the Lady and consider seriously his relations with the Emperor. He begged the Council, therefore, to prevent such rumours from being circulated if
they did not wish Chapuys to contradict them himself.

The Ambassador was keeping within the truth when
he said that Charles was not meditating war. Chapuys's
instructions when first sent to England had been not to
make matters worse than they were, not to threaten war
nor to imply in any way that there was danger of war.[1]
He had himself, however, insisted that there was no

[1] Chapuys to Charles V., May 26, 1533.—*Spanish Calendar*, vol. iv.
part 2, p. 687.

alternative. He had encouraged Catherine's friends with hope of eventual help, and continued to convey to the Emperor their passionate wish that ' his Majesty's ' hand would soon reach England,' before ' the accursed ' woman ' made an end of the Queen and of them—to tell him that, were his forces once on land, they might raise as many men as they pleased, and the London citizens would stand by, ' keep the enlistment money,' and wait to see which party won. As long, however, as his master was undecided, he would not, he said, take measures which would do no good, and only lead to inconvenience. He had merely given the Council ' a ' piece of his mind,' and had said what no one else would say, for fear of Lady Anne.

The answer to his letter which he expected from the King did not arrive, but instead of it an invitation to dinner from the Duke of Norfolk, which he refused lest his consent should be misconstrued. Ultimately, however, Cromwell came to him with the King's permission. Cromwell, strange to say, had been a strong advocate for the Imperial alliance, in opposition to the French, and with Cromwell the Ambassador's relations were more easy than with the Duke. Their conversations were intimate and confidential. Chapuys professed a hope that the King's affection for the Lady would pass off, and promised, for himself, to pour no more oil on the fire till he received fresh orders. If they wished for peace, however, he said they must be careful of their behaviour to the Queen, and he complained of the removal of her arms from her barge in the river. Such petty acts of persecution ought to be avoided. The removal of the arms was the work of some too zealous friend of Anne. Cromwell had not heard of it, and said that the King would be greatly displeased. Meanwhile he trusted that Spanish notions of honour would not interfere with a friendship so useful to both countries. If it came to war, England would not be found an easy conquest. He defended the King's action. The Pope would not do him justice, so he had slapped the Pope in the face. No doubt he had been influenced by love for the Lady. Neither the King himself, nor all the preachers in the world, would convince him that love had nothing to do with it. But the King was well read in the canon law, and if his conscience was satisfied it was enough.

As Cromwell was so frank, Chapuys asked him when and where the marriage with Anne had been concluded. Cromwell either would not or could not tell him, saying merely that Norfolk had not been present at the ceremony, but others of the Council had, and there was no doubt that it had really taken place.

So matters stood in England, every one waiting to learn how the Emperor would act. Anne Boleyn was duly crowned at Whitsuntide—a splendid official pageant compensating for the secrecy of her marriage. The streets were thronged with curious spectators, but there was no enthusiasm. The procession was like a funeral. The Pope was about to meet the King of France at Nice. Norfolk was commissioned to attend the interview, and, as Henry still hoped that the Duke

would bring back an acquiescence in his wishes from
Clement, Chapuys saw him before his departure. The
Duke said the peace of the world now depended on
the Emperor. He repeated that his niece's marriage
had been no work of his. Her father and he had
always been against it, and, but for them, it would have
happened a year before. She had been furious with
both of them. She was now *enceinte,* and had told
her father and himself and Suffolk that she was in
better plight than they wished her to be. To attempt
to persuade the King to take Catherine back either by
threat or argument would be labour thrown away,
such ' were his scruples of conscience and his despair
' of having male succession by her.'

At Cromwell's intercession, the Bishop of Rochester
was now released from confinement, and politics were
quiet till the effect was seen of the Nice conference.
Anxious consultations were held at Rome before the
Pope set out. The Cardinals met in consistory. Henry's
belief had been that Francis was prepared to stand by
him to the uttermost, and would carry Clement with
him. He was now to find either that he had been
misled or had wilfully deceived himself. Cardinal
Tournon, who was supposed to have carried an ulti-
matum from the meeting at Calais, had required the
Pope to suspend the process against Henry:[1] if the
Pope replied that the offence was too great, and that
he must deprive him, Francis did not say that he

---

[1] Chapuys to Charles V., May 29, 1533.—*Spanish Calendar,* vol.
iv. part 2, p. 699.

would risk excommunication himself by taking an open part, but had directed the Cardinal to urge the removal of the suit to a neutral place, as had been often proposed. The Pope told the Count de Cifuentes that this suggestion had been already discussed with the Emperor, and that the Emperor had not entirely disapproved;[1] but the cunning and treacherous Clement had formed a plan of his own by which he thought he could save England and punish Henry. Francis being less firm than he had feared, he thought that, by working on French ambition, he could detach Francis completely from his English ally. The French were known to be eager to recover Calais. What if Calais could be offered them as a bait? They might turn their coats as they had so often done before.[2] Cunning and weakness generally go together. It was an ingenious proposal and throws a new light on Clement's character. Nothing came of it, for the Emperor, with a view to the safety of Flanders and the eventual recovery of the English alliance, declined to sanction a change of ownership on his own frontier. Finding no encouragement, Clement relapsed into his usual attitude. The Imperialists continued to press for the delivery of sentence before the Pope should leave Rome. The Pope continued to insist on knowing the Emperor's intentions.

A Spanish lawyer, Rodrigo Davalos, had been sent

---

[1] Cifuentes to Charles V., May 29, 1533.—*Spanish Calendar* vol. iv. part 2, p. 702

[2] The Cardinal of Jaen to Charles V., June 16, 1533.—*Ibid.* p. 709.

to Rome to dissuade the Pope from the Nice interview, and to quicken the action of the Rota.

'Queen Catherine's suit,' he said, 'had been carried ' on as if it were that of the poorest woman in the world. 'Since Cifuentes and he had been there the process had 'been pushed on, but the Advocates and Proctors had 'not received a real. Their hands required anointing 'to make them stick to their business. The Cardinals 'were at sixes and sevens, and refused to pull together, ' do what Davalos would.'[1]

Davalos, being a skilful manipulator and going the right way to work, pressed the process forward in the Rota without telling the Pope what he was doing, since Clement would have stopped it had he not been kept in ignorance. But, 'God helping, no excuse was left.' The forms were all concluded, and nothing remained but to pass the long-talked-of sentence. The Pope was so 'importuned' by the French and English Ambassadors to suspend it till after the meeting at Nice that Davalos could not say whether he would get it after all; but he told the Pope that further hesitation would be regarded by the Emperor as an outrage, and would raise suspicion through the whole world. The Pope promised, but where good-will was wanting trifles were obstacles. Davalos confessed that he had no faith in his promise. He feared the Pope must have issued some secret brief, which stood in his way.[2]

Clement, however, was driven on in spite of himself.

---

[1] Davalos to Charles V., June 30 and July 5, 1533.—*Spanish Cal-* *endar*, vol. iv. part 2, pp. 725-28.
[2] *Ibid.*

Judgment on the principal cause could not be wrung from him. Cardinal Salviati was of opinion that they would never give it till the Emperor would promise that it should be executed.[1] But a Brief *super Attentatis,* which was said to be an equivalent, Clement was required to sign, and did sign—a Brief on which Charles could act if occasion served, the Pope himself swearing great oaths that Henry had used him ill, and that he would bribe Francis to forsake him by the promise of Calais.

One more touch must be added to complete the comedy of distraction. A proposal of the Spanish Council to send a special embassy to London to remonstrate with the King had been definitely rejected by the Emperor. It was revived by Chapuys, with whom it had probably originated. He imagined that the most distinguished representatives of the Spanish nation might appear at the English Court and protest against the ill-usage of the daughter of Ferdinand and Isabella. If the King refused them satisfaction, they might demand to be heard in Parliament. The King would then be placed in the wrong before his own people. The nobles of Aragon and Castile would offer their persons and their property to maintain the Queen's right; and Chapuys said, '*Not a Spaniard would hesi-*'*tate if they were privately assured first that they would*'*not be taken at their word.*'[3]

[1] Davalos to Charles V., June 30 and July 5, 1533.—*Spanish Calendar,* vol. iv. part 2, p. 749.

[2] *Ibid.* p. 734.
[3] Chapuys to Charles V., June 28, 1533.—*Ibid.* pp. 718-20.

Leaving the Catholic Powers in confusion and uncertainty, we return to England. Catherine had rejected every proposal which had been made to her. There could not be two queens in the same country, and, after Anne's coronation, a deputation waited upon her to intimate that her style must be changed. She must now consent to be termed Princess Dowager, when an establishment would be provided for her as the widow of the King's brother. Her magnificent refusal is well known to history. Cromwell spoke with unbounded admiration of it. Yet it was inconvenient, and increased the difficulty of providing for her, since she declined to accept any grants which might be made to her under the new title, or to be attended by any person who did not treat her and address her as queen. It would have been better if she had required to be allowed to return to Castile; but both the Spanish Council and the Emperor had decided that she must remain in England. The Princess had been allowed to rejoin her. The mother and daughter had made short expeditions together, and had been received with so much enthusiasm that it was found necessary again to part them. Stories were current of insulting messages which Catherine had received from the Lady Anne, false probably, and meant only to create exasperation. The popular feeling was warmly in her favour. She was personally liked as much as Anne was hated; and the King himself was not spared. As a specimen of the license of language, 'a Mrs. 'Amadas, witch and prophetess, was indicted for having 'said that the Lady Anne should be burned, for she was

'a harlot. Master Norris [Sir Henry Norris, Equerry
'to Henry] was bawd between her and the King. The
'King had kept both the mother and the daughter, and
'Lord Wiltshire was bawd to his wife and to his two
'daughters.'[1] In July the news arrived from Rome
of the Brief *de Attentatis,* and with it the unpleasant
intelligence that Francis could not be depended on, and
that the hopes expected from the meeting at Nice would
not be realised. The disappointment was concealed
from Anne, for fear of endangering the expected child.
Norfolk, who had waited in Paris to proceed in the
French King's train, was ordered to return to England.
Henry was not afraid, but he was discovering that he
had nothing to rely upon but himself and the nation.
The terms on which France and the Empire stood
towards each other were so critical that he did not
expect the Emperor to quarrel with England if he
could help it. Chapuys seemed studiously to seek
Cromwell. Of Cromwell's fidelity to himself Henry
was too well assured to feel uneasy about their intimacy,
and therefore they met often and as freely exchanged
their thoughts. Chapuys found Cromwell 'a man of
'sense, well versed in affairs of State, and able to judge
'soundly,' with not too good an opinion of the Lady
Anne, who returned his dislike. Anne was French;
Cromwell was Imperialist beyond all the rest of the
Council.

'I told him,' wrote the Ambassador to Charles, after

---

[1] *Calendar, Foreign and Domestic,* vol. vi. p. 399.

one of these conversations, 'I often regretted your
'Majesty had not known him in Wolsey's time. He
'would have been a greater man than the Cardinal, and
'the King's affairs would have gone much better. He
'seemed pleased, so I continued. Now was the time
'for him to do his master better service than ever man
'did before. Sentence had been given in Rome against
'the King, and there was no further hope that your
'Majesty and the Pope would agree to the divorce.
'I presumed that the King being so reasonable,
'virtuous, and humane a prince, would not persist
'longer and blemish the many gifts which God had
'bestowed on him. I prayed him to move the King.
'He could do more with him than any other man.
'He was not in the Council when the accursed business
'was first mooted. The Queen trusted him, and, when
'reinstated, would not forget his service. Cromwell
'took what I said in good part. He assured me that
'all the Council desired your Majesty's friendship. He
'would do his best, and hoped that things would turn
'out well. If I can believe what he says, there is still
'a hope that the King may change. I will set the net
'again and try if I can catch him; but one cannot be
'too cautious. The King is disturbed by what has
'passed at Rome. He fears the Pope will seduce the
'French King from him.' [1]

Who was this Cromwell that had grown to such
importance ? Granvelle had asked. 'He is the son,'

---

[1] Chapuys to Charles V., Aug. 3, 1533.—*Spanish Calendar*, vol. iv.
part 2, pp. 759-60.

replied Chapuys, ' of a farrier in Chelsea, who is buried
' in the parish church there. His uncle, father of
' Richard Cromwell, was cook to the Archbishop of
' Canterbury. This Thomas Cromwell was wild in his
' youth, and had to leave the country. He went to
' Flanders and to Rome. Returning thence he married
' the daughter of a wool merchant, and worked at his
' father-in-law's business. After that he became a
' solicitor. Wolsey, finding him diligent and a man
' of ability for good or ill, took him into service and
' employed him in the suppression of religious houses.
' When Wolsey fell he behaved extremely well. The
' King took him into his secret Council. Now he is
' above everyone, except the Lady, and is supposed to
' have more credit than ever the Cardinal had. He is
' hospitable and liberal, speaks English well, and Latin,
' French, and Italian tolerably.' [1]

The intimacy increased. Cromwell, though Imperial in politics and no admirer of Anne Boleyn, was
notoriously Henry's chief adviser in the reform of the
clergy; but to this aspect of him Chapuys had no
objection. Neither the Ambassador nor Charles, nor
any secular statesman in Europe, was blind to the
enormities of Churchmen or disposed to lift a finger for
them, if reform did not take the shape of Lutheranism.
Charles himself had said that, if Henry had no objects
beyond the correction of the spiritualty, he would rather
aid than obstruct him. Between Chapuys and Cromwell

---

[1] Chapuys to Granvelle, Nov. 21, 1535.—*Calendar, Foreign and
Domestic*, vol. ix. p. 289.

there was thus common ground; and Cromwell's hint that the King might perhaps reconsider his position may not have been wholly groundless.

The action of the Rota, pressed through by Davalos, had taken Henry by surprise. He had not expected that the Pope would give a distinct judgment against him. He had been equally disappointed in the support which he expected from Francis. That he should now hesitate for an instant was natural and inevitable; but the irresolution, if real, did not last. Norfolk wrote to the King from Paris 'to care nothing for the Pope: 'there were men enough at his side in England to 'defend his right with the sword.' [1] Henry appealed to a General Council, when a council could be held which should be more than a Papal delegacy. The revenues of the English sees which were occupied by Campeggio and Ghinucci he sequestrated, as a sign of the abandonment of a detestable system.

His own mind, meanwhile, was fastened on the approaching confinement of Anne. With the birth of a male heir to the crown he knew that his difficulties would vanish. Nurses and doctors had assured him of a son, and the event was expected both by him and by others with passionate eagerness. A Prince of Wales would quiet the national uncertainty. It would be the answer of Heaven to Pope and Emperor, and a Divine sanction of his revolt. There is danger in interpreting Providence before the event. If the anticipation is

---

[1] Chapuys to Charles V., Aug. 23, 1533.—*Spanish Calendar*, vol. iv. part 2, p. 777.

disappointed, the weight of the sentence may be thrown into the opposing scale.

To the bitter 'mortification of the King and the 'Lady, to the reproach of physicians, astrologers, 'sorcerers, and sorceresses who affirmed that the child 'would be a male,' [1] to the delight of Chapuys and the perplexity of a large section of the English people who were waiting for Providence to speak, on the 7th of September the girl who was afterwards to be Queen Elizabeth was brought into the world.

This was the worst blow which Henry had received. He was less given to superstition than most of his subjects, but there had been too much of appeals to Heaven through the whole of the controversy. The need of a male heir had been paraded before Christendom as the ground of his action. He had already discovered that Anne was not what his blindness to her faults had allowed him to believe ; he was fond of the Princess Mary, and Anne had threatened to make a waiting-maid of her. The new Queen had made herself detested in the Court by her insolence ; there had been 'lover's quarrels,' [2] from which Catherine's friends had gathered hopes, and much must have passed behind the scenes of which no record survives. A lady of the bedchamber had heard Henry say he would 'rather beg 'from door to door than forsake her;' [3] on the other hand, Anne acknowledged afterwards that his love had

---

[1] Chapuys to Charles V. Sept. 10, 1533.—*Spanish Calendar*, vol. iv. part 2, p. 789.

[2] *Ibid.* p. 788.
[3] *Ibid.*, Nov. 3, 1533.—*Ibid.* p. 842.

not been returned, and she could hardly have failed to let him see it. Could she be the mother of a prince she was safe, but on this she might well think her security depended. All Henry's male children, except the Duke of Richmond, had died at the birth or in infancy; and words which she let fall to her sister-in-law, Lady Rochford, implied a suspicion that the fault was in the King.[1] It is not without significance that in the subsequent indictment of Sir Henry Norris it was alleged that on the 6th of October, 1533, less than a month after Anne's confinement, she solicited Norris to have criminal intercourse with her, and that on the 12th the act was committed. But to this subject I shall return hereafter.

Anyway, the King made the best of his misfortune. If the first adventure had failed, a second might be more successful. The unwelcome daughter was christened amidst general indifference, without either bonfires or rejoicings. She was proclaimed Princess, and the title was taken away from her sister Mary. Chapuys, after what Cromwell had said to him, trusted naturally that the King's mind would be affected by his disappointment. They met again. Chapuys urged that it would be easier to set things straight than at an

[1] The King's infirmities were not a secret. In 1533, upon Elizabeth's birth, a Señor de Gambaro, who was an intimate friend of the Duke of Norfolk, wrote at Rome for Cifuentes a curious account of the situation and prospects of things in England. Among other observations he says: 'The [expected] child 'will be weak, owing to his 'father's condition.'—Avisos de las cosas de Inglaterra dados por Sr. de Gambaro en Roma. *Calendar, Foreign and Domestic,* vol. vi. p. 683.

earlier stage. The King, being of a proud temper,
would have felt humiliated if he had been baffled. He
might now listen to reason. It was said of Englishmen
that when they had made a mistake they were more
ready to confess it than other people; and, so far from
losing in public esteem, he would only gain, if he now
admitted that he had been wrong. The Emperor would
send an embassy requesting him affectionately to take
Catherine back; his compliance would thus lose all
appearance of compulsion. The expectation was
reasonable. Cromwell, however, had to tell him in
earnest language that it could not be; and the Catholic
party in England, who had hoped, as Chapuys hoped,
and found themselves only further embittered by the
exclusion of Mary from the succession, became desperate
in turn. From this period their incipient treason developed into definite conspiracy, the leader among the
disaffected and the most influential from his reputed
piety and learning being Fisher, Bishop of Rochester,
whose subsequent punishment has been the text for so
many eloquent invectives. Writing on the 27th of
September to the Emperor, Chapuys says: 'The good
'Bishop of Rochester has sent to me to notify that the
'arms of the Pope against these obstinate men are
'softer than lead, and that your Majesty must set your
'hand to it, in which you will do a work as agreeable
'to God as a war against the Turk.'[1] This was not
all. The Bishop had gone on to advise a measure which

---

[1] *Calendar, Foreign and Domestic,* vol. vi. p. 486. *Spanish Calendar,*
vol. iv. part 2, p. 813.

would lead immediately and intentionally to a revival
of the Wars of the Roses. 'If matters come to a
' rupture, the Bishop said it would be well for your
' Majesty to attach to yourself the son of the Princess
' Mary's governess [the Countess of Salisbury, mother
' of Reginald Pole], daughter of the Duke of Clarence,
' to whom, according to the opinion of many, the king-
' dom would belong. He is now studying at Padua.
' On account of the pretensions which he and his
' brother would have to the crown, the Queen would
' like to bestow the Princess on him in marriage, and
' the Princess would not refuse. He and his brothers
' have many kinsmen and allies, of whose services your
' Majesty might make use and gain the greater part of
' the realm.'[1]

The Bishop of Rochester might plead a higher
allegiance as an excuse for conspiring to dethrone his
Sovereign. But those who play such desperate games
stake their lives upon the issue, and if they fail must
pay the forfeit. The Bishop was not the only person
who thus advised Chapuys. Rebellion and invasion
became the settled thought of the King's opponents,
and Catherine was expected to lend her countenance.
The Regent's Council at Brussels, bolder than the
Spanish, were for immediate war. A German force
might be thrown across the Channel. The Flemish
nobles might hesitate, but would allow ships to carry an
army to Scotland. The army might then march south ;

---

[1] *Calendar, Foreign and Domestic,* vol. vi. p. 486. *Spanish
Calendar,* vol. iv. part 2, p. 813.

Catherine would join it, and appear in the field.[1]
Catherine herself bade Chapuys charge the Pope in
her name to proceed to the execution of the sentence [2]
'in the most rigorous terms of justice possible;' the
King, she said, would then be brought to reason when
he felt the bit. She did not advocate violence in words,
though what she did advocate implied violence and made
it inevitable. Fisher was prepared for any extremity.
'The good and Holy Bishop of Rochester,' Chapuys
repeated, 'would like your Majesty to take active
'measures immediately, as I wrote in my last, which
'advice he has sent to me again lately to repeat.[3]
'Without this they fear disorder. The smallest force
'would suffice.'

Knowing Charles's unwillingness, the Ambassador
added a further incitement. Among the preachers, he
said, there was one who spread worse errors than
Luther. The Prelates all desired to have him punished,
but the Archbishop of Canterbury held him up, the
King would not listen to them; and, were it not that
he feared the people, would long since have professed
Lutheranism himself.[4]

---

[1] News from Flanders.—*Calendar Foreign and Domestic*, vol.
vi. p. 493.

[2] *I. e.* the calling in the secular arm, which had not been actually
done in the Brief *de Attentatis*.

[3] Chapuys to Charles V., Oct.
10, 1533.—*Calendar, Foreign and Domestic*, vol. vi. p. 511.

[4] *Ibid.*

CHAPTER XIV.

Interview between the Pope and Francis at Marseilles—Proposed
compromise—The divorce case to be heard at Cambray—The
Emperor consents—Catherine refuses—The story of the Nun
of Kent—Bishop Fisher in the Tower—Imminent breach with
the Papacy—Catherine and the Princess Mary—Separation of
the Princess from her mother—Catherine at Kimbolton—
Appeals to the Emperor—Encouragement of Lutheranism—
Last efforts at Rome—Final sentence delivered by the Pope—
The Pope's authority abolished in England.

THE Pope's last brief had been sufficiently definite
to enable the Emperor to act upon it if Henry
still disobeyed. English scruples, however, required a
judgment on the divorce itself before force was openly
tried. Clement went, as he had intended, to France
in October, and met the French King at Marseilles.
Norfolk, as has been said, was not allowed to be present;
but Gardiner and Bonner attended as inferior agents to
watch the proceedings. Cifuentes followed the Papal
Court for Charles, and the English Nuncio, who had
been at last recalled, was present also. The main
result of the interview was the marriage of the Duke
of Orleans to the Pope's niece, Catherine de' Medici, a
guarantee that Francis was not to follow England into

schism but was to remain Catholic. The engagements
with which he had tempted Henry into committing
himself were thus abandoned, and the honour which
had been saved at Pavia was touched, if it was not lost.
It had strength enough, however, to lead him still to
exert himself to bring Clement to reason. The bribe
of Calais was not tried upon him, having been emphatically negatived by the Emperor. The Chancellor
of France presented in Henry's name a formal complaint
of the Pope's conduct. It was insisted that when he
commissioned Campeggio to go to England, he had
formally promised not to revoke the cause to Rome,
and this promise he had violated. The Pope's answer
was curious. He admitted the promise, but he said it
was conditional on Queen Catherine's consent, *though
this clause was not inserted in the commission lest it
might suggest to her to complain.*[1] The answer was
allowed to pass. Other objections were similarly set
aside, and then the Cardinal de Tarbes, professing to
speak in Henry's name, proposed that the Pope should
appoint another commission to hear the cause at
Cambray, himself nominating the judges. If the Pope
would comply he was authorised to say that the King
would obey, and, pending the trial, would separate from
Anne and recall Catherine to the court. Cifuentes had
again urged the Pope to declare Henry deprived. The
Pope had refused on the ground that, unless the
Emperor would bind himself to execute the sentence

---

[1] Cifuentes to Charles V., Oct. 23, 1533.—*Calendar, Foreign and
Domestic,* vol. vi. p. 534.

in arms, the Holy See would lose reputation.[1] He had, therefore, a fair excuse for listening to the French suggestion. The Cardinals deliberated, and thought it ought to be accepted. If the King would really part with Anne, the cause might be even heard in England itself, and no better course could be thought of. The proposal was referred, through the Papal Nuncio, to the Emperor, and the Emperor wrote on the margin of the Nuncio's despatch to him that he could give no answer till he had communicated with Catherine, but that he would write and recommend her to follow the course pointed out by his Holiness.[2]

The Spanish party suspected a trick. They thought that there might be an appearance of compliance with the Pope's brief. Catherine might be allowed a room in the Palace till the cause was removed from Rome. It was all but gained in the Rota; if referred back in the manner proposed, it would be delayed by appeals and other expedients till it became interminable. Their alternative was instant excommunication. But the Pope had the same answer. How could he do that? He did not know that the Emperor would take up arms. Were he to issue the censures, and were no effect to follow, the Apostolic See would be discredited. De Tarbes was asked to produce his commission from Henry to make suggestions in his name. It was found when examined to be insufficient. Henry himself,

---

[1] Cifuentes to Charles V., Oct. 23, 1533.—*Calendar, Foreign and Domestic,* vol. vi. p. 534.

[2] The Papal Nuncio to Charles V., Oct. 22.—*Spanish Calendar,* vol. iv. part 2, p. 830.

when he learnt what had been done, 'changed colour, 'crushed the letter in his hands, and exclaimed that 'the King of France had betrayed him.'[1] But he had certainly made some concession or other. The time allowed in the last brief had run out. The French Cardinals did not relinquish their efforts. They demanded a suspension of six months, till Henry and Francis could meet again and arrange something which the Pope could accept. The Pope, false himself, suspected every one to be as false as he was. He suspected that a private arrangement was being made between Henry and the Emperor, and Cifuentes himself could not or would not relieve his misgivings. In the midst of the uncertainty a courier came in from England with an appeal *ad futurum Concilium*—when a council could be held that was above suspicion. The word 'council' always drove Clement distracted. He complained to Francis, and Francis, provoked at finding his efforts paralysed, said angrily that, were it not for his present need of the King of England's friendship lest others should forestall him there, he would play him a trick that he should remember. The suspension of the censures for an indefinite time was granted, however, after a debate in the Consistory. The English Council, when the proposal for the hearing of the cause at Cambray was submitted to them, hesitated over their answer. They told Chapuys that such a compromise as the Pope offered might once have been entertained, but nothing

---

[1] Chapuys to Charles V., Nov. 3, 1533.—*Spanish Calendar,* vol. iv. part 2, pp. 839-41.

now would induce the King to sacrifice the interests
of his new-born daughter; 'all the Ambassadors in
'the world would not move him, not even the Pope
'himself, if he came to visit him.'[1]

Nevertheless, so anxious were all parties now at the
last moment to find some conditions or other to prevent the Division of Christendom that the Cardinal de
Tarbes's proposition, or something like it, might have
been accepted. The Emperor, however, had made his
consent contingent on Catherine's acquiescence, and
Catherine herself refused—refused resolutely, absolutely,
and finally. Charles had written to her as he had
promised. Chapuys sent her down the letter with a
draft of the terms proposed, and he himself strongly
exhorted her to agree. He asked for a distinct 'Yes'
or 'No,' and Catherine answered 'No.' Her cause
should be heard in Rome, she said, and nowhere but in
Rome; the removal to Cambray meant only delay, and
from delay she had suffered long enough; should Anne
Boleyn have a son meanwhile, the King would be more
obstinate than ever. The Pope must be required to end
the cause himself and to end it quickly. The Emperor
knew her determination and might have spared his
application.[2] She wrote to Chapuys 'that, sentence
'once pronounced, the King, for all his bravado and
'obstinacy, would listen to reason, and war would be

[1] Chapuys to Charles V., Dec.
6, 1533.—*Spanish Calendar*, vol.
iv. part 2, p. 871.

[2] *Ibid.*, Nov. 20, 1533.—*Ibid.*,

p. 859. Catherine to Charles V.,
Nov. 21.—*Calendar, Foreign and
Domestic*, vol. vi. p. 578.

'unnecessary.' 'On that point,' the Ambassador said, 'she would not find a single person to agree with her.' [1]

Catherine had pictured to herself a final triumph, and she could not part with the single hope which had cheered her through her long trial. If any chance of accommodation remained after her peremptory answer, it was dispelled by the discovery of the treason connected with the Nun of Kent. The story of Elizabeth Barton has been told by me elsewhere. Here it is enough to say that from the beginning of the divorce suit an hysterical woman, professing to have received Divine revelations, had denounced the King's conduct in private and public, and had influenced the judgment of peers, bishops, statesmen, and privy councillors. She had been treated at first as a foolish enthusiast, but her prophecies had been circulated by an organisation of itinerant friars, and had been made use of to feed the disaffection which had shown itself in the overtures to Chapuys. The effect which she had produced had been recently discovered. She had been arrested, had made a large confession, and had implicated several of the greatest names in the realm. She had written more than once to the Pope. She had influenced Warham. She had affected the failing intellect of Wolsey. The Bishop of Rochester, the Marquis and Marchioness of Exeter, had admitted her to intimate confidence. Even Sir Thomas More had at one time half believed that she was inspired. Catherine, providentially, as Chapuys thought,

---

[1] Chapuys to Charles V., Nov. 24, 1533.—*Spanish Calendar*, vol. iv. part 2, p. 864.

had declined to see her, but was acquainted with all that passed between her and the Exeters.

When brought before the Council she was treated *comme une grosse dame*—as a person of consideration. The occasion was of peculiar solemnity, and great persons were in attendance from all parts of the realm. The Chancellor, in the Nun's presence, gave a history of her proceedings. He spoke of the loyalty and fidelity which had been generally shown by the nation during the trying controversy. The King had married a second wife to secure the succession and provide for the tranquillity of the realm. The woman before them had instigated the Pope to censure him, and had endeavoured to bring about a rebellion to deprive him of his throne. The audience, who had listened quietly so far, at the word 'rebellion' broke out into cries of 'To the 'stake! to the stake!' The Nun showed no alarm, but admitted quietly that what the Chancellor said was true. She had acknowledged much, but more lay behind, and Chapuys confessed himself alarmed at what she might still reveal. Cromwell observed to him that 'God must have directed the sense and wit of the 'Queen to keep clear of the woman.' But Catherine's confessor had been among the most intimate of her confederates; and to be aware of treason and not reveal it was an act of treason in itself. Sir Thomas More cleared himself. Fisher, the guiltiest of all, was sent to the Tower for misprision.

The Pope's final sentence was now a certainty. Francis had cleared his conscience by advocating the compromise. Nothing more could be done, he said, unless Cranmer's judgment was revoked. He chose to forget that the compromise had been rejected by Catherine herself. He complained that as fast as he studied to gain the Pope the English studied to lose him. He had devised a plan, and the English spoilt it. He regretted that he had ever meddled in the matter. The Pope could not help himself, but must now excommunicate the King and call on Christendom to support him.[1]

Henry could no longer doubt that he was in serious danger. To the risk of invasion from abroad, disaffection at home had to be added. How far it extended he did not yet know. All along, however, he had been preparing for what the future might bring. The fleet was in high order; the fortifications at Dover and Calais had been repaired; if the worst came he meant to be ready for it; the stoppage of trade might be serious; it was to this that Catherine looked as her most effective weapon; but English commerce was as important to Spain and Flanders as the Flemish woollens to the London citizens, and the leading merchants on both sides came to an understanding that an Interdict would be disregarded. The Lutherans had the courage of their opinions and could be depended on to fight. The laws against heretics were allowed to sleep. Their numbers increased, and the French Ambassador observed to Chapuys that they would not

---

[1] Gardiner to Henry VIII., Nov. 1533.—*Calendar, Foreign and Domestic*, vol. vi. p. 571.

easily be eradicated. Many who were orthodox in the faith were bitter against Rome and Romanism. The Duke of Norfolk was the loudest of them all. Flanders could not live, he said to a deputation of alarmed citizens, without the English trade; and as to the Pope, the Pope was a wretch and a bastard, a liar and a bad man; he would stake wife and children and his own person to be revenged on him.[1] An order of Council came out that the Pope henceforward was to be styled only Bishop of Rome. Chapuys could not understand it. The Duke, he thought, was strangely changed; he had once professed to be a staunch Catholic. Norfolk had not changed. The peculiar Anglican theory was beginning to show itself that a Church might still be Catholic though it ceased to be Papal.

Irritated though he was at his last failure, Francis did not wholly abandon his efforts. A successful invasion of England by the Emperor would be dangerous or even fatal to France. He wrote to Anne· He sent his letter by the hands of her old friend, Du Bellay, and she was so pleased that she kissed him when he presented it. Du Bellay sought out Chapuys. 'Could nothing be done,' he asked, 'to prevent Eng-'land from breaking with the Papacy? Better England, 'France, and the Empire had spent a hundred thousand 'crowns than allow a rupture. The Emperor had done 'his duty in supporting his aunt; might he not now 'yield a little to avoid worse?' Chapuys could give

---

[1] Chapuys to Charles, Dec. 9, 1533.—*Spanish Calendar,* vol. iv. part 2, p. 875.

him no hope. The treatment of Catherine alone would force the Emperor to take further measures.

That Catherine, so far, had no personal ill-usage to complain of had been admitted by the Spanish Council, and alleged as an argument against interference by force in her favour. Chapuys conceived, and probably hoped, that this objection was being removed.

What to do with her was not the least of the perplexities in which Henry had involved himself. By the public law of Christendom, a marriage with a brother's widow was illegal. By the law as it has stood ever since in England, the Pope of Rome neither has, nor ever had, a right to dispense in such cases. She was not, therefore, Henry's queen. She deserved the most indulgent consideration; her anger and her resistance were legitimate and natural; but the fact remained. She had refused all compromise. She had insisted on a decision, and an English Court had given judgment against her. If she was queen, Elizabeth was a bastard, and her insistence upon her title was an invitation to civil war. She was not standing alone. The Princess Mary, on her father's marriage with Anne, had written him a letter, which he had praised as greatly to her credit; but either Anne's insolence or her mother's persuasion had taken her back to Catherine's side. Her conduct may and does deserve the highest moral admiration; but the fidelity of the child to her mother was the assertion of a right to be next in succession to the crown. There was no longer a doubt that a dangerous movement was on foot for an insurrection, supported from abroad. If Catherine escaped with Mary to the Continent, war would instantly follow. If there was a rebellion at home, their friends intended to release them, and to use their names in the field. It was found necessary again to part them. The danger would be diminished if they were separated; together they confirmed each other's resolution. Catherine was sent to Kimbolton with a reduced household —her confessor, her doctor, her own personal servants and attendants—who had orders to call her Princess, but obeyed as little as they pleased. Mary was attached to the establishment of her baby sister Elizabeth under charge of Anne Boleyn's aunt, Mrs. Shelton.

History with a universal voice condemns the King's conduct as cruel and unnatural. It was not cruel in the sense of being wanton; it was not unnatural in the sense that he had no feeling. He was in a dilemma, through his own actions, from which he could not otherwise extricate himself. Catherine was not his wife, and he knew it; he had been misled by Wolsey into the expectation that the Pope would relieve him; he had been trifled with and played upon; he was now threatened with excommunication and deposition. Half his subjects, and those the boldest and most determined, had rallied to his side; his cause had become the occasion of a great and beneficent revolution, and incidental difficulties had to be dealt with as they rose. Catherine he had long ceased to love, if love had ever existed between them, but he respected her character and admired her indomitable courage. For his daughter

he had a real affection, as appeared in a slight incident
which occurred shortly after her removal. Elizabeth
was at Hatfield, and Mary, whose pride Anne had
threatened to humble, was with her. Mrs. Shelton's
orders were to box Mary's ears if she presumed to call
herself Princess. The King knew nothing of these
instructions. He had found his daughter always dutiful
except when under her mother's influence, and one
day he rode down to Hatfield to see her. The Lady
Anne, finding that he had gone without her knowledge,
'considering the King's easiness and lightness, if any
'one dared to call it so,' and afraid of the effect which
a meeting with his daughter might have upon him,
sent some one in pursuit to prevent him from seeing or
speaking with her. The King submitted to his imperious mistress, saw Anne's child, but did not see
Mary. She had heard of his arrival, and as he was
mounting his horse to ride back she showed herself on
the leads, kneeling as if to ask his blessing. The King
saw her, bowed, lifted his bonnet, and silently went his
way.[1]

The French Ambassador met him afterwards in
London. The King said he had not spoken to his
daughter on account of her Spanish obstinacy. The
Ambassador saying something in her favour, 'tears
'rushed into the King's eyes, and he praised her
'many virtues and accomplishments.' 'The Lady,'
said Chapuys, 'is aware of the King's affection for his

---

[1] Chapuys to Charles, Jan. 17, 1534.—*Calendar, Foreign and Domestic*, vol. vii. p. 31.

'daughter, and therefore never ceases to plot against
'her.' The Earl of Northumberland, once Anne's
lover, told him that she meant to poison the Princess.
Chapuys had thought it might be better if she avoided
irritating her father; he advised her to protect herself
by a secret protest, and to let her title drop on condition that she might live with her mother. Lady
Anne, however, it was thought, would only be more
malicious, and a show of yielding would discourage
her friends. Another plan was to carry her off abroad;
but war would then be inevitable, and Chapuys could
not venture to recommend such an attempt without the
Emperor's express consent.[1]

Catherine also was, or professed to be, in fear of
foul play. Kimbolton was a small but not inconvenient
residence. It was represented as a prison. The King
was supposed to be eager for her death; and, in the
animosity of the time, he, or at least his mistress, was
thought capable of any atrocity. The Queen was out
of health in reality, having shown signs of dropsy, and
the physicians thought her life uncertain. She would
eat nothing which her new servants provided; the
little food she took was prepared by her chamberwoman,
and her own room was used as a kitchen.[2] Charles
had intimated that, if she was ill-used, he might be
driven to interfere; and every evil rumour that was
current was treasured up to exasperate him into action.

---

[1] Chapuys to Charles V., Feb.
11, 1534.—*Spanish Calendar*, vol.
v. p. 31.

[2] *Ibid.*, Jan. 17, 1534.—*Calendar, Foreign and Domestic*, vol.
vii. pp. 31—33.

No words, Chapuys said in a letter to the Emperor, could describe the grief which the King's conduct to the Queen and Princess was creating in the English people. They complained bitterly of the Emperor's inaction. They waited only for the arrival of a single ship of war to rise *en masse ;* and, if they had but a leader to take command, they said, they would do the work themselves. They reminded him of Warwick, who dethroned the King's grandfather, and Henry VII., who dethroned Richard. Some even said the Emperor's right to the throne was better than the present King's; for Edward's children were illegitimate, and the Emperor was descended from the House of Lancaster. If the Emperor would not move, at least he might stop the Flanders trade, and rebellion would then be certain. There was not the least hope that the King would submit. The accursed Anne had so bewitched him that he dared not oppose her. The longer the Emperor delayed, the worse things would grow from the rapid spread of Lutheranism.[1]

Wise sovereigns, under the strongest provocation, are slow to encourage mutiny in neighbouring kingdoms. Charles had to check the over-zeal of his Ambassador, and to tell him that 'the present was no time for 'vigorous action or movement of any kind.' Chapuys promised for the future 'to persuade the Queen to 'patience, and to do nothing which might lead to the

---

[1] Chapuys to Charles V., Dec. 16, 1533.—*Spanish Calendar,* vol. iv. part 2, p. 883.

CHAPTER XVI.

Prosecution of Lord Dacre—Failure of the Crown—Rebellion in Ireland—Lord Thomas Fitzgerald—Delight of the Catholic party—Preparations for a rising in England—The Princess Mary—Lord Hussey and Lord Darcy—Schemes for insurrection submitted to Chapuys—General disaffection among the English Peers—Death of Clement VII.—Election of Paul III.—Expectation at Rome that Henry would now submit—The expectation disappointed — The Act of Supremacy—The Italian conjuror—Reginald Pole—Violence and insolence of Anne Boleyn—Spread of Lutheranism—Intended escape of the Princess Mary out of England.

THE English Peers are supposed to have been the servile instruments of Henry VIII.'s tyrannies and caprices, to have been ready to divorce or murder a wife, or to execute a bishop, as it might please the King to command. They were about to show that there were limits to their obedience, and that when they saw occasion they could assert their independence. Lord Dacre of Naworth was one of the most powerful of the northern nobles. He had distinguished himself as a supporter of Queen Catherine, and was particularly detested by the Lady Anne. His name appears prominently in the lists supplied to Chapuys of those who could be counted upon in the event of a rising. The

M

Government had good reason, therefore, to watch him with anxiety. As Warden of the Marches he had been in constant contact with the Scots, and a Scotch invasion in execution of the Papal censures had been part of Chapuys's scheme. Dacre was suspected of underhand dealings with the Scots. He had been indicted at Carlisle for treason in June, and had been sent to London for trial. He was brought to the bar before the Peers, assisted by the twelve Judges. An escape of a prisoner was rare when the Crown prosecuted; the Privy Council prepared the evidence, drew up their case, and in bringing a man to the bar made themselves responsible for the charge; failure, therefore, was equivalent to a vote of censure. The prosecution of Dacre had been set on foot by Cromwell, who had perhaps been informed of particulars of his conduct which it was undesirable to bring forward. The Peers looked on Cromwell as another Wolsey—as another intruding commoner who was taking liberties with the ancient blood. The Lady Anne was supposed to have borne malice against Dacre. The Lady Anne was to be made to know that there were limits to her power. Dacre spoke for seven hours to a sympathetic court; he was unanimously acquitted, and the City of London celebrated his escape with bonfires and illuminations. The Court had received a sharp rebuff. Norfolk, who sat as High Steward, had to accept a verdict of which he alone disapproved.[1] At Rome the acquittal was regarded as

---

[1] Chapuys to Charles V., July 27, 1534.—*Calendar, Foreign and Domestic*, vol. vii. p. 389.

perhaps the beginning of some commotion with which God was preparing to punish the King of England.[1]

More serious news arrived from Ireland. While the English Catholics were muttering discontent and waiting for foreign help, Lord Thomas Fitzgerald, 'the youth of promise' whom Chapuys had recommended to Charles's notice, had broken into open rebellion, and had forsworn his allegiance to Henry as an excommunicated sovereign. Fitzgerald was a ferocious savage, but his crimes were committed in the name of religion. In my history of this rebellion I connected it with the sacred cause of More and Fisher, and was severely rebuked for my alleged unfairness. The fresh particulars here to be mentioned prove that I was entirely right, that the rising in Ireland was encouraged by the same means, was part of the same conspiracy, that it was regarded at Rome and by the Papal party everywhere as the first blow struck in a holy war.

It commenced with the murder of the Archbishop of Dublin, a feeble old man, who was dragged out of his bed and slaughtered by Fitzgerald's own hand. It spread rapidly through the English Pale, and Chapuys recorded its progress with delight. The English had been caught unprepared. Skeffington, the Deputy, was a fool. Ireland, in Chapuys's opinion, was practically recovered to the Holy See, and with the smallest assistance from the Emperor and the Pope the heretics and all their works would be made an end of there.[2]

---

[1] Cifuentes to Charles V., Aug. 1, 1534.—*Spanish Calendar*, vol. v. p. 229.

[2] Chapuys to Charles V., Aug. 11, 1534.—*Spanish Calendar*, vol. v. pp. 243-4.

A fortnight later he wrote still more enthusiastically. Kildare's son was absolute master of the island. He had driven the King to ask for terms; he had refused to listen, and was then everywhere expelling the English or else killing them.

The pleasure felt by all worthy people, Chapuys said, was incredible. Such a turn of events was a good beginning for a settlement in England, and the Catholic party desired his Majesty most passionately not to lose the opportunity. On all sides the Ambassador was besieged with entreaties. ' An excellent nobleman had ' met him by appointment in the country, and had ' assured him solemnly that the least move on the ' Emperor's part would end the matter. The Irish ' example had fired all their hearts. They were longing ' to follow it.'

As this intelligence might fail to rouse Charles, the Ambassador again added as a further reason for haste that the Queen and Princess were in danger of losing their lives. Cromwell had been heard to say that their deaths would end all quarrels. Lord Wiltshire had said the same, and the fear was that when Parliament reassembled the ladies might be brought to trial under the statute.[1]

If Cromwell and Lord Wiltshire used the words ascribed to them, no evil purpose need have been implied or intended. Catherine was a confirmed invalid; the Princess Mary had just been attacked with an alarming illness. Chapuys had dissuaded Mary at last

---

[1] Chapuys to Charles V., Aug. 29.—*Spanish Calendar*, p. 250.

from making fresh quarrels with her governess; she
had submitted to the indignities of her situation with
reluctant patience, and had followed unresistingly in the
various removals of Elizabeth's establishment. The
irritation, however, had told on her health, and at the
time of Chapuys's conversation with the 'excellent
'nobleman' her life was supposed to be in danger from
ordinary causes. That Anne wished her dead was natural
enough; Anne had recently been again disappointed,
and had disappointed the King in the central wish of
his heart. She had said she was *enceinte*, but the signs
had passed off. It was rumoured that Henry's feelings
were cooling towards her. He had answered, so Court
scandal said, to some imperious message of hers that
she ought to be satisfied with what he had done for
her; were things to begin again, he would not do as
much. Report said also that there were *nouvelles
amours*; but, as the alleged object of the King's attention was a lady devoted to Queen Catherine, the *amour*
was probably innocent. The Ambassador built little
upon this; Anne's will to injure the Princess he
knew to be boundless, and he believed her power over
Henry still to be great. Mary herself had sent him
word that she had discovered practices for her
destruction.

Any peril to which she might be exposed would
approach her, as Chapuys was obliged to confess, from
one side only. He ascertained that 'when certain
'members of the Council had advised harsh measures
'to please the Lady Anne,' the King had told them

that he would never consent, and no one at the Court
—neither the Lady nor any other person—dared speak
against the Princess. ' The King loved her,' so Cromwell said, ' a hundred times more than his latest born.'
The notion that the statute was to be enforced against
her life was a chimera of malice. In her illness he
showed the deepest anxiety; he sent his own physician
to attend on her, and he sent for her mother's physician
from Kimbolton. Chapuys admitted that he was naturally kind—' d'aymable et cordiale nature '—that his
daughter's death would be a serious blow to himself,
however welcome to Anne and to politicians, and that,
beyond his natural feeling, he was conscious that,
occurring under the present circumstances, it would be
a stain on his reputation.

More than once Henry had interfered for Mary's
protection. He had perhaps heard of what Anne had
threatened to do to her on his proposed journey to
Calais. She had been the occasion, at any rate, of sharp
differences between them. He had resented, when he
discovered it, the manner in which she had been
dragged to the More, and had allowed her, when staying
there, to be publicly visited by the ladies and gentlemen
of the Court, to the Lady's great annoyance. Nay,
Mary had been permitted to refuse to leave her room
when Anne had sent for her, and the strictest orders
had been given through Cromwell that anyone who
treated her disrespectfully should be severely punished.[1]

---

[1] Chapuys to Charles V., Oct. 24, 1534.—*Spanish Calendar*, vol. v.
pp. 294 et seq.

True as all this might be, however, Chapuys's feelings towards the King were not altered, his fears
diminished, or his desire less eager to bring about a
rebellion and a revolution. Lord Thomas Fitzgerald's
performances in Ireland were spurring into energy the
disaffected in England. The nobleman to whom
Chapuys had referred was Lord Hussey of Lincolnshire,
who had been Chamberlain to the Princess Mary when
she had an establishment of her own as next in succession to the crown. Lord Hussey was a dear friend of
her mother's. Having opened the ground he again
visited the Ambassador 'in utmost secrecy.' He told
him that he and all the honest men in the realm were
much discouraged by the Emperor's delay to set things
straight, as it was a thing which could so easily be done.
The lives of the Queen and Princess were undoubtedly
threatened; their cause was God's cause, which the
Emperor was bound to uphold, and the English people
looked to him as their natural sovereign. Chapuys
replied that if the Emperor were to do as Lord Hussey
desired, he feared that an invasion of England would
cause much hurt and suffering to many innocent people.
Lord Hussey was reputed a wise man. Chapuys asked
him what would he do himself if he were in the Emperor's place. Lord Hussey answered that the state of
England was as well known to Chapuys as to himself.
Almost everyone was looking for help to the Emperor.
There was no fear of his injuring the people; their
indignation was so great that there would be no resistance. The war would be over as soon as it was begun.

The details, he said, Lord Darcy would explain better than he could do. The Emperor should first issue a declaration. The people would then take arms, and would be joined by the nobles and the clergy.

Fisher had used the same language. Fisher was in the Tower, and no longer accessible. Lord Darcy of Templehurst has been already seen in drawing the indictment against Wolsey. He was an old crusader; he had served under Ferdinand and Isabella, was a Spaniard in sympathy, and was able, as he represented, to bring eight thousand men into the field from the northern counties. On Lord Hussey's recommendation Chapuys sent a confidential servant to Darcy, who professed himself as zealous as his friend. Darcy said that he was as loyal as any man, but things were going on so outrageously, especially in matters of religion, that he, for one, could not bear it longer. In the north there were six hundred lords and gentlemen who thought as he did. Measures were about to be taken in Parliament to favour the Lutherans. He was going himself into Yorkshire, where he intended to commence an opposition. If the Emperor would help him, he would take the field behind the crucifix, and would raise the banner of Castile. Measures might be concerted with the Scots; a Scotch army might cross the border as soon as he had himself taken arms; an Imperial squadron should appear simultaneously at the mouth of the Thames, and a battalion of soldiers from Flanders should be landed at Hull, with arms and money for the poorer gentlemen. He and the northern lords would supply their own forces. Many of the other Peers, he said, entirely agreed with him. He named especially Lord Derby and Lord Dacre.[1]

This letter is of extreme importance, as explaining the laws which it was found necessary to pass in the ensuing Parliament. A deeply-rooted and most dangerous conspiracy was actively forming—how dangerous the Pilgrimage of Grace afterwards proved—in which Darcy and Hussey were the principal leaders. The Government was well served. The King and Cromwell knew more than it was prudent to publish. The rebellion meditated was the more formidable because it was sanctified by the name of religion, with the avowed purpose of executing the Papal Brief. Fitzgerald's rising in Ireland was but the first dropping of a storm designed to be universal. Half the Peers who surrounded Henry's person, and voted in Parliament for the reforming statutes, were at heart leagued with his enemies. He had a right to impose a test of loyalty on them, and force them to declare whether they were his subjects or the Pope's.

For a moment it seemed as if the peril might pass over. It became known in England in October that Clement VII. had ended his pontificate, and that Cardinal Farnese reigned in his stead as Paul III. On Clement's death the King, according to Chapuys, had counted on a schism in the Church, and was disappointed at the facility with which the election had

---

[1] Chapuys to Charles V., Sept. 30, 1534.—*Calendar, Foreign and Domestic*, vol. vii. p. 466.   *Spanish Calendar*, vol. v. p. 608.

been carried through ; but Farnese had been on Henry's side in the divorce case, and the impression in the English Council was that the quarrel with Rome would now be composed. The Duke of Norfolk, who had been the loudest in his denunciations of Clement, was of opinion that the King, as a Catholic prince, would submit to his successor. Even Cromwell laid the blame of the rupture on Clement personally, and when he heard that he was gone, exclaimed that ' the Great ' Devil was dead.' Henry knew better than his Minister that ' the Great Devil' was not this or that pontiff, but the Papacy itself. He had liberated his kingdom ; he did not mean to lead it back into bondage. ' Let no ' man,' he said to Norfolk, ' try to persuade me to such ' a step. I shall account no more of the Pope than ' of any priest in my realm.' [1] Farnese undoubtedly expected that Henry would make advances to him, and was prepared to meet them; he told Casalis that he had taken a legal opinion as to whether his prede- cessor's judgment in the divorce case could be reopened, and a decision given in the King's favour ; the lawyers had assured him that there would be no difficulty, and the Pope evidently wished the King to believe that he might now have his way if he would place himself in the Pope's hands. Henry, however, was too wary to be caught. He must have deeds, not words, he said. If the Pope was sincere, he would revoke his predecessor's sentence of his own accord. Francis, by whose influence

---

[1] Chapuys to Charles V., Oct. 13, 1534.—*Spanish Calendar*, vol. v. p. 279.

Farnese had been elected, tried to bring Henry to submission, but to no purpose. The King was no longer to be moved by vague phrases like those to which he had once trusted to his cost. Surrounded by treachery though he knew himself to be, he looked no longer for palliatives and compromises, and went straight on upon his way. The House of Commons was with him, growing in heartiness at each succeeding session. The Peers and clergy might conspire in secret. In public, as estates of the realm, they were too cowardly to oppose.

Parliament met in November. The other Acts which were passed by it this year are relatively unimportant, and may be read elsewhere. The great business of the session, which has left its mark on history, was to pass the Act of Supremacy, detailing and explaining the meaning of the title which Convocation two years previously had conferred upon the King. Unentangled any longer with saving clauses, the sovereign authority under the law in all causes, ecclesiastical and civil, was declared to rest thenceforward in the Crown, and the last vestiges of Roman jurisdiction in England were swept off and disappeared. No laws, no injunctions, no fancied rights over the consciences of English subjects were to be pleaded further as a rule to their conduct which had not been sanctioned by Crown and Parliament. No clergy, English or foreign, were to exercise thenceforward any power not delegated to them and limited under the law of the land, except what could not be taken from them—their

special privilege of administering the sacraments.
Double loyalty to the Crown and to the Papacy was
thenceforward impossible. The Pope had attempted to
depose the King. The Act of Supremacy was England's
answer.

But to enact a law was not enough. With Ireland
in insurrection, with half the nobles and more than half
the clergy, regular and secular, in England inviting a
Spanish invasion, the King and Commons, who were in
earnest in carrying through the reforms which they had
begun, were obliged to take larger measures to distin-
guish their friends from their enemies. If the Catholics
had the immense majority to which they pretended, the
Constitution gave them the power of legitimate opposition. If they were professing with their lips and sus-
taining with their votes a course of policy which they
were plotting secretly to overthrow, it was fair and
right to compel them to show their true colours.
Therefore the Parliament further enacted that to deny
the royal supremacy—in other words, to maintain the
right of the Pope to declare the King deprived—should
be high treason, and the Act was so interpreted that
persons who were open to suspicion might be interro-
gated, and that a refusal to answer should be accepted
as an acknowledgment of guilt. In quiet times such a
measure would be unnecessary, and therefore tyrannical.
Facta arguantur, dicta impune sint. In the face of
Chapuys's correspondence it will hardly be maintained
that the reforming Government of Henry VIII. was in
no danger. The Statute of Supremacy must be judged

by the reality of the peril which it was designed to meet. If the Reformation was a crime, the laws by which it defended itself were criminal along with it. If the Reformation was the dawning of a new and brilliant era for Imperial England, if it was the opening of a fountain from which the English genius has flowed out over the wide surface of the entire globe, the men who watched over its early trials and enabled the movement to advance, undishonoured and undisfigured by civil war, deserve rather to be respected for their resolution than reviled as arbitrary despots. To try the actions of statesmen in a time of high national peril by the canons of an age of tranquillity is the highest form of historical injustice.

The naked truth—and nakedness is not always indecent—was something of this kind. A marriage with a brother's wife was forbidden by the universal law of Christendom. Kings, dukes, and other great men who disposed as they pleased of the hands of their sons and daughters, found it often desirable, for political or domestic reasons, to form connections which the law prohibited, and therefore they maintained an Italian conjuror who professed to be able for a consideration to turn wrong into right. To marriages so arranged it was absurd to attach the same obligations as belonged to unions legitimately contracted. If, as often happened, such marriages turned out ill, the same conjuror who could make could unmake. This function, also, he was repeatedly called on to exercise, and, for a consideration also, he was usually compliant. The King of England had been married as a boy to Catherine of Aragon, carrying out an arrangement between their respective fathers. The marriage had failed in the most important object for which royal marriages are formed: there was no male heir to the crown, nor any prospect of one. Henry, therefore, as any other prince in Europe would have done, applied to the Italian for assistance. The conjuror was willing, confessing that the case was one where his abilities might properly be employed. But another of his supporters interfered, and forced him to refuse. The King of England had always paid his share for the conjuror's maintenance. He was violently deprived of a concession which it was admitted that he had a right to claim. But for the conjuror's pretensions to make the unlawful lawful, he would not have been in the situation in which he found himself. What could be more natural than that, finding himself thus treated, he should begin to doubt whether the conjuror, after all, had the power of making wrong into right? whether the marriage had not been wrong from the beginning? And, when the magical artist began to curse, as his habit was when doubts were thrown on his being the Vicar of the Almighty, what could be more natural also than to throw him and his tackle out of window?

The passing of the Act increased the anxiety about the position of the Princess Mary. In the opinion of most reasonable persons her claim to the succession was superior to that of Elizabeth, and, if she had submitted to her father, it would probably have been allowed and established. In the eyes of the disaffected, however, she was already, by Clement's sentence, the legitimate possessor of the throne. Reginald Pole, Lady Salisbury's son and grandson of the Duke of Clarence, was still abroad. Henry had endeavoured to gain him over, but had not succeeded. He was of the blood of the White Rose, and, with his brother, had gone by instinct into opposition. His birth, in those days of loyalty to race, gave him influence in England, and Catherine, as has been seen, had fixed upon him as Mary's husband. He had been brought already under Charles's notice as likely to be of use in the intended rebellion. The Queen, wrote Chapuys to the Emperor, knew no one to whom she would better like her daughter to be married; many right-minded people held that the right to the crown lay in the family of the Duke of Clarence, Edward's children having been illegitimate; if the Emperor would send an army across with Lord Reginald attached to it, every one would declare for him; his younger brother Geoffrey was a constant visitor to himself; once more he insisted that nothing could be more easy than the conquest of the whole kingdom.[1]

The object with Chapuys was now to carry Mary abroad, partly that she might be married to Pole, partly for her own security. Notwithstanding the King's evident care for her health and good treatment, he could not look into the details of her daily life, and Anne was growing daily more dangerous. Both

[1] Chapuys to Charles V., Nov. 3, 1534.—*Calendar, Foreign and Domestic*, vol. vii. p. 519.

Catherine and the Princess had still many friends among the ladies of the Court. To one of these, young and beautiful—and, therefore, certainly not the plain Jane Seymour—the King was supposed to have paid attentions. Like another lady who had been mentioned previously, she was devoted to Catherine's interests, and obviously not, therefore, a pretender to Henry's personal affections. Anne had affected to be jealous, and under other aspects had reason for uneasiness. She had demanded this lady's dismissal from the Court, and had been so violent that ' the King had left her in ' displeasure, complaining of her importunacy and vex- ' atiousness.' The restoration of Mary to favour was a constant alarm to Anne, and she had a party of her own which had been raised by her patronage, depended on her influence, and was ready to execute her pleasure. Thus the petty annoyances of which both Catherine and her daughter complained were not discontinued. The household at Kimbolton was reduced; a confi- dential maid who had been useful in the Queen's corre- spondence was discovered and dismissed. Mary was left under the control of Mrs. Shelton, who dared not openly displease Anne. It was Anne that Chapuys blamed.

Anne hated the Princess. The King had a real love for her. In her illness he had been studiously kind. When told it had been caused by mental trouble, he said, with a sigh, ' that it was a pity her obstinacy ' should prevent him from treating her as he wished ' and as she deserved. The case was the harder, as he ' knew that her conduct had been dictated by her

' mother, and he was therefore obliged to keep them
' separate.' [1]

The Privy Councillors appear to have remonstrated
with Anne on her behaviour to Mary. Passionate
scenes, at any rate, had occurred between her and
Henry's principal Ministers. She spoke to her uncle,
the Duke of Norfolk, in terms 'which would not be
' used to a dog.' Norfolk left the room in indignation,
muttering that she was a '*grande putaine.*' The malcontents increased daily and became bolder in word and
action. Lord Northumberland, Anne's early lover, of
whom Darcy had been doubtful, professed now to be so
disgusted with the malice and arrogance of the Lady
that he too looked to the Emperor's coming as the only
remedy. Lord Sandys, Henry's chamberlain, withdrew
to his house, pretending sickness, and sent Chapuys a
message that the Emperor had the hearts of the English
people, and, at the least motion which the Emperor
might make, the realm would be in confusion.[2] The
news from Fitzgerald was less satisfactory. His resources were failing, and he wanted help, but he was
still standing out. England, however, was more and
more sure; the northern counties were unanimous, in
the south and west the Marquis of Exeter and the
Poles were superior to any force which could be brought
against them; the spread of Lutheranism was creating
more exasperation than even the divorce. Moderate

---

[1] Chapuys to Charles V., Dec. 19, 1534.—*Spanish Calendar*, vol. v. p. 343.

[2] Chapuys to Charles V., Jan. 14, 1535.—*Calendar, Foreign and Domestic*, vol. viii. p. 14.

men had hoped for an arrangement with the new Pope. Instead of it, the heretical preachers were more violent than ever, and the King was believed to have encouraged them. Dr. Brown, an Augustinian friar, and General of the Mendicant Order, who, as some believed, had married the King and Anne, had dared to maintain in a sermon 'that the Bishops and all others who did 'not burn the Bulls which they had received from the 'Pope, and obtain others from the King, deserved to be 'punished. Their authority was derived from the King 'alone. Their sacred chrism would avail them nothing 'while they obeyed the Idol of Rome, who was a limb 'of the Devil.'

'Language so abominable,' said Chapuys in reporting it, 'must have been prompted by the King, or else 'by Cromwell, who made the said monk his right hand 'in all things unlawful;' Cromwell and Cranmer being of Luther's opinion that there was no difference between priests and bishops, save what the letters patent of the Crown might constitute. 'Cromwell,' Chapuys said, 'had been feeling his way with some of the Bench on 'the subject.' At a meeting of Council he had asked Gardiner and others whether the King could not make and unmake bishops at his pleasure. They were obliged to answer that he could, to save their benefices.[1]

Outrages so flagrant had shocked beyond longer endurance the conservative mind of England. Darcy, at the beginning of the new year (a year which, as he

---

[1] Chapuys to Charles V., Jan. 28, 1535.—*Calendar, Foreign and Domestic*, vol. viii. p. 38.

hoped, was to witness an end to them), sent Chapuys a present of a sword, as an indication that the time was come for sword-play.[1] Let the Emperor send but a little money; let a proclamation be drawn in his name that the nation was in arms for the cause of God and the Queen, the comfort of the people, and the restoration of order and justice, and a hundred thousand men would rush to the field. The present was the propitious moment. If action was longer delayed, it might be too late.[2]

To the enthusiastic and the eager the cause which touches themselves the nearest seems always the most important in the world. Charles V. had struggled long to escape the duty which the Pope and destiny appeared to be combining to thrust upon him. With Germany unsettled, with the Turks in Hungary, with Barbarossa's corsair-fleet commanding the Mediterranean and harassing the Spanish coast, with another French war visibly ahead, and a renewed invasion of Italy, Charles was in no condition to add Henry to the number of his enemies. Chapuys and Darcy, Fisher and Reginald Pole allowed passion to persuade them that the English King was Antichrist in person, the centre of all the disorder which disturbed the world. All else could wait, but the Emperor must first strike down Antichrist, and

---

[1] ' Veuillant denoter par icelle, 'puisque n'a moyen de m'envoyer ' dire seurement, que la saison sera 'propice pour jouer des cousteaulx.' —Chapuys to Charles V., Jan. 1,

1535.—*Calendar, Foreign and Domestic*, vol. viii. p. 1 ; and *MS.* *Vienna.*

[2] Chapuys to Charles V., Jan. 28, 1535.—*Ibid.* vol. viii. p. 38.

then the rest would be easy. Charles was wiser than
they, and could better estimate the danger of what he
was called on to undertake; but he could not shut his
ears entirely to entreaties so reiterated. Before anything could be done, however, means would have to be
taken to secure the persons of the Queen and Princess
—of the Princess especially, as she would be in most
danger. So far he had discouraged her escape when it
had been proposed to him, since, were she once in his
hands, he had thought that war could no longer be
avoided. He now allowed Chapuys to try what he could
do to get her out of the country, and meanwhile to report
more particularly on the landing of an invading force.

The escape itself presented no great difficulty. The
Princess was generally at the Palace at Greenwich.
Her friends would let her out at night; an armed
barge could be waiting off the walls, and a Flemish
man-of-war might be ready at the Nore, of size sufficient
to beat off boats that might be sent in pursuit. Should
she be removed elsewhere, the enterprise would not be
so easy. In the event of an insurrection while she was
still in the realm, Chapuys said the first step of the
Lords would be to get possession of her mother and
Mary. If they failed, the King would send them to the
Tower; but in the Tower they would be out of danger,
as the Constable, Sir William Kingston, was their
friend. In any case he did not believe that hurt would
be done them, the King feeling that, if war did break
out, they would be useful as mediators, like the wife
and mother of Coriolanus.

CHAPTER XVII.

Prospects of civil war—England and Spain—Illness of the Princess
Mary—Plans for her escape—Spirit of Queen Catherine—The
Emperor unwilling to interfere—Negotiations for a new treaty
between Henry and Charles—Debate in the Spanish Council
of State—The rival alliances—Disappointment of the confederate Peers—Advance of Lutheranism in England—Cromwell and Chapuys—Catherine and Mary the obstacles to peace
—Supposed designs on Mary's life.

ENGLAND, to all appearance, was now on the eve
of a bloody and desperate war. The conspirators
were confident of success; but conspirators associate
exclusively with persons of their own opinions, and
therefore seldom judge accurately of the strength of
their opponents. Chapuys and his friends had been
equally confident about Ireland. Fitzgerald was now a
fugitive, and the insurrection was burning down; yet
the struggle before Henry would have been at least as
severe as had been encountered by his grandfather
Edward, and the country itself would have been torn to
pieces; one notable difference only there was in the
situation—that the factions of the Roses had begun the
battle of themselves, without waiting for help from
abroad; the reactionaries under Henry VIII., con-

fessedly, were afraid to stir without the avowed support
of the Emperor; and Charles, when the question came
seriously before him, could not have failed to ask
himself why, if they were as strong as they pretended,
and the King's party as weak as they said it was, they
endured what they could easily prevent.

These reflections naturally presented themselves
both to the Emperor and to the Spanish Council when
they had to decide on the part which they would take.
If what Chapuys represented as a mere demonstration
should turn into serious war, England and France
would then unite in earnest; they would combine
with Germany; and Europe would be shaken with a
convulsion of which it was impossible to foresee the
end. The decision was momentous, and Charles paused
before coming to a resolution. Weeks passed, and
Chapuys could have no positive answer, save that he
was to give general encouragement to the Queen's
friends, and let them know that the Emperor valued
their fidelity. Weary of his hesitation, and hoping to
quicken his resolution, Catherine sent Chapuys word
that the Princess was to be forced to swear to the Act
of Supremacy, and that, on her refusal, she was to be
executed or imprisoned for life. Catherine wrote what
she, perhaps, believed, but could not know. But the
suspense was trying, and the worst was naturally looked
for. News came that English sailors had been burnt
by the Inquisition at Seville as heretics. Cromwell
observed to Chapuys that 'he had heard the Emperor
'was going to make a conquest of the realm.' The

Ambassador had the coolness to assure him that he was
dreaming; and that such an enterprise had never been
thought of. Cromwell knew better. He had learnt,
for one thing, of the plans for Mary's escape. He knew
what that would mean, and he had, perhaps, prevented
it. The project had been abandoned for the moment.
Instead of escaping, she had shown symptoms of the
same dangerous illness by which she had been attacked
before. There was the utmost alarm, and, as a pregnant evidence of the condition of men's minds, the
physicians refused to prescribe for her, lest, if she died,
they should be suspected of having poisoned her. The
King's physician declined, Queen Catherine's physician
declined—unless others were called in to assist—and
the unfortunate girl was left without medical help, in
imminent likelihood of death, because every one felt
that her dying at such a time would be set down to foul
play. The King sent for Chapuys and begged that he
would select a doctor, or two doctors, of eminence to
act with his own. Chapuys, with polite irony, replied
that it was not for him to make a selection; the King
must be better acquainted than he could be with the
reputation of the London physicians; and the Emperor
would be displeased if he showed distrust of his
Majesty's care for his child. Cromwell, who was present,
desired that if the Princess grew worse Chapuys would
allow one of his own people to be with her. Henry
continued to express his grief at her sufferings. Some
members of the Council 'had not been ashamed to say'
that as men could find no means of reconciling the

King with the Emperor, God might open a door by
taking the Princess to himself. It was a very natural
thought. Clement had said the same about Catherine.
But the aspiration would have been better left unex-
pressed.[1] Chapuys's suspicions were not removed. He
perceived the King's anxiety to be unfeigned; but he
detested him too sincerely to believe that in anything
he could mean well. The Princess recovered. Catherine
took advantage of the attack to entreat again that her
daughter might be under her own charge. It was cruel
to be obliged to refuse.

Chapuys presented the Queen's request. The King,
he said, heard him patiently and graciously, and,
instead of the usual answer that he knew best how to
provide for his daughter, replied, gently, that he would
do his utmost for the health of the Princess, and, since
her mother's physician would not assist, he would find
others. But to let Chapuys understand that he was
not ignorant of his secret dealings, he said he could not
forget what was due to his own honour. The Princess
might be carried out of the kingdom, or might herself
escape. She could easily do it if she was left in her
mother's charge. He had perceived some indications,
he added significantly, that the Emperor wished to have
her in his hands.

Ambassadors have a privilege of lying. Chapuys
boldly declared that there was no probability of the
Emperor attempting to carry off the Princess. The

---

[1] Chapuys to Charles V., Feb. 9, 1535.—*Calendar Foreign and
Domestic*, vol. viii. pp. 68—72.

controversy had lasted five years, and there had been no indication of any such purpose. The King said that it was Catherine who had made the Princess so obstinate. Daughters owed some obedience to their mothers, but their first duty was to the father. This Chapuys did not dispute, but proposed as an alternative that she should reside with her old governess, Lady Salisbury. The King said the Countess was a foolish woman, and of no experience.[1]

The difficulty was very great. To refuse so natural a request was to appear hard and unfeeling; yet to allow Catherine and Mary to be together was to furnish a head to the disaffection, of the extent of which the King was perfectly aware. He knew Catherine, and his words about her are a key to much of their relations to one another. 'She was of such high courage,' he said, ' that, with her daughter at her side, she might raise ' an army and take the field against him with as much ' spirit as her mother Isabella.' [2]

Catherine of Aragon had qualities with which history has not credited her. She was no patient, suffering saint, but a bold and daring woman, capable, if the opportunity was offered her, of making Henry repent of what he had done. But would the opportunity ever come ? Charles was still silent. Chapuys

---

[1] Chapuys to Charles V., Feb. 25, 1535.—*Calendar, Foreign and Domestic*, vol. viii. p. 100.

[2] 'Car estant la Royne si haul-'tain de cœur, luy venant en fan-'tasye, à l'appuy de la faveur de 'la Princesse, elle se pourroit 'mettre au champ et assembler 'force gents et luy faire la guerre 'aussy hardiment que fit la Royne 'sa mere.'—Chapuys à l'Empereur, Mar. 23, 1535.—*MS. Vienna.*

continued to feed the fire with promises. Granvelle, Charles's Minister, might be more persuasive than himself. To Granvelle the Ambassador wrote 'that the 'Concubine had bribed some one to pretend a revelation 'from God that she was not to conceive children while 'the Queen and the Princess were alive. The Concu- 'bine had sent the man with the message to the King, 'and never ceased' [Wolsey had called Anne 'the night 'crow'] 'to exclaim that the ladies were rebels and 'traitresses, and deserved to die.'[1]

Norfolk, irritated at Anne's insolence to him, withdrew from Court in ill-humour. He complained to Reginald Pole's brother, Lord Montague, that his advice was not attended to, and that his niece was intolerable. The Marquis of Exeter regretted to Chapuys that the chance had not been allowed him so far to shed his blood for the Queen and Princess. Let the movement begin, and he would not be the last to join. Mary, notwithstanding the precautions taken to keep her safe, had not parted with her hope of escape. If she could not be with her mother, she thought the Emperor might perhaps intercede with the King to remove her from under Mrs. Shelton's charge. The King might be brought to consent; and then, Chapuys said, with a pinnace and two ships in the river, she might still be carried off when again at Greenwich, as he could find means to get her out of the house at any hour of the night.[2]

---

[1] Chapuys to Granvelle, March 23, 1535.—*Spanish Calendar*, vol. v. p. 432 ; and *MS. Vienna*.

[2] Chapuys to Charles V., Feb. 25, 1534.—*Calendar, Foreign and Domestic*, vol. viii. p. 105.

At length the suspense was at an end, and the long-waited-for decision of the Emperor arrived. He had considered, he said, the communications of Lord Darcy and Lord Sandys; he admitted that the disorders of England required a remedy; but an armed interference was at the present time impossible.[1] It was a poor consolation to the English Peers and clergy; and there was worse behind. Not only the Emperor did not mean to declare war against Henry, but, spite of Catherine, spite of excommunication, spite of heresy, he intended, if possible, to renew the old alliance between England and the House of Burgundy. Politics are the religion of princes, and if they are wise the peace of the world weighs more with them than orthodoxy and family contentions. Honour, pride, Catholic obligations recommended a desperate stroke. Prudence and a higher duty commanded Charles to abstain. Sir John Wallop, the English representative at Paris, was a sincere friend of Queen Catherine, but was unwilling, for her sake, to see her plunge into an insurrectionary whirlpool. Viscount Hannaert, a Flemish nobleman with English connections, was Charles's Minister at the same Court. Together they discussed the situation of their respective countries. Both agreed that a war between Henry and the Emperor would be a calamity to mankind, while in alliance they might hold in check the impatient ambition of France. Wallop suggested that they might agree by mutual consent to suspend

---

[1] *Spanish Calendar*, Feb. 26, 1535, vol. v. p. 402.

their differences on the divorce; might let the divorce pass in silence for future settlement, and be again friends.

The proposal was submitted to the Spanish Council of State. The objections to it were the wrongs done, and still being done, to the Queen and Princess in the face of the Pope's sentence, and the obligation of the Emperor to see that sentence enforced. An arrangement between the Emperor and the King of England on the terms suggested would be ill received in Christendom, would dispirit the two ladies, and their friends in England who had hitherto supported the claims of the Princess Mary to the succession; while it might, further, encourage other princes to divorce their wives on similar grounds. In favour of a treaty, on the other hand, were the notorious designs of the French King. France was relying on the support of England. If nothing was done to compose the existing differences, the King of England might be driven to desperate courses. The Faith of the Church would suffer. The General Council, so anxiously looked for, would be unable to meet. The French King would be encouraged to go to war. Both he and the King of England would support the German schism, and the lives of the Princess and her mother would probably be sacrificed. A provisional agreement might modify the King of England's action, the Church might be saved, the ladies' lives be secured, and doubt and distrust be introduced between England and France. The Emperor could then deal with the Turks, and other difficulties could be tided over till a Council could meet and settle everything. [1]

Chapuys had written so confidently on the strength of the insurrectionary party that it was doubted whether choice between the alternative courses might not better be left for him to decide. Charles, who could better estimate the value of the promises of disaffected subjects, determined otherwise. The Ambassador, therefore, was informed that war would be inconvenient. Lord Darcy's sword must remain in the scabbard, and an attempt be made for reconciliation on the lines suggested by Sir John Wallop. Meanwhile, directions were given to the Inquisitors at Seville to be less precipitate in their dealings with English seamen.

From the first it had been Cromwell's hope and conviction that an open quarrel would be escaped. The French party in the English Council—Anne Boleyn, her family, and friends—had been urging the alliance with France and a general attack on Charles's scattered dominions. Cromwell, though a Protestant in religion, distrusted an associate who, when England was once committed, might make his own terms and leave Henry to his fate. In politics Cromwell had been consistently Imperialist. He had already persuaded the King to allow the Princess to move nearer to Kimbolton, where her mother's physician could have charge of her. He sent thanks to Charles in the King's name for his interference with the Holy Office. He left nothing

---

[1] *Calendar, Foreign and Domestic,* Feb. 26, 1535, vol. viii. p. 106.

undone to soften the friction and prepare for a reconciliation. Catherine and Mary he perceived to be the
only obstacle to a return to active friendship. If the
broken health of one, and the acute illness of the other,
should have a fatal termination, as a politician he could
not but feel that it would be an obstacle happily
removed.

Chapuys's intrigue with the confederate Peers had
been continued to the latest moment. All arrangements had been made for their security when the rising
should break out. Darcy himself was daily looking
for the signal, and begged only for timely notice of the
issue of the Emperor's manifesto to escape to his castle
in the north.[1] The Ambassador had now to trim his
sails on the other tack. The Emperor was ready to
allow the execution of Clement's sentence to stand over
till the General Council, without prejudice to the rights
of parties, provided an engagement was made for the
respectful treatment of the Queen and Princess, and a
promise given that their friends should be unmolested.
To Catherine the disappointment was hard to bear.
The talk of a treaty was the death-knell of the hopes
on which she had been feeding. A close and confidential intercourse was established between Chapuys
and Cromwell to discuss the preliminary conditions,
Chapuys, ill liking his work, desiring to fail, and on the
watch for any point on which to raise a suspicion.

The Princess was the first difficulty. Cromwell

---

[1] *Spanish Calendar*, vol. v. pp. 421-2.

had promised that she should be moved to her mother's neighbourhood. She had been sent no nearer than Ampthill. Cromwell said that he would do what he could, but the subject was disagreeable to the King, and he could say no more. He entered at once, however, on the King's desire to be again on good terms with the Emperor. The King had instructed him to discuss the whole situation with Chapuys, and it would be unfortunate, he said, if the interests of two women were allowed to interfere with weighty matters of State. The Queen had been more than once seriously ill, and her life was not likely to be prolonged. The Princess was not likely to live either; and it did not appear that either in Spain or France there was much anxiety for a material alteration in their present position. Meanwhile, the French were passionately importuning the King to join in a war against the Emperor. Cromwell said that he had been himself opposed to it, and the present moment, when the Emperor was engaged with the Turks, was the last which the King would choose for such a purpose. The object to be arrived at was the pacification of Christendom and the general union of all the leading Powers. The King desired it as much as he, and had, so far, prevented war from being declared by France.

It was true that the peace of the world was of more importance than the complaints of Catherine and Mary. Catherine had rejected a compromise when the Emperor himself recommended it, and Mary had defied her father and had defied Parliament at her mother's bidding. There were limits to the sacrifices which they were entitled to demand. Chapuys protested against Cromwell's impression that the European Powers were indifferent. The strongest interest was felt in their fate, he said, and many inconveniences would follow should harm befall them. The world would certainly believe that they had met with foul play. The Emperor would be charged with having caused it by neglecting to execute the Pope's sentence, and it would be said also that, but for the expectations which the Emperor had held out to them of defending their cause, they would themselves have conformed to the King's wishes; they would then have been treated with due regard and have escaped their present miseries. Cromwell undertook that the utmost care and vigilance should be observed that hurt should not befall them. The Princess, he said, he loved as much as Chapuys himself could love her, and nothing that he could do for them should be neglected; but the Ambassador and the Emperor's other agents were like hawks who soared high to stoop more swiftly on their prey. Their object was to have the Princess declared next in succession to the crown, and that was impossible owing to the late statutes.

Chapuys reported what had passed to his master, but scarcely concealed his contempt for the business in which he was engaged. ' I cannot tell,' he wrote, ' what sort of a treaty could be made with this King as ' long as he refuses to restore the Queen and Princess, ' or repair the hurts of the Church and the Faith,

'which grow worse every day. No later than Sunday
'last a preacher raised a question whether the body of
'Christ was contained, or not, in the consecrated wafer.
'Your Majesty may consider whither such propositions
'are tending.' [1]

A still more important conversation followed a few
days later. It can hardly be doubted, in the face of
Chapuys's repeated declaration, that both Catherine
and her daughter were in personal danger. Anne
Boleyn felt her position always precarious as long as
they were alive and refused to acknowledge her
marriage. She perhaps felt that it would go hard with
herself in the event of a successful insurrection. She
had urged, as far as she dared, that they should be
tried under the statute; but Henry would not allow
such a proposal to be so much as named to him. Other
means, however, might be found to make away with
them, and Sir Arthur Darcy, Lord Darcy's son, thought
they would be safer in the King's hands in the Tower
than in their present residence. 'The devil of a con-
'cubine would never rest till she had gained her object.'

The air was thick with these rumours when Chapuys
and Cromwell again met. The overtures had been
commenced by the Emperor. Cromwell said the King
had given him a statement in writing that he was
willing to renew his old friendship with the Emperor
and make a new treaty with him, if proper safeguards
could be provided for his honour and reputation; but

---

[1] Chapuys to Charles V., March 7, 1535.—*Spanish Calendar*, vol. v.
pp. 413—422.

it was to be understood distinctly that he would not permit the divorce question to be reopened; he would rather forfeit his crown and his life than consent to it or place himself in subjection to any foreign authority; this was his firm resolution, which he desired Chapuys to make known to the Emperor.

The Spanish Ministry had been willing that the Pope's sentence should be revised by a General Council. Why, Chapuys asked, might not the King consent also to refer the case to the Council? The King knew that he was right. He had once been willing—why should he now refuse? A Council, it had been said, would be called by the Pope, and would be composed of clergy who were not his friends; but Chapuys would undertake that there should be no unfair dealing. Were the Pope and clergy to intend harm, all the Princes of Christendom would interfere. The Emperor would recommend nothing to which the King would not be willing to subscribe. The favourable verdict of a Council would restore peace in England, and would acquit the Emperor's conscience. The Emperor, as matters stood, was bound to execute the sentence which had been delivered, and could not hold back longer without a hope of the King's submission.

Cromwell admitted the reasonableness of Chapuys's suggestion. The Emperor was showing by the advances which he had commenced that he desired a reconciliation. A Council controlled by the princes of Europe might perhaps be a useful instrument. Cromwell promised an answer in two days.

Then, after a pause, he returned to the subject of
which he had spoken before. In a matter of so much
consequence to the world as the good intelligence between himself and the King of England, he said that
the Emperor ought not to hesitate on account of the
Queen and the Princess. They were but mortal. If
the Princess was to die, her death would be no great
misfortune, when the result of it would be the union
and friendship of the two Princes.[1] He begged
Chapuys to think it over when alone and at leisure.
He then went on to inquire (for Chapuys had not
informed him that the Emperor had already made
up his mind to an arrangement) whether the ladies'
business might not be passed over silently in the new
treaty, and be left in suspense for the King's life.
A General Council might meet to consider the other
disorders of Christendom, or a congress might be
held, previously appointed jointly by the King and the
Emperor, when the ladies' rights might be arranged
without mystery. Then once more, and, as Chapuys
thought, with marked emphasis, he asked again what
harm need be feared if the Princess were to die. The

[1] 'Il me dit que vostre Majesté
'ne se debvoit arrester pour empe-
'scher ung si inestimable bien que
'produiroit en toute la Chrestienté
'l'union et la bonne intelligence
'dentre vostre Majesté et le Roy son
'maistre pour l'affaire des Royne et
'Princesse qui n'estoient que mor-
'telles ; et que ne seroit grand
'dommage de la mort de la dicte
'Princesse au pris du bien que sor-
'tiroit de la dicte union et intelli-
'gence; en quoy il me prioit vouloir
'considerer quand seroy seul et
'desoccupé.' Chapuys to Charles
V., March 23, 1535.—*Vienna MS.*;
and *Spanish Calendar*, vol. v. p.
426. This and other of Chapuys's
most important letters I tran-
scribed myself at Vienna.

world might mutter, but why should it be resented by the Emperor ?[1]

Chapuys says that he replied that he would not dwell on the trouble which might arise if the Princess suddenly died in a manner so suspicious. God forbid that such a thing should be ! How could the Emperor submit to the reproach of having consented to the death of his cousin, and sold her for the sake of a peace ?

Chapuys professed to believe, and evidently wished the Emperor to believe, that Cromwell was seriously proposing that the Princess Mary should be made away with. A single version of a secret conversation is an insufficient evidence of an intended monstrous crime. We do not know in what language it was carried on. Cromwell spoke no language but English with exactness, and Chapuys understood English imperfectly. The recent and alarming illness of the Princess, occasioned by restraint, fear, and irritation, had made her condition a constant subject of Chapuys's complaints, and Cromwell may have been thinking and speaking only of her dying under the natural consequences of prolonged confinement. Chapuys's unvarying object was to impress on the Emperor that her life was in danger. But Cromwell, he admitted, had been uniformly friendly to Mary, and, had foul play been really contemplated, the Emperor's Ambassador was the last person to whom the intention would have been communicated.

---

[1] 'Me replicquant de nouveaulx quel dommage ou danger 'seroyt que la dicte Princesse feust 'morte, oyres que le peuple en 'murmurast, et quelle raison auroit 'vostre Majesté d'en fayre cas.'

The conversation did not end with Chapuys's answer. Cromwell went on, he said (still dwelling on points most likely to wound Charles), to rage against popes and cardinals, saying that he hoped the race would soon be extinct, and that the world would be rid of their abomination and tyranny. Then he spoke again of France, and of the pressure laid on Henry to join with the French in a war. Always, he said, he had dissuaded his master from expeditions on the Continent. He had himself refused a large pension which the French Government had offered him, and he intended at the next Parliament to introduce a Bill prohibiting English Ministers from taking pensions from foreign princes on pain of death.

Men who have been proposing to commit murders do not lightly turn to topics of less perilous interest.

Some days passed before Chapuys saw Cromwell again ; but he continued to learn from him the various intrigues which were going on. Until the King was sure of his ground with Charles, the French faction at the Court continued their correspondence with Francis. The price of an Anglo-French alliance was to be a promise from the French King to support Henry in his quarrel with Rome at the expected Council, and Chapuys advised his master not to show too much eagerness for the treaty, as he would make the King more intractable.

The Emperor's way of remedying the affairs of England could not be better conceived, he said, provided the English Government met him with an honest

response, provided they would forward the meeting of
the Council, and treat the Queen and Princess better,
who were in great personal danger. This, however,
he believed they would never do. The Queen had
instructed him to complain to the Emperor that her
daughter was still left in the hands of her enemies, and
that if she was to die it would be attributed to the
manner in which she had been dealt with; the Queen,
however, was satisfied that the danger would disappear
if the King and the Emperor came to an understanding; and, if she could be assured that matters
would be conducted as the Emperor proposed, he
would be able to persuade her to approve of the whole
plan.

Chapuys never repeated his suspicion that danger
threatened Mary from Cromwell, and, if he had really
believed it, he would hardly have failed to make further
mention of so dark a suggestion. He was not scrupulous about truth : diplomatists with strong personal
convictions seldom are. He had assured the King that
a thought had never been entertained of an armed
interference in England, while his letters for many
months had been full of schemes for insurrection and
invasion. He was eager for the work to begin. He
was incredulous of any other remedy, and, if he dared,
would have forced the Emperor's hand. He depended
for his information of what passed at the Court upon
Anne Boleyn's bitterest enemies, and he put the worst
interpretation upon every story which was brought to
him. Cromwell, he said, had spoken like Caiaphas. It

is hardly credible that Cromwell would have ventured
to insult the Emperor with a supposition that he would
make himself an accomplice in a crime. But though I
think it more likely that Chapuys misunderstood or
misrepresented Cromwell than that he accurately
recorded his words, yet it is certain that there were
members of Henry's Council who did seriously desire
to try and to execute both Mary and her mother.
Both of them were actively dangerous. Their friends
were engaged in a conspiracy for open rebellion in their
names, and, under the Tudor princes, nearness of blood
or station to the Crown was rather a danger than a
protection. Royal pretenders were not gently dealt
with, even when no immediate peril was feared from
them. Henry VII. had nothing to fear from the Earl
of Warwick, yet Warwick lay in a bloody grave.
Mary herself executed her cousin Jane Grey, and was
hardly prevented from executing her sister Elizabeth.
Elizabeth, in turn, imprisoned Catherine Grey, and let
her die as Chapuys feared that Mary was now about to
die. The dread of another war of succession lay like
a nightmare on the generations which carried with
them an ever-present memory of the Wars of the
Roses.

CHAPTER XVIII.

MORE than a year had now passed since Clement
delivered judgment on the divorce case. So
far the discharge had been ineffective, and the Brief
of Execution, the direct command to the Catholic
Powers to dethrone Henry and to his subjects to
renounce their allegiance, was still withheld. The
advances which the new Pope had made to England
having met with no response, Paul III. was ready to
strike the final blow, but his hand had been held by
Charles, who was now hoping by a treaty to recover
the English alliance. Catherine had consented, but
consented reluctantly, to an experiment from which she
expected nothing. Chapuys himself did not wish it to

succeed, and was unwilling to part with the expectations
which he had built on Darcy's promises. The Spanish
Council, in recommending the course which the
Emperor had taken, had foreseen the dispiritment which
it might produce among the Queen's friends, and the
injury to the Holy See by the disregard of a sentence
which Charles had himself insisted on. The treaty
made no progress. The sacrifice appeared to be fruit-
less, and Catherine appealed to Charles once more in
her old tone. She would be wanting in her duty to
herself, she said, and she would offend God, if she did
not seek the help of those who alone could give her
effectual assistance. She must again press upon his
Majesty the increasing perils to the Catholic Faith and
the injury to the English realm which his neglect to
act was producing. The sentence of Clement had been
powerless. She entreated him with all her energy as a
Christian woman to hesitate no longer. Her daughter
had been ill, and had not yet recovered. Had her
health been strong, the treatment which she received
would destroy it, and, if she died, there would be a
double sin. The Emperor need not care for herself.
She was accustomed to suffering and could bear anything. But she must let him know that she was as
poor as Job, and was expecting a time when she would
have to beg for alms for the love of God.[1]

Mary was scarcely in so bad a case as her mother
represented. Her spirit had got the better of her

---

[1] Queen Catherine to Charles
V., April 8.—*MS. Vienna; Cal-* *endar, Foreign and Domestic,* vol.
viii. p. 197.

illness and she was again alert and active. The King had supplied her with money and had sent her various kind messages, but she was still eager to escape out of the realm, and Charles had again given a qualified consent to the attempt being made if it was sure of success. With Mary in his hands, he could deal with Henry to better advantage. A favourable opportunity presented itself. Three Spanish ships were lying in the Lower Pool; Mary was still at Greenwich, and their crews were at her disposition. Chapuys asked if she was ready. She was not only ready but eager. She could leave the palace at night with the help of confederates, be carried on board, and disappear down the river.

Accident, or perhaps a whispered warning, deranged her plans. By a sudden order she was removed from Greenwich to Eltham. The alteration of residence was not accompanied with signs of suspicion. She was treated with marked respect. A State litter of some splendour was provided for her. The governess, Mrs. Shelton, however, was continued at her side, and the odious presence redoubled her wish to fly. Before she left Greenwich she sent a message to Chapuys imploring his advice and his assistance. She begged him for the love of God to contrive fresh means for removing her from the country. The enterprise, he thought, would be now dangerous, but not impossible, and success would be a glorious triumph. The Princess had told him that in her present lodging she could not be taken away at night, but she might walk in the day in fine weather, and might be surprised and carried off as if against her consent. The river would not be many miles distant, and, if she could be fallen in with when alone, there might be less difficulty than even at Greenwich, because she could be put on board below Gravesend.[1]

As a ship would be required from Flanders, Chapuys communicated directly with Granvelle. He was conscious that, if he was himself in England when the enterprise was attempted, his own share in it would be suspected and it might go hard with him. He proposed, therefore, under some excuse of business in the Low Countries, to cross over previously.

It would be a splendid *coup*, he said, and, considering how much the Princess wished it and her remarkable prudence and courage, the thing could, no doubt, be managed. Could she be once seized and on horseback, and if there was a galley at hand and a large ship or two, there would be no real difficulty. The country-people would help her, and the parties sent in pursuit would be in no hurry.[2]

Either the difficulties proved greater than were expected, or Charles was still hoping for the treaty, and would not risk an experiment which would spoil the chances of an accommodation. Once more he altered his mind and forbade the venture, and Chapuys had to

---

[1] Chapuys to Charles V., April 4, 1535.—*MS. Vienna; Calendar, Foreign and Domestic*, vol. viii. p. 193.

[2] Chapuys to Granvelle, April 5, 1535.—*Calendar, Foreign and Domestic*, vol. viii. p. 194; and *MS. Vienna.*

take up again a negotiation from which he had no
expectation of good. He met Cromwell from time to
time, his master's pleasure being to preserve peace on
tolerable terms; and the Ambassador continued to
propose the reference of the divorce case to the General
Council, on which Cromwell had seemed not unwilling
to listen to him. If Henry could be tempted by vague
promises to submit his conduct to a Council called by
the Pope, he would be again in the meshes out of which
he had cut his way. The cunning Ambassador urged on
Cromwell the honour which the King would gain if a
Council confirmed what he had done; and when Cromwell
answered that a Council under the Emperor's influence
might rather give an adverse sentence, he said that, if
it was so, the King would have shown by a voluntary
submission that his motives had been pure, and might
have perfect confidence in the Emperor's fairness.
Cromwell said he would consult the King; but the real
difficulty lay in the pretensions of the Princess. Cromwell was well served; he probably knew, as well as
Chapuys, of the intended rape at Eltham, and all that
it would involve. 'Would to God——' he broke out
impatiently, and did not finish the sentence; but
Chapuys thought he saw what the finish would have
been.[1] Henry may be credited with some forbearance
towards his troublesome daughter. She defied his laws.
Her supporters were trying to take his crown from him,
and she herself was attempting to escape abroad and

---

[1] Chapuys to Charles V., April 17, 1535.—*Calendar, Foreign and
Domestic,* vol. viii. p. 209.

levy war upon him. Few of his predecessors would have hesitated to take ruder methods with so unmalleable a piece of metal. She herself believed that escape was her only chance of life. She was in the power of persons who, she had been told, meant to poison her, while no means were neglected to exasperate the King's mind against her. He, on his side, was told that she was incurably obstinate, while everything was concealed that might make him more favourably disposed towards her. In the midst of public business with which he was overwhelmed, he could not know what was passing inside the walls at Eltham. He discovered occasionally that he had been deceived. He complained to Cromwell ' that ' he had found much good in his daughter of which he ' had not been properly informed.' But if there was a conspiracy against Mary, there was also a conspiracy against himself, in a quarter where it could have been least expected.

Dr. Butts, the King's physician, whose portrait by Holbein is so familiar to us, was one of the most devoted friends of Queen Catherine. During Mary's illness, Dr. Butts had affected to be afraid of the responsibility of attending upon her. He had consented afterwards, though with apparent reluctance, and had met in consultation Catherine's doctor, who had also allowed himself to be persuaded. Henry sent Butts down to Eltham with his own horses. The Royal physician found his patient better than he expected, and, instead of talking over her disorders, he talked of the condition of the realm with his brother practitioner.

'The doctor is a very clever man,' wrote Chapuys,
reporting the account of the conversation which he
received from the Queen's physician, 'and is intimate
'with the nobles and the Council. He says that there
'are but two ways of assisting the Queen and Princess
'and of setting right the affairs of the realm : one
'would be if it pleased God to visit the King with some
'little malady.'[1] 'The second method was force, of
'which, he said, the King and his Ministers were in
'marvellous fear. If it came to war, he thought the
'King would be specially careful of the Queen and
'Princess, meaning to use them, should things turn
'to the worst, as mediators for peace. But if neither
'of these means were made use of, he really believed
'they were in danger of their lives. He considered it
'was lucky for the King that the Emperor did not
'know how easy the enterprise of England would
'be; and the present, he said, was the right time
'for it.'

His private physician, it is to be remembered, was
necessarily, of all Henry's servants, the most trusted by
him; and the doctor was not contented with indirect
suggestions, for he himself sent a secret message to
Chapuys that twenty great peers and a hundred knights
were ready, they and their vassals, to venture fortune

---

[1] 'Le premier estoit si Dieu
'vouloit visiter le Roy de quelque
'petite maladie.' The word *petite*
implied perhaps in Chapuys's mind
that Dr. Butts contemplated a
disorder of which he could control
the dimensions, and the word, if
he used it, is at least as suspicious
as Cromwell's language about
Mary.

CH. 18.]   *POPULAR OPINION.*   367

and life, with the smallest assistance from the Emperor, to rise and make a revolution.[1]

Dr. Butts with his *petite maladie* was a 'giant traitor,' though, happily for himself, he was left undiscovered. Human sympathies run so inevitably on the side of the sufferers in history, that we forget that something also is due to those whom they forced into dealing hardly with them. Catherine and the faithful Catholics who conspired and lost their lives for her cause and the Pope's, are in no danger of losing the favourable judgment of the world; the tyranny and cruelty of Henry VIII. will probably remain for ever a subject of eloquent denunciation; but there is an *altera pars*— another view of the story, which we may be permitted without offence to recognise. Henry was, on the whole, right; the general cause for which he was contending was a good cause. His victory opened the fountains of English national life, won for England spiritual freedom, and behind spiritual freedom her political liberties. His defeat would have kindled the martyr-fires in every English town, and would have burnt out of the country thousands of poor men and women as noble as Catherine herself. He had stained the purity of his action by intermingling with it a weak passion for a foolish and bad woman, and bitterly he had to suffer for his mistake;

---

[1] 'Affirmant pour tout certain 'qu'il y avoit une xx des prin-'cipaulx Seigneurs d'Angleterre et 'plus de cent Chevaliers tout dis-'posés et prests à employer per-'sonnes, biens, armes, et subjects, 'ayant le moindre assistance de 'vostre Majesté.' Chapuys to Charles V., April 25, 1535.— *Calendar, Foreign and Domestic,* vol. viii. p. 222; and *MS. Vienna.*

but the revolt against, and the overthrow of, ecclesiastical despotism were precious services, which ought to be remembered to his honour; and, when the good doctor to whom he trusted his life, out of compassion for an unfortunate lady was, perhaps, willing to administer a doubtful potion to him, or to aid in inviting a Catholic army into England to extinguish the light that was dawning there, only those who are Catholics first and Englishmen afterwards will say that it was well done on the doctor's part.

The temper of the nation was growing dangerous, and the forces on both sides were ranging themselves for the battle. Bishop Fisher has been seen sounding on the same string. He, with More, had now been for many months in the Tower, and his communications with Chapuys having been cut off, he had been unable to continue his solicitations; but the Ambassador had undertaken for the whole of the clergy on the instant that the Emperor should declare himself. The growth of Lutheranism had touched their hearts with pious indignation; their hatred of heresy was almost the sole distinction which they had preserved belonging to their sacred calling. The regular orders were the most worthless; the smaller monasteries were nests of depravity; the purpose of their existence was to sing souls out of purgatory, and the efficacy of their musical petitionings being no longer believed in, the King had concluded that monks and nuns could be better employed, and that the wealth which maintained them could be turned to better purpose—to the purpose

especially of the defence of the realm against them and
their machinations. The monks everywhere were the
active missionaries of treason. They writhed under
the Act of Supremacy. Their hope of continuance
depended on the restoration of the Papal authority.
When they were discovered to be at once useless and
treacherous, it was not unjust to take their lands from
them and apply the money for which those lands could
be sold, to the fleet and the fortresses on the coast.

In this, the greatest of his reforms, Cromwell had
been the King's chief adviser. He had been employed
under Wolsey in the first suppression of the most
corrupt of the smaller houses. In the course of his
work he had gained an insight into the scandalous
habits of their occupants, which convinced him of the
impolicy and uselessness of attempting to prolong their
existence. Institutions however ancient, organisations
however profoundly sacred, cannot outlive the recognition that the evil which they produce is constant and
the advantage visionary.

That the monastic system was doomed had become
generally felt; that the victims of the intended overthrow should be impatient of their fate was no more
than natural. The magnitude of the design, the interests which were threatened, the imagined sanctity
attaching to property devoted to the Church, gave an
opportunity for outcry against sacrilege. The entire
body of monks became in their various orders an army
of insurrectionary preachers, well supplied with money,
terrifying the weak, encouraging the strong, and appeal-

ing to the superstitions so powerful with a people like the English, who were tenacious of their habits and associations.

The Abbots and Priors had sworn to the supremacy, but had sworn reluctantly, with secret reservations to save their consciences. With the prospect of an Imperial deliverer to appear among them, they were recovering courage to defy their excommunicated enemy. Those who retained the most of the original spirit of their religion were the first to recover heart for resistance. The monks of the London Charterhouse, who were exceptions to the general corruption, and were men of piety and character, came forward to repudiate their oaths and to dare the law to punish them. Their tragical story is familiar to all readers of English history. Chapuys adds a few particulars. Their Prior, Haughton, had consented to the Act of Supremacy; but his conscience told him that in doing so he had committed perjury. He went voluntarily, with three of the brotherhood, to Cromwell, and retracted his oath, declaring that the King in calling himself Head of the Church was usurping the Pope's authority. They had not been sent for; their house was in no immediate danger; and there was no intention of meddling with them. Their act was a gratuitous defiance, and under the circumstances of the country was an act of war. The effect, if not the purpose, was, and must have been, to encourage a spirit which would explode in rebellion. Cromwell warned them of their danger, and advised them to keep their scruples to themselves. They said they would rather encounter a hundred thousand deaths. They were called before a Council of Peers. The Knights of the Garter were holding their annual Chapter, and the attendance was large. The Duke of Norfolk presided, having returned to the Court, and the proceedings were unusually solemn. The monks were required to withdraw their declaration ; they were told that the statute was not to be disputed. They persisted. They were allowed a night to reflect, and they spent it on their knees in prayer. In the morning they were recalled ; their courage held, and they were sentenced to die, with another friar who had spoken and written to similar purpose.

They had thrown down a challenge to the Government ; the challenge was accepted, and the execution marked the importance of the occasion. They were not a handful of insignificant priests ; they were the advanced guard of insurrection ; and to allow them to triumph was to admit defeat. They were conducted through the streets by an armed force. The Duke of Norfolk, the Duke of Richmond, Henry's illegitimate son, Lord Wiltshire, and Lord Rochford attended at the scaffold. Sir Henry Norris was also there, masked, with forty of the Royal Guard on horseback. At the scaffold they were again offered a chance of life ; again they refused, and died gallantly. The struggle had begun for the Crown of England. In claiming the supremacy for the Pope, these men had abjured their allegiance to the King whom the Pope had excom-

municated. Conscience was nothing — motive was
nothing. Conscience was not allowed as a plea when a
Lutheran was threatened with the stake. In all civil
conflicts high motives are to be found on both sides,
and in earnest times words are not used without
meaning. The Statute of Supremacy was Henry's
defence against an attempt to deprive him of his crown
and deprive the kingdom of its independence. To
disobey the law was treason; and the penalty of
treason was death.[1]

Chapuys in telling the story urged it as a proof to
Charles that there was no hope of the King's repent-
ance. It was now expected that More and Fisher, and
perhaps the Queen and Princess, would be called on
also to acknowledge the supremacy, and, if they refused,
would suffer the same fate. The King's Ministers,
Chapuys said, were known to have often reproached the
King, and to have told him it was a shame for him and
the kingdom not to punish them as traitors. Anne
Boleyn was fiercer and haughtier than ever she was.[2]
Sir Thomas More was under the same impression that
Anne had been instigator of the severities. She would
take his head from him, he said, and then added, pro-
phetically, that her own would follow. The presence of
her father and brother and her favourite Norris at the
execution of the Carthusians confirmed the impression.
The action of the Government had grounds more sufficient than a woman's urgency. More and Fisher re-

---

[1] Chapuys to Charles V., May 5, 1535.—*Spanish Calendar*, vol. v.
p. 452.   [2] *Ibid.*

ceived notice that they would be examined on the statute, and were allowed six weeks to prepare their answer. Chapuys did not believe that any danger threatened Catherine, or threatened her household. She herself, however, anticipated the worst, and only hoped that her own fate might rouse the Emperor at last.

The Emperor was not to be roused. He was preparing for his great expedition to Tunis to root out the corsairs, and had other work on hand. In vain Chapuys had tried to make him believe that Cromwell meditated the destruction of the Princess Mary; in vain Chapuys had told him that words were useless, and that 'cautery was the only remedy'—that the English Peers were panting for encouragement to take arms. He had no confidence in insurgent subjects who could not use the constitutional methods which they possessed to do anything for themselves. He saw Henry crushing down resistance with the relentless severity of the law. He replied to Chapuys's entreaties that, although he could not in conscience abandon his aunt and cousin, yet the Ambassador must temporise. He had changed his mind about Mary's escape : he said it was dangerous, unadvisable, and not to be thought of.[1] The present was not the proper moment. He wrote a cautious letter to the King, which he forwarded for Chapuys to deliver. In spite of Charterhouse monks and Lutheran preachers, the Ambassador was to take up again the negotiations for the treaty.

---

[1] Charles V. to Chapuys, May 10, 1535.—*Spanish Calendar*, vol. v. p. 459.

Thus Cromwell and he recommenced their secret meetings. A country-house was selected for the purpose, where their interviews would be unobserved. Chapuys had recommended that Henry should assist in calling a General Council. Cromwell undertook that Henry would consent, provided the Council was not held in Italy, or in the Pope's or the Emperor's dominions, and provided that the divorce should not be among the questions submitted to it. The Emperor, he said, had done enough for his honour, and might now leave the matter to the King's conscience. With respect to the Queen and Princess, the King had already written to Sir John Wallop, who was to lay his letters before the Spanish Ambassador in Paris. The King had said that, although the Emperor, in forsaking a loyal friend for the sake of a woman, had not acted well with him, yet he was willing to forget and forgive. If the Emperor would advise the ladies to submit to the judgment of the Universities of Europe, which had been sanctioned by the English estates of the realm, and was as good as a decree of a Council, they would have nothing to complain of.[1] Chapuys observed that such a letter ought to have been shown to himself before it was sent; but that was of no moment. The King of France, Cromwell went on, would bring the Turk, and the Devil too, into Christendom to recover Milan; the King and the Emperor ought to draw together to hold France in check; and yet, to give Chapuys a hint that

---

[1] *Spanish Calendar*, vol. v. p. 459.

he knew what he had been doing, he said he had heard, though he did not believe it, that the Emperor and the King of the Romans had thought of invading England, in a belief that they would make an easy conquest of it. They would find the enterprise more costly than they expected, and, even if they did conquer England, they could not keep it. Chapuys, wishing to learn how much had been discovered, asked what Cromwell meant. Cromwell told him the exact truth. The scheme had been to stop the trade between England and Flanders. A rebellion was expected to follow, which, Cromwell admitted, was not unlikely ; and then, in great detail and with a quiet air of certainty, he referred to the solicitations continually made to the Emperor to send across an army.

Leaving Chapuys to wonder at his sources of information so accurate, Cromwell spoke of an approaching conference at Calais, which was to be held at the request of the French King. He did not think anything would come of it. He had himself declined to be present, but one of the proposals to be made would be an offer of the Duke of Angoulême for the young Princess Elizabeth. The Council, he said, had meantime been reviewing the old treaty for the marriage of the Emperor to the Princess Mary, and the King had spoken in the warmest terms of the Emperor. Perhaps as a substitute for the French connection, and provided the divorce was not called in question again, he thought that the Princess Elizabeth might be betrothed to Philip, and a marriage could be found out of the realm for the

Princess Mary with the Emperor's consent and appro-
bation. The King, in this case, would give her the
greatest and richest dower that was ever given to any
Queen or Empress.[1]

Chapuys observed that the divorce must be disposed
of before fresh marriages could be thought of. Cromwell wished him to speak himself to the King. Chapuys
politely declined to take so delicate a negotiation out of
Cromwell's hands. For himself, he had not yet abandoned hope of a different issue. Lord Darcy was still
eager as ever, and wished to communicate directly with
the Emperor. From Ireland, too, the news was less
discouraging. The insurrection had burnt down, but
was still unsubdued. Lord Thomas found one of his
difficulties to lie in the incompleteness of the Papal
censures. The formal Bull of Deposition was still
unpublished. The young chief had written to the
Pope to say that, but for this deficiency, he would have
driven the English out of the island, and to beg that it
might be immediately supplied. He had himself, too,
perhaps, been in fault. The murder of an archbishop
who had not been directly excommunicated was an
irregularity and possibly a crime. He prayed that the
Pope would send him absolution. Paul as he read the
letter showed much pleasure. He excused his hesitation as having risen from a hope that the King of
England would repent. For the future he said he
would do his duty, and at once sent Lord Thomas the

---

[1] Chapuys to Charles V., May 8, 1535.—*Spanish Calendar*, vol. v.
p. 457.

required pardon for an act which had been really meritorious.[1]

The absolution may have benefited Lord Thomas's soul. It did not save him from the gallows.

Again Cromwell and Chapuys met. Again the discussion returned to the insoluble problem. The Spanish Council of State had half recommended that the divorce should be passed over, as it had been at Cambray. Chapuys laboured to entangle Henry in an engagement that it should be submitted to the intended General Council. The argument took the usual form. Cromwell said that the King could not revoke what he had done, without disgrace. Chapuys answered that it was the only way to avoid disgrace, and the most honourable course which he could adopt. The King ought not to be satisfied in such a matter with the laws and constitutions of his own country. If he would yield on this single point, the taking away the property of the clergy might in some degree be confirmed. The ground alleged for it being the defence of the realm, there would be less occasion for such measures in future; the Emperor would allow the King to make his submission in any form that he might choose, and everything should be made as smooth as Henry could desire.

Cromwell, according to Chapuys, admitted the soundness of the argument, but he said that it was neither in his power, nor in any man's power, to

---

[1] Dr. Ortiz to Charles V., May 27, 1535.—*Spanish Calendar,* vol. v. p. 462.

persuade the King, who would hazard all rather than yield. Even the present Pope, he said, had, when Cardinal, written an autograph letter to the King, telling him that he had a right to ask for a divorce, and that Clement had done him great wrong.

The less reason then, Chapuys neatly observed, for refusing to lay the matter before a General Council.

The Ambassador went through his work dutifully, though expecting nothing from it, and his reports of what passed with the English Ministers ended generally with a recommendation of what he thought the wiser course. Lord Hussey, he said, had sent to him to say that he could remain no longer in a country where all ranks and classes were being driven into heresy; and would, therefore, cross the Channel to see the Emperor in person, to urge his own opinion and learn the Emperor's decision from his own lips. If the answer was unfavourable, he would tell his friends, that they might not be deceived in their expectations. They would then act for themselves.[1]

It is likely that Chapuys had been instructed to reserve the concessions which Charles was prepared to make till it was certain that, without them, the treaty would fail. France meanwhile was outbidding the Emperor, and the King was using, without disguise, the offers of each Power to alarm the other. Cromwell at the next meeting told Chapuys that Francis was ready to support the divorce unreservedly if Henry

---

[1] Chapuys to Charles V., May 23, 1535.—*Calendar, Foreign and* | *Domestic,* vol. viii. p. 280 ; *Spanish Calendar,* vol. v. p. 465.

would assist him in taking Milan. The French, he said, should have a sharp answer, could confidence be felt in the Emperor's overtures. A sharp struggle was going on in the Council between the French and Imperial factions. Himself sincerely anxious for the success of the negotiation in which he was engaged, Cromwell said he had fallen into worse disgrace with Anne Boleyn than he had ever been. Anne had never liked him. She had told him recently 'she would like 'to see his head off his shoulders.'[1] She was equally angry with the Duke of Norfolk, who had been too frank in the terms in which he had spoken of her. If she discovered his interviews with Chapuys, she would do them both some ill turn.

The King himself agreed with Cromwell in preferring the Emperor to Francis, but he would not part company with France till he was assured that Charles no longer meant his harm. Charles, it will be remembered, had himself written to Henry, and the letter had by this time arrived. Chapuys feared that, if he presented it at a public audience, the Court would conclude that the Emperor was reconciled, and had abandoned the Queen and Princess, so he applied for a private reception. The King granted it, read the letter, spoke graciously of the expedition against the Turks, and then significantly of his own armaments and the new fortifications at Dover and Calais. He believed (as Chapuys had heard from the Princess Mary) that, if

---

[1] *Spanish Calendar*, vol. v. p. 484.

he could tide over the present summer, the winter
would then protect him, and that in another year he
would be strong enough to fear no one. Seeing that he
said nothing of the treaty, Chapuys began upon it, and
said that the Emperor was anxious to come to terms
with him, so far as honour and conscience would allow.
Henry showed not the least eagerness. He replied
with entire frankness that France was going to war for
Milan. Large offers had been made to him, which, so
far, he had not accepted ; but he might be induced to
listen, unless he could be better assured of the Emperor's
intention.[1]

It was evident that Henry could neither be cajoled
nor frightened. Should Charles then give up the
point for which he was contending ? Once more the
Imperial Privy Council sat to consider what was to be
done. It had become clear that no treaty could be
made with Henry unless the Emperor would distinctly
consent that the divorce should not be spoken of. The
old objections were again weighed—the injuries to the
Queen and to the Holy See, the Emperor's obligations,
the bad effect on Christendom and on England which
a composition on such terms would produce, the encouragement to other Princes to act as Henry had done
—stubborn facts of the case which could not be evaded.
On the other hand were the dangerous attitude of
Francis, the obstinacy of Henry, the possibility that
France and England might unite, and the inability of

---

[1] Chapuys to Charles V., June 5, 1535.—*Spanish Calendar*, vol. v.
p. 483.

the Emperor to encounter their coalition. Both Francis
and Henry were powerful princes, and a quarrel would
not benefit the Queen and her daughter if the Emperor
was powerless to help them. The divorce was the
difficulty. Should the Emperor insist on a promise
that it should be submitted to a General Council? It
might be advisable, under certain circumstances, to
create disturbances in England and Ireland, so as to
force the King into an alliance on the Emperor's terms.
But if Henry could be induced to suspend or modify his
attacks on the Faith and the Church, to break his connection with France and withdraw from his negotiations
with the Germans, if securities could be taken that the
Queen and Princess should not be compelled to sign or
promise anything without the Emperor's consent, the
evident sense of the Spanish Council of State was that
the proceedings against the King should be suspended,
perhaps for his life, and that no stipulations should be
insisted on, either for the King's return to the Church
or for his consent to the meeting of the General Council.
God might perhaps work on the King's conscience
without threat of force or violence ; and the Emperor,
before starting on his expedition to Tunis, might tell
the English Ambassador that he wished to be the
King's friend, and would not go to war with any
Christian prince unless he was compelled. The Queen's
consent would, of course, be necessary ; she and the
Princess would be more miserable than ever if they
were made to believe that there was no help for them.

---

[1] *Spanish Calendar*, vol. v. p. 486.

But their consent, if there was no alternative, might be assumed when a refusal would be useless.

If the willingness to make concessions was the measure of the respective anxieties for an agreement between the two countries, Spain was more eager than England, for the Emperor was willing to yield the point on which he had broken the unity of Christendom and content himself with words, while Henry would yield nothing, except the French alliance, for which he had cared little from the time that France had refused to follow him into schism.

An alliance of the Emperor with an excommunicated sovereign in the face of a sentence which he had himself insisted on, and with a Bull of Deposition ready for launching, would be an insult to the Holy See more dangerous to it than the revolt of a single kingdom. The treaty might, however, have been completed on the terms which Wallop and the Imperial Ambassador had agreed on at Paris, and which the Imperial Council had not rejected. The Pope saw the peril, struck in, and made it impossible. In the trial and execution of the Carthusians Henry had shown to Europe that he was himself in earnest. The blood of martyrs was the seed of the Church, and Paul calculated rightly that he could not injure the King of England more effectually than by driving him to fresh severities and thus provoking an insurrection. No other explanation can be given for his having chosen this particular moment for an act which must and would produce the desired consequence. Bishop Fisher and Sir Thomas

More had been allowed six weeks to consider whether they would acknowledge the Statute of Supremacy. More was respected by every one, except the Lutherans, whom he confessed that he hated; Fisher was regarded as a saint by the Catholic part of England; and the King, who was dependent after all on the support of his subjects and could not wish to shock or alienate them, would probably have pressed them no further, unless challenged by some fresh provocation. Fisher had waded deep into treason, but, if the King knew it, there was no evidence which could be produced. Before the six weeks were expired the Court and the world were astonished to hear that Paul had created the Bishop of Rochester a cardinal, and that the hat was already on the way. Casalis, who foresaw the consequences, had protested against the appointment, both to the Pope and the Consistory. Paul pretended to be frightened. He begged Casalis to excuse him to the King. He professed, what it was impossible to believe, that he had intended to pay England a compliment. A General Council was to meet. He wished England to be represented there by a Prelate whom he understood to be distinguished for learning and sanctity. The Roman Pontiffs have had a chequered reputation, but the weakest of them has never been suspected of a want of worldly acuteness. The condition of England was as well understood at Rome as it was understood by Chapuys, and, with Dr. Ortiz at his ear, Paul must have been acquainted with the disposition of every peer and prelate in the realm. Fisher's name had been familiar

through the seven years' controversy as of the one
English bishop who had been constant in resistance to
every step of Henry's policy. Paul, who had just
absolved Silken Thomas for the Archbishop of Dublin's
murder, had little to learn about the conspiracy, or
about Fisher's share in it. The excuse was an insolence more affronting than the act itself. It was
impossible for the King to acknowledge himself defied
and defeated. He said briefly that he would send
Fisher's head to Rome, for the hat to be fitted on it.
Sir Thomas More, as Fisher's dearest friend, connected
with him in opposition to the Reformation and sharing
his imprisonment for the same actions, was involved
along with him in the fatal effects of the Pope's cunning
or the Pope's idiocy. The six weeks ran out. The
Bishop and the ex-Chancellor were called again before
the Council, refused to acknowledge the supremacy, and
were committed for trial.

The French and English Commissioners had met
and parted at Calais. Nothing had been concluded
there, as Cromwell said with pleasure to Chapuys,
prejudicial to the Emperor ; but as to submitting the
King's conduct to a Council, Cromwell reiterated that
it was not to be thought of. Were there no other
reason, the hatred borne to him by all the English
prestraylle for having pulled down the tyranny of the
Church and tried to reform them, would be cause
sufficient. The Council would be composed of clergy.
More than this, and under the provocation of the fresh
insult, Cromwell said that neither the King nor his

subjects would recognise any Council convoked by the Pope. A Council convoked by the Emperor they would acknowledge, but a Papal Council never. They intended to make the Church of England a true and singular mirror to all Christendom.[1]

Paul can hardly have deliberately contemplated the results of what he had done. He probably calculated either that Henry would not dare to go to extremities with a person of so holy a reputation as Bishop Fisher, or that the threat of it would force Fisher's and the Queen's friends into the field in time to save him. They had boasted that the whole country was with them, and the Pope had taken them at their word. Yet his own mind misgave him. The Nuncio at Paris was directed to beg Francis to intercede. Francis said he would do his best, but feared the ' hat ' would prove the Bishop's death. Henry, Francis said, was not always easy to deal with. He almost treated him as a subject. He was the strangest man in the world, he feared he could do no good with him.[2] There was not the least likelihood that the King would allow the interposition either of Francis or of any one. The crime created by the Act of Supremacy was the denial by word or act of the King's sovereignty, ecclesiastical or civil, and the object was to check and punish seditious speaking or preaching. As the Act was first

---

[1] Chapuys to Charles V., June 30, 1535.—*Spanish Calendar*, vol. v. p. 500.

[2] The Bishop of Faenza to M. Ambrogio, June 6, 1535.—*Calendar, Foreign and Domestic*, vol. viii. p. 320.

drafted, to speak at all against the supremacy brought
an offender under the penalties. The House of Commons
was unwilling to make mere language into high treason,
and a strong attempt was made to introduce the word
' maliciously.' Men might deny that the King was
Head of the Church in ignorance or inadvertence ; and
an innocent opinion was not a proper subject for severity.
But persons who had exposed themselves to suspicion
might be questioned, and their answers interpreted by
collateral evidence, to prove disloyal intention. Chapuys's
letters leave no doubt of Fisher's real disloyalty. But
his desire to bring in an Imperial army was shared by
half the Peers, and, if proof of it could be produced,
their guilty consciences might drive them into open
rebellion. It was ascertained that Fisher and More
had communicated with each other in the Tower on the
answers which they were to give. But other points
had risen for which Fisher was not prepared. Among
the papers found in his study were letters in an unknown hand addressed to Queen Catherine, which
apparently the Bishop was to have forwarded to her,
but had been prevented by his arrest. They formed
part of a correspondence between the Queen and some
foreign prince, carried on through a reverend father
spoken of as E. R. . . . alluding to things which ' no
' mortal man was to know besides those whom it be-
hoved,' and to another letter which E. R. had received
of the Bishop himself. Fisher was asked who wrote
these letters : ' Who was E. R. ? Who was the Prince ? '
What those things were which no mortal was to know ?

If trifles, why the secrecy, and from whom were they to be concealed ? What were the letters which had been received from the Bishop himself to be sent oversea ? The letters found contained also a request to know whether Catherine wished the writer to proceed to other princes in Germany and solicit them; and again a promise that the writer would maintain her cause among good men there, and would let her know what he could succeed in bringing to pass with the princes.

The Bishop was asked whether, saving his faith and allegiance, he ought to have assisted a man who was engaged in such enterprises, and why he concealed a matter which he knew to be intended against the King ; how the letter came into his hands, who sent it, who brought it. If the Bishop refused to answer or equivocated, he was to understand that the King knew the truth, for he had proof in his hands. The writer was crafty and subtle and had promised to spend his labour with the princes that they should take in hand to defend the Lady Catherine's cause.

The King held the key to the whole mystery. The mine had been undermined. The intended rebellion was no secret to Henry or to Cromwell. Catherine, a divorced wife and a Spanish princess, owed no allegiance in England. But Fisher was an English subject, and conscience is no excuse for treason, until the treason succeeds.

Fisher answered warily, but certainly untruly, that he could not recollect the name either of the Prince who wrote the letter which had been discovered or of the messenger who brought it. It was probably some German prince, but, as God might help him, he could not say which, unless it was Ferdinard, King of Hungary. E. R. was not himself, nor did he ever consent that the writer should attempt anything with the German princes against the King.

He had been careful. He had desired Chapuys from the beginning that his name should not be mentioned, except in cipher. He had perhaps abstained from directly advising an application to Ferdinand, who could not act without the Emperor's sanction. His messages to Charles through his Ambassador even Fisher could scarcely have had the hardiness to deny ; but these messages, if known, were not alleged. The Anglo-Imperial alliance was on the anvil, and the question was not put to him.[1]

Of Fisher's malice, however, as the law construed it, there was no doubt. He persisted in his refusal to acknowledge the supremacy of the Crown. Five days after his examination he was tried at Westminster Hall, and in the week following he was executed on Tower Hill. He died bravely in a cause which he believed to be right. To the last he might have saved himself by submission, but he never wavered. He knew that he could do better service to the Queen and the Catholic Church by his death than by his life. Cromwell told Chapuys that ' the Bishop of Rome was ' the cause of his punishment, for having made a

---

[1] Examination of Fisher in the Tower, June 12, 1535.—*Calendar,* *Foreign and Domestic,* vol. viii. pp. 331 et seq.

'cardinal of the King's worst enemy.' He was 'greatly 'pitied of the people.' The pity would have been less had his real conduct been revealed.

A nobler victim followed. In the lists of those who were prepared to take arms against the King there is no mention of the name of Sir Thomas More; but he had been Fisher's intimate friend and companion, and he could hardly have been ignorant of a conspiracy with which Fisher had been so closely concerned; while malice might be inferred without injustice from an acquaintance with dangerous purposes which he had not revealed. He paid the penalty of the society to which he had attached himself. He, even more than the Bishop of Rochester, was the chief of the party most opposed to the Reformation. He had distin-guished himself as Chancellor by his zeal against the Lutherans, and, if that party had won the day, they would have gone to work as they did afterwards when Mary became Queen. No one knew better than More the need in which the Church stood of the surgeon's hand; no one saw clearer the fox's face under the monk's cowl: but, like other moderate reformers, he detested impatient enthusiasts who spoilt their cause by extravagance. He felt towards the Protestantism which was spreading in England as Burke felt towards the Convention and the Jacobin Club, and while More lived and defied the statute, the vast middle party in the nation which was yet undecided found encourage-ment in opposition from his example. His execution has been uniformly condemned by historians as an act

of wanton tyranny.   It was not wanton, and it was not
an act of tyranny.   It was an inevitable and painful
incident of an infinitely blessed revolution.

The received accounts of his trials are confirmed
with slight additions by a paper of news from England
which was sent to the Imperial Court.

More was charged with having deprived the King
of the title of 'Supreme Head of the Church,' which
had been granted to him by the last Parliament.   He
replied that, when questioned by the King's Secretary
what he thought of the statute, he had answered that,
being a dead man to the world, he cared nothing for
such things, and he could not be condemned for silence.
The King's Attorney said that all good subjects were
bound to answer without dissimulation or reserve,
and silence was the same as speech.   Silence, More
objected, was generally taken to mean consent.   Whatever his thoughts might be, he had never uttered them.

He was charged with having exchanged letters with
the Bishop of Rochester in the Tower on the replies
which they were to give on their examination.   Each
had said that the statute was a sword with two edges,
one of which slew the body, the other the soul.   As
they had used the same words, it was clear that they
were confederated.

More replied that he had answered as his conscience
dictated, and had advised the Bishop to do the same.
He did not believe that he had ever said or done anything maliciously against the statute.

The jury consulted only for a quarter of an hour

and returned a verdict of 'guilty.' Sentence passed as
a matter of course, and then More spoke out. As he
was condemned, he said he would now declare his
opinion. He had studied the question for seven years,
and was satisfied that no temporal lord could be head
of the spiritualty. For each bishop on the side of the
Royal Supremacy he could produce a hundred saints.
For their Parliament he had the Councils of a thousand
years. For one kingdom he had all the other Christian
Powers. The Bishops had broken their vows; the
Parliament had no authority to make laws against the
unity of Christendom, and had capitally sinned in
making them. His crime had been his opposition to
the second marriage of the King. He had faith, however, that, as St. Paul persecuted St. Stephen, yet both
were now in Paradise, so he and his judges, although at
variance in this world, would meet in charity hereafter.[1]

The end came quickly. The trial was on the 1st
of July; on the 6th the head fell of one of the most
interesting men that England ever produced. Had the
supremacy been a question of opinion, had there been
no conspiracy to restore by arms the Papal tyranny, no
clergy and nobles entreating the landing of an army
like that which wasted Flanders at the command of the
Duke of Alva, no Irish nobles murdering archbishops
and receiving Papal absolution for it, to have sent Sir
Thomas More to the scaffold for believing the Pope to
be master of England would have been a barbarous

---

[1] News from England, July 1, 1535.—*Spanish Calendar*, vol. v. p.
507.

murder, deserving the execration which has been poured
upon it.   An age which has no such perils to alarm its
slumbers forgets the enemies which threatened to waste
the country with fire and sword, and admires only the
virtues which remain fresh for all time ; we, too, if exposed to similar possibilities, might be no more merciful
than our forefathers.

The execution of Fisher and More was the King's
answer to Papal thunders and domestic conspirators,
and the effect was electric.   Darcy again appealed to
Chapuys, praying that the final sentence should be instantly issued.   He did not wish to wait any longer for
Imperial aid.   The Pope having spoken, the country
would now rise of itself.   The clergy would furnish all
the money needed for a beginning, and a way might be
found to seize the gold in the Treasury.   Time pressed.
They must get to work at once.   If they loitered
longer, the modern preachers and prelates would corrupt
the people, and all would be lost.[1]   Cifuentes wrote
from Rome to the Emperor that the Bishop of Paris
was on his way thither with proposals from Francis for
an arrangement with England which would be fatal to
the Queen, the Church, and the morals of Christendom.
He begged to be allowed to press the Pope to hold in
readiness a brief deposing Henry ; a brief which, if
once issued, could not be recalled.[2]

---

[1] Chapuys to Charles V.,
July 11, 1535.—*Spanish Calendar*, vol. v. p. 512.

[2] Cifuentes to Charles V.
July 16, 1535.—*Ibid.* p. 515.

CHAPTER XIX.

Campaign of the Emperor in Africa—Uncertainties at Rome—
Policy of Francis—English preparations for war—Fresh
appeals to the Emperor—Delay in the issue of the censures—
The Princess Mary—Letter of Catherine to the Pope—Dis-
affection of the English Catholics—Libels against Henry—
Cromwell and Chapuys—Lord Thomas Fitzgerald—Dangerous
position of Henry—Death of the Duke of Milan—Effect on
European policy—Intended Bull of Paul III.—Indecision of
Charles—Prospect of war with France—Advice of Charles to
Catherine—Distrust of the Emperor at the Papal Court—War-
like resolution of the Pope restrained by the Cardinals.

CIFUENTES had been misinformed when he feared
that Francis was again about to interpose in Henry's
behalf at Rome. The conference at Calais had broken
up without definite results. The policy of France was
to draw Henry off from his treaty with the Emperor;
Henry preferred to play the two great Catholic Powers
one against the other, and commit himself to neither;
and Francis, knowing the indignation which Fisher's
execution would produce at Rome, was turning his
thoughts on other means of accomplishing his purpose.
The Emperor's African campaign was splendidly successful—too successful to be satisfactory at the Vatican.
The Pope, as the head of Christendom, was bound to

express pleasure at the defeat of the Infidels, but he
feared that Charles, victorious by land and sea, might
give him trouble in his own dominions.[1] A settled
purpose, however, remained to punish the English
King, and Henry had need to be careful. The French
faction in the Council wished him to proceed at once to
extremities with the Princess, which would effectually
end the hopes of an Imperial alliance. Anne Boleyn
was continually telling the King that the Queen and
Princess were his greatest danger. 'They deserved
'death more than those who had been lately executed,
'since they were the cause of all the mischief.'[2]
Chapuys found himself no longer able to communicate
with Mary, from the increased precaution in guarding
her. It was alleged that there was a fear of her being
carried off by the French.

The Imperial party at Rome, not knowing what to
do or to advise, drew a curious memorandum for
Charles's consideration. The Emperor, they said, had
been informed when the divorce case was being tried at
Rome, *that England was a fief of the Church of Rome,*
and, as the King had defied the Apostolic See, he deserved to be deprived of his crown. The Emperor had
not approved of a step so severe. But the King had
now beheaded the Bishop of Rochester, whom the Pope
had made a cardinal. On the news of the execution
the Pope and Cardinals had moved that he should be
deprived at once and without more delay for this and

---

[1] *Spanish Calendar*, vol. v. p. 532.

[2] Chapuys to Charles V., July 25, 1535.—*Ibid.* vol. v. p. 518.

for his other crimes. Against taking such action was the danger to the Queen, of which they were greatly afraid, and also the sense that if, after sentence, the crown of England devolved on the Holy See, injury might be done to the prospects of the Princess. It might be contrived that the Pope in depriving the King might assign the crown to his daughter, or the Pope in Consistory might declare secretly that they were acting in favour of the Princess and without prejudice to her claim. To this, however, there was the objection that the King might hear of it through some of the Cardinals. Something at any rate had to be done. All courses were dangerous. The Emperor was requested to decide.[1]

A new ingredient was now to be thrown into the political cauldron. So far from wishing to reconcile England with the Papacy, the Pope informed Cifuentes that Francis was now ready and willing to help the Apostolic See in the execution of the Sentence against the King of England. Francis thought that the Emperor ought to begin, since the affair was his personal concern; but when the first step was taken Francis himself would be at the Pope's disposition. The meaning of this, in the opinion of Cifuentes, was merely to entangle the Emperor in a war with England, and so to leave him. The Pope himself thought so too. Francis had been heard to say that when the Emperor had opened the campaign he would come next and do

---

[1] Memorandum on the Affairs of England.—*Spanish Calendar*, vol. v. p. 522.

what was most for his own interest. The Pope, however, said, as Clement had said before him, that, if Charles and Francis would only act together against England, the 'execution' could be managed satisfactorily. Cifuentes replied that he had no commission to enter into that question. He reported what had passed to his master, and said that he would be in no haste to urge the Pope to further measures.[1]

Henry had expected nothing better from France. He had dared the Pope to do his worst. He stood alone, with no protection save in the jealousy of the rival Powers, and had nothing to trust to save his own ability to defend his country and his crown. His chief anxiety was for the security of the sea. A successful stoppage of trade would, as Cromwell admitted, lead to confusion and insurrection. Ship after ship was built and launched in the Thames. The busy note of preparation rang over the realm. The clergy, Lord Darcy had said, were to furnish money for the rising. The King was taking precautions to shorten their resources, and turn their revenues to the protection of the realm. Cromwell's visitors were out over England examining into the condition of the religious houses, exposing their abuses and sequestrating their estates. These dishonoured institutions had been found to be 'very stews ' of unnatural crime' through the length and breadth of England. Their means of mischief were taken away from such worthless and treacherous communities.

---

[1] Memorandum on the Affairs of England.—*Spanish Calendar*, vol. v. p. 535.

Crown officials were left in charge, and their final fate
was reserved for Parliament.

Henry, meanwhile, confident in his subjects, and
taking lightly the dangers which threatened him, went
on progress along the Welsh borders, hunting, visiting,
showing himself everywhere, and received with apparent
enthusiasm. The behaviour of the people perplexed
Chapuys. 'I am told,' he wrote, 'that in the districts
' where he has been, a good part of the peasantry, after
' hearing the Court preachers, are abused into the belief
' that he was inspired by God to separate himself from
' his brother's wife. They are but idiots. They will
' return soon enough to the truth when there are any
' signs of change.' They would not return, nor were
they the fools he thought them. The clergy, Chapuys
himself confessed it, had made themselves detested by
the English commons for their loose lives and the
tyranny of the ecclesiastical courts. The monasteries,
too many of them, were nests of infamy and fraud, and
the King whom the Catholic world called Antichrist
appeared as a deliverer from an odious despotism.

At Rome there was still uncertainty. The Imperial
memorandum explains the cause of the hesitation.
The Emperor was engaged in Africa, and could decide
nothing till his return. The great Powers were divided
on the partition of the bear's skin, while the bear
was still unstricken. Why, asked the impatient
English Catholics, did not the Pope strike and make
an end of him when even Francis, who had so long
stayed his hand, was now urging him to proceed?

Francis was probably as insincere as Cifuentes believed him to be. But the mere hope of help from such a quarter gave fresh life to the wearied Catherine and her agents.

'The Pope,' wrote Dr. Ortiz to the Emperor, 'has ' committed the deprivation of the King of England and ' the adjudication of the realm to the Apostolic See as a ' fief of the Church to Cardinals Campeggio, Simoneta, ' and Cesis. The delay in granting the executorials in ' the principal cause is wonderful. Although the depo- ' sition of the King was spoken of so hotly in the Con- ' sistory, and they wrote about it to all the Princes, they ' will only proceed with delay and with a monition to ' the King to be intimated in neighbouring countries. ' This is needless. His heresy, schism, and other crimes ' are notorious. He may be deprived without the delay ' of a monition. If it is pressed, it is to be feared it will ' be on the side of France. It is a wonderful revenge ' which the King of France has taken on the King of ' England, to favour him until he has fallen into schism ' and heresy, and then to forsake him in it, to delude ' him as far as the gallows, and to leave him to hang. ' The blood of the saints whom that King has martyred ' calls to God for justice.' [1]

Catherine, sick with hope deferred and tired of the Emperor's hesitation, was catching at the new straw which was floating by her. Ortiz must have kept her informed of the French overtures at the Vatican. She

---

[1] Ortiz to the Empress, Sept. 1, 1535.—*Calendar, Foreign and Domestic* vol. ix. p. 84.

prayed the Regent Mary to use her influence with the French Queen. Now was the time for Francis to show himself a true friend of his brother of England, and assist in delivering him from a state of sin.[1]

Strange rumours were current in France and in England to explain the delay of the censures. The Pope had confessed himself alarmed at the completeness of Charles's success at Tunis. It was thought that the Emperor, fresh from his victories, might act on the advice of men like Lope de Soria, take his Holiness himself in hand and abolish the Temporal Power; that the Pope knew it, and therefore feared to make matters worse by provoking England further.[2]

Pope and Princes might watch each other in distrust at a safe distance; but to the English conspirators the long pause was life or death. Delays are usually fatal with intended rebellion. The only safety is in immediate action. Enthusiasm cools, and secrets are betrayed. Fisher's fate was a fresh spur to them to move, but it also proved that the Government knew too much and did not mean to flinch.

Chapuys tried Granvelle again. 'Every man of 'position here,' he said, 'is in despair at the Pope's 'inaction. If something is not done promptly, there

---

[1] 'Cuando se viese con la Señora 'Reyna su hermana, despues de 'dadas mis afectuosas encomiendas, 'rogarle de mi parte quisiese tener 'mencion de my con el Christianis-'imo Rey su marido y hacer quanto 'pudiese ser, que el sea buen amigo 'al Rey mi Señor procurando de 'quitarle del pecado, en que esta.' Catherine to the Regent Mary, Aug. 8, 1535.—Vienna MS.

[2] Chapuys to Charles V., Sept. 25, 1535.—Calendar, Foreign and Domestic, vol. ix. pp. 140, 141.

' will be no hope for the ladies, or for religion either,
' which is going daily to destruction. Things are come
' to such a pass that at some places men even preach
' against the Sacrament. The Emperor is bound to
' interfere. What he has done in Africa he can do in
' England with far more ease and with incomparably
' more political advantage.' [1]

Granvelle could but answer that Henry was a
monster, and that God would undoubtedly punish him;
but that for himself he was so busy that he could
scarcely breathe, and that the Emperor continued to
hope for some peaceful arrangement.

Cifuentes meanwhile kept his hand on Paul. His
task was difficult, for his orders were to prevent the issue
of the executorials for fear France should act upon
them, while Catholic Christendom would be shaken to
its base if it became known that it was the Emperor
who was preventing the Holy See from avenging itself.
Even with the Pope Cifuentes could not be candid, and
Ortiz, working on Paul's jealousy and unable to com-
prehend the obstacle, had persuaded his Holiness to
draw up ' the brief of execution,' and furnish a copy to
himself.[2]

---

[1] Chapuys to Granvelle, Sept.
25, 1535.—*Vienna MS.; Calendar,
Foreign and Domestic,* vol. ix. p.
141.

[2] The executory brief was not
identical with the Bull of Deposition. The first was the final act
of Catherine's process, a declaration
that Henry, having disobeyed the

sentence on the divorce delivered
by Clement VII., was excommunicated, and an invitation to the
Catholic Powers to execute the
judgment by force. The second
involved a claim for the Holy See
on England as a fief of the Church
—an intimation that the King of
England had forfeited his crown

'In the matter of the executory letters,' Cifuentes
wrote to Charles, 'I have strictly followed your Majesty's
'instructions. They have been kept back for a year
'and a half without the least appearance that the delay
'proceeded from us, but, on the contrary, as if we
'were disappointed that they were not drawn when
'asked for. Besides his Holiness's wish to wait for the
'result of the offers of France, another circumstance
'has served your Majesty's purpose. There were
'certain clauses to which I could not consent in the
'draft shown to me, as detrimental to the right of the
'Queen and Princess and to your Majesty's pre-eminence.

'Now that all hope has vanished of the return of
'the King of England to obedience, Dr. Ortiz, not
'knowing that you wished the execution to be delayed,
'has taken out the executory letters and almost
'despatched them while I was absent at Perugia. The
'letters are ready, nothing being wanted but the Pope's
'seal. I have detained them for a few days, pretending
'that I must examine the wording. They will remain
'in my possession till you inform me of your pleasure.' [1]

The issue of the Pope's censures either in the form
of a letter of execution or of a Bull of Deposition was
to be the signal of the English rising, with or without
the Emperor. Darcy and his friends were ready and

---

and that his subjects' allegiance
had reverted to their Supreme
Lord. The Pope and Consistory
preferred the complete judgment,
as more satisfactory to themselves.
The Catholic Powers objected to it

for the same reason. The practical
effect would be the same.

[1] Cifuentes to Charles V., Oct.
8, 1535.—*Spanish Calendar*, vol.
v. p. 547.

resolved to begin. But without the Pope's direct
sanction the movement would lose its inspiration. The
Irish rebellion had collapsed for the want of it. Lord
Thomas Fitzgerald had surrendered and was a prisoner
in the Tower.

It was not the part of a child, however great her
imagined wrongs, deliberately to promote an insurrection against her father. Henry II.'s sons had done it,
but times were changed. The Princess Mary was
determined to justify such of Henry's Council as had
recommended the harshest measures against her. She
wrote a letter to Chapuys which, if intercepted, might
have made it difficult for the King to save her.

'The condition of things,' she said, ' is worse than
' wretched. The realm will fall to ruin unless his
' Majesty, for the service of God, the welfare of Chris-
' tendom, the honour of the King my father, and
' compassion for the afflicted souls in this country, will
' take pity on us and apply the remedy. This I hope
' and feel assured that he will do if he is rightly
' informed of what is taking place. In the midst of
' his occupations in Africa he will have been unable to
' realise our condition. The whole truth cannot be
' conveyed in letters. I would, therefore, have you
' despatch one of your own people to inform him of
' everything, and to supplicate him on the part of the
' Queen my mother and myself for the honour of God
' and for other respects to attend to and provide for us.
' In so acting he will accomplish a service most agree-
' able to Almighty God. Nor will he win less fame

' and glory to himself than he has achieved in the
' conquest of Tunis or in all his African expedition.' [1]

Catherine simultaneously addressed herself to the
Pope in a letter equally characteristic. The 'brief of
' execution' was the natural close of her process, which,
after judgment in her favour, she was entitled to
demand. The Pope wished her to apply for it, that it
might appear to be granted at her instance and not on
his own impulse.

' Most Holy and Blessed Father,' she wrote, ' I kiss
' your Holiness's hands. My letters have been filled
' with complaints and importunities, and have been
' more calculated to give you pain than pleasure. I
' have therefore for some time ceased from writing
' to your Holiness, although my conscience has re-
' proached me for my silence. One only satisfaction
' I have in thinking of the present state of things : I
' thank unceasingly our Lord Jesus Christ for having
' appointed a vicar like your Holiness, of whom so much
' good is spoken at a time when Christendom is in so
' great a strait. God in his mercy has preserved you
' for this hour. Once more, therefore, as an obedient
' child of the Holy See, I do entreat you to bear this
' realm in special mind, to remember the King, my

---

[1] ' Et luy supplier de la part de
' la Royne, ma mère, et myenne,
' en l'honneur de Dieu et pour
' aultres respects, que dessus vou-
' loit entendre et pourvoyr aux
' affaires dycy. En quoy fera tres
' agréable service à Dieu, et n'en
' acquerra moins de gloire qu'en la
' conqueste de Tunis et de toute
' l'affaire d'Afrique.' *De la Princesse d'Angleterre à l'Ambassadeur*, October, 1535. — *MS.
Vienna ; Spanish Calendar*, vol.
v. p. 559.

' lord and husband, and my daughter. Your Holiness
' knows, and all Christendom knows, what things are
' done here, what great offence is given to God, what
' scandal to the world, what reproach is thrown upon
' your Holiness. If a remedy be not applied shortly,
' there will be no end to ruined souls and martyred
' saints. The good will be firm and will suffer. The
' lukewarm will fail if they find none to help them, and
' the rest will stray out of the way like sheep that have
' lost their shepherd. I place these facts before your
' Holiness because I know not any one on whose
' conscience the deaths of these holy and good men and
' the perdition of so many souls ought to weigh more
' heavily than on yours, inasmuch as your Holiness
' neglects to encounter these evils which the Devil, as
' we see, has sown among us.

'I write frankly to your Holiness, for the discharge
' of my own soul, as to one who, I hope, can feel with
' me and my daughter for the martyrdoms of these
' admirable persons. I have a mournful pleasure in
' expecting that we shall follow them in the manner of
' their torments. And so I end, waiting for the remedy
' from God and from your Holiness. May it come
' speedily! If not, the time will be past. Our Lord
' preserve your Holiness's person !' [1]

On the same day and by the same messenger she
wrote to Charles, congratulating him on his African
victory, and imploring him, now that he was at liberty,

---

[1] Queen Catherine to the Pope, October 10, 1535.—*MS. Vienna.*

to urge the Pope into activity. In other words, she was desiring him to carry fire and sword through England, when if she herself six years before would have allowed the Pope's predecessor to guide her and had retired into 'religion,' there would have been no divorce, no schism, no martyrs, no dangers of a European convulsion on her account. Catherine, as other persons have done, had allowed herself to be governed by her own wounded pride, and called it conscience.

Chapuys conveyed the Queen's arguments both to Charles and to Granvelle. He again assured them that the Princess and her mother were in real danger of death. If the Emperor continued to hesitate, he said, after his splendid victories in Africa, there would be general despair. The opportunity would be gone, and an enterprise now easy would then be difficult, if not impossible.

Now was the time. The execution of More and Fisher, the suppression of the monasteries, the spoliation of the Church, had filled clerical and aristocratic England with fear and fury. The harvest had failed; and the failure was interpreted as a judgment from Heaven on the King's conduct. So sure Chapuys felt that the Emperor would now move that he sent positive assurances to Catherine that his master would not return to Spain till he had restored her to her rights. Even the Bishop of Tarbes, who was again in London, believed that Henry was lost at last. The whole nation, he said, peers and commons, and even the King's own servants, were devoted to the Princess and her mother, and would join any prince who would take up their cause. The discontent was universal, partly because the Princess was regarded as the right heir to the crown, partly for fear of war and the ruin of trade. The autumn had been wet: half the corn was still in the fields. Queen Anne was universally execrated, and even the King was losing his love for her. If war was declared, the entire country would rise.[1]

The Pope, it has been seen, had thought of declaring Mary to be Queen in her father's place. Such a step, if ventured, would inevitably be fatal to her. Her friends in England wished to see her married to some foreign prince—if possible, to the Dauphin—that she might be safe and out of the way. The Princess herself, and even the Emperor, were supposed to desire the match with the Dauphin, because in such an alliance the disputes with France might be forgotten, and Charles and the French King might unite to coerce Henry into obedience.

The wildest charges against Henry were now printed and circulated in Germany and the Low Countries. Cromwell complained to Chapuys. 'Worse,' he said, ' could not be said against Jew or Devil.' Chapuys replied ironically that he was sorry such things should be published. The Emperor would do his best to stop them, but in the general disorder tongues could not be controlled.

So critical the situation had become in these autumn

---

[1] The Bishop of Tarbes to the Bailly of Troyes, October, 1535.— *Calendar, Foreign and Domestic*, vol. ix. p. 187.

months that Cromwell, of course with the King's consent, was obliged to take the unusual step of interfering with the election of the Lord Mayor of London, alleging that, with the State in so much peril, it was of the utmost consequence to have a well-disposed man of influence and experience at the head of the City.

'Cromwell came to me this morning,' Chapuys wrote to his master on the 13th of October; 'he said the King was informed that the Emperor intended to attack him in the Pope's name (he called his Holiness "bishop of "Rome," but begged my pardon while he did so), and that a Legate or Bishop was coming to Flanders to stir the fire. The King could not believe that the Emperor had any such real intention after the friendship which he had shown him, especially when there was no cause. In breaking with the Pope he had done nothing contrary to the law of God, and religion was nowhere better regulated and reformed than it was now in England. The King would send a special embassy to the Emperor, if I thought it would be favourably received. I said I could not advise so great a Prince. I believed that, if the object of such an embassy was one which your Majesty could grant in honour and conscience, it would not only be well received but would be successful. Otherwise, I could neither recommend nor dissuade.' [1]

By the same hand which carried this despatch Chapuys forwarded the letters of Catherine and Mary,

[1] Chapuys to Charles V., October 13, 1535. — *Calendar,* | *Foreign and Domestic,* vol. ix. p. 196.

adding another of his own to Granvelle, in which he
said 'that if the Emperor wished to give peace and
'union to Christendom, he must begin in England. It
'would be easy, for every one was irritated. The King's
'treasure would pay for all, and would help, besides, for
'the enterprise against the Turk. It was time to
'punish him for his folly and impiety.'[1]

Charles seemed to have arrived at the same conclusion. He had already written from Messina, on his
return from Tunis, both to Chapuys and to his Ambassador in Paris, that, as long as Henry retained his
concubine, persisted in his divorce, and refused to
recognise the Princess as his heir, he could not honourably treat with him.[2] The Pope, when Catherine's
letter reached him, was fuming with fresh anger at the
fate of the Irish rebellion. Lord Thomas, spite of Papal
absolution and blessing, was a prisoner in the Tower.
He had surrendered to his uncle, Lord Leonard Grey,
under some promise of pardon. He had been carried
before the King. For a few days he was left at liberty,
and might have been forgiven if he would have made a
satisfactory submission; but he calculated that 'a new
'world' was not far off, and that he might hold out in
safety. Such a wild cat required stricter keeping. The
Tower gates closed on him, and soon after he paid for
the Archbishop's life with his own.

Ortiz, when he heard that Fitzgerald was imprisoned,
said that the choice lay before him to die a martyr or

<hr>

[1] Chapuys to Granvelle, October 13, 1535.—*Calendar, Foreign*
and Domestic, vol. ix. p. 199.
[2] *Ibid.* pp. 225, 228.

else to be perverted. God, he hoped, would permit the
first. The spirit of one of the murdered Carthusians
had appeared to the brotherhood and informed them
of the glorious crown which had been bestowed on
Fisher. [1]

In this exalted humour Catherine's letter found
Paul and the Roman clergy. The Pope had already
informed Cifuentes that he meant to proceed to
'deprivation.' The letters of execution had been so
drawn or re-drawn as to involve the forfeiture of
Henry's throne,[2] and Ortiz considered that Providence
had so ordered it that the Pope was now acting *motu
proprio* and not at the Queen's solicitation. Cifuentes
was of opinion, however, that Paul meant to wait for the
Queen's demand, that the responsibility might be hers.
Chapuys's courier was ordered to deliver Catherine's
letter into the Pope's own hands. Cifuentes took the
liberty of detaining it till the Emperor's pleasure was
known. But no one any longer doubted that the time
was come. France and England were no longer united,
and the word for action was to be spoken at last.

At no period of his reign had Henry been in greater
danger. At home the public mind was unsettled. A
large and powerful faction of peers and clergy were
prepared for revolt, and abroad he had no longer an
ally. England seemed on the eve of a conflict the
issue of which no one could foresee. At this moment
Providence, or the good luck which had so long be-

---

[1] *Spanish Calendar*, October
24, 1535, vol. v. p. 559.

[2] Ortiz to the Emperor, November 4, 1535.—*Ibid.* vol. v. p. 565.

friended him, interposed to save the King and save the Reformation.

Sforza, Duke of Milan and husband of Christina of Denmark, died childless on the 24th of October. Milan was the special subject of difference between France and the Empire. The dispute had been suspended while the Duke was alive. His death re-opened the question, and the war long looked for for the Milan succession became inevitable and immediately imminent.

The entire face of things was now changed. Francis had, perhaps, never seriously meant to join in executing the Papal sentence against England; but he had intended to encourage the Emperor to try, that he might fish himself afterwards in the troubled waters, and probably snatch at Calais. He now required Henry for a friend again, and the old difficulties and the old jealousies were revived in the usual form. Both the great Catholic Powers desired the suspension of the censures. The Emperor was again unwilling to act as the Pope's champion while he was uncertain of the French King. Francis wished to recover his position as Henry's defender. The Pope was an Italian prince as well as sovereign of the Church, and his secular interest was thought to be more French than Imperial.

No sooner was Sforza gone than the Cardinal Du Bellay and the Bishop of Mâcon were despatched from Paris to see and talk with Paul. They found him still too absorbed in the English question to attend to

anything besides. He was in the high exalted mood
of Gregory VII., imagining that he was about to reassert
the ancient Papal prerogative and again dispose of
kingdoms.

The Pope, wrote the French Commissioners, having
heard that there were famine and plague in England,
had made up his mind to act, and was incredibly
excited. The sentence was prepared and was to issue
unexpectedly like a bolt out of the blue sky. They
enclosed a copy of it, and waited for instructions from
Francis as to the line which they were to take. To
set things straight again would, they said, be almost
impossible; but they would do their best to prevent
extremities, and to show the King of England that they
had endeavoured to serve him. Nothing like the
sentence which Paul had constructed had been ever
seen before. Some articles had been inserted to force
Francis to choose between the Pope and the King.
They were malicious, unjust, and *terriblement enormes.*[1]

The new Hildebrand, applying to himself the words
of Jeremiah, 'Behold, I have set thee over nations and
'kingdoms, that thou mayest root out and destroy,' had
proceeded to root out Henry. He had cursed him; he
cursed his abettors. His body when he died was to lie
unburied and his soul lie in hell for ever. His subjects
were ordered to renounce their allegiance, and were to
fall under interdict if they continued to obey him.
No true son of the Church was to hold intercourse or

---

[1] Du Bellay and the Bishop of
Mâcon to Francis I., November
12, 1535.—*Calendar, Foreign and
Domestic,* vol. ix. p. 273.

alliance with him or his adherents, under pain of sharing his damnation; and the Princes of Europe and the Peers and commons of England were required, on their allegiance to the Holy See, to expel him from the throne.[1]

This was the 'remedy' for which Catherine had been so long entreating, out of affection for her misguided lord, whose soul she wished to save. The love which she professed was a love which her lord could have dispensed with.

The Papal Nuncio reported from Paris the attitude which France intended to assume. He had been speaking with the Admiral Philip de Chabot about England. The Admiral had admitted that the King had doubtless done violent things, and that the Pope had a right to notice them. France did not wish to defend him against the Pope, but, if he was attacked by the Emperor, would certainly take his part. The Nuncio said that he had pointed out that the King of England had God for an enemy; that he was, therefore, going to total ruin; and that the Pope had hoped to find in Francis a champion of the Church. The Admiral said that, of course, England ought to return to the faith: the Pope could deal with him hereafter; but France must take care of her own interests.[2]

Charles, too, was uneasy and undecided. Until the Milan question had been reopened the French had

---

[1] Froude's *History of England,* vol. ii. p. 288.

[2] Bishop of Faenza to M. Ambrogio, November 15, 1535.— *Calendar, Foreign and Domestic,* vol. ix. p. 276.

spoken as if they would no longer stand between Henry and retribution, but he was now assured that they would return to their old attitude. They had stood by Henry through the long controversy of the divorce. Even when Fisher was sent to the scaffold they had not broken their connection with him. The King, he knew, was frightened, and would yield, if France was firm; but, unless the Pope had a promise from the French King under his own hand to assist in executing the censures, the Pope would find himself disappointed; and the fear was that Francis would draw the Emperor into a war with England and then leave him to make his own bargain.[1]

Kings whose thrones and lives are threatened cannot afford to be lenient. Surrounded by traitors, uncertain of France, with the danger in which he stood immeasurably increased by the attitude of Catherine and her daughter, the King, so the Marchioness of Exeter reported to Chapuys, had been heard to say that they must bend or break. The anxiety which they were causing was not to be endured any longer. Parliament was about to meet, and their situation would have then to be considered.[2]

---

[1] Charles V. to Cifuentes, Nov. 1535.—*Calendar, Foreign and Domestic*, vol. ix. p. 277.

[2] 'Tout à cest instant la Marquise de Exeter m'a envoyé dire 'que le Roy a dernierement dit à 'ses plus privés conseillers qu'il 'ne voulloit plus demeurer en les 'fascheuses crainctes et grevements 'qu'il avoit de long temps eus à 'cause des Royne et Princesse ; et 'qu'ils y regardassent à ce prochain 'Parlement l'en faire quicte, jurant 'bien et tres obstinément qu'il 'n'actendroit plus longuement de 'y pourvoir.' Chapuys to Charles V., Nov. 6, 1535.—*MS. Vienna.*

The Marchioness entreated him to let the Emperor know of this, and tell him that, if he waited longer, he would be too late to save them. Chapuys took care that these alarming news should lose nothing in the relating. Again, after a fortnight, Lady Exeter came to him, disguised, to renew the warning. The ‘she-devil ‘ of a Concubine,’ she said, was thinking of nothing save of how to get the ladies despatched. The Concubine ruled the Council, and the King was afraid to contradict her. The fear was, as Chapuys said, that he would make the Parliament a joint party with him in his cruelties, and that, losing hope of pardon from the Emperor, they would be more determined to defend themselves.[1]

The danger, if danger there was, to Catherine and Mary, was Chapuys's own creation. It was he who had encouraged them in defying the King, that they might form a visible rallying-point to the rebellion. Charles was more rational than the Ambassador, and less credulous of Henry's wickedness. ‘ I cannot believe what ‘ you tell me,’ he replied to his Ambassador's frightful story. ‘ The King cannot be so unnatural as to put to ‘ death his own wife and daughter. The threats you ‘ speak of can only be designed to terrify them. They ‘ must not give way, if it can be avoided ; but, if they ‘ are really in danger, and there is no alternative, you ‘ may tell them from me that they must yield. A sub-

---

[1] ‘ Afin que par ce moyen, per- ‘ dant l'espoir de la clemence et ‘ misericorde de Vostre Majeste, ‘ toutefois fussent plus determinez ‘ à se defendre.' Chapuys à l'Empereur. —*MS. Vienna,* Nov. 23.

' mission so made cannot prejudice their rights. They
' can protest that they are acting under compulsion, in
' fear for their lives. I will take care that their pro-
' testation is duly ratified by their proctors at Rome.'[1]
Chapuys was a politician, and obeyed his orders. But
that either Catherine or her daughter should give way
was the last wish either of him or of Ortiz, or any of
the fanatical enthusiasts. Martyrs were the seed of the
Church. If Mary abandoned her claim to the succession, her name could no longer be used as a battle-cry.
The object was a revolution which would shake Henry
from his throne. On the scaffold, as a victim to her
fidelity to her mother and to the Holy See, she would
give an impulse to the insurrection which nothing could
resist.

The croaks of the raven were each day louder.
Lady Exeter declared that the King had said that the
Princess should be an example that no one should
disobey the law. There was a prophecy of him that
at the beginning of his reign he would be gentle as
a lamb, and at the end worse than a lion. That
prophecy he meant to fulfil.[2]

Ortiz, who had his information from Catherine herself, said that she was preparing to die as the Bishop of
Rochester and the others had died. She regretted
only that her life had not been as holy as theirs.
The ' kitchen-wench '—as Ortiz named Anne—had

---

[1] The Emperor to Chapuys.—
MS. Vienna.
[2] Chapuys to Granvelle, Nov.

21, 1535.—*Calendar, Foreign and
Domestic*, vol. ix. p. 290.

often said of the Princess that either Mary would be her death or she would be Mary's, and that she would take care that Mary did not laugh at her after she was gone.[1]

Stories flying at such a time were half of them the creation of rage and panic, imperfectly believed by those who related them, and reported to feed a fire which it was so hard to kindle; but they show the spirit of which the air was full. At Rome there was still distrust. Francis had shown the copy of the intended sentence to the different Ambassadors at Paris. He had said that the Pope was claiming a position for the Apostolic See which could not be allowed, and must be careful what he did.[2] Paul agreed with the Emperor that, before the sentence was delivered, pledges to assist must be exacted from Francis, but had thought that he might calculate with sufficient certainty on the hereditary enmity between France and England. Cifuentes told him that he must judge of the future by the past. The French were hankering after Italy, and other things were nothing in comparison. The Pope hinted that the Emperor was said to be treating privately with Henry. Cifuentes could give a flat denial to this, for the treaty had been dropped. If the Emperor, however, resolved to undertake the execution, Francis was not to be allowed to hear of it, as he would use the knowledge to set Henry on his guard.[3]

---

[1] Ortiz to the Empress, Nov. 22, 1535.—*Calendar, Foreign and Domestic*, vol. ix. pp. 293-4.

[2] Bishop of Faenza to M. Am-brogio, Dec. 9.—*Ibid.* vol. ix. p. 317.

[3] Cifuentes to Charles V., Nov. 30, 1535.—*Ibid.* vol. ix. p. 303.

Chapuys was a master of the art of conveying false impressions while speaking literal truth.

Francis, who, in spite of Cifuentes, learnt what was being projected at Rome, warned Henry that the Emperor was about to invade England. He even said that the Emperor had promised that, if he would not interfere, the English crown might be secured to a French prince by a marriage with Mary. Cromwell questioned Chapuys on such ' strange news.' Lying cost Chapuys nothing. The story was true, but he replied that it was wild nonsense. Not only had the Emperor never said such a thing, but he had never even thought of anything to the King's prejudice, and had always been solicitous for the honour and tranquillity of England. The Emperor wished to increase, not diminish, the power of the King, and even for the sake of the Queen and Princess he would not wish the King to be expelled, knowing the love they bore him. Cromwell said he had always told the King that the Emperor would attempt nothing against him unless he was forced. Chapuys agreed : so far, he said, from promoting hostilities against the King, the Emperor, ever since the sentence on the divorce, had held back the execution, and, if further measures were taken, they would be taken by the Pope and Cardinals, not by the Emperor.[1]

In this last intimation Chapuys was more correct than he was perhaps aware of.

---

[1] Chapuys to Charles V., Dec. 18, 1535.—*Calendar, Foreign and Domestic*, vol. ix. p. 333.

The Pope, sick of the irresolutions and mutual animosities of the great Catholic Powers, had determined to act for himself. Catherine's friends had his ear. They at all events knew their own minds. On the 10th of December he called a consistory, said that he had suffered enough in the English cause, and would bear it no more. He required the opinions of the Cardinals on the issue of the executorial brief. The scene is described by Du Bellay, who was one of them, and was present. The Cardinals, who had been debating and disagreeing for seven years, were still in favour of further delays. They all felt that a brief or bull deposing the King was a step from which there would be no retreat. The Great Powers, they were well aware, would resent the Pope's assumption of an authority so arrogant. All but one of them said that before the executory letters were published a monition must first be sent to the King. The language of the letters, besides, was too comprehensive. The King's subjects and the King's allies were included in the censures, and, not being in fault, ought not to suffer. Voices, too, were heard to say that kings were privileged persons, and ought not to be treated with disrespect.

The Pope, before dissatisfied with their objections, now in high anger at the last suggestion, declared that he would spare neither emperors, nor kings, nor princes. God had placed him over them all; the Papal authority was not diminished—it was greater than ever, and would be greater still when there was a pope who

dared to act without faction or cowardice. He reproached the Cardinals with embroiling a clear matter.
The brief, he maintained, was a good brief, faulty
perhaps in style, but right in substance, and approved
it was to be, and at once.

It hit all round—hit the English people who continued loyal to their sovereign, hit the Continental
Powers who had treaties with Henry which they had
not broken. The Cardinals thought the Pope would
spoil everything. Campeggio said such a Bull touched
the French King, and must not appear. The Archbishop of Capua went with the Pope : 'Issue at once,'
he said, 'or the King will be sending protests, as he did
'in Clement's time.' The Pope spoke in great anger,
but to no purpose. The majority of the Cardinals was
against him, and the Bull was allowed to sleep till a
more favourable time. 'It is long,' said Du Bellay,
'since there has been a Pope less loved by the College,
'the Romans, and the world.'[1]

---

[1] Cardinal du Bellay to the Car-
dinals of Lorraine and Tournon, | Dec. 22, 1535.—*Calendar, Foreign
and Domestic,* vol. ix. pp. 341-3.

CHAPTER XX.

Illness of Queen Catherine—Her physician's report of her health
—Her last letter to the Emperor—She sends for Chapuys—
Interview between Chapuys and Henry—Chapuys at Kim-
bolton—Death of Catherine—Examination of the body—
Suspicion of poison—Chapuys's opinion—Reception of the
news at the Court—Message of Anne Boleyn to the Princess
Mary—Advice of Chapuys—Unpopularity of Anne—Court
rumours.

WHILE the Pope was held back by the Cardinals,
and the Great Powers were watching each other,
afraid to move, the knot was about to be cut, so far as
it affected the fortunes of Catherine of Aragon, in a
manner not unnatural and, by Cromwell and many others,
not unforeseen. The agitation and anxieties of the protracted conflict had shattered her health. Severe attacks
of illness had more than once caused fear for her life,
and a few months previously her recovery had been
thought unlikely, if not impossible. Cromwell had
spoken of her death to Chapuys as a contingency which
would be useful to the peace of Europe, and which he
thought would not be wholly unwelcome to her nephew.
Politicians in the sixteenth century were not scrupulous, and Chapuys may perhaps have honestly thought

that such language suggested a darker purpose. But Cromwell had always been Catherine's friend within the limits permitted by his duty to the King and the Reformation. The words which Chapuys attributed to him were capable of an innocent interpretation; and it is in the highest degree unlikely that he, of all men, was contemplating a crime of which the danger would far outweigh the advantage, and which would probably anticipate for a few weeks or months only a natural end, or that, if he had seriously entertained such an intention, he would have made a confidant of the Spanish Ambassador. Catherine had been wrought during the autumn months into a state of the highest excitement. Her letters to the Pope had been the outpourings of a heart driven near to breaking; and if Chapuys gave her Charles's last message, if she was told that it was the Emperor's pleasure that she and her daughter must submit, should extremities be threatened against them, she must have felt a bitter conviction that the remedy which she had prayed for would never be applied, and that the struggle would end in an arrangement in which she would herself be sacrificed.

The life at Kimbolton was like the life at an ordinary well-appointed English country-house. The establishment was moderate, but the castle was in good condition and well furnished; everything was provided which was required for personal comfort; the Queen had her own servants, her confessor, her physician, and two or three ladies-in-waiting; if she had not more state about her,

it was by her own choice, for, as has been seen, she
had made her recognition as queen the condition of her
accepting a more adequate establishment. Bodily hard-
ships she had none to suffer, but she had a chronic disorder of long standing, which had been aggravated by
the high-strung expectations of the last half-dozen years.
Sir John Wallop, the English ambassador at Paris, had
been always ' her good servant '; Lady Wallop was her
creatura and was passionately attached to her. From
the Wallops the Nuncio at the French Court heard in
the middle of December that she could not live more
than six months. They had learnt the ' secret ' of her
illness from her own physician, and their evident grief
convinced him that they were speaking the truth.
Francis also was aware of her condition ; the end was
known to be near, and it was thought in Court circles
that when she was gone ' the King would leave his
' present queen and return to the obedience of the
' Church.' [1]

The disorder from which Catherine was suffering
had been mentioned by Cromwell to Chapuys. The
Ambassador asked to be allowed to visit her. Cromwell said that he might send a servant at once to
Kimbolton, to ascertain her condition, and that he
would ask the King's permission for himself to follow.
The alarming symptoms passed off for the moment ;
she rallied from the attack, and on the 13th of
December she was able to write to Ortiz, to tell him of

---

[1] The Bishop of Faenza to M.   *dar, Foreign and Domestic*, vol.
Ambrogio, Dec. 13, 1535.—*Calen-*   ix. p. 326.

the comfort and encouragement which she had received from his letters, and from the near prospect of the Pope's action. In that alone lay the remedy for the sufferings of herself and her daughter and 'all the 'good.' The Devil, she said, was but half tied, and slackness would let him loose. She could not and dared not speak more clearly; Ortiz was a wise man, and would understand.[1]

On the same day she wrote her last letter to the Emperor. The handwriting, once bold and powerful, had grown feeble and tremulous, and the imperfectly legible lines convey only that she expected something to be done at the approaching parliament which would be a world's scandal and her own and her daughter's destruction.[2]

Finding herself a little better, she desired Chapuys to speak to Cromwell about change of air for her, and to ask for a supply of money to pay the servants' wages. Money was a gratuitous difficulty : she had refused to take anything which was addressed to her as princess dowager, and the allowance was in arrears. She had some confidence in Cromwell, and Charles, too, believed, in spite of Chapuys's stories, that Cromwell meant well to Catherine, and wished to help her. He wrote himself to Cromwell to say that his loyal service would not be forgotten.[3]

---

[1] Queen Catherine to Dr. Ortiz, Dec. 13, 1535.—*Calendar, Foreign and Domestic,* vol. ix. p. 325.

[2] Queen Catherine to Charles V., Dec. 13, 1535.—*MS. Vienna.*

[3] The Emperor to Thomas Cromwell, Dec. 13, 1535.— *Spanish Calendar,* vol. ix. p. 588.

Chapuys heard no more from Kimbolton for a fort-night, and was hoping that the attack had gone off like those which had preceded it ; on the 29th, how-ever, there came a letter to him from the Spanish physician, saying that she was again very ill, and wished to see him. Chapuys went to Cromwell immediately. Cromwell assured him that no objection would be raised, but that, before he set out, the King desired to speak with him. He hurried to Greenwich, where the Court was staying, and found Henry more than usually gracious, but apparently absorbed in politics. He walked up and down the room with his arm around the Ambassador's neck, complained that Charles had not written to him, and that he did not know what to look for at his hands. The French, he said, were making advances to him, and had become so pressing, since the death of the Duke of Milan, that he would be forced to listen to them, unless he could be satisfied of the Emperor's intentions. He was not to be deluded into a position where he would lose the friendship of both of them. Francis was burning for war. For himself he meant honourably, and would be perfectly open with Chapuys . he was an Englishman, he did not say one thing when he meant another. Why had not the Emperor let him know distinctly whether he would treat with him or not ?

Chapuys hinted a fear that he had been play-ing with the Emperor only to extort better terms from France. A war for Milan there might possibly be, but the Emperor after his African successes was

stronger than he had ever been, and had nothing to
fear.

All that might be very well, Henry said, but if he
was to throw his sword into the scale the case might
be different. Hitherto, however, he had rejected the
French overtures, and did not mean to join France in
an Italian campaign if the Emperor did not force him.
As to the threats against himself, English commerce
would of course suffer severely if the trade was stopped
with the Low Countries, but he could make shift
elsewhere; he did not conceal his suspicions that the
Emperor meant him ill, or his opinion that he had
been treated unfairly in the past.[1]

Chapuys enquired what he wished the Emperor to
do. To abstain, the King replied, from encouraging the
Princess and her mother in rebellion, and to require the
revocation of the sentence which had been given on the
divorce. The Emperor could not do that, Chapuys rejoined, even if he wished to do it. The King said he
knew the Pope had called on the Emperor to execute
the sentence; he did not believe, however, that Madame,
as he called Catherine, had long to live, and, when she
was gone, the Emperor would have no further excuse
for interfering in English affairs. Chapuys replied that

---

[1] ' Et que vostre Ma^te luy avoit
' usé de la plus grande ingratitude
' que l'on sçauroit dire, solicitant
' à l'appetit d'une femme tant de
' choses contre luy, que luy avoit
' faict innumerables maux et fas-
' cheries, et de telle importance,
'que vostre Ma^te par menasses et
' force avoit faict donner la sentence
' contre luy, comme le mesme Pape
' l'avoit confessé.' Chapuys à
l'Empereur, Dec. 30, 1535.—*MS.
Vienna; Spanish Calendar,* vol.
v. p. 595.

the Queen's death would make no difference. The
sentence had been a necessity. The King ended the
conversation by telling him that he might go to see her,
if he liked; but she was *in extremis,* and he would
hardly find her alive. At the Princess's request,
Chapuys asked if she also might go to her mother. At
first Henry refused, but said, after a moment, he would
think about it, and added, as Chapuys afterwards recol-
lected, a few words of kindness to Catherine herself.

Unfeeling and brutal, the world exclaims. More
feeling may have been shown, perhaps, than Chapuys
cared to note. But kings whose thrones are menaced
with invasion and rebellion have not much leisure for
personal emotions. Affection for Catherine Henry had
none, however, and a pretence of it would have been
affectation. She had harassed him for seven years;
she had urged the Pope to take his crown from him;
she had done her worst to stir his subjects into
insurrection, and bring a Spanish fleet and army into
English waters and upon English soil. Respect her
courage he did, but love for her, if in such a marriage
love had ever existed, must have long disappeared, and
he did not make a show of a regret which it was
impossible for him to feel. He perhaps considered
that he had done more than enough in resisting the
advice of his Council to take stronger measures.

After despatching the letter describing the interview
at Greenwich, the Ambassador started with his suite for
Kimbolton, and with a gentleman of Cromwell's household in attendance. Immediately on his arrival Cathe-

rine sent for him to her bedside, and desired that this
gentleman should be present also, to hear what passed
between them. She thanked Chapuys for coming.
She said, if God was to take her, it would be a consolation to her to die in his arms and not like a wild animal.
She said she had been taken seriously ill at the end of
November with pain in the stomach and nausea; a
second and worse attack of the same kind had followed
on Christmas Day; she could eat nothing, and believed
that she was sinking. Chapuys encouraged her—expressed his hopes for her recovery—said that he was
commissioned to tell her that she might choose a residence for herself at any one of the royal manors, that
the King would give her money, and was sorry to hear
of her illness. He himself entreated her to keep up
her spirits, as on her recovery and life the peace of
Christendom depended. The visit excited her, she was
soon exhausted, and they then left her to rest. After
an interval she sent for the Ambassador again, and
talked for two hours with him alone. She had
brightened up; the next morning she was better; he
remained four days at Kimbolton, which were spent
in private conversation. She was the same Catherine
that she had always been—courageous, resolute, and
inflexible to the end. She spoke incessantly of the
Emperor, and of her own and her daughter's situation.
She struck perpetually on the old note: the delay of
the 'remedy' which was causing infinite evil, and
destroying the souls and bodies of all honest and
worthy people.

Chapuys explained to her how the Emperor had been circumstanced, and how impossible it had been for him to do more than had been done. He comforted her, however, with dilating on the Pope's indignation at the execution of Fisher, and his determination to act in earnest at last. He told her how Francis, who had been the chief difficulty, was now becoming alienated from the King, and satisfied her that the delay had not been caused by forgetfulness of herself and the Princess. With these happier prospects held out to her she recovered her spirits and appeared to be recovering her health. At the end of the four days she was sleeping soundly, enjoying her food, laughing and exchanging Castilian jokes with a Spaniard whom Chapuys had brought with him. She was so much better, so happy, and so contented, that the Ambassador ceased to be alarmed about her. He thought it would be imprudent to abuse the King's permission by remaining longer unnecessarily. The physician made no objection to his going, and promised to let him know if there was again a change for the worse; but this person evidently no longer believed that there was any immediate danger, for his last words to Chapuys were to ask him to arrange for her removal from Kimbolton to some better air. Catherine, when the Ambassador took leave, charged him to write to the Emperor, to Granvelle, and to Secretary Covos, and entreat them, for God's sake, to make an end one way or the other, for the uncertainty was ruining the realm and would be her own and her daughter's destruction.

This was on the night of Tuesday, the 4th of January. Chapuys was to leave the next morning. Before departing he ascertained that she had again slept well, and he rode off without disturbing her. Through the Wednesday and Thursday she continued to improve, and on the Thursday afternoon she was cheerful, sate up, asked for a comb, and dressed her hair. That midnight, however, she became suddenly restless, begged for the Sacrament, and became impatient for morning when it could be administered. Her confessor, Father Ateca (who had come with her from Spain, held the see of Llandaff, and had been left undisturbed through all the changes of the late years), offered to anticipate the canonical hour, but she would not allow him. At dawn on Friday she communicated, prayed God to pardon the King for the wrongs which had been inflicted upon her, and received Extreme Unction; she gave a few directions for the disposition of her personal property, and then waited for the end. At two o'clock in the afternoon she passed peacefully away (Friday, Jan. 7, 1536).

A strange circumstance followed. The body was to be embalmed. There were in the house three persons who, according to Chapuys, had often performed such operations, neither of them, however, being surgeons by profession. These men, eight hours after the death, opened the stomach in the usual way, but without the presence either of the confessor or the physician. Chapuys says that these persons were acting by the

King's command,[1] but there is nothing to indicate that
the confessor and physician might not have been
present at the operation had they thought it necessary.
Chapuys had previously asked the physician if the
Queen could have been poisoned. The physician said
that he feared so, as she had not been well since she
had taken some Welsh ale; if there had been poison,
however, it must have been very subtle, as he had
observed no symptom which indicated it; when the
body was opened they would know.[2] The physician
had thus looked forward to an examination, and had he
really entertained suspicions he would certainly have
made an effort to attend. If he was prohibited, or if
the operation had been hurried through without his
knowledge, it is not conceivable that, after he had left
England and returned to his own country, he would not
have made known a charge so serious to the world.
This he never did. It is equally remarkable that on
removing from Kimbolton he was allowed to attend
upon the Princess Mary—a thing impossible to understand if he had any mystery of the kind to communicate to her, or if the Government had any fear of what
he might say. When the operation was over, however,

[1] Chapuys to Charles V., Jan.
21, 1536.—MS. Vienna; Spanish
Calendar, vol. v. part 2, p. 18.

[2] 'Je demanday par plusieurs
'fois au medecin s'il y avoit quelque
'soubçon de venin. Il me dict
'qu'il s'en doubtoit, car depuys
'qu'elle avoit beu d'une cervise de

'Galles elle n'avoit fait bien; et
'qu'il failloit que ne fust poison
'terminé et artificieux, car il ne
'veoit les signes de simple et pur
'venin.' Chapuys à l'Empereur,
Jan. 9, 1536. — MS. Vienna;
Calendar, Foreign and Domestic,
vol. x. p. 22.

one of the men went to the Father Ateca and told him
in confession, as if in fear of his life, that the body and
intestines were natural and healthy, but that the heart
was black. They had washed it, he said; they had
divided it, but it remained black and was black
throughout. On this evidence the physician concluded
that the Queen, beyond doubt, had died of poison.[1]

A reader who has not predetermined to believe the
worst of Henry VIII. will probably conclude differently.
The world did not believe Catherine to have been
murdered, for among the many slanders which the embittered Catholics then and afterwards heaped upon
Henry, they did not charge him with this. Chapuys,
however, believed, or affected to believe, that by some
one or other murdered she had been. It was a terrible
business, he wrote. The Princess would die of grief,
or else the Concubine would kill her. Even if the
Queen and Princess had taken the Emperor's advice and
submitted, the Concubine, he thought, under colour of
the reconciliation which would have followed, would
have made away with them the more fearlessly, because
there would then be less suspicion. He had not been
afraid of the King. The danger was from the Concubine, who had sworn to take their lives and would
never have rested till it was done. The King and his
Mistress, however, had taken a shorter road. They
were afraid of the issue of the brief of execution.
With Catherine dead the process at Rome would drop,

---

[1] Chapuys to Charles V., Jan.
9, and Jan. 21, 1536.—*MS.* | *Vienna ; Spanish Calendar*, vol.
v. part 2, pp. 2—10.

the chief party to the suit being gone. Further action would have to be taken by the Pope on his own account, and no longer upon hers, and the Pope would probably hesitate; while, as soon as the mother was out of the way, there would be less difficulty in working upon the daughter, whom, being a subject, they would be able to constrain.[1]

It was true that the threatened Papal brief, being a part and consequence of the original suit, would have to be dropped or recalled. Henry could not be punished for not taking back his wife when the wife was dead. To that extent her end was convenient, and thus a motive may be suggested for making away with her. It was convenient also, as was frankly avowed, in removing the principal obstacle to the reconciliation of Henry and the Emperor; but, surely, on the condition that the death was natural. Had Charles allowed Chapuys to persuade him that his aunt had been murdered, reconciliation would have been made impossible for ever, and Henry would have received the just reward of an abominable crime. Chapuys's object from the beginning had been to drive the Emperor into war with England, and if motive may be conjectured for the murder of Catherine, motive also can be found for Chapuys's accusations, which no other evidence, direct or indirect, exists to support.

If there had been foul play there would have been an affectation of sorrow. There was none at all. When

---

[1] Chapuys to Charles V., Jan. 21, 1536.—*MS. Vienna; Calendar, Foreign and Domestic*, vol. x. p. 47.

the news arrived, Anne Boleyn and her friends showed
unmixed pleasure. The King (Chapuys is again the
only witness, and he was reporting from hearsay)
thanked God there was now no fear of war; when the
French knew that there was no longer any quarrel
between him and the Emperor, he could do as he
pleased with them. Chapuys says these were his first
words on receiving the tidings that Catherine was gone
—words not unnatural if the death was innocent, but
scarcely credible if she had been removed by assassination.

The effect was of general relief at the passing away
of a great danger. It was thought that the Pope would
now drop the proceedings against the King, and Cromwell said that perhaps before long they would have a
Legate among them. Even Chapuys, on consideration,
reflected that he might have spoken too confidently
about the manner of Catherine's end. Her death, he
imagined, had been brought about partly by poison
and partly by despondency. Had he reflected further,
he might have asked himself how poison could have
been administered at all, as the Queen took nothing
which had not been prepared by her own servants, who
would all have died for her.

Undoubtedly, however, the King breathed more
freely when she was gone. There was no longer a
woman who claimed to be his wife, and whose presence
in the kingdom was a reflection on the legitimacy of his
second daughter. On the Sunday following, the small
Elizabeth was carried to church with special ceremony.

In the evening there was a dance in the hall of the palace, and the King appeared in the middle of it with the child in his arms. All allowance must be made for the bitterness with which Chapuys described the scene. He was fresh from Catherine's bedside. He had witnessed her sufferings; he had listened to the story of her wrongs from her own lips. He had talked hopefully with her of the future, and had encouraged her to expect a grand and immediate redress; and now she was dead, worn out with sorrow, if with nothing worse, an object at least to make the dullest heart pity her, while of pity there was no sign. What was to be done? He himself had no doubt at all. The enemy was off his guard, and now was the moment to strike.

Anne Boleyn sent a message to Mary that she was ready, on her submission, to be her friend and a second mother to her. Mary replied that she would obey her father in everything, saving her honour and conscience, but that it was useless to ask her to abjure the Pope. She was told that the King himself would use his authority and command her to submit. She consulted Chapuys on the answer which she was to give should such a command be sent. He advised her to be resolute but cautious. She must ask to be left in peace to pray for her mother's soul; she must say that she was a poor orphan, without experience or knowledge; the King must allow her time to consider. He himself despatched a courier to the Regent of the Netherlands with plans for her escape out of England. The Pope, he said, must issue his Bull without a day's delay, and in it, for the sake of Catherine's honour, it must be stated that she died queen. Instant preparations must be made for the execution of the sentence. Meanwhile he recommended the Emperor to send some great person to remonstrate against the Princess's treatment and to speak out boldly and severely. The late Queen, he wrote, used to say that the King and his advisers were like sheep to those who appeared like wolves, and lions to those who were afraid of them. Mildness at such a moment would be the ruin of Christendom. If the Emperor hesitated longer, those who showed no sorrow at the mother's death would take courage to make an end with the daughter. There would be no need of poison. Grief and hard usage would be enough.[1]

The King with some hesitation had consented to Chapuys's request that Catherine's physician should be allowed to attend the Princess. The presence of this man would necessarily be a protection, and either Anne's influence was less supreme than the Ambassador had feared, or her sinister designs were a malicious invention. It is unlikely, however, that warnings so persistently repeated and so long continued should have been wholly without foundation, and, if the inner secrets of the Court could be laid open, it might be found that the Princess had been the subject of many an altercation between Anne and the King. Even Chapuys always acknowledged that it was from her, and not from Henry,

---

[1] Chapuys to Charles V., Jan. 21 and Jan. 29.—*Spanish Calendar,* vol. v. part 2, pp. 10—26.

that the danger was to be feared. He had spoken
warmly of Mary, had shown affection for her when her
behaviour threatened his own safety. He admired the
force of character which she was showing, and had
silenced peremptorily the Ministers who recommended
severity. But if he was her father, he was also King
of England. If he was to go through with his policy
towards the Church, the undisguised antagonism of a
child whom three-quarters of his subjects looked on as
his legitimate successor was embarrassing and even
perilous. Had Anne Boleyn produced the prince so
much talked of, all would then have been easy. He
would not then be preferring a younger daughter to an
elder. Both would yield to a brother with whom all
England would be satisfied, and Mary would cease to
have claims which the Emperor would feel bo° :d to
advocate. The whole nation was longing for a p. ѕce ;
but the male heir, for which the King had plunged into
such a sea of troubles, was still withheld. He had
interpreted the deaths of the sons whom Catherine had
borne him into a judgment of Heaven upon his first
marriage; the same disappointment might appear to a
superstitious fancy to be equally a condemnation of the
second. Anne Boleyn's conduct during the last two
years had not recommended her either to the country
or perhaps to her husband. Setting aside the graver
charges afterwards brought against her, it is evident
that she had thrown herself fiercely into the political
struggles of the time. To the Catholic she was a
diablesse, a tigress, the author of all the mischief which

was befalling them and the realm. By the prudent
and the moderate she was almost equally disliked; the
nation generally, and even Reformers like Cromwell
and Cranmer, were Imperialist; Anne Boleyn was
passionately French. Personally she had made herself
disliked by her haughty and arrogant manners. She
had been received as Queen after her marriage was
announced with coldness, if not with hostility. Had
she been gracious and modest, she might have partially
overcome the prejudice against her. But she had been
carried away by the vanity of her elevation; she had
insulted the great English nobles; she had spoken to
the Duke of Norfolk 'as if he was a dog;' she had
threatened to take off Cromwell's head. Such manners
and such language could not have made Henry's difficulties less, or been pleasing to a sovereign whose
authority depended on the goodwill of his people. He
had fallen in love with an unworthy woman, as men will
do, even the wisest; yet in his first affection he had not
been blind to her faults, and, even before his marriage,
had been heard to say that, if it was to be done again,
he would not have committed himself so far. He had
persisted, perhaps, as much from pride, and because he
would not submit to the dictation of the Emperor, as
from any real attachment. Qualities that he could
respect she had none. Catherine was gone; from that
connection he was at last free, even in the eyes of the
Roman Curia; but whether he was or was not married
lawfully to Anne was a doubtful point in the mind of
many a loyal Englishman; and to the best of his own

friends, to the Emperor, and to all Europe, his separation
from a woman whom the Catholic world called his concubine, and a marriage with some other lady which
would be open to no suspicion and might result in the
much-desired prince, would have been welcomed as a
peace-offering. She had done nothing to reconcile the
nation to her. She had left nothing undone to exasperate it. She was believed, justly or unjustly, to
have endeavoured to destroy the Princess Mary. She
was credited by remorseful compassion with having
been the cause of her mother's death. The isolation
and danger of England were all laid to her account.
She was again *enceinte*. If a prince was born, all faults
would be forgotten; but she had miscarried once since
the birth of Elizabeth, and a second misfortune might
be dangerous. She had failed in her attempts to conciliate Mary, who, but for an accident, would have made
good her escape out of England. When the preparations were almost complete, the Princess had been
again removed to another house, from which it was
found impossible to carry her away. But Chapuys
mentions that, glad as Anne appeared at the Queen's
death, she was less at ease than she pretended. Lord
and Lady Exeter had brought him a Court rumour of
words said to have been uttered by the King, ' that he
' had been drawn into the marriage by witchcraft; God
' had shown his displeasure by denying him male
' children by her, and therefore he might take another
' wife.'

Lord and Lady Exeter were no trustworthy authorities—on this occasion even Chapuys did not believe them—but stories of the kind were in the wind. It was notorious that everything was not well between the King and Lady Anne. A curious light is thrown on the state of Anne's mind by a letter which she wrote to her aunt, Mrs. Shelton, after Mary's rejection of her advances. Mrs. Shelton left it lying open on a table. Mary found it, copied it, and replaced it, and the transcript, in Mary's handwriting, is now at Vienna.

'MRS. SHELTON,—My pleasure is that you seek to 'go no further to move the Lady Mary towards the 'King's grace, other than as he himself directed in his 'own words to her. What I have done myself has been 'more for charity than because the King or I care what 'course she takes, or whether she will change or not 'change her purpose. When I shall have a son, as 'soon I look to have, I know what then will come to 'her. Remembering the word of God, that we should 'do good to our enemies, I have wished to give her 'notice before the time, because by my daily experience 'I know the wisdom of the King to be such that he 'will not value her repentance or the cessation of her 'madness and unnatural obstinacy when she has no 'longer power to choose. She would acknowledge her 'errors and evil conscience by the law of God and the 'King if blind affection had not so sealed her eyes that 'she will not see but what she pleases.

'Mrs. Shelton, I beseech you, trouble not yourself

' to turn her from any of her wilful ways, for to me she
' can do neither good nor ill. Do your own duty to-
' wards her, following the King's commandment, as I
' am assured that you do and will do, and you shall find
' me your good lady, whatever comes.

'Your good Mistress,

'ANNE R.'

CHAPTER XXI.

Funeral of Catherine—Miscarriage of Anne—The Princess Mary
and the Act of Supremacy—Her continued desire to escape—
Effect of Catherine's death on Spanish policy—Desire of the
Emperor to recover the English alliance—Chapuys and
Cromwell—Conditions of the treaty—Efforts of the Emperor
to recover Henry to the Church—Matrimonial schemes—
Likelihood of a separation of the King from Anne—Jane
Seymour—Anne's conduct—The Imperial treaty—Easter at
Greenwich—Debate in Council—The French alliance or the
Imperial—The alternative advantages—Letter of the King to
his Ambassador in Spain.

CATHERINE was buried with some state in Peter-
borough Cathedral on the 29th of January. In
the ceremonial she was described as the widow of Prince
Arthur, not as the Queen of England, and the Spanish
Ambassador, therefore, declined to be present. On
the same day Anne Boleyn again miscarried, and
this time of a male infant. She laid the blame of
her misfortune on the Duke of Norfolk. The King
had been thrown from his horse; Norfolk, she said,
had alarmed her by telling her of the accident too
suddenly. This Chapuys maliciously said that the King
knew to be untrue, having been informed she had heard

the news with much composure. The disappointment worked upon his mind; he said he saw plainly God would give him no male children by that woman; he went once to her bedside, spoke a few cold words, and left her with an intimation that he would speak to her again when she was recovered. Some concluded that there was a defect in her constitution; others whispered that she had been irritated at attentions which the King had been paying to Jane Seymour, who in earlier days had been a lady-in-waiting to Catherine. Anne herself, according to a not very credible story of Chapuys's, was little disturbed; her ladies were lamenting; she consoled them by saying that it was all for the best; the child that had been lost had been conceived in the Queen's lifetime, and the legitimacy of it might have been doubtful; no uncertainty would attach to the next.[1] It is not likely that Anne felt uncertain on such a point, or would have avowed it if she had. She might have reasons of her own for her hopes of another chance. Henry seemed to have no hope at all; he sent Chapuys a message through Cromwell that Mary's situation was now changed; her train should be increased, and her treatment improved—subject, however, of course, to her submission.

Mary had made up her mind, under Chapuys's

---

[1] 'L'on m'a dict que la Concu-bine consoloit ses demoiselles qui pleuroient, leur disant que c'estoit pour le mieulx, car elle en seroit tant plus tost enceinte, et que le fils qu'elle porterait ne seroit dubi-eulx comme fust esté icellui, estant conceu du vivant de la Royne.' Chapuys to Granvelle, Feb. 25, 1536.—*MS. Vienna; Calendar, Foreign and Domestic,* vol. x. p. 135.

advice, that if a prince was born, she would acknowledge the Act of Supremacy and the Act of Succession with a secret protest, as the Emperor had recommended her. She had no intention, however, of parting with her pretensions, and alienating her friends, as long as there was no brother whose claims she could not dispute. Chapuys had imagined, and Mary had believed, that the Emperor would have resented the alleged poisoning of Catherine; that, instead of her death removing the danger of war, as Henry supposed, war had now become more certain than ever. With this impression, the Princess still kept her mind fixed on escaping out of the country, and continued to press Chapuys to take her away. She had infinite courage; a Flemish ship was hovering about the mouth of the Thames ready to come up, on receiving notice, within two or three miles of Gravesend. The house to which she had been removed was forty miles from the place where she would have to embark; it was inconvenient for the intended enterprise, and was, perhaps, guarded, though she did not know it. She thought, however, that, if Chapuys would send her something to drug her women with, she could make her way into the garden, and the gate could be broken open. 'She was so eager,' Chapuys said, 'that, if he had told her to cross the Channel in a 'sieve, she would venture it;' the distance from Gravesend was the difficulty: the Flemish shipmaster was afraid to go higher up the river: a forty miles' ride would require relays of horses, and the country through which she had to pass was thickly inhabited. Means, however, might be found to take her down in a boat, and if she was once out of England, and under the Emperor's protection, Chapuys was convinced that the King would no longer kick against the pricks.

Mary herself was less satisfied on this point. Happy as she would be to find herself out of personal danger, she feared her father might still persist in his heresies, and bring more souls to perdition; 'she would, there-'fore, prefer infinitely,' she said, 'the general and total 'remedy so necessary for God's service.' She wished Chapuys to send another messenger to the Emperor, to stir him up to activity. But Chapuys, desperate of rousing Charles by mere entreaties, encouraged her flight out of the country as the surest means of bringing Henry to a reckoning. The difficulty would not be very great; the King had shown an inclination to be more gentle with her; Mrs. Shelton had orders to admit her mother's physician to her at any time that he pleased; and others of the household at Kimbolton were to be transferred to her service; these relaxations would make the enterprise much easier, and Chapuys was disposed to let it be tried. The Emperor's consent, however, was of course a preliminary condition, and his latest instructions had been unfavourable. The Ambassador, therefore, referred the matter once more to Charles's judgment, adding only, with a view to his own safety, that, should the escape be carried out, his own share in it would immediately be suspected; and the King, who had no fear of any one in the world, would undoubtedly kill him. He could be of no use in the execution of the plot, and would, therefore, make an excuse to cross to Flanders before the attempt was made.[1]

Chapuys's precipitancy had been disappointed before, and was to be disappointed again; he had worked hard to persuade Charles that Catherine had been murdered; Charles, by the manner in which he received the intelligence, showed that his Minister's representations had not convinced him. In sending word to the Empress that the Queen was dead, the Emperor said that accounts differed as to her last illness: some saying that it was caused by an affection of the stomach, which had lasted for some days; others that she had drunk something suspected to have contained poison. He did not himself say that he believed her to have been poisoned, nor did he wish it to be repeated as coming from him. The Princess, he heard, was inconsolable; he hoped God would have pity on her. He had gone into mourning, and had ordered the Spanish Court to do the same.[2]

In Spain there was an obvious consciousness that nothing had been done of which notice could be taken. Had there been a belief that a Spanish princess had been made away with in England, as the consummation of a protracted persecution, so proud a people would indisputably have demanded satisfaction. The effect was exactly the opposite. Articles had been drawn by the Spanish Council for a treaty with France as a settlement

---

[1] Chapuys to Charles V., Feb. 17, 1536.—*Calendar, Foreign and Domestic,* vol. x. p. 116.

[2] Charles V. to the Empress, Feb. 1, 1536.—*Spanish Calendar,* vol. v. part 2, p. 33.

of the dispute about Milan. One of the conditions was the stipulation to which Cromwell had referred in a conversation with Chapuys, that *France* was to undertake the execution of the Papal sentence and the reduction of England to the Church. The Queen being dead, the Emperor's Council recommended that this article should now be withdrawn, and the recovery of the King be left to negotiation.[1] Instead of seeing in Catherine's death an occasion for violence, they found in it a fresh motive for a peaceful arrangement.

It was assumed that if the Princess escaped, and if Henry did not then submit, war would be the immediate consequence. The Emperor, always disinclined towards the 'remedy' which his Ambassador had so long urged upon him, acted as Cromwell expected. The adventurous flight to Gravesend had to be abandoned, and he decided that Mary must remain quiet. In protecting Catherine while alive he had so far behaved like a gentleman and a man of honour. He was her nearest relation, and it was impossible for him to allow her to be pushed aside without an effort to prevent it. But as a statesman he had felt throughout that a wrong to his relation, or even a wrong to the Holy See, in the degraded condition of the Papacy, was no sufficient cause for adding to the confusions of Christendom. He had rather approved than condemned the internal reforms in the Church of England; and, after taking time to reflect and perhaps inquire more particularly into the

---

[1] Report of the Privy Council of Spain, Feb. 26, 1536.—*Spanish Calendar*, vol. v. part 2, p. 60.

circumstances of Catherine's end, he behaved precisely as he would have done if he was satisfied that her death was natural: he gave Chapuys to understand, in a letter from Naples,[1] that, if a fresh opening presented itself, he must take up again the abandoned treaty; and the secret interviews recommenced between the Ambassador and the English Chief Secretary.

These instructions must have arrived a week after the plans had been completed for Mary's escape, and Chapuys had to swallow his disappointment and obey with such heart as he could command. The first approaches were wary on both sides. Cromwell said that he had no commission to treat directly, and that, as the previous negotiations had been allowed to drop, the first overtures must now come from the Emperor; the Queen being gone, however, the ground of difference was removed, and the restoration of the old alliance was of high importance to Christendom; the King and the Emperor united could dictate peace to the world; France was on the eve of invading Italy, and had invited the King to make a simultaneous attack upon Flanders; a party in the Council wished him to consent; the King, however, preferred the friendship of the Emperor, and, Catherine being no longer alive, there was nothing to keep them asunder.

Chapuys, who never liked the proposal of a treaty at all, listened coldly; he said he had heard language of that kind before, and wished for something more

_____

[1] *Calendar, Foreign and Domestic,* vol. x. p. 224.

precise; Cromwell replied that he had been speaking merely his own opinion; he had no authority and therefore could not enter into details; if there was to be a reconciliation, he repeated that the Emperor must make the advances.

The Emperor, Chapuys rejoined, would probably make four conditions: the King must be reconciled to the Church as well as to himself; the Princess must be restored to her rank and be declared legitimate; the King must assist in the war with the Turks, and the league must be offensive as well as defensive.

Cromwell's answer was more encouraging than Chapuys perhaps desired. The fourth article, he said, would be accepted at once, and on the third the King would do what he could; no great objection would be made to the second; the door was open. Reconciliation with Rome would be difficult, but even that was not impossible. If the Emperor would write under his own hand to the Dukes of Norfolk and Suffolk, and to the Duke of Richmond, who in mind and body singularly resembled his father, much might be done.

A confidential Minister would not have ventured so far without knowing Henry's private views, and such large concessions were a measure of the decline of Anne Boleyn's influence. As regarded the Princess Mary, Chapuys had found that there was a real disposition to be more kind to her, for the King had sent her a crucifix which had belonged to her mother, containing a piece of the true cross, which Catherine had desired that she should have,[1] and had otherwise shown signs of a father's affection.

The Emperor himself now appears upon the scene, and the eagerness which he displayed for a reconciliation showed how little he had really seen to blame in Henry's conduct. So long as Catherine lived he was bound in honour to insist on her acknowledgment as queen; but she was gone, and he was willing to say no more about her. He saw that the intellect and energy of England were running upon the German lines. Chapuys, and perhaps other correspondents more trustworthy, had assured him that, if things went on as they were going, the hold of the Catholic Church on the English people would soon be lost. The King himself, if he wished it, might not be able to check the torrent, and the opinion of his vassals and his own imperious disposition might carry him to the extreme lengths of Luther. The Emperor was eager to rescue Henry before it was too late from the influences under which his quarrel with the Pope had plunged him. He praised Chapuys's dexterity; he was pleased with what Cromwell had said, and proceeded himself to take up the points of the proposals.

'The withdrawal of the King from the Church of 'Rome,' he said, 'was a matter of great importance. 'His pride might stand in the way of his turning back: 'he might be ashamed of showing a want of resolution 'before the world and before his subjects, and he was

---

[1] Chapuys to Charles V., Feb. 25, 1536.—*Calendar, Foreign and Domestic,* vol. x. pp. 131 et seq.

'obstinate in his own opinions.' Charles, therefore, directed Chapuys to lay before him such considerations as were likely to affect his judgment, the peril to his soul, the division and confusion sure to arise in his realm, and the evident danger should the Pope go on to the execution of the sentence and call in the assistance of the princes of Christendom. Under the most favourable aspect, both he and his supporters would be held in continual anxiety; and, though he might be able to maintain what he had begun as long as he himself lived, he could not do it without great difficulty, and would inevitably leave an inheritance of calamity to those who came after him. Chapuys was to advise him, therefore, to take timely measures for the security of the realm, and either refer his differences with the Pope to a General Council, or trust to Charles himself to negotiate for him with the Holy See, which he might assure himself that Charles would do on honourable and favourable terms. The chief objections likely to be raised by Henry would be the Pope's sentence in the divorce case, the interests of his country in the annates question, and other claims upon the realm which the Pope pretended. The first could be disposed of in the arrangement to be made for the Princess; the annates could be moderated, and a limit fixed for the Pope's other demands; as to the supreme authority over the Church of England, Chapuys might persuade the King that the relative positions of the Crown and the Holy See might be determined to his own honour and the profit and welfare of the

realm.[1] The Emperor, indeed, was obliged to add he
could give no pledge to the prejudice of the Church
without the Pope's consent, but Chapuys might promise
that he would use his utmost exertions to bring about a
reasonable composition. Charles evidently did not intend
to allow the pretensions of the Papacy to stand in the
way of the settlement of Europe. If the Ambassador
saw that a reconciliation with Rome was hopeless, sooner
than lose the treaty the Emperor was ready to consent
to leave that point out in order to carry the others,
provided the King did not require him directly to
countenance what he had done. As to the Princess,
care would have to be taken not to compromise the
honour of the late Queen or the legitimacy and rights
of her daughter. If her father would not consent to
recognise formally her claim on the succession, that too
might be left in suspense till the King's death ; and
Charles was willing to undertake that, as long as Henry
lived, no action was to be taken against him, and none
permitted to be taken on the part of any one, not even
of the Pope, to punish him for his treatment of Catherine
—not though her end had been hastened, as some
suspected, by sinister means. A marriage could be
arranged for Mary between the King and the Emperor ;
and, should the King himself decide to abandon the
Concubine and marry again in a fit and convenient
manner, Chapuys was to offer no opposition, and the

---

[1] 'Et aussy quant à l'auctorité 'de l'Eglise Anglicane l'on pourroit 'persuader au Roy que la chose 's'appoincteroit à son honneur, 'proufit, et bien du royaulme.'

Emperor said that he would not object to help him in conformity with the treaty.[1]

It was obvious to every one that, if Henry separated from Anne, an immediate marriage with some other person would follow. Charles was already weighing the possibility, and when the event occurred it will be seen that he lost not a moment in endeavouring to secure Henry's hand for another of his own relations. Princes and statesmen are not scrupulous in arranging their political alliances, but, considering all that had happened and all that was about to happen, the readiness of Charles V. to bestow a second kinswoman on the husband of Queen Catherine may be taken to prove that his opinion of Henry's character was less unfavourable than that which is generally given by historians.

Cromwell had been premature in allowing a prospect of the restoration of the Papal authority in England. Charles, in his eagerness to smooth matters, had suggested that a way might be found to leave the King the reality of the supremacy, while the form was left to the Pope. But no such arrangement was really possible, and Henry had gone on with his legislative measures against the Church as if no treaty was under consideration. Parliament had met again, and had passed an Act for the suppression of the smaller

---

[1] That is, as part of it. Charles V. to Chapuys, March 28, 1536.— *MS. Vienna; Calendar, Foreign and Domestic,* vol. x. pp. 224 et seq.; *Spanish Calendar,* vol. v. part 2, pp. 71 et seq. There are some differences in the translations in the two Calendars. When I refer to the MS. at Vienna, I use copies made there by myself.

monasteries.   That the Emperor should be suing to
him for an alliance while he was excommunicated by
the Pope, and was deliberately pursuing a policy which
was exasperating his own clergy, was peculiarly agreeable
to Henry, and he enjoyed the triumph which it gave
him; a still greater triumph would be another marriage
into the Imperial family; and a wish that he should
form some connection, the legality of which could not
be disputed, was widely entertained and freely uttered
among his own subjects. Chapuys, before Charles's
letter could have reached him, had been active in
encouraging the idea. He had spoken to Mary about
it, and Mary had been so delighted at the prospect of
her father's separation from Anne, that she said she
would rejoice at it, though it cost her the succession.[1]
That the King was likely to part with Anne was the
general talk of London. Chapuys called on Cromwell,
alluded to the rumour which had reached him, and
intimated how much mischief would be avoided if the
King could make up his mind to take another wife,
against whom no objection could be brought. Cromwell
said that he had never himself been in favour of the
marriage with Anne, but, seeing the King bent on it,
he had assisted him to the best of his power; he
believed, however, that, the thing having been done,
the King would abide by it; he might pay attentions
to other ladies, but they meant nothing.

Cromwell's manner seemed peculiar, and Chapuys

---

[1] Chapuys to Charles V., April 1, 1536.—*Calendar, Foreign and
Domestic*, vol. x. p. 243.

observed him more closely. The Secretary was leaning against a window, turning away his face as if to conceal a smile. There had been a report that some French princess was being thought of, and perhaps Chapuys made some allusion to it; for Cromwell said that Chapuys might assure himself that, if the King did take another wife, he would not look for her in France.

The smile might have had a meaning which Chapuys could not suspect. The Secretary was by this time acquainted with circumstances in Anne's conduct which might throw another aspect on the situation, but the moment had not come to reveal them. It is likely enough that the King had been harassed and uncertain. The air was thick with stories claiming to be authentic. Lady Exeter had told Chapuys that the King had sent a purse and a letter to Jane Seymour, of whom Anne had been jealous. Jane Seymour had returned the letter unopened and the money along with it, and had prayed the bearer to say to the King that he must keep his presents till she made some honourable marriage.

Lady Exeter and her friends made their own comments. Anne's enemies, it was said, were encouraging the intimacy with Jane, and had told the lady to impress upon the King that the nation detested his connection with Anne and that no one believed it lawful; as if it were likely that a woman in the position in which Jane Seymour was supposed to stand could have spoken to him on such a subject, or would have recommended herself to Henry if she did. At the same time it is possible and even probable that Henry, observing her quiet, modest, and upright character, may have contrasted her with the lady to whom he had bound himself, may have wished that he could change one for the other, and may even have thought of doing it; but that, as Cromwell said, he had felt that he must make no more changes, and must abide by the destiny which he had imposed on himself.[1]

For, in fact, it was not open to Henry to raise the question of the lawfulness of his marriage with Anne, or to avail himself of it if raised by others. He had committed himself far too deeply, and the Parliament had been committed along with him, to the measures by which the marriage was legalised. Yet Anne's ascendency was visibly drawing to an end, and clouds of a darker character were gathering over her head. In the early days of her married life outrageous libels had been freely circulated, both against her and against the King. Henry had been called a devil. The Duke of Norfolk had spoken of his niece as a *grande putaine*. To check these effusive utterances the severest penalties had been threatened by proclamation against all who dared to defame the Queen's character, and no one had ventured to whisper a word against her. But her conduct had been watched; light words, light actions had been observed and carefully noted. Her overbearing manner had left her without a friend save her own immediate connections and personal allies. 'Men's

---

[1] Chapuys to Charles V., April 1, 1536.—*Calendar, Foreign and Domestic*, vol. x. p. 242.

'mouths had been shut when they knew what ought
'not to have been concealed.'[1] A long catalogue of
misdeeds had been registered, with dates and particulars,
treasured up for use by the ladies of the household, as
soon as it should become safe to speak; and if her
conduct had been really as abandoned as it was afterwards alleged to have been, the growing alienation of
the King may be easily understood. It was impossible
for any woman to have worn a mask so long and never
to have given her husband occasion for dissatisfaction.
Incidents must have occurred in the details of daily life,
if not to rouse his suspicions, yet to have let him see
that the woman for whom he had fought so fierce a
battle had never been worth what she had cost him.

Anne Boleyn's fortunes, however, like Catherine's,
were but an episode in the affairs of England and of
Christendom, and the treaty with the Emperor was
earnestly proceeded with as if nothing were the matter.
The great concerns of nations are of more consequence
to contemporary statesmen than the tragedies or
comedies of royal households. Events rush on; the
public interests which are all-absorbing while they last
are superseded or forgotten; the personal interests
remain, and the modern reader thinks that incidents
which most affect himself must have been equally
absorbing to every one at the time when they occurred.
The mistake is natural, but it is a mistake notwithstanding. The great question of the hour was the

---

[1] *Calendar, Foreign and Domestic,* June 2, 1536, vol. x. pp. 428
et seq.

alternative alliance with the Empire or with France, and the result to be expected from the separation of England from Rome.

The Emperor wrote, as Cromwell had suggested, to the three Dukes. Chapuys paid Cromwell a visit at his country-house in the middle of April, to discuss again the four conditions. Cromwell had laid them before the King, and had to report his answer. The reconciliation with Rome was declared impossible. Henry said that the injuries to England by the Pope's sentence had been too great, and the statutes too recent to be repealed. The Pope himself was now making overtures, and was disposed to gratify the King as much as possible. Something, therefore, might be done in the future, but for the present the question could not be entertained. Cromwell offered to show the Ambassador the Pope's letters, if he wished to see them. Chapuys observed sarcastically that, after all that had passed, the King ought to be highly gratified at finding his friendship solicited by the Pope and the Emperor, the two parties whom he had most offended. It might be hoped that, having enjoyed his triumph, the King would now recollect that something was due to the peace of Christendom. Cromwell did not attempt a repartee, and let the observation pass. He said, however, that he hoped much from time. On the other points, all consideration would be shown for the Princess, but the King could not consent to make her the subject of an article in the treaty; no difficulty would be made about assistance in the Turkish war; as to France, the Council were unanimous in recommending the Imperial alliance, and had represented their views to the King. The King was pausing over his resolution, severely blaming the course which Francis was pursuing, but less willing to break with France than Cromwell had himself expected. Francis, Cromwell said, had stood by the King as a friend in the worst of his difficulties, and the King did not like to quarrel with him; he, however, intended to speak to Chapuys himself.

The Court was keeping Easter at Greenwich, and thither the Ambassador repaired. Easter Sunday falling on the 16th of April, the Chapter of the Garter was to be held there, and the assembly was large and splendid. Anne Boleyn was present in state as Queen, with her brother Lord Rochford, the demeanour of both of them undisturbed by signs of approaching storm. When Chapuys presented himself, Rochford paid him particular attention. The Ambassador had been long absent from the Court circle. Cromwell told him that the King would be pleased if he would now pay his respects to Anne, which he had never hitherto done, adding that, if he objected, it would not be insisted on. Chapuys excused himself. For various reasons, he said, he thought it not desirable. Cromwell said that his answer would be taken in good part, and hoped that the rest of their business would run smoothly.

Henry himself passed by as Cromwell was speaking to Chapuys. He bowed, took off his cap, and motioned to the Ambassador to replace his own. He then inquired after his health, asked how the Emperor was, how things were going in Italy—in short, was particularly courteous.

Service followed in the chapel. Rochford conducted Chapuys thither, and, as his sister was to be present and an encounter could not be avoided, people were curious to see how she and the Ambassador would behave to each other. Anne was ' affable ' enough, and curtseyed low as she swept past.

After mass the King and several members of the Council dined in Anne's apartments. As it was presumed that Chapuys would not desire to form one of the party, he was entertained by the household. Anne asked why he had not been invited. The King said there was reason for it.

Dinner over, Henry led Chapuys into his private cabinet, Cromwell following with the Chancellor Audeley. No one else was present at the beginning of the conference. The King drew the Ambassador apart into a window, when Chapuys again produced at length his four points. The King listened patiently as Chapuys expatiated on the action of the French, remarking only that Milan and Burgundy belonged to France and not to the Emperor. The observation showed Chapuys that things were not yet as he could have wished. He inquired whether, if the treaty were made, England would be prepared to assist the Emperor should France attack the Duke of Gueldres. Henry answered that he would do his part better than others had done their parts with him; he then called up

Cromwell and Audeley, and made Chapuys repeat what
he had said. This done, Chapuys withdrew to another
part of the room, and fell into conversation with Sir
Edward Seymour, who had since entered. He left
Henry talking earnestly with the two Ministers, and
between him and them Chapuys observed that there
was a strong difference of opinion. The King's voice
rose high. Cromwell, after a time, left him, and, saying that he was thirsty, seated himself on a chest out of
the King's sight and asked for water. The King then
rejoined the Ambassador, and told him that his communications were of such importance that he must
have them in writing. Chapuys objected that this
was unusual. He had no order to write anything, and
dared not go beyond his instructions. Henry was civil,
but persisted, saying that he could give no definite
answer till he had the Emperor's offer in black and
white before him. Generally, however, he said that his
quarrel with Rome did not concern the Emperor. If
he wished to treat with the Pope, he could do it without the Emperor's interposition ; the Princess was
his daughter, and would be used according to her
deserts ; a subvention for the Turkish war might be
thought of when the alliance with Charles was renewed.
Finally he said that he would not refuse his friendship
to those who sought it in becoming terms, but he *was
not a child, to be whipped first and then caressed and
invited back again and called sweet names.* He drummed
with his finger on his knee as he spoke. He insisted
that he had been injured and expected an acknowledg-

ment that he had been injured. The overtures, he repeated, must come from the Emperor. The Emperor must write him a letter requesting him to forget and forgive the past, and no more should then be said about it; but such a letter he must and would have. Chapuys restrained his temper. He said it was unreasonable to expect the Emperor to humiliate himself. Henry only grew more excited, called Charles ungrateful, declared that but for himself he would never have been on the Imperial throne, or even have recovered his authority in Spain when the commons had revolted; and, in return, the Emperor had stirred up Pope Clement to deprive him of his kingdom.

Chapuys said it was not the Emperor's doing. The Pope had done it himself, at the solicitation of other parties.

So the conference ended, and not satisfactorily. Henry was not a child to be whipped and caressed. Charles wanted him now, because he was threatened by France; and he, of his own judgment, preferred the Imperial alliance, like the rest of his countrymen; but Charles had coerced the Pope into refusing a concession which the Pope had admitted to be just, and the King knew better than his Council that the way to secure the Emperor's friendship was not to appear too eager for it.

The sharpness with which the King had spoken disappointed and even surprised Cromwell, who, when the audience was over, could hardly speak for vexation. His impression apparently was that the French faction

had still too much influence with the King, and the
French faction was the faction of Anne. He recovered
his spirits when Chapuys informed him of the concessions which the Emperor was prepared to make, and
said that he still hoped for 'a good result.'

The next morning, Wednesday, 19th of April, the
Privy Council met again in full number. They sate for
three hours. The future of England, the future of
Europe, appeared to them at that moment to be hanging on the King's resolution. They went in a body to
him and represented on their knees that they believed
the Imperial alliance essential to the safety of the
country, and they implored him not to reject a hand
so unexpectedly held out to him on a mere point of
honour. Henry, doubtless, felt as they did. Since
his quarrel with Charles he had hardly known a quiet
hour; he had been threatened with war, ruin of trade,
interdict, and internal rebellion. On a return to the
old friendship the sullen clergy, the angry Peers, would
be compelled into submission, for the friend on whom
they most depended would have deserted them; the
traders would no longer be in alarm for their ventures;
the Pope and his menaces would become a laughing-
stock, and in the divorce controversy the right would
be tacitly allowed to have been with the King, since it
was to be passed over without being mentioned. Immense advantages. But the imperious pride of Henry
insisted on the form as well as the substance—on
extorting a definite confession in words as well as a
practical acknowledgment. All the troubles which had

fallen on him—the quarrel with the Papacy, the
obstinate resistance of Catherine and Mary, the threats
of invasion and insurrection—he looked upon as
Charles's work. It was true that the offered friendship
was important to England, but England's friendship
was important to the Emperor, and the Emperor must
ask for it. He told the kneeling Councillors that he
would sooner lose his crown than admit, even by implication, that he had given Charles cause to complain of
him. He was willing to take the Emperor's hand, but
he would not seek or sue for it. The Emperor himself
must write to him.

Cromwell, in describing what had passed to Chapuys,
said that he was sorry that things had gone no better,
but that he was not discouraged. The King had
directed him to thank Chapuys for his exertions, and,
for himself, he trusted that the Ambassador would persevere. If the Emperor would send even a letter of
credit, the King would be satisfied. In all his private
conversations, although he had taken the responsibility
on himself, he had acted under the King's instructions.
The Ambassador asked him, if this was so, what could
have caused the change. He answered that kings had
humours and peculiarities of their own, unknown to
ordinary mortals. In spite of what had passed, the
King was writing at that moment to Francis, to require
him to desist from his enterprise against Italy.

Chapuys replied that he would endeavour to obtain
the letter from the Emperor which the King demanded.
He wrote to Charles, giving a full and perhaps accurate

account of all that had passed; but he ended with
advice of his own which showed how well Henry
had understood Chapuys's own character, and the
slippery ground on which he was standing. Chapuys
had disliked the treaty with England from the beginning. He told his master that Henry's real purpose
was to make him force out of the Pope a revocation of
the sentence on the divorce. He recommended the
Emperor once more to leave Henry to reap the fruit of
his obstinacy, to come to terms with France, and allow
the Pope to issue the Bull of Deposition—with a proviso
that neither he nor Francis would regard any child as
legitimate whom the King might have, either by the
Concubine or by any other woman whom he might
marry during the Concubine's life, unless by a dispensation from the Pope, which was not likely to be asked
for. He did not venture to hope that the Emperor
would agree, but such a course, he said, would bring
the King to his senses, and force would be unnecessary.[1]

To Granvelle the Ambassador wrote more briefly to
the same purpose. 'God knew,' he said, 'how he had
'worked to bring the King to a right road; but he had
'found him unspeakably obstinate. The King seemed
'determined to compel the Emperor to acknowledge
'that Clement's sentence had been given under pressure
'from himself. Cromwell had behaved like an honest
'man, and had taken to his bed for sorrow. Cromwell

---

[1] Chapuys to Charles V., April 21, 1536.—*Calendar, Foreign and Domestic,* vol. x. pp. 287 et seq.; *Spanish Calendar,* vol. v. part 2, pp. 85 et seq.

'knew how necessary the Emperor's friendship was to
'the King, but God or the Devil was preventing it.' [1]

Henry gave his own version of the story to the
English Ministers at Charles's court.

' The Emperor's Ambassador,' he said, 'has been
' with us at Greenwich with offers to renew the alliance,
' the conditions being that we would allow the Emperor
' to reconcile us with the Pope, that we will declare our
' daughter Mary legitimate and give her a place in the
' succession, that we will help him against the Turks,
' and declare war against France should France invade
' Milan.

' Our answer was that the breach of amity came
' first from the Emperor himself. We gave him the
' Imperial crown when it lay with us to dispose of.
' We lent him money in his difficulties, &c. In return
' he has shown us nothing but ingratitude, stirring the
' Bishop of Rome to do us injury. If he will by express
' writing desire us to forget his unkind doings, or will
' declare that what we consider unkindness has been
' wrongly imputed to him, we will gladly embrace his
' overtures; but as we have sustained the wrong we
' will not be suitors for reconciliation. As to the
' Bishop of Rome, we have not proceeded on such slight
' grounds as we would revoke or alter any part of
' our doings, having laid our foundation on the Law of
' God, nature, and honesty, and established our work
' thereupon with the consent of the Estates of the

----

[1] April 21.—*Calendar, Foreign and Domestic.*

'Realm in open and high court of Parliament. A
'proposal has been made to us by the Bishop himself
'which we have not yet embraced, nor would it be
'expedient that a reconciliation should be compassed
'by any other means. We should not think the
'Emperor earnestly desired a reconciliation with us, if
'he desired us to alter anything for the satisfaction of
'the Bishop of Rome, our enemy.

'As to our daughter Mary, if she will submit to the
'laws we will acknowledge and use her as our daughter;
'but we will not be directed or pressed therein. It is
'as meet for us to order things here without search for
'foreign advice as for the Emperor to determine his
'affairs without our counsel. About the Turks we can
'come to no certain resolution; but if a reconciliation
'of the affairs of Christendom ensue, we will not fail to
'do our duty. Before we can treat of aid against the
'French King the amity with the Emperor must first
'be renewed.' [1]

---

[1] Henry VIII. to Pate, April 25, 1536. Abridged.—*Calendar, Foreign and Domestic*, vol. x. p. 306.

CHAPTER XXII.

Easter at Greenwich—French and Imperial factions at the English court—Influence of Anne Boleyn—Reports of Anne's conduct submitted to the King—Flying rumours—Secret Commission of Inquiry—Arrests of various persons—Sir Henry Norris and the King—Anne before the Privy Council—Sent to the Tower—Her behaviour and admissions—Evidence taken before the Commission—Trials of Norris, Weston, Brereton, and Smeton—Letter of Weston—Trial of Anne and her brother—Executions—Speech of Rochford on the scaffold—Anne sentenced to die—Makes a confession to Cranmer—Declared to have not been the King's lawful wife—Nature of the confession not known—Execution.

AT the moment when the King was bearing himself so proudly at the most important crisis of his reign, orthodox historians require us to believe that he was secretly contriving to rid himself of Anne Boleyn by a foul and false accusation, that he might proceed immediately to a new marriage with another lady. Men who are meditating enormous crimes have usually neither leisure nor attention for public business. It is as certain as anything in history can be certain that to startle Europe with a domestic scandal while mighty issues were at stake on which the fate of England depended was the last subject with which England's

King was likely to have been occupied. He was
assuming an attitude of haughty independence, where
he would need all his strength and all the confidence
of his subjects. To conspire at such a moment against
the honour and life of a miserable and innocent woman
would have occurred to no one who was not a maniac.
Rumour had been busy spreading stories that he was
weary of Anne and meant to part with her; but a few
days previously he had dissolved the Parliament which
for seven years had been described as the complacent
instrument of his will. He could not be equally assured
of the temper of another, hastily elected, in the uneasy
condition of the public mind; and, without a Parliament, he could take no action which would affect the
succession. However discontented he might be with
his present Queen, the dissolution of Parliament is a
conclusive proof that at the time of Chapuys's visit to
Greenwich he was not contemplating a matrimonial
convulsion. Probably, in spite of all the stories set
flowing into Chapuys's long ears by the ladies of the
household, he had resolved to bear his fortune, bad as
it was, and was absolutely ignorant of the revelation
which was about to break upon him. Husbands are
proverbially the last to know of their wives' infidelities;
and the danger of bringing charges which could not be
substantiated against a woman in Anne's position would
necessarily keep every lip shut till the evidence could
be safely brought forward. Cromwell appears to have
been in possession of important information for many
weeks. The exposure, however, might still have been

delayed but for the unfavourable answer of the King to the Emperor's advances, which had so much distressed the advocates of a renewal of the amity. France was now going to war, and making large offers for the English alliance. Henry, though his affection for Anne had cooled, still resented the treatment which he had received from Charles, and had a fair opportunity of revenging himself. The wisest of his Ministers were against continental adventures, and wished him earnestly to accept the return of a friendship the loss of which had cost the country so dear. But the French faction at the Court, Anne and her relations, and the hot-tempered young men who surrounded him, were still able to work upon his wounded pride. Could they plunge the country into war at the side of Francis, they would recover their ascendency. Any day might see some fatal step taken which could not be recovered. Both Anne and Rochford were bold, able, and unscrupulous, and Cromwell, with a secret in his hand which would destroy them, saw that the time was come to use it.

That it was not accident which connected the outburst of the storm on Anne's head with the political negotiations is certain from Cromwell's own words. He told Chapuys that it was the disappointment which he felt at the King's reply to him on the Wednesday after Easter that had led him to apply the match to the train.[1]

---

[1] 'Et que à luy avoit esté 'donnée l'auctorité de descouvrir 'et parachever les affaires de .a 'dicte Concubine, en quoy il avoit

A casual incident came to his assistance. A Privy
Councillor, whose name is not mentioned, having
remarked sharply on the light behaviour of a sister who
was attached to the Court, the young lady admitted her
offence, but said it was nothing in comparison with the
conduct of the Queen. She bade her brother examine
Mark Smeton, a groom of the chamber and a favourite
musician.[1] The Privy Councillor related what he had
heard to two friends of the King, of whom Cromwell
must have been one. The case was so serious that they
agreed that the King must be informed. They told
him. He started, changed colour, thanked them, and
directed an inquiry to be held in strict secrecy. The
ladies of the bedchamber were cross-questioned. Lady
Worcester[2] was 'the first accuser.' 'Nan Cobham'

' eu une merveilleuse peine ; et que
' sur le desplesir et courroux qu'il
'avoit eu sur la response que le
' Roy son maistre m'avoit donnée
' le tiers jour de Pasques il se mit
'à fantasier et conspirer le dict
' affaire,' &c. Chapuys to Charles
V., June 6, 1536.—*MS. Vienna ;
Spanish Calendar*, vol. v. part 2,
p. 137. From the word 'conspirer' it has been inferred that
the accusation of Anne and her
accomplices was a conspiracy of
Cromwell's, got up in haste for
an immediate political purpose.
Cromwell must have been marvellously rapid, since within four
days he was able to produce a
case to lay before a Special Commission composed of the highest

persons in the realm assisted by
the Judges, involving the Queen
and a still powerful faction at the
Court. We are to believe, too,
that he had the inconceivable
folly to acknowledge it to Chapuys,
the most dangerous person to
whom such a secret could be
communicated. Cromwell was
not an idiot, and it is impossible
that in so short a time such an
accumulation of evidence could
have been invented and prepared
so skilfully as to deceive the
Judges.

[1] *Calendar, Foreign and Domestic*, June 2, vol. x. p. 428.

[2] Daughter of Sir Anthony
Brown, Master of the Horse.

and a maid gave other evidence; but 'Lady Worcester
'was the first ground.'[1]

Nothing was allowed to transpire to disturb the
festivities at Greenwich. On St. George's Day, April
23, the Queen and her brother received an intimation
that they were in less favour than usual. The Chapter
of the Garter was held. An order was vacant; Anne
asked that it should be given to Lord Rochford, and
the request was refused; it was conferred on her cousin,
Sir Nicholas Carew, to her great vexation. In this,
however, there was nothing to alarm her. The next
day, the 24th, a secret committee was appointed to
receive depositions, consisting of the Chancellor, the
Judges, Cromwell, and other members of Council; and
by this time whispers were abroad that something was
wrong, for Chapuys, writing on the 29th of April, said
that 'it would not be Carew's fault if Anne was not out
'of the saddle before long, as he had heard that he was
'daily conspiring against her and trying to persuade
'Mistress Seymour and her friends to work her ruin.
'Four days ago [*i. e.* on April 25] Carew and other
'gentlemen sent word to the Princess to take courage,
'as the King was tired of the Concubine and would not
'endure her long.'[2] Geoffrey Pole, Reginald's brother,
a loose-tongued gentleman, told Chapuys that the
Bishop of London (Stokesley) had been lately asked
whether the King could dismiss the Concubine; the

[1] John Husee to Lady Lisle,
May 24, 1536.—*Calendar, Foreign
and Domestic*, vol. x. p. 397.

[2] Chapuys to Charles V., April
29.—*Spanish Calendar*, p. 105.

Bishop had declined to give an opinion till the King asked for it, and even then would not speak till he knew the King's intention. The Bishop, Chapuys said, was one of the promoters of the first divorce, and was now penitent, the Concubine and all her family being accursed Lutherans.[1]

Such stories were but surmise and legend. I insert them to omit nothing which may be construed into an indication of conspiracy. The Commission meanwhile was collecting facts which grew more serious every day. On Thursday, the 27th, Sir William Brereton, a gentleman of the King's Privy Chamber, was privately sent to the Tower, and on the 30th was followed thither by the musician Smeton. The next morning, the 1st of May, high festival was held at Greenwich. A tournament formed a part of the ceremony, with the Court in attendance. Anne sat in a gallery as Queen of the day, while her knights broke lances for her, caring nothing for flying scandal, and not suspecting the abyss which was opening under her feet. Sir Henry Norris and Lord Rochford were in the lists as defender and challenger, when suddenly the King rose; the pageant was broken up in confusion; Henry mounted his horse and, followed by a small train, rode off for London, taking Norris with him. Sir Henry Norris was one of Henry's most intimate personal friends. He was his equerry, and often slept in his room or in an adjoining closet. The inquiries of the Commission had not yet implicated him as a principal, but it had appeared that

---

[1] Chapuys to Charles V., April 29.—*Spanish Calendar*, p. 105.

circumstances were known to him which he ought to have revealed. The King promised to forgive him if he would tell the truth, but the truth was more than he could dare to reveal. On the following day he, too, was sent to the Tower, having been first examined before the Commissioners, to whom—perhaps misled by some similar hope of pardon held out to him by Sir William Fitzwilliam—he confessed more than it was possible to pardon, and then withdrew what he had acknowledged.[1] So far, Smeton only had confessed to 'any actual thing,' and it was thought the King's honour would be touched if the guilt of the rest was not proved more clearly.

Anne had been left at Greenwich. On the next morning she was brought before the Council there, her uncle, the Duke of Norfolk, presiding. She was informed that she was charged with adultery with various persons. Her answers, such as they were, the Duke set aside as irrelevant. She complained afterwards that she had been 'cruelly handled' by the Council. It was difficult not to be what she would consider cruel. She, too, was conducted up the river to the Tower, where she found that to Smeton and Brereton and Norris another gentleman of the household, Sir Francis Weston, had now been added. A small incident is mentioned which preserves a lost practice of the age. 'On the evening of the day on which the Concu- 'bine was sent to the Tower, the Duke of Richmond 'went to his father to ask his blessing, according to the

---

[1] *History of England,* vol. ii. p. 363.

'English custom. The King said, in tears, that he, and
'his sister the Princess, ought to thank God for having
'escaped the hands of that woman, who had planned to
'poison them.'[1]

Chapuys made haste to inform the Emperor of the
welcome catastrophe. The Emperor, he said, would
recollect the expressions which he had reported as used
by Cromwell regarding the possible separation of the
King and the Concubine. Both he and the Princess
had been ever since anxious that such a separation
should be brought about. What they had desired had
come to pass better than any one could have hoped, to
the great disgrace of the Concubine, who, by the judgment of God, had been brought in full daylight from
Greenwich to the Tower, in charge of the Duke of
Norfolk and two chamberlains. Report said it was for
continued adultery with a spinet-player belonging to
her household. The player had been committed to the
Tower also, and, after him, Sir H. Norris, the most
familiar and private companion of the King, for not
having revealed the matter.[2]

Fresh news poured in as Chapuys was writing.
Before closing his despatch he was able to add that Sir
Francis Weston and Lord Rochford were arrested also.
The startling story flew from lip to lip, gathering volume
as it went. Swift couriers carried it to Paris. Viscount

---

[1] Chapuys to Charles V., May 19, 1536.—*Spanish Calendar*, vol. v. part 2, p. 125.

[2] Chapuys to Charles V., May 2, 1536.—*MSS. Vienna; Calendar, Foreign and Domestic*, vol. x. p. 330; *Spanish Calendar*, vol. v. part 2, p. 107.

Hannaert, the Imperial Ambassador there,[1] wrote to Granvelle that Anne had been surprised in bed with the King's organist.[2] In the course of the investigation, witnesses had come forward to say that nine years previously a marriage had been made and consummated between Anne and Percy Earl of Northumberland. Percy, however, swore, and received the sacrament upon it, before the Duke of Norfolk and the Archbishops of Canterbury and York, that no contract or promise of marriage of any kind had passed between them.[3] Anne's attendants in the Tower had been ordered to note what she might say. She denied that she was guilty, sometimes with hysterical passion, sometimes with a flighty levity; but not, so far as her words are recorded, with the clearness of conscious innocence. She admitted that with Norris. Weston, and Smeton she had spoken foolishly of their love for herself, and of what might happen were the King to die. Smeton, on his second examination, confessed that he had on three several occasions committed adultery with the Queen. Norris repudiated his admissions to Sir William Fitzwilliam— what they were is unknown—and offered to maintain his own innocence and the Queen's with sword and

---

[1] In transcribing the MS. twenty years ago at Vienna I mistook the name for Howard, which it much resembled in the handwriting of the time. I am reminded correctly that there was no Viscount Howard in the English Peerage.

[2] 'Le Visconte Hannaert a 'escript au Sr de Granvelle que au 'mesme instant il avoit entendu de 'bon lieu que la concubine du dict 'Roy avoit esté surprise couchée 'avec l'organiste du dict Roy.'

[3] The Earl of Northumberland to Cromwell, May 13, 1536.— *Calendar, Foreign and Domestic,* vol. x. p. 356.

lance.   Weston and Brereton persisted in absolute
denial.

Meanwhile the Commission continued to take
evidence.   A more imposing list of men than those
who composed it could not have been collected in
England.   The members of it were the Lord Chancellor, the Duke of Norfolk, the Duke of Suffolk, Lord
Wiltshire, Anne's and Rochford's father, the Earls of
Oxford, Westmoreland, and Sussex, Lord Sandys,
Thomas Cromwell, Sir William Fitzwilliam, the Lord
High Admiral, Sir William Paulet, Lord Treasurer,
and nine judges of the courts at Westminster.   Before
these persons the witnesses were examined and their
depositions written down.   'The confessions,' Cromwell
wrote afterwards to Gardiner, 'were so abominable that
'a great part of them were not given in evidence, but
'were clearly kept secret.' [1]

The alleged offences had been committed in two
counties.   The Grand Juries of Kent and Middlesex
returned true bills on the case presented to them.   On
the 7th of May writs were sent out for a new Parliament, to be chosen and to meet immediately.   The
particular charges had been submitted to the Grand
Juries with time, place, and circumstance.   The details
have been related by me elsewhere.[2]   In general the
indictment was that for a period of more than two years,
from within a few weeks after the birth of Elizabeth to

---

[1] Cromwell to Gardiner, July
5, 1536.—*Calendar, Foreign and
Domestic*, vol. xi. p. 17.

[2] *History of England*, vol. ii.
p. 380.

the November immediately preceding, the Queen had repeatedly committed acts of adultery with Sir Henry Norris, Sir William Brereton, Sir Francis Weston, Mark Smeton, and her brother Lord Rochford. In every case the instigation and soliciting were alleged to have been on the Queen's side. The particulars were set out circumstantially, the time at which the solicitations were made, how long an interval elapsed between the solicitation and the act, and when and where the several acts were committed. Finally it was said that the Queen had promised to marry some one of these traitors whenever the King should depart this life, affirming that she would never love the King in her heart.

Of all these details evidence of some kind must have been produced before the Commission, and it was to this that Cromwell referred in his letter to Gardiner. The accused gentlemen were all of them in situations of trust and confidence at the Court, with easy access to the Queen's person, and, if their guilt was real, the familiarity to which they were admitted through their offices was a special aggravation of their offences.

In a Court so jealous, and so divided, many eyes were on the watch and many tongues were busy. None knew who might be implicated, or how far the Queen's guilt had extended. Suspicion fell on her cousin, Sir Francis Bryan, who was sharply examined by Cromwell. Suspicion fell also on Anne's old lover, Sir Thomas Wyatt, Surrey's friend, to whom a letter survives, written on the occasion by his father, Sir Henry. The old man told his son he was sorry that he was too ill to do his duty to his King in that dangerous time when the King had suffered by false traitors. He prayed God long to give *him* grace, to be with him and about him that had found out the matter, and the false traitors to be punished to the example of others.[1]

Cranmer had been much attached to Anne. The Catholic party being so bitter against her, she had made herself the patroness of the Protestant preachers, and had protected them against persecution. The Archbishop had regarded her as an instrument of Providence, and when the news reached him of the arrest and the occasion of it he was thunderstruck. He wrote an anxious and beautiful letter to the King, expressing a warm belief and hope that the Queen would be able to clear herself. Before he could send it he was invited to meet the Council in the Star Chamber. On his return he added a postscript that he was very sorry such faults could be proved by the Queen as he heard of their relation.[2]

On Friday the 12th of May the four commoners were brought up for trial. The Court sat in Westminster Hall, Lord Wiltshire being on the bench with the rest. Their guilt, if proved, of course involved the guilt of his daughter. The prisoners were brought to the bar and the indictment was read. Smeton pleaded guilty of adultery, but not guilty of the inferential charge of compassing the death of the King. The

---

[1] Sir Henry Wyatt to Thomas Wyatt, May 7, 1536.—*Calendar, Foreign and Domestic*, vol. x. p. 345.   'Him' refers to Cromwell.

[2] *History of England*, vol. ii. pp. 367—371.

other three held to their denial. Weston was married. His mother and his young wife appeared in court, 'oppressed with grief,' to petition for him, offering 'rents and goods' for his deliverance;[1] but it could not avail. The jury found against them all, and they were sentenced to die. Two letters to Lord and Lady Lisle from a friend in London convey something of the popular feeling.

'John Husee to Lady Lisle.

May 13.

'Madam, I think verily if all the books and chronicles 'were totally revolved and to the uttermost persecuted 'and tried, which against women hath been penned, 'contrived, and written since Adam and Eve, those 'same were, I think, verily nothing in comparison of 'that which hath been done and committed by Anne 'the Queen, which though I presume be not all things 'as it is now rumoured, yet that which hath been by 'her confessed, and other offenders with her, by her 'own alluring, procurement, and instigation, is so 'abominable and detestable, that I am ashamed that 'any good woman should give ear thereunto. I pray 'God give her grace to repent while she now liveth. 'I think not the contrary but she and all they shall 'suffer.'[2]

'To Lord Lisle.

Same date.

'Here are so many tales I cannot tell what to write. 'Some say young Weston shall scape, and some that

---

[1] *Calendar, Foreign and Domestic,* vol. x. p. 430.   [2] *Ibid.* p. 357.

' none shall die but the Queen and her brother; others,
' that Wyatt and Mr. Page are as like to suffer as the
' rest. If any escape, it will be young Weston, for whom
' importunate suit is made.'

Great interest was felt in Sir F. Weston. The appearance of his wife and mother in court had created
general compassion for him. He was young, rich,
accomplished. He was well known in Paris, had been
much liked there. M. d'Intevelle, who had been his
friend, hurried over to save him, and the Bishop of
Tarbes, the resident Ambassador, earnestly interceded.
Money, if money could be of use, was ready to be
lavished. But, like Norris, Weston had been distinguished by Henry with peculiar favour; and if he had
betrayed the confidence that was placed in him he had
nothing to plead which would entitle him to special
mercy. A letter has been preserved, written by Weston
to his family after his sentence, inclosing an inventory
of his debts, which he desired might be paid. If any
one can believe, after reading it, that the writer was
about to die for a crime of which he knew that he was
innocent, I shall not attempt to reason with such a
person.

' Father, mother, and wife,
    ' I shall humbly desire you, for the salvation of my
' soul, to discharge me of this bill, and forgive me all
' the offences that I have done unto you, and in especial
' to my wife, which I desire for the love of God to
' forgive me and to pray for me; for I believe prayer

' will do me good. God's blessing have my children and
' mine.

> ' By me, a great offender to God.'[1]

On Sunday the 14th a report of the proceedings up
to that moment was sent by Cromwell to Sir John
Wallop and Gardiner at Paris. The story, he said,
was now notorious to every one, but he must inform
them further how the truth had been discovered and
how the King had proceeded. The Queen's incontinent
living was so rank and common that the ladies of the
Privy Chamber could not conceal it. It came to the
ears of some of the Council, who told his Majesty,
though with great fear, as the case enforced. Certain
persons of the household and others who had been about
the Queen's person were examined; and the matter
appeared so evident that, besides the crime, there brake
out a certain conspiracy of the King's death, which
extended so far that they that had the examination
of it quaked at the danger his Grace was in, and on
their knees gave God laud and praise that he had
preserved him so long from it. Certain men were
committed to the Tower, Mark and Norris, and the
Queen's brother. Then she herself was apprehended;
after her, Sir Francis Weston and Brereton. Norris,
Weston, Brereton, and Mark were already condemned
to death, having been arraigned at Westminster on
the past Friday. The Queen and her brother were to

---

[1] Autograph letter of Sir Francis Weston, May 13, 1536.—*Calendar, Foreign and Domestic*, vol. x. p. 358.

R

be arraigned the next day. He wrote no particulars. The things were so abominable that the like was never heard.[1]

Anne Boleyn was already condemned by implication. The guilt of her paramours was her own. She herself was next brought to the bar, with her brother, to be tried by the Peers. The court was held at the Tower. Norfolk presided as High Steward. Lord Wiltshire was willing to sit, but the tragedy was terrible enough without further aggravation, and the world was spared the spectacle of a father taking part in the conviction of his own children on a charge so hideous. The Earl of Northumberland did sit, though ill from anxiety and agitation. Twenty-five other Peers took their places also.

The account of the proceedings is preserved in outline in the official record; a further detailed description was furnished by Chapuys to the Emperor, containing new and curious particulars.

On Monday the 15th of May, Chapuys wrote, the Concubine and her brother were condemned for treason by the principal nobles of England. The Duke of Norfolk passed sentence, and Chapuys was told that the Earl of Wiltshire was ready to assist at the trial, as he had done at that of the rest. The *putaine* and her brother were not taken to Westminster, as the others had been, but were brought to the bar at the Tower. No secret was made of it, however, for over

---

[1] Cromwell to Wallop and Gardiner, May 14, 1536.—*Calen-* *dar, Foreign and Domestic,* vol. x. p. 359.

two thousand persons were present. The principal charge against her was that she had cohabited with her brother and the other accomplices, that a promise had passed between her and Norris that she would marry him after the King's decease—a proof that they had desired his death; that she had exchanged medals with Norris, implying that they were leagued together; that she had poisoned the late Queen, and intended to poison the Princess.[1] To most of these charges she returned an absolute denial; others she answered plausibly, but confessed having given money to Weston and to other gentlemen. She was likewise charged, and the brother also, with having ridiculed the King, showing in many ways she had no love for him, and was tired of her life with him. The brother was accused of having had connection with his sister. No proof of his guilt was produced, except that of having been once alone with her for many hours, and other small follies. He replied so well that many who were present were betting two to one he would be acquitted.

Another charge against him was that the Concubine had told his wife that the King was unequal to his duties.[2] This was not read out in court; it was given

---

[1] 'Qu'elle avoit faict empoisoner la feue Royne et machyné 'de faire de mesme à la Princesse.' Chapuys was not present, but was writing from report, and was not always trustworthy. No trace is found of these accusations in the Record, but they may have been mentioned in the pleadings.

[2] 'Que le Roy n'estoit habille 'en cas de copuler avec femme, et 'qu'il n'avoit ni vertu ni puissance.' Historians, to make their narrative coherent, assume an intimate acquaintance with the motives for each man's or woman's actions. Facts may be difficult to ascertain, but motives, which cannot be

to Rochford in writing, with a direction not to make
it public, but to say merely yes or no. To the great
annoyance of Cromwell and others, who did not wish
suspicions to be created which might prejudice the
King's issue, Rochford read it aloud.[1]

He was accused also of having used words implying
a doubt whether Anne's daughter was the King's, to
which he made no answer.

The brother and sister were tried separately and did
not see each other. The Concubine was sentenced to
be burnt alive or beheaded, at the King's pleasure.
When she heard her fate she received it calmly, saying
that she was ready to die, but was sorry that others

---

ascertained at all unless when acknowledged, they are able to dis-
cern by intuition. They have
satisfied themselves that the
charges against Anne Boleyn were
invented because the King wished
to marry Jane Seymour. I pretend
to no intuition myself. I do not
profess to be wise beyond what I
find written. In this instance I
hazard a conjecture—a conjecture
merely—which occurred to me
long ago as an explanation of some
of the disasters of Henry's marriages, and which the words, alleged to have been used by Anne
to Lady Rochford, tend, *pro tanto*,
to confirm.

Henry was already showing
signs of the disorder which eventu-
ally killed him. Infirmities in his
constitution made it doubtful, both
to others and to himself, whether

healthy children, or any children at
all, would in future be born to him.
It is possible—I do not say more
—that Anne, feeling that her own
precarious position could only be
made secure if she became the
mother of a prince, had turned for
assistance in despair at her disappointments to the gentlemen by
whom she was surrounded. As an
hypothesis, this is less intolerable
than to suppose her another
Messalina. In every instance of
alleged offence the solicitation is
said to have proceeded from herself, and to have been only yielded
to after an interval of time.

[1] 'Au grand despit de Cromwell
'et d'aucungs autres qui ne voul-
'droient en cest endroit s'engen-
'droit suspicion qui pourroit preju-
'diquer à la lignée que le dict Roy
'pretend avoir.'—*MSS. Vienna.*

who were innocent and loyal should suffer on her account. She begged for a short respite, to dispose her conscience. The brother said that, since die he must, he would no longer plead 'not guilty,' but would confess that he deserved death, and requested only that his debts might be paid out of his property.[1]

Two days after the trial of the Queen and Rochford, the five gentlemen suffered on Tower Hill. The Concubine, wrote Chapuys, saw them executed from the windows of the Tower, to enhance her misery. The Lord Rochford declared himself innocent of everything with which he was charged, although he confessed that he had deserved death for having contaminated himself with the new sects of religion, and for having infected many others. For this he said that God had justly punished him. He prayed all the world to keep clear of heresy, and his words would cause the recovery and conversion of innumerable souls.[2] This is a good instance of Chapuys's manner, and is a warning against an easy acceptance of his various stories. It is false that Rochford declared himself innocent of the adultery. It is false that he said that he deserved death for heresy. He said nothing—not a word—about heresy. What he did say is correctly given in Wriothesley's Chronicle, which confirms the report sent from London to the

---

[1] Chapuys to Charles V., May 19, 1536.—*MSS. Vienna; Spanish Calendar*, vol. v. part 2, pp. 122 et seq. In one or two instances my translation will be found to differ slightly from that of S Gayangas.

[2] Chapuys to Charles V., May 19.—*Spanish Calendar*, vol. v. part 2, p. 128.

Regent of the Netherlands.[1]   The Spanish writer says
that his address was '*muy bien Catolica*,' but it will be
seen that he carefully avoided a denial of the crime for
which he suffered.

'Masters all, I am come hither not to preach a
'sermon, but to die, as the law hath found me, and to
'the law I submit me, desiring you all, and specially
'my masters of the Court, that you will trust in God
'specially, and not in the vanities of the world; for if I
'had so done I think I had been alive as ye be now.
'Also I desire you to help to the setting forth of the true
'Word of God; I have been diligent to read it and set
'it forth truly; but if I had been as diligent to observe
'it and done and lived thereafter as I was to read it
'and set it forth, I had not come hereto.   Wherefore I
'beseech you all to be workers and live thereafter, and
'not to read it and live not thereafter.   As for my
'offences, it cannot avail you to hear them that I die
'here for; but I beseech God that I may be an example
'to you all, and that all you may beware by me, and
'heartily I require you all to pray for me and to forgive
'me if I have offended you, and I forgive you all, and
'God save the King.'[2]

Of the other four, Smeton and Brereton admitted
the justice of their sentence, Brereton adding that, if
he had to die a thousand deaths, he deserved them all.
Norris was almost silent.   Weston lamented in general

---

[1] *History of England*, vol. ii.
p. 394.
[2] *Wriothesley's Chronicle* (Cam-
den Society's Publications), vol. i.
p. 39.

terms the wickedness of his past life. From not one of the five came the indignant repudiation of a false accusation which might have been surely looked for from innocent men, and especially to be looked for when the Queen's honour was compromised along with theirs.

A Protestant spectator of the execution, a follower of Sir H. Norris, and a friend and schoolfellow of Brereton, said that at first he and all other friends of the Gospel had been unable to believe that the Queen had behaved so abominably. 'As he might be saved 'before God, he could not believe it, till he heard them 'speak at their death; but in a manner all confessed 'but Mr. Norris, who said almost nothing at all.' [1]

Dying men hesitate to leave the world with a lie on their lips. It appears to me, therefore, that these five gentlemen did not deny their guilt, because they knew that they were guilty. The unfortunate Anne was still alive: and while there was life there was hope. A direct confession on their part would have been a confession for her as well as themselves, and they did not make it; but, if they were really innocent, that they should have suffered as they did without an effort to clear themselves or her is one more inexplicable mystery in this extraordinary story.

Something even more strange was to follow.

At her trial Anne had been 'unmoved as a stone, 'and had carried herself as if she was receiving some

---

[1] Constantine's Memorial.—*Archæologia*, vol. xxiii. pp. 63—66.

'great honour.' She had been allowed a chair, and
had bowed to the Peers as she took her seat. She said
little, ' but her face spoke more than words, and no one
' to look on her would have thought her guilty.' 'She
' protested that she had not misconducted herself.'
When Norfolk delivered sentence her face did not
change. She said merely that she would not dispute
the judgment, but appealed to God.[1] Smeton had
repeated his own confession on the scaffold. She turned
pale when she was told of it. ' Did he not acquit me
' of the infamy he has laid on me?' she said. 'Alas, I
fear his soul will suffer for it!'[2]

But she had asked for time to prepare her conscience
and for spiritual help; she called herself a Lutheran,
and on the Tuesday, the day after her trial, Cranmer
went to the Tower to hear her confession. She then
told the Archbishop something which, if true, invalidated
her marriage with the King; if she had not been his
wife, her intrigues were not technically treason, and
Cranmer perhaps gave her hope that this confession
might save her, for she said afterwards to Sir William
Kingston that she expected to be spared and would
retire into a nunnery.[3] The confession, whatever it
might be, was produced on the following day by the
Archbishop sitting judicially at Lambeth,[4] and was
there considered by three ecclesiastical lawyers, who

---

[1] *Calendar, Foreign and Domestic,* June 2, vol. x. p. 430.
[2] *Ibid.* p. 431.
[3] Kingston to Cromwell, May

16, 1536,—*Calendar, Foreign and
Domestic,* vol. x. p. 371.
[4] 28 Hen. VIII. cap. 7.

gave as their opinion that she had never been the
King's lawful wife, and this opinion was confirmed by
the Chancellor, the Duke of Suffolk, the Earl of Oxford,
and a committee of bishops. The confession itself
belonged to the secrets which Cromwell described as
'too abominable to be made known,' and was never
published. The judgment of the Archbishop itself was
ratified on the 28th of June by the two Houses of
Convocation. It was laid before Parliament and was
made the basis of a new arrangement of the succession.
But the Statute merely says ' that God, from whom no
' secret things could be hid, had caused to be brought
' to light evident and open knowledge of certain im-
' pediments unknown at the making of the previous
' Act, and since that time confessed by the Lady Anne
' before the Archbishop of Canterbury, sitting judicially
' for the same, whereby it appeared that the marriage
' was never good nor consonant to the laws.'

Conjecture was, of course, busy over so singular a
mystery. Some said that the Archbishop had declared
Elizabeth to have been Norris's bastard, and not the
daughter of the King. Others revived the story of
Henry's supposed intrigue with Anne's sister, Mary,
and Chapuys added a story which even he did not
affect to believe, agreeable as it must have been to him.
' Many think,' he said, ' that the Concubine had become
' so audacious in vice, because most of the new bishops
' had persuaded her that she need not go to confession ;
' and that, according to the new sect, it was lawful to
' seek aid elsewhere, even from her own relations, when

'her husband was not able to satisfy her.'[1]   The Wriothesley Chronicle says positively that, on the 17th of May, in the afternoon, at a solemn court kept at Lambeth by the Archbishop of Canterbury and the doctors of the law, the King was divorced from his wife, Queen Anne; and there at the same court was a privy contract approved that she had made to the Earl of Northumberland, afore the King's time, and so she was discharged, and was never lawful Queen of England.[2]

There are difficulties in accepting either of these conjectures. Chapuys, like Dr. Lingard after him, decided naturally for the hypothesis most disgraceful to the King. The Mary Boleyn story, authoritatively confirmed, at once covered Henry's divorce process with shame, and established the superior claim of Mary to the succession.[3] But in the Act of Parliament the

---

[1] Chapuys to Granvelle, May 19, 1536.—*Calendar, Foreign and Domestic*, vol. x. p. 380.

[2] *Wriothesley's Chronicle*, vol. i. pp. 40, 41.

[3] Chapuys's words are worth preserving. He was mistaken in his account of the Statute. It did not declare Mary legitimate, and it left Henry power to name his own successor should his marriage with Jane Seymour prove unfruitful. So great an error shows the looseness with which he welcomed any story which fell in with his wishes. He says: 'Le statut declairant la Princesse 'legitime heretiere, la fille de la 'Concubine, a esté revoqué, et elle 'declairé bastarde, non point 'comme fille de M. Norris, comme 'se pouvoit plus honnestement 'dire, mais pour avoir esté le mar- 'riage entre la dicte Concubine et 'le dict Roy illegitime à cause qu'il 'avoit cogneu charnellement la 'sœur de la dicte Concubine : pour 'laquelle cause l'Archevesque de 'Canterburi, ung ou deux jours 'avant que la dicte Concubine fut 'executée, donna et prefera la 'sentence de divorce, de quoy, 'comme sçavez trop mieulx, n'es- 'toit grand besoign, puisque l'epée

cause is described as something unknown in 1533, when
the first Statute was passed; and the alleged intrigue
had then been the common subject of talk in Catholic
circles and among the Opposition members of Parliament. The Act says that the cause was a fact confessed
by the Lady Anne. The Lady Anne might confess her
own sins, but her confession of the sins of others was
not a confession at all, and could have carried no
validity unless supported by other evidence. Chapuys's
assertion requires us to suppose that Henry, being
informed of Anne's allegation, consented to the establishment of his own disgrace by making it the subject
of a legal investigation; that he thus himself allowed a
crime to be substantiated against him which covered
him with infamy, and which no other attempt was ever
made to prove. How did Chapuys know that this was
the cause of the divorce of Anne? If it was communicated to Parliament, it must have become the common
property of the realm, and have been no longer open
to question. If it was not communicated, but was
accepted by Parliament itself on the authority of the
Council, who were Chapuys's informants and how did
they know? Under Chapuys's hypothesis the conduct
of King, Council, Parliament, and Convocation becomes

'et la mort les auroit prochaine-
'ment et absolument divorcés : et
'puisque aussy le vouloient faire,
'le pretext eust esté plus honneste
'd'alleguer qu'elle avoit este mariée
'à aultre encores vivant. Mais
'Dieu a voulu descouvrir plus
'grande abomination, qui est plus
'que inexcusable actendu qu'il ne
'peut alleguer ignorance neque
'juris neque facti. Dieu veuille
'que telle soit la fin de toutes ses
'folies !' Chapuys à Granvelle,
July 8, 1536.—*MS. Vienna.*

gratuitous folly—folly to which there was no temptation and for which there was no necessity. The King had only to deny the truth of the story, and nothing further would have been made of it. The real evidence for the *liaison* with Mary Boleyn is the ineradicable conviction of a certain class of minds that the most probable interpretation of every act of Henry is that which most combines stupidity and wickedness. To argue such a matter is useless. Those who believe without reason cannot be convinced by reason.

The Northumberland explanation is less improbable, but to this also there are many objections. Northumberland himself had denied on oath, a few days before, that any contract had ever passed between Anne and himself. If he was found to have perjured himself, he would have been punished, or, at least, disgraced; yet, a few months later, in the Pilgrimage of Grace, he had the King's confidence, and deserved it by signal loyalty. The Norris story is the least unlikely. The first act of criminality with Anne mentioned in the indictment was stated to have been committed with Norris four weeks after the birth of Elizabeth, and the intimacy may have been earlier; while the mystery observed about it may be better accounted for, since, if it had been avowed, Elizabeth's recognition as the King's daughter would have been made ever after impossible, and the King did believe that she was really his own daughter.

But here, again, there is no evidence. The explanation likeliest of all is that it was something different

from each of these—one of the confessions which had
been kept back as 'too abominable.' It is idle to
speculate on the antecedents of such a woman as Anne
Boleyn.

If she had expected that her confession would save
her, she was mistaken.   To marry a king after a
previous unacknowledged intrigue was in those days
constructive treason, since it tainted the blood royal.[1]
The tragedy was wound up on Friday, the 19th of
May; the scene was the green in front of the Tower.
Foreigners were not admitted, but the London citizens
had collected in great numbers, and the scaffold had
been built high that every one might see.   The Chancellor, the Duke of Suffolk, the young Duke of
Richmond—then himself sick to death—Cromwell, and
other members of the Council, were present by the
King's order.   Throughout the previous day Anne had
persisted in declaring her innocence.   In the evening
she had been hysterical, had talked and made jokes.
The people would call her 'Queen Anne *sans tête*,' she
said, and 'laughed heartily.'   In the morning at nine
o'clock she was led out by Sir William Kingston,
followed by four of her ladies.   She looked often over
her shoulder, and on the fatal platform was much
'amazed and exhausted.'

When the time came for her to speak, she raised her
eyes to heaven and said, ' Masters, I submit me to the
' law, as the law has judged me, and as for my offences,

---

[1] This was distinctly laid down in the case of Catherine Howard.

'I accuse no man. God knoweth them. I remit
'them to God, beseeching him to have mercy on my
'soul. I beseech Jesu save my sovereign and master,
'the King, the most godly, noble, and gentle Prince
'there is.'[1] She then laid her head on the block and
so ended ; she, too, dying without at the last denying
the crime for which she suffered. Of the six who were
executed not one made a protestation of innocence. If
innocent they were, no similar instance can be found in
the history of mankind.

---

[1] *Wriothesley's Chronicle,* pp. 41, 42.

CHAPTER XXIII.

Competition for Henry's hand—Solicitations from France and
from the Emperor—Overtures from the Pope—Jane Seymour
—General eagerness for the King's marriage—Conduct of
Henry in the interval before Anne's execution—Marriage with
Jane Seymour—Universal satisfaction—The Princess Mary
—Proposal for a General Council—Neutrality of England in
the war between France and the Empire.

HUMAN nature is said to be the same in all ages
and countries. Manners, if it be so, signally
vary. Among us, when a wife dies, some decent interval
is allowed before her successor is spoken of. The
execution for adultery of a Queen about whom all
Europe had been so long and so keenly agitated might
have been expected to be followed by a pause. No
pause, however, ensued after the fall of Anne Boleyn.
If Henry had been the most interesting and popular of
contemporary princes, there could not have been greater
anxiety to secure his vacant hand. Had he been the
most pious of Churchmen, the Pope could not have
made greater haste to approach him with offers of
friendship. There was no waiting even for the result
of the trial. No sooner was it known that Anne had
been committed to the Tower for adultery than the
result was anticipated as a certainty. It was assumed

as a matter of course that the King would instantly
look for another wife, and Francis and the Emperor
lost not a moment in trying each to be beforehand with
the other. M. d'Inteville had come over to intercede
for Sir Francis Weston, but he brought a commission
to treat for a marriage between Henry and a French
princess. To this overture the King replied at once
that it could not be, and, according to Chapuys, added
ungraciously, and perhaps with disgust, that he had
experienced already the effects of French education.[1]
The words, perhaps, were used to Cromwell, and not
to the French Ambassador; but Chapuys was hardly
less surprised when Cromwell, in reporting them, coolly
added that the King could not marry out of the realm,
because, if a French princess misconducted herself,
they could not punish her as they had punished the
last.[2] The Ambassador did not understand irony, and
was naturally startled, for he had received instructions
to make a similar application on behalf of his own
master. Charles was eager to secure the prize, and,
anticipating Anne's fate, he despatched a courier to
Chapuys on hearing of her arrest, with orders to seize

---

[1] 'Le Roy respondit qu'il avoit
'trop experimenté en la dicte Con-
'cubine, que c'estoit de la nourri-
'ture de France.' Chapuys à
l'Empereur, June 6.—*MS. Vienna.*

[2] 'Me dict qu'icelluy Baily de
'Troyes et l'autre Ambassadeur
'avoient proposé le mariage de
'l'aisnée fille de France avec ce
'Roy, mais que c'estoit peine per-
'due. Car ce Roy ne se marieroit
'oncques hors de son royaulme, et,
'luy demandant raison pourquoy, il
'm'en dit avec assez mine assurance
'que se venant à mesfaire de son
'corps une Reine estrangere qui fut
'de grand sang et parentage, l'on
'ne pourroit chastier et s'en faire
'quitte comme il avoit fait de la
'derniere.' Chapuys à l'Empereur.
—*MS. Vienna*, June 6.

the opportunity. 'If Hannaert's news be true,' he wrote on the 15th of May, the day of the trial at West-minster, 'the King, now that God has permitted this 'woman's damnable life to be discovered, may be more 'inclined to treat with us, and there may be a better 'foundation for an arrangement in favour of the 'Princess. But you must use all your skill to prevent a 'marriage with France. The King should rather choose 'one of his own subjects, either the lady for whom 'he has already shown a preference or some other.'

So far Charles had written when Chapuys's mes-senger arrived with later news. George has just come, the Emperor then continued, and I have heard from him what has passed about the Concubine. It is supposed that she and the partners of her guilt will be executed, and that the King, being of amorous complexion and anxious, as he has always pretended, for a male heir, will now marry immediately. Overtures will certainly be made to him from France. You will endeavour, either as of yourself or through Cromwell, to arrange a match for him with the Infanta of Portugal, my niece, who has a settlement by will of 400,000 ducats. Simultaneously you will propose another marriage between the Princess Mary and the Infant of Portugal, Don Louis, my brother-in-law. You will point out that these alliances will remove past unpleasantness, and will unite myself, the King, and our respective countries. You will show the advantage that will accrue to the realm of England should a prince be the result, and we may reasonably hope that it will be so, the Infanta being young and well nurtured. If you find the King disinclined to this marriage, you may propose my niece, the Duchess Dowager of Milan, a beautiful young lady with a good dowry.[1]

On the same 15th of May Granvelle, no less eager, wrote to Chapuys also. M. l'Ambassadeur, my good brother and friend, I have received your letters and have heard what your messenger had to tell me. You have done well to keep us informed about the Concubine. It is indeed fine music and food for laughter.[2] God is revealing the iniquity of those from whom so much mischief has risen. We must make our profit of it, and manage matters as the Emperor directs. Use all your diligence and dexterity. Immense advantage will follow, public and private. You will yourself not fail of your reward for your true and faithful services.[3]

So anxious was Charles for fresh matrimonial arrangements with Henry, that he wrote again to the same purpose three days later—a strange wish if he believed Catherine to have been murdered, or her successor to be on the eve of execution because the King was tired of her. To Charles and Granvelle, as to Chapuys himself, the unfortunate Anne was the English Messalina. The Emperor and all the contemporary world saw in her nothing but a wicked woman at last detected and brought to justice.[4]

---

[1] Charles V. to Chapuys, May 15, 1536.—*MS. Vienna; Calendar, Foreign and Domestic,* vol. x. p. 370.

[2] 'Qui à la verité est une 'musique de hault genre et digne 'de rire.'   [3] *MS. Vienna.*

[4] Chapuys to Granvelle, May 19, 1536.—*Calendar, Foreign and Domestic,* vol. x. p. 380.

What came of these advances will be presently seen; but, before proceeding, a glance must be given at the receipt of the intelligence of Anne's fall at the Holy See. This also was *chose de rire.* Chapuys had sent to Rome in the past winter a story that Henry had said Anne Boleyn had bewitched him. The Pope had taken it literally, and had supposed that when the witch was removed the enchantment would end. He sent for Sir Gregory Casalis on the 17th of May, and informed him of what he had heard from England. He said that he had always recognised the many and great qualities of the King; and those qualities he did not doubt would now show themselves, as he had been relieved from his unfortunate marriage. Let the King reattach himself to Holy Church and take the Pope for an ally; they could then give the law both to the Emperor and to the King of France, and the entire glory of restoring peace to Christendom would attach to Henry himself. The King, he said, had no cause to regard him as an enemy; for he had always endeavoured to be his friend. In the matrimonial cause he had remonstrated in private with his predecessor. At Bologna he had argued for four hours with the Emperor, trying to persuade him that the King ought not to be interfered with.[1] Never had he desired to offend the King,

---

[1] 'In causâ matrimonii et in 'consistoriis et publice et privatim 'apud Clementem VII. se omnia 'quæ potuit pro vestrâ Majestate 'egisse : et Bononiæ Imperatori per 'horas quatuor accurate persuadere 'conatum fuisse, non esse Majesta-'tem vestram per illam causam im-'pugnandam.' Sir Gregory Casalis to Henry VIII., May 27, 1536.— *Calendar, Foreign and Domestic,* vol. x. pp. 406 et seq.

although so many violent acts had been done in England against the Holy See. He had made the Bishop of Rochester a cardinal solely with a view to the General Council, and because the Bishop had written a learned book against Luther. On the Bishop's execution, he had been compelled to say and do certain things, but he had never intended to give effect to them.

If the Pope had thought the King to have been right in his divorce suit, it was not easy to understand why he had excommunicated him and tried to deprive him of his crown because he had disobeyed a judgment thus confessed to have been unjust. Casalis asked him if he was to communicate what he had said to the King, The Pope, after reflecting a little, said that Casalis might communicate it as of himself; that he might tell the King that the Pope was well-disposed towards him, and that he might expect every favour from the Pope. Casalis wrote in consequence that on the least hint that the King desired a reconciliation, a Nuncio would be sent to England to do everything that could be found possible; after the many injuries which he had received, opinion at Rome would not permit the Pope to make advances until he was assured that they would be well received; but some one would be sent in Casalis's name bringing credentials from his Holiness.

Never since the world began was a dastardly assassination, if Anne Boleyn was an innocent woman, rewarded with so universal a solicitation for the friendship

of the assassin. In England the effect was the same.
Except by the Lutherans, Anne had been universally
hated, and the King was regarded with the respectful
compassion due to a man who had been cruelly injured.
The late marriage had been tolerated out of hope for
the birth of the prince who was so passionately longed
for. Even before the discovery of Anne's conduct, a
considerable party, with the Princess Mary among
them, had desired to see the King separated from her
and married to some other respectable woman. Jane
Seymour had been talked about as a steady friend
of Catherine, and, when Catherine was gone, of the
Princess. The King had paid her attentions which, if
Chapuys's stories were literally true—as probably
they were not—had been of a marked kind. In all
respects she was the opposite of Anne. She had plain
features, pale complexion, a low figure—in short, had no
personal beauty or any pretensions to it, with nothing
in her appearance to recommend her, except her youth.
She was about twenty-five years of age. She was not
witty either, or brilliant; but she was modest, quiet,
with a strong understanding and rectitude of principle,
and, so far as her age and her opportunities allowed,
she had taken Mary's part at the Court. Perhaps this
had recommended her to Henry. Whether he had
himself ever seriously thought of dismissing Anne and
inviting Jane Seymour to take her place is very
dubious ; nor has any one a right to suppose that under
such conditions Jane Seymour would have regarded
such a proposal as anything but an insult. How soon

after the detection of Anne's crime the intention was formed is equally uncertain.[1] Every person at home and abroad regarded it as obvious that he must marry some one, and marry at once. He himself professed to be unwilling, 'unless he was constrained by his subjects.'

In Chapuys's letters, truth and lies are so inter-mixed that all his personal stories must be received with distrust. Invariably, however, he believed and reported the most scandalous rumours which he could hear. Everybody, he said, rejoiced at the execution of the *putaine;* but there were some who spoke variously of the King. He had heard, from good authority, that in a conversation which passed between Mistress Seymour and the King before the arrest of the Con-cubine, the lady urged him to restore the Princess to the Court. The King told her she was a fool; she ought to be thinking more of the children which they might expect of their own, than of the elevation of the other. The lady replied that in soliciting for the Princess, she was consulting for the good of the King, of herself, of her children should she have any, and of all the realm, as, without it, the English nation would never be satisfied. Such a conversation is not in itself likely to have been carried on *before* Anne's arrest, and

---

[1] Cromwell, writing to Gardiner to inform him of the marriage, said that 'the nobles 'and Council upon their knees 'had moved him to it.' If their entreaty had been no more than a farce, Cromwell would hardly have mentioned it so naturally in a private letter to a brother Privy Councillor. — *Calendar, Foreign and Domestic,* vol. xi. p. 16.

certainly not where it could be overheard by others; especially as Chapuys admitted that the King said publicly he would not marry any one unless the Parliament invited him. One would like to know what the trustworthy authority might have been. Unfortunately for the veracity of his informant, he went on with an account of the King's personal behaviour, the accuracy of which can be tested.

'People,' he said, 'had found it strange that the 'King, after having received such ignominy, should 'have gone about at such a time banqueting with 'ladies, sometimes remaining after midnight, and 'returning by the river, accompanied by music and 'the singers of his chamber. He supped lately,' the Ambassador continued, 'with several ladies at the 'house of the Bishop of Carlisle, and showed extrava-'gant joy.' The Bishop came the next morning to tell Chapuys of the visit, and added a story of the King having said that he had written a tragedy on Anne's conduct which he offered the Bishop to read.[1] Of John Kite, the Bishop of Carlisle, little is known, save that Sir William Kingston said he used to play 'Penny 'Gleek' with him. But it happens that a letter exists, written on the same day as Chapuys's, which describes Henry's conduct at precisely the same period.

John Husee, the friend and agent of Lord Lisle, was in London on some errand from his employer. His business required him to speak to the King, and

---

[1] Chapuys to Charles V., May 19, 1536.—*Calendar, Foreign and Domestic,* vol. x. p. 378.

he said that he had been unable to obtain admittance, the King having remained in strict seclusion from the day of Anne's arrest to her execution. 'His Grace,' Husee wrote, ' came not abroad this fortnight, except it ' was in the garden or in his boat, when it may become ' no man to interrupt him. Now that this matter is ' past I hope to see him.' [1]

Chapuys was very clever : he may be believed, with limitations, when writing on business or describing conversations of his own with particular persons; but so malicious was he, and so careless in his matters of fact or probability, that he cannot be believed at all when reporting scandalous anecdotes which reached him from his 'trustworthy authorities.'

It is, however, true that, before the fortnight had expired, the King had resolved to do what the Council recommended—marry Jane Seymour, and marry her promptly, to close further solicitation from foreign Powers. There is no sign that she had herself sought so questionable an elevation. A powerful party in the State wished her to accept a position which could have few attractions, and she seems to have acquiesced without difficulty. Francis and Charles were offering their respective Princesses; the readiest way to answer them without offence was to place the so much coveted hand out of the reach of either. On the 20th of May, the morning after Anne was beheaded, Jane Seymour was brought secretly by water to the palace at Westminster,

---

[1] John Husee to Lord Lisle, May 19.—*Calendar, Foreign and Domestic*, vol. x. p. 385.

and was then and there formally betrothed to the King.
The marriage followed a few days later. On Ascension
Day, the 25th of May, the King, in rejecting the offered
match from Francis, said that he was not then actually
married. On the 29th or 30th, Jane was formally introduced as Queen.

Chapuys was disappointed in his expectation of
popular displeasure. Not a murmur was heard to
break the expression of universal satisfaction. The
new Queen was a general favourite; every one knew
that she was a friend of the Princess Mary, and every
one desired to see Mary replaced in her rights. Fortunately for the Princess, the attempt at escape had
never been carried out. She had remained quietly
watching the overthrow of her enemy, and trusting the
care of her fortunes to Cromwell, who, she knew, had
always been her advocate. She had avoided writing to
him to intercede for her, because, as she said, ' I per-
' ceived that nobody dared speak for me as long as that
' woman lived who is now gone, whom God in his mercy
' forgive.' [1] The time had now come for her to be
received back into favour. Submission of some kind
it would be necessary for her to make; and the form in
which it was to be done was the difficulty. The King
could not replace in the line of the succession a daughter
who was openly defying the law. Cromwell drew for
Mary a sketch of a letter which he thought would be
sufficient. It was to acknowledge that she had offended

---

[1] The Princess Mary to Cromwell, May 26, 1536.—*Calendar,
Foreign and Domestic.*

her father, to beg his blessing and his forgiveness, and
to promise obedience for the future, to congratulate him
on his marriage, and to ask permission to wait on the
new Queen. He showed the draft to Chapuys, for
the Princess to transcribe and send. Chapuys objected
that the surrender was too absolute. Cromwell said
that he might alter it if he pleased, and a saving
clause was introduced, not too conspicuous. She was to
promise to submit in all things 'under God.' In this
form, apparently, the letter was despatched, and was
said to have given great satisfaction both to Henry and
the new Queen. Now it was thought that Mary would
be restored to her rank as Princess. She would be
excluded from the succession only if a son or daughter
should be born of the new marriage; but this did
not alarm Chapuys, for 'according to the opinion of
many,' he said, ' there was no fear of any issue of either
sex.'

On Ascension Day, the Ambassador had been admitted to an audience, the first since the unprosperous
discussion at Greenwich. The subject of the treaty
with the Emperor had been renewed under more
promising auspices. The King had been gracious.
Chapuys had told him that the Emperor desired to
explain and justify the actions of which the King had
complained; but before entering on a topic which
might renew unpleasant feelings, he said that the
Emperor had instructed him to consult the King's
wishes; and he undertook to conform to them. The
King listened with evident satisfaction; and a long

talk followed, in the course of which the Ambassador
introduced the various proposals which the Emperor
had made for fresh matrimonial connections. The King
said that Chapuys was a bringer of good news; his
own desire was to see a union of all Christian princes;
if the Emperor was in earnest, he hoped that he would
furnish the Ambassador with the necessary powers to
negotiate, or would send a plenipotentiary for that
particular purpose.

The offer of the Infanta of Portugal for the King
himself was, of course, declined, the choice being
already made ; but Cromwell said afterwards that Don
Luis might perhaps be accepted for the Princess, the
position of the Princess being the chief point on which
the stability of all other arrangements must depend.
As to the 'General Council,' it was not to be supposed
that the King wanted to set up a 'God of his own,' or
to separate himself from the rest of Christendom.   He
was as anxious as any one for a Council, but it must
be a Council called by the Emperor as chief of Christian
Europe.   It is to be observed that Henry, as Head of
the Church of England, took upon himself the entire
ordering of what was or was not to be.   Even the form
of consulting the clergy was not so much as thought of.
Chapuys could not answer for as much indifference on
the Emperor's part.   The Council, he thought, must
be left in the Pope's hands at the outset.   The Council
itself, when it assembled, could do as it pleased.   He
suggested, however, that Cromwell should put in writing his conception of the manner in which a Council

could be called by the Emperor, which Cromwell promised to do.

All things were thus appearing to run smooth. Four days later, when the marriage with Jane Seymour had been completed, Chapuys saw Henry again. The King asked him if he had heard further from the Emperor. Chapuys was able to assent. Charles's eager letters had come in by successive posts, and one had just arrived in which he had expressed his grief and astonishment at the conduct of Anne Boleyn, had described how he had spoken to his own Council about the woman's horrible ingratitude, and had himself offered thanks to God for having discovered the conspiracy, and saved the King from so great a danger. Henry made graceful acknowledgments, replied most politely on the offer of the Infanta, for which he said he was infinitely obliged to the Emperor, and conducted the Ambassador into another room to introduce him to the Queen.

Chapuys was all courtesy. At Henry's desire he kissed and congratulated Jane. The Emperor, he said, would be delighted that the King had found so good and virtuous a wife. He assured her that the whole nation was united in rejoicing at her marriage. He recommended the Princess to her care, and hoped that she would have the honourable name of peacemaker.

The King answered for her that this was her nature. She would not for the world that he went to war.

Chapuys was aware that Henry was not going to

war on the side of Francis—that danger had passed; but that he would not go to war at all was not precisely what Chapuys wished to hear. What Charles wanted was Henry's active help against the French. The fourth condition of the proposed treaty was an alliance offensive and defensive. Henry merely said he would mediate, and, if France would not agree to reasonable terms, he would then declare for the Emperor.[1]

The Emperor, like many other persons, had attributed the whole of Henry's conduct to the attractions of Anne Boleyn. He had supposed that after his eyes had been opened he would abandon all that he had done, make his peace with the Pope, and return to his old friends with renewed heartiness. He was surprised and disappointed. Mediation would do no good at all, he said. If the King would join him against France, the Emperor would undertake to make no peace without including him, and would take security for the honour and welfare of the realm. But he declined to quarrel with the Pope to please the King; and if the King would not return to the obedience of the Holy See or submit his differences with the Pope to the Emperor and the Council, he said that he could make no treaty at all with him. He directed Chapuys, however, to continue to discuss the matter in a friendly way, to gain time till it could be seen how events would turn.[2]

---

[1] Chapuys to Charles V., June 6.—*Calendar, Foreign and Domestic*, vol. x. p. 440; *Spanish Calendar*, vol. v. pp. 137 et seq.

[2] Charles V. to Chapuys, June 30, 1536.—*Calendar, Foreign and Domestic*, vol. x. p. 511.

How events did turn is sufficiently well known. The war broke out—the French invaded Italy; the Emperor, unable to expel them, turned upon Provence, where he failed miserably with the loss of the greater part of his army.

Henry took no part. The state of Europe was considered at length before the English Council. Chapuys was heard, and the French Ambassador was heard; and the result was a declaration of neutrality—the only honourable and prudent course where the choice lay between two faithless friends who, if the King had committed himself to either, would have made up their own quarrels at England's expense.

CHAPTER XXIV.

Expectation that Henry would return to the Roman Communion
—Henry persists in carrying out the Reformation—The
Crown and the clergy—Meeting of a new Parliament—Fresh
repudiation of the Pope's authority—Complications of the
succession—Attitude of the Princess Mary—Her reluctant
submission—The King empowered to name his successor by
will—Indication of his policy—The Pilgrimage of Grace—
Cost of the Reformation — The martyrs, Catholic and
Protestant.

WHETHER Henry, on the exposure of the character of the woman for whom, in the world's
opinion, he had quarrelled with Rome and broken the
union of Christendom, would now reverse his course
and return to the communion of the Apostolic See, was
the question on which all minds were exercising themselves. The Pope and the European Powers were
confident, believing the reports which had reached
them of the discontent in England. Cranmer feared
it, as he almost confessed in the letter which he wrote
to the King when he first heard of the arrest of Anne.
She had been conspicuously Lutheran; her family
and her party were Lutheran, and the disgrace
might naturally extend to the cause which they represented. The King was to show that he had not, as he

said himself, 'proceeded on such light grounds.' The divorce had been the spark which kindled the mine; but the explosive force was in the temper of the English nation. The English nation was weary of a tribunal which sold its decrees for money, or allowed itself to be used as a tool by the Continental Sovereigns. It was weary of the iniquities of its own Church Courts, which had plundered rich and poor at their arbitrary pleasure—of a clergy which, protected by the immunities which Becket had won for them, and restrained by no laws save those which they themselves allowed, had made their lives a scandal and their profession an offence. The property which had been granted them in pious confidence for holy uses was squandered in luxurious self-indulgence; and they had replied to the reforms which were forced upon them by disloyalty and treason. They had been coerced into obedience; they had been brought under the control of the law, punished for their crimes in spite of their sacred calling under which they had claimed exemption, and been driven into the position of ordinary citizens. Their prelates were no longer able to seize and burn *ex officio* obnoxious preachers, or imprison or ruin under the name of heretics rash persons who dared to speak the truth of them.

In exasperation at the invasion of these time-honoured privileges, they denounced as sacrilege the statutes which had been required to restrain them. They had conspired to provoke the Pope to excommunicate their Sovereign, and solicited the Catholic Powers

to invade their country and put the Reformers down
with fire and sword. The King, who had been the instrument of their beneficent humiliation, did not intend
either to submit the internal interests of the country to
the authority of a foreign bishop, or to allow the black
regiments at home to recover the power which they had
so long abused.

Cromwell's commissioners were still busy on the
visitation of the religious houses. Each day brought
in fresh reports of their condition. These communities,
supposed to be special servants of God, had become
special servants of the Devil. The eagerness with
which the Pope solicited Henry's return, the assurance
that he had always been his friend—had always maintained that Henry was right in the divorce case, when
he had a Bull ready in his desk taking his crown from
him—was in itself sufficient evidence of the fitness
of such a ruler to be the Supreme Judge in Christendom. Just as little could the Emperor be trusted,
whose affectations of friendship were qualified by
secret reservations. The King had undertaken a
great and beneficent work in his own realm and meant
to go through with it. The Pope might do as he
pleased. The Continental Princes might quarrel or
make peace, hold their Councils, settle as they liked
their own affairs, in their own way; England was
sufficient for herself. He had called his people under
arms; he had fortified the coasts; he had regenerated
the navy. The nation, or the nobler part of it, he
believed to be loyal to himself—to approve what he

S

had done and to be ready to stand by him. He was
not afraid of attack from abroad. If there was a re-
bellious spirit at home, if the clergy were mutinous
because the bit was in their mouths, if the Peers of
the old blood were alarmed at the growth of religious
liberty and were discontented because they could no
longer deal with it in the old way, the King was convinced that he was acting for the true interests of the
country, that Parliament would uphold him, and that
he could control both the ecclesiastics and the nobles.
The world should see that the reforms which he had
introduced into England were not the paltry accidents
of a domestic scandal, but the first steps of a revolution
deliberately resolved on and sternly carried out which
was to free the Island for ever from the usurped
authority of an Italian Prelate and from the poisonous
influences within the realm of a corrupt and demoralising
superstition.

The call of Parliament after Anne's execution was
the strongest evidence of confidence in his people
which Henry had yet given. He had much to
acknowledge and much to ask. He had to confess
that, although he had been right in demanding a
separation from his brother's wife, he had fatally mistaken the character of the woman whom he had chosen
to take her place. The succession which he had hoped
to establish he had made more intricate than before.
He had now three children, all technically illegitimate.
The Duke of Richmond was the son of the only mistress
with whom he was ever known to have been really

connected. The Duke was now eighteen years old. He had been educated as a Prince, but had no position recognised by the law. Elizabeth's mother had acknowledged to having committed herself before her marriage with the King, and many persons doubted whether Elizabeth was the King's true daughter. Mary's claim was justly considered as the best, for, though her mother's marriage had been declared illegal, she had been born *bonâ fide parentum.* What Parliament would do in such extraordinary circumstances could not be foreseen with any certainty, and the elections had to be made with precipitancy and without time for preparation. The writs were issued on the 7th of May. The meeting was to be on the 8th of June. The Crown could influence or control the elections at some particular places. At Canterbury Cromwell named the representatives who were to be chosen,[1] as, till the Reform Bill of 1832, they continued to be named by the patrons of boroughs. Yet it would be absurd to argue from single instances that the Crown could do what it pleased. Even with leisure to take precautions and with the utmost exercise of its powers, it could only affect the returns, in the great majority of the constituencies, through the Peers and landowners, and the leading citizens in the corporations. With only four weeks to act in, a Queen to try and execute, and a King to marry in the interval, no ingenuity and no industry could have sufficed to secure a House of

---

[1] *Calendar, Foreign and Domestic,* June 6, 1536, vol. x. p. 389.

Commons whose subserviency could be counted on, if subserviency was what the King required. It is clear only that, so far as concerned the general opinion of the country, the condemnation of Anne Boleyn had rather strengthened than impaired his popularity. As Queen she had been feared and disliked. Her punishment was regarded as a creditable act of justice, and the King was compassionated as a sufferer from abominable ingratitude.

Little is known in detail of the proceedings of this Parliament. The Acts remain : the debates are lost. The principal difficulties with which it had to deal concerned Anne's trial and the disposition of the inheritance of the Crown. On the matter of real importance, on the resolution of King and Legislature to go forward with the Reformation, all doubts were promptly dispelled. An Act was passed without opposition reasserting the extinction of the Pope's authority, and another taking away the protection of sanctuary from felonious priests. The succession was a harder problem. Day after day it had been debated in the Council. Lord Sussex had proposed that, as all the children of the King were illegitimate, the male should be preferred to the female and the crown be settled on the Duke of Richmond.[1] Richmond was personally liked. He resembled his father in appearance and character, and the King himself was supposed to favour this solution. With the outer world the favourite was the Princess

---

[1] Chapuys to Charles V., June 6, 1536.—*Calendar, Foreign and Domestic*, vol. x. p. 441.

Mary. Both she and her mother were respected for
a misfortune which was not due to faults of theirs,
and the Princess was the more endeared by the danger
to which she was believed to have been exposed
through the machinations of Anne. The new Queen
was her strongest advocate, and the King's affection
for her had not been diminished even when she
had tried him the most. He could not have been
ignorant of her correspondence with Chapuys : he probably knew that she had wished to escape out of the
realm, and that the Pope, who was now suing to him,
had meant to bestow his own crown upon her. But her
qualities were like his own, tough and unmalleable, and
in the midst of his anger he had admired her resolution.
Every one expected that she would be restored to her
rank after Anne's death. The King had apparently
been satisfied with her letter to him. Cromwell was
her friend, and Chapuys, who had qualified her submission, was triumphant and confident. He was led to
expect that an Act would be introduced declaring her
the next heir—nay, he had thought that such an Act
had been passed. Unfortunately for him the question
of her acknowledgment of the Act of Supremacy was
necessarily revived. Had she or had she not accepted
it ? The Act had been imposed, with the Statute of
Treasons attached, as a test of loyalty to the Reformation.
It was impossible to place her nearest to the throne as
long as she refused obedience to a law essential to the
national independence. To refuse was to confess of
a purpose of undoing her father's work, should he

die and the crown descend to her. She had supposed
that 'she was out of her trouble' while she had saved
her conscience by the reservation in her submission.
Chapuys found her again 'in extreme perplexity and
'anger.' The reservation had been observed. The
Duke of Norfolk, Lord Sussex, a Bishop, and other
Privy Councillors, had come with a message to her, like
those which had been so often carried ineffectually to
her mother, to represent the necessity of obedience.
Chapuys said that she had confounded them with her
wise answers, and that, when they could not meet her
arguments, they 'told her that, if she was their daughter,
' they would knock her head against the wall till it was
' as soft as a baked apple.' In passing through Mary
and through Chapuys the words, perhaps, received some
metaphorical additions. It is likely enough, however,
that Norfolk, who was supporting her claims with
all his power, was irritated at the revival of the old
difficulties which he had hoped were removed. The
Princess 'in her extreme necessity' wrote for advice to
the Ambassador. The Emperor was no longer in a
condition to threaten, and to secure Mary's place as
next in the succession was of too vital importance to
the Imperialists to permit them to encourage her in
scruples of conscience. Chapuys answered frankly that,
if the King persisted, she must do what he required.
The Emperor had distinctly said so. Her life was
precious, she must hide her real feelings till a time
came for the redress of the disorders of the realm.
Nothing was demanded of her expressly against God or

the Articles of Faith, and God looked to intentions rather than acts.

Mary still hesitated. She had the Tudor obstinacy, and she tried her will against her father's. The King was extremely angry. He had believed that she had given way and that the troubles which had distracted his family were at last over. He had been exceptionally well-disposed towards her. He had probably decided to be governed by the wishes of the people and to appoint her by statute presumptive heir, and she seemed determined to make it impossible for him. He suspected that she was being secretly encouraged. To defend her conduct, as Cromwell ventured to do, provoked him the more, for he felt, truly, that to give way was to abandon the field. Lady Hussey was sent to the Tower; Lord Exeter and Sir William Fitzwilliam were suspended from attendance on the Council; and even Cromwell, for four or five days, counted himself a lost man. Jane Seymour interceded in vain. To refuse to acknowledge the supremacy was treason, and had been made treason for ample reason. Mary, as the first subject in the realm, could not be allowed to deny it. Henry sent for the Judges, to consider what was to be done, and the Court was once more in terror. The Judges advised that a strict form of submission should be drawn, and that the Princess should be required to sign it. If she persisted in her refusal, she would then be liable to the law. The difficulty was overcome, or evaded, in a manner characteristic of the system to which Mary so passionately adhered. Chapuys drew a secret protest that, in submitting, she was yielding only to force. Thus guarded, he assured her that her consent would not be binding, that the Pope would not only refrain from blaming her, but would highly approve. She was still unsatisfied, till she made him promise to write to the Imperial Ambassador at Rome to procure a secret absolution from the Pope for the full satisfaction of her conscience. Thus protected, she disdainfully set her name to the paper prepared by the Judges, without condescending to read it, and the marked contempt, in Chapuys's opinion. would serve as an excuse for her in the future.[1]

While the crisis lasted the Council were in permanent session. Timid Peers were alarmed at the King's peremptoriness, and said that it might cost him his throne. The secret process by which Mary had been brought to yield may have been conjectured, and her resistance was not forgotten, but she had signed what was demanded, and it was enough. In the Court there was universal delight. Chapuys congratulated Cromwell, and Cromwell led him to believe that the crown would be settled as he wished. The King and Queen drove down to Richmond to pay the Princess a visit. Henry gave her a handsome present of money and said that now she might have anything that she pleased. The Queen gave her a diamond. She was to return to the Court and resume her old station. One cloud only remained. If it was generally understood that the heir

---

[1] Chapuys to Charles V., July 1, 1536.—*Spanish Calendar*, vol. v. part 2, pp. 184 et seq.

presumptive in her heart detested the measures in
which she had formally acquiesced, the country could
no longer be expected to support a policy which would
be reversed on the King's death. Mary's conduct left
little doubt of her real feelings, and therefore it was
not held to be safe to give her by statute the position
which her friends desired for her. The facility with
which the Pope could dispense with inconvenient
obligations rendered a verbal acquiescence an imperfect
safeguard. Parliament, therefore, did not, after all, entail
the crown upon her, in the event of the King's present
marriage being unfruitful, but left her to deserve it and
empowered the King to name his own successor.

Chapuys, however, was able to console himself with
the reflection that the Bastard, as he called Elizabeth,
was now out of the question. The Duke of Richmond
was ill—sinking under the same weakness of constitution which had been so fatal in the Tudor family, and
of which he, in fact, died a few weeks later. The
prevailing opinion was that the King could never have
another child. Mary's prospects, therefore, were tolerably secure. ' I must admit,' Chapuys wrote on the 8th
of July, ' that her treatment improves every day. She
' never had so much liberty as now, or was served
' with so much state even by the little Bastard's
' waiting-women. She will want nothing in future but
' the name of Princess of Wales,[1] and that is of no

---

[1] Chapuys to Charles V., July 8, 1536.—*Spanish Calendar*, vol. v. part 2, p. 221. In using the words, ' Princess of Wales,' Chapuys adds a curious fact, if fact it be—' Nowhere that I know

'consequence, for all the rest she will have more abun-
'dantly than before.'

Mary, in fact, now wanted nothing save the Pope's
pardon for having abjured his authority. Chapuys
had undertaken that it would be easily granted. The
Emperor had himself asked for it, yet not only could
not Cifuentes obtain the absolution, but he did not so
much as dare to speak to Paul on the subject. The
absolution for the murder of an Archbishop of Dublin
had been bestowed cheerfully and instantly on Fitzgerald. Mary was left with perjury on her conscience,
and no relief could be had. There appeared to be some
technical difficulty. 'Unless she retracted and abjured
'in the presence of the persons before whom she took
'the oath, it was said that the Pope's absolution
'would be of no use to her.' There was, perhaps,
another objection. Cifuentes imperfectly trusted Paul.
He feared that if he pressed the request the secret
would be betrayed and that Mary's life would be in
danger.[1]

Time, perhaps, and reflection alleviated Mary's re-
morse and enabled her to dispense with the Papal
anodyne, while Cromwell further comforted the Ambassador in August by telling him that the King felt
he was growing old, that he was hopeless of further

'of,' he says, 'is the title of Prin-
'cess given to a King's daughter
'as long as there is hope of male
'descent. It was the Cardinal of
'York who, for some whim or
'other of his own, broke through
'the rule and caused Henry's
'daughter by Catherine to be
'called "Princess of Wales."'

[1] Cifuentes to Charles V.,
August 4, 1536.—*Spanish Calendar*, vol. v. part 2, p. 221.

offspring, and was thinking seriously of making Mary his heir after all.[1]

Age the King could not contend with, but for the rest he had carried his policy through. The first act of the Reformation was closing, and he was left in command of the situation. The curtain was to rise again with the Lincolnshire and Yorkshire rebellion, to be followed by the treason of the Poles. But there is no occasion to tell a story over again which I can tell no better than I have done already, nor does it belong to the subject of the present volume. The Pilgrimage of Grace was the outbreak of the conspiracy encouraged by Chapuys to punish Henry, and to stop the progress of the Reformation; Chapuys's successors in the time of Elizabeth followed his example; and with them all the result was the same—the ruin of the cause which with such weapons they were trying to maintain, and the deaths on the scaffold of the victims of visionary hopes and promises which were never to be made good.

All the great persons whom Chapuys names as willing to engage in the enterprise—the Peers, the Knights, who, with the least help from the Emperor, would hurl the King from his throne, Lord Darcy and Lord Hussey, the Bishop of Rochester, as, later on, the Marquis of Exeter, Lord Montague and his mother—sank one after another into bloody graves. They mistook their imaginations for facts, their passions for

---

[1] Chapuys to Charles V., August 12, 1536.

arguments, and the vain talk of an unscrupulous Ambassador for solid ground on which to venture into
treason. In their dreams they saw the phantom of the
Emperor coming over with an army to help them.
Excited as they had been, they could not part with
their hopes. They knew that they were powerful in
numbers. Their preparations had been made, and many
thousands of clergy and gentlemen and yeomen had
been kindled into crusading enthusiasm. The flame
burst out sporadically and at intervals, without certain
plan or purpose, at a time when the Emperor could not
help them, even if he had ever seriously intended it,
and thus the conflagration, which at first blazed through
all the northern counties, was extinguished before it
turned to civil war. The common people who had been
concerned in it suffered but lightly. But the roots had
penetrated deep; the conspiracy was of long standing;
the intention of the leaders was to carry out the Papal
censures, and put down what was called heresy. The
rising was really formidable, for the loyalty of many
of the great nobles was not above suspicion, and, if
not promptly dealt with, it might have enveloped the
whole island. Those who rise in arms against Govern-
ments must take the consequences of failure, and the
leaders who had been the active spirits in the sedition
were inexorably punished. In my History of the time
I have understated the number of those who were
executed. Care was taken to select only those who
had been definitely prominent. Nearly three hundred
were hanged in all—in batches of twenty-five or thirty,

in each of the great northern cities ; and, to emphasise the example and to show that the sacerdotal habit would no longer protect treason, the orders were to select particularly the priests and friars who had been engaged. The rising was undertaken in the name of religion. The clergy had been the most eager of the instigators. Chapuys had told the Emperor that of all Henry's subjects the clergy were the most disaffected, and the most willing to supply money for an invasion. They were therefore legitimately picked out for retribution, and in Lincoln, York, Hull, Doncaster, Newcastle, and Carlisle, the didactic spectacle was witnessed of some scores of reverend persons swinging for the crows to eat, in the sacred dress of their order. A severe lesson was required to teach a superstitious world that the clerical immunities existed no longer and that priests who broke the law would suffer like common mortals; but it must be clearly understood that, if these men could have had their way, the hundreds who suffered would have been thousands, and the victims would have been the poor men who were looking for a purer faith in the pages of the New Testament.

When we consider the rivers of blood which were shed elsewhere before the Protestant cause could establish itself, the real wonder is the small cost in human life of the mighty revolution successfully accomplished by Henry. With him, indeed, Chapuys must share the honour. The Catholics, if they had pleased, might have pressed their objections and their remonstrances in Parliament; and a nation as disposed for compromise as the English might have mutilated the inevitable changes. Chapuys's counsels tempted them into more dangerous and less pardonable roads. By encouraging them in secret conspiracies he made them a menace to the peace of the realm. He brought Fisher to the block. He forced the Government to pass the Act of Supremacy as a defence against treason, and was thus the cause also of the execution of Sir Thomas More and the Charterhouse monks.

To Chapuys, perhaps, and to his faithful imitators later in the century—De Quadra and Mendoza—the country owes the completeness of the success of the Reformation. It was a battle fought out gallantly between two principles—a crisis in the eternal struggle between the old and the new. The Catholics may boast legitimately of their martyrs. But the Protestants have a martyrology longer far and no less honourable, and those who continue to believe that the victory won in England in the sixteenth century was a victory of right over wrong, have no need to blush for the actions of the brave men who, in the pulpit or in the Council Chamber, on the scaffold or at the stake, won for mankind the spiritual liberty which is now the law of the world.

INDEX.

INDEX.

THE END.

Richard Clay & Sons, Limited, London and Bungay.